VOLUME 1

Exploring Inclusive & Equitable Pedagogies

Creating Space for All Learners

Melissa N. Mallon, Jane Nichols,
Elizabeth Foster, Ariana Santiago,
Maura Seale, and Robin Brown,
editors

Association of College and Research Libraries
A division of the American Library Association
Chicago, Illinois 2023

CONTENTS

SECTION 6. INSTRUCTOR IDENTITY AND POSITIONALITY

SECTION 7. PROFESSIONAL DEVELOPMENT

Acknowledgements

The coeditors (Ariana, Elizabeth, Jane, Maura, Melissa, and Robin) wish to thank all of our colleagues who proposed chapters for this volume. We are especially grateful for the contributing authors that spent a substantial amount of time and energy on their chapters during a time of global upheaval and anxiety. Their care and dedication to their work shines through, and we are grateful to have learned from them.

We collectively acknowledge our fellow coeditors' care and compassion as we worked on this book and appreciate the expertise shared and inspiration provided along the way. We would also like to thank Erin Nevius, content strategist at ACRL, for her wonderful editorial guidance and support over the course of this project.

Finally, we would like to thank the thousands of academic librarians out there for their commitment to creating inclusive and welcoming classroom environments that support the whole student experience.

Introduction

"We challenge you to be the instructors our students need."[1]

With this beautifully concise and prescient call to action, we join an ever-growing contingent of teaching librarians to urge our fellow instructors to explore and center equitable and inclusive pedagogies in their classrooms and libraries. To become the instructors our students need, we must adopt the mindsets and develop the underlying skills to enact inclusive and equitable teaching and learning, a theme which underpins this collection. In the contributed chapters that follow, readers will find reflections, practices, and models that deepen our collective understanding of equitable and inclusive theories and practices, presenting new grounding for both our individual teaching and our instruction programs. Adopting this framing positions library instructors to respond to Cooke and Sweeney's[2] call while opening doors for further exploration of new pedagogical ways of thinking.

Defining Inclusive and Equitable Pedagogies

Inclusive and equity-minded pedagogy is inspired by a rich array of theories including Black feminist thought, critical race theory, cultural humility, cultural competence, disabilities studies, universal design for learning, and critical information literacy, among others.[3] bell hooks and Paolo Friere's[4] anti-oppressive approaches to education are foundational to our theoretical understanding of inclusive and equitable pedagogies. Tuitt[5] integrates their theories as he outlines multiple concepts that inclusive and equitable pedagogues draw on for their daily work; concepts reflected in chapters throughout these volumes. When we base our instruction on inclusive and equitable pedagogies, we endeavor to connect authentically with students as well as to connect classroom learning to the context of their lives; we share power with students; we promote their voices, narratives, ways of learning, knowing, and being; and we strive to create a culture of care, empathy, and humility.[6] Inclusive pedagogy is further characterized by theory-based instructional design, centering students and their varied learning styles, while asking educators to be flexible and reflective.[7] As inclusive pedagogues, just as we ask students to bring their full humanity, we create space for our full humanity as well.[8] When we clearly share our objectives and expectations for a learning experience, students may better understand us and the learning context we aspire to create.[9]

In 2018 Tuitt, Haynes, and Stewart enhanced this definition based on their classroom experiences in light of ongoing shifts in higher education and society and in particular the growing Movement for Black Lives.[10] These shifts underscored their desire to "realize education as the practice of freedom"; meaning our educational practices embrace "intentional praxis", "voice and lived experience", "interdisciplinary and diverse content", 'anti-racist equity mindedness", "identity affirming and socially just learning environments", "courageous transparency", and "resilient emotional labor of love".[11] All are themes reflected throughout these volumes.

Centering Foundational Conversations

Librarians have considered multiple aspects of equity, diversity, inclusion, and more recently, antiracism, as they relate to our profession and everyday work, to library and information science education, and to instructional activities. Several librarians have depicted the lived experiences that BIPOC library workers can face in the library and information science profession, providing much needed insight into their lived reality of systems of oppression as well as strategies for intervention (while also acknowledging that they are not representing all voices).[12] Additional efforts at changing our field and by extension, our instruction, are understanding and "problematiz(ing)" whiteness in order to develop our collective knowledge about the many manifestations of white supremacy's impact.[13] Cooke and Sweeney's *Teaching for Justice: Implementing Social Justice in the LIS Classroom*[14] centers social justice theory and pedagogy in the LIS classroom; a key location of change for the profession. Librarians have also shared new directions, or cartographies, for our work in the classroom, at the reference desk, in archives and special collections, and as a way to support librarianship in Black and Brown communities.[15] Critical librarianship, or critlib, has long been and continues to be a productive lens to interrogate librarianship as a field, including our practices, history, socioeconomics, culture, geographic locations, and our presumed neutral positionality for the purpose of becoming socially just.[16] Instruction librarians seeking to engage in equitable and inclusive practices have also applied critical theories to interrogate instructional practices while sharing the strategies and mindsets they adopted to inform their pedagogy;[17] this work has been extended to assessment practices where we are invited to consider the role of relational care when assessing our students, our instruction, and our selves.[18] Leung and López-McKnight's edited collection, *Knowledge Justice: Disrupting Library and Information Studies through Critical Race Theory*, marks a watershed of librarians applying critical race theory to librarianship and opening the possibility of our field becoming explicitly anti-racist.[19]

This collection expands on these foundational works by exploring myriad questions, such as:

- How do theories and practices related to equitable and inclusive pedagogies inspire our teaching?
- How have librarians engaged in equitable and inclusive teaching?
- How might librarians implement equitable and inclusive pedagogy in ways specific to library instruction?

Authors apply a range of theories related to equitable and inclusive pedagogies (rather than focusing on a single theory, such as social justice theory) while also featuring examples of inclusive teaching in action. This blended focus provides academic library educators with both the theoretical foundations and practical applications to adopt more inclusive teaching practices.

Book Structure

Chapters in this collection share theories and practices applicable to the range of instructional activities we undertake in our classrooms, libraries, on campus, in our communities, and especially in response to online teaching and learning. By sharing how they have re-imagined and re-interpreted their approach to these activities through the lenses of inclusive, equitable, anti-racist, anti-oppressive pedagogies, the authors in this two-volume set model inclusive and equitable ways of thinking and teaching.

We, the editors, shaped sections to expand the conversation by sharing theoretical understandings and practical applications that librarian instructors can pick up, adopt, wrangle with, and shape for their contexts. Chapters reflect the range of instructional activities in which librarians engage including special collections, information literacy, digital scholarship, and outreach and community building activities. Authors showcase the various types of academic libraries where we work: small four-year colleges, community colleges, large research universities. Some institutions have earned the minority-serving designation and others are predominately white (historically and currently). Taking an inclusive approach to content, chapters take a variety of formats such as: reflective/personal, narrative, analytical/academic, case study, autoethnography, and a zine.

Chapters are categorized into seven sections covering a variety of inclusive and equitable pedagogies: Anti-Racist Approaches; Intentional Information Literacy;

Engendering Care and Empathy; Community Building; Universal Design (including accessibility and disability studies); Instructor Identity and Positionality; and Professional Development. This organization emerged from submissions reflecting authors' current environments and is shaped by national and global concerns including the COVID-19 pandemic, systemic racism, and underfunding of social safety nets.

Sections: Volume 1

ANTI-RACIST APPROACHES

In this section, eight chapters discuss theories and practices which authors draw on to inform their journey towards becoming anti-racist teachers and community builders. Their willingness to reflect on their own positionality, privilege, and power combined with their actions contributes to dismantling whiteness in their instruction and outreach activities. Librarians may lead or participate in campus-based programs aimed at raising awareness of anti-racist pedagogies and culturally responsive practices, signaling broad based support as well as movement towards integration into individual practitioners' teaching. Individual exploration and reflection on one's theoretical approach to instruction provides rich grounding for our pedagogy. Authors share their reflections on dialogic pedagogy, epistemic justice, algorithmic literacy, and oppressive authority and how they applied these theories to a range of teaching activities.

INTENTIONAL INFORMATION LITERACY

Key to successful library educators' practice is a willingness to regularly apply, assess, and modify their pedagogy. Throughout this section, authors share how they intentionally integrate theory into their practice and reflect on outcomes for improvement. Three chapters focus on how to reframe traditional realms of library instruction in order to be more inclusive. Three chapters bring critical information literacy into conversation with other pedagogical theories and practices. Two chapters use theory to destabilize dominant understandings of academic research practices and create more inclusive classrooms and consultations.

ENGENDERING CARE AND EMPATHY

The chapters in this section emphasize empathy and care as a means of advancing equity and inclusion in the classroom. Several authors discuss how using special collections and archival materials can advance empathy by highlighting the voices and stories of those marginalized or with hidden narratives. We learn about outreach programs that similarly provide opportunities for academic communities to engage with and build empathy for their fellow humans. Finally, several authors in this section write about creating a culture of care in the classroom, particularly focusing on the student experience as researcher and contributor of new knowledge.

Sections: *Volume 2*
COMMUNITY BUILDING

In our daily work, we take an expansive approach to community building and the seven chapters in this section reflect that expansiveness. Chapters discuss equitable and inclusive community building in the many instructional settings familiar to library educators. The range of contexts include writing center and library instruction; individual consultations; online, hybrid, and in-person workshops; and digital scholarship projects as part of credit courses. The opportunity to create community extends to library ambassador programs where student ambassadors connect with each other and the students they present to; in particular when this model is paired with a campus student mentorship program. Course-based activities whose outcomes center trust, connection, and joy when using archival materials to produce a primary source reader are the foundations for supporting community among students and their instructors. (This chapter is delightfully presented in a zine format.) Given the centrality of our spaces, gathering student input to inform a space redesign is a natural opportunity for community building both as part of the process and the resulting effort. Developing and sustaining a practice of reflecting on one's teaching praxis as well as offering students opportunities to reflect on their research practices makes space to deepen connections among librarians and students.

UNIVERSAL DESIGN FOR LEARNING

Applying universal design for learning (UDL) principles extends equitable and inclusive instruction to address multiple learning styles as well as disabilities. Across eight chapters, library educators demonstrate how they employ UDL concepts to support student learning. Core to UDL principles is offering multiple options for learners to engage in content. Doing so, practitioners aim to reach as many students as possible and their varied learning styles and abilities. UDL has become increasingly relevant as libraries shift library instruction online, whether due to the worldwide pandemic or the rise of distance learning. Many educators adopt CAST's (formerly the Center for Applied Special Technology) helpful and practical articulation of UDL principles; a match for teaching librarians given the multidisciplinary nature of our work. Authors detail the practical implications of accessibility and UDL for library instruction and note that there is much work to do to ensure that digital learning tools and experiences are completely accessible.

INSTRUCTOR IDENTITY AND POSITIONALITY

The identity and positionality of library instructors can have a significant impact on the inclusivity of learning environments. The four chapters in this section each explore instructor identity and positionality from different perspectives, including: early-career librarians developing intentional teaching practices; reflecting on one's own social identities as an instructor, and incorporating cultural humility and funds of knowledge into praxis; the challenges unique to one-shot library instruction, with guidance on adapting inclusive teaching strategies; and as adjunct instructors in MLIS programs integrating inclusive pedagogies within the limitations of the adjunct role. It is critical to reflect on your own identities and positionality, especially terms of how they might impact students and your ability to create inclusive and equitable learning spaces.

PROFESSIONAL DEVELOPMENT

Regular professional development is crucial for librarians to continue to grow in their understanding and application of inclusive and equitable pedagogies. The four chapters in this final section share strategies and activities librarians have engaged to develop their and their colleagues' expertise. Librarians describe benefits experienced when exchanging knowledge and practices from in-house professional development activities. Key to success is creating strong relationships whether with fellow teaching librarians, library colleagues, or teaching faculty in the disciplines. Learning to effectively develop and sustain such relationships can start in the library and information science graduate school setting when working in well-crafted group projects.

Concluding Remarks

We thank all of our contributors for their willingness to engage in this project, particularly in a time period of unknown churn. We were delighted and inspired by the myriad possibilities for learning, becoming, and trying out pedagogies that support inclusivity and equity. We hope this collection inspires, educates, and stirs you to "recover, illuminate, theorize, reenvision, and enact alternative possibilities for a liberatory librarianship"[20] and praxis. Doing so will help us become the teachers our students need us to be while opening the door for their creations.

To move beyond our profession's comfort zone, we must engage in action: "Anti-racism is about action, and enacting your critical consciousness. This is the part where you engage in tangible, community-based actions."[21]

Notes

1.   Cooke and Sweeney, *Teaching for Justice: Implementing Social Justice in the LIS Classroom*, 288.
2.   Ibid.
3.   Crenshaw, "Mapping the Margins."; Leung and López-McKnight, *Knowledge Justice*; Tervalon and Murray-Garcia, "Cultural Humility versus Cultural Competence"; Hurley, Kostelecky, and Townsend, "Cultural Humility in Libraries"; Foster, "Cultural Competence in Library Instruction"; Hodge, "Integrating Cultural Humility into Public Services Librarianship."; CAST, "Universal Design for Learning Guidelines Version 2.2."; Elmborg, "Critical Information Literacy."; Nicholson and Seale, *The Politics of Theory and the Practice of Critical Librarianship.*;.

4. Hooks, *Teaching To Transgress.*, Freire, *Pedagogy of the Oppressed.*
5. Tuitt, "Afterword."
6. Tuitt., 245-250
7. Tuitt. 251-254
8. Tuitt. 255-256
9. Tuitt. 256
10. Tuitt, Frank, Chayla Haynes, and Saran Stewart. "Transforming the Classroom at Traditionally White Institutions to Make Black Lives Matter." *To Improve the Academy* 37, no. 1 (2018). http://dx.doi.org/10.3998/tia.17063888.0037.108.
11. Ibid.
12. Chou, Pho, and Roh, *Pushing the Margins*; ; Brown, Feretti, Leung, and Méndez-Brady, "We Here: Speaking Our Truth." *Library Trends.*
13. Schlesselman-Tarango, *Topographies of Whiteness*; Brown, Feretti, Leung, and Méndez-Brady, "We Here: Speaking Our Truth." *Library Trends*
14. Cooke and Sweeney, *Teaching for Justice: Implementing Social Justice in the LIS Classroom.*
15. Schlesselman-Tarango.
16. James Elmborg, "Critical Information Literacy: Implications for Instructional Practice." *The Journal of Academic Librarianship* 32, no. 2 (2006): 192–199; Nicholson and Seale, *The Politics of Theory and the Practice of Critical Librarianship*; Drabinski, "Critical Librarianship in a Global Context";
17. Downey, A., *Critical information literacy: Foundations, inspirations, and ideas*; Pagowsky and McElroy, *Critical Library Pedagogy Handbook*; Accardi et. al., *Critical Library Instruction: Theories and Methods*; Tewell, "A decade of critical information literacy: A review of the literature."
18. Arellano Douglas, Veronica. "Moving from Critical Assessment to Assessment as Care." *Communications in Information Literacy*
19. Leung and López-McKnight, *Knowledge Justice.*
20. Honma, 2021, p. 48
21. "Reading is only a step on the path to anti-racism," PublishersWeekly.com, https://www.publishersweekly.com/pw/by-topic/industry-news/libraries/article/83626-reading-is-only-a-step-on-the-path-to-anti-racism.html

Bibliography

Accardi, Maria T., Emily Drabinski, and Alana Kumbier. Critical Library Instruction : Theories and Methods. Edited by Maria T. Accardi, Emily Drabinski, and Alana Kumbier. Duluth, Minnesota: Library Juice Press, 2010.

Arellano Douglas, Veronica. "Moving from Critical Assessment to Assessment as Care." Communications in Information Literacy 14, no. 1 (June 2020). https://doi.org/10.15760/comminfolit.2020.14.1.4.

Brown, Jennifer, Jennifer A. Ferretti, Sofia Leung, and Marisa Méndez-Brady. "We Here: Speaking Our Truth." *Library Trends* 67, no. 1 (2018): 163–81. https://doi.org/10.1353/lib.2018.0031.

CAST. "Universal Design for Learning Guidelines version 2.2.". Universal Design for Learning Guidelines. 2018. http://udlguidelines.cast.org.

Chou, Rose L., Annie Pho, and Charlotte Roh. *Pushing the Margins: Women of Color and Intersectionality in LIS*. Library Juice Press, 2018.Cooke, Nicole A. "Reading Is Only a Step on the Path to Anti-Racism." *PublishersWeekly.com*. Accessed January 19, 2022. https://www.publishersweekly.com/pw/by-topic/industry-news/libraries/article/83626-reading-is-only-a-step-on-the-path-to-anti-racism.html.

Cooke, Nicole A., and Miriam E. Sweeney. *Teaching for Justice: Implementing Social Justice in the LIS Classroom*. Library Juice Press, 2017.

Crenshaw, Kimberle. "Mapping the Margins: Intersectionality, Identity Politics, and Violence against Women of Color." *Stan. L. Rev.* 43 (1990): 1241.

Downey, A. (2016). *Critical information literacy: Foundations, inspirations, and ideas*. Sacramento, CA: Library Juice Press.

Elmborg, James. "Critical Information Literacy: Implications for Instructional Practice." *The Journal of Academic Librarianship* 32, no. 2 (2006): 192–99.

Foster, Elizabeth. "Cultural Competence in Library Instruction: A Reflective Practice Approach." *portal: Libraries and the Academy* 18, no. 3 (2018): 575–93.

Freire, Paulo. 1972. *Pedagogy of the Oppressed*. [New York]: Herder and Herder.

Hodge, Twanna. "Integrating Cultural Humility into Public Services Librarianship." *International Information & Library Review* 51, no. 3 (July 3, 2019): 268–74. https://doi.org/10.1080/10572317.2019.1629070.

Homna, Todd. "Introduction to Part I." In *Knowledge Justice: Disrupting Library and Information Studies through Critical Race Theory*, edited by Sofia Y. Leung and Jorge R. López-McKnight, 0. The MIT Press, 2021. https://doi.org/10.7551/mitpress/11969.003.0004.

hooks, bell. *Teaching to Transgress: Education as the Practice of Freedom*. Taylor & Francis. New York, NY: Routledge, 1994

Hurley, David A., Sarah R. Kostelecky, and Lori Townsend. "Cultural Humility in Libraries." *Reference Services Review* 47, no. 4 (November 11, 2019): 544–55. https://doi.org/10.1108/RSR-06-2019-0042.

Leung, Sofia Y., and Jorge R. López-McKnight, eds. *Knowledge Justice: Disrupting Library and Information Studies Through Critical Race Theory*. MIT Press, 2021. https://doi.org/10.7551/mitpress/11969.001.0001.

Nicholson, Karen P., and Maura Seale. *The Politics of Theory and the Practice of Critical Librarianship*. Library Juice Press, 2018.

Pagowsky, Nicole, and Kelly McElroy. *Critical Library Pedagogy Handbook*. Edited by Nicole Pagowsky and Kelly McElroy. Chicago, Illinois: Association of College and Research Libraries, a division of the American Library Association, 2016.

Schlesselman-Tarango, Gina. *Topographies of Whiteness: Mapping Whiteness in Library and Information Science*. Library Juice Press Sacramento, CA, 2017.

Tervalon, Melanie, and Jann Murray-Garcia. "Cultural Humility versus Cultural Competence: A Critical Distinction in Defining Physician Training Outcomes in Multicultural Education." *Journal of Health Care for the Poor and Underserved* 9, no. 2 (1998): 117–25.

Tewell, Eamon. "A decade of critical information literacy: A review of the literature." *Communications in information literacy* 9, no. 1 (2015): 2. https://doi.org/10.15760/comminfolit.2015.9.1.174

Tuitt, Franklin A. "Afterword: Realizing a More Inclusive Pedagogy." in A. Howell and F. A. Tuitt (Eds.), *Race and Higher Education: Rethinking Pedagogy in Diverse College Classrooms*, 243-68. Cambridge, MA: Harvard Education Publishing Group, 2003.

Tuitt, Frank, Chayla Haynes, and Saran Stewart. *Race, Equity, and the Learning Environment : The Global Relevance of Critical and Inclusive Pedagogies in Higher Education*. Vol. First edition. Sterling, Virginia: Stylus Publishing. 2016.

Tuitt, Frank, Chayla Haynes, and Saran Stewart. "Transforming the Classroom at Traditionally White Institutions to Make Black Lives Matter." *To Improve the Academy* 37, no. 1 (2018). http://dx.doi.org/10.3998/tia.17063888.0037.108

SECTION 1
Anti-racist Approaches

Introduction

Elizabeth Foster

The chapters in this section are connected by the authors' efforts to critically self-reflect on their power, privilege, and positionality, as well as systems and notions that have long been held to be true due to the profession's role in perpetuating whiteness. Teaching with intention to combat these long-standing ideas and to create equity and inclusivity requires librarians to step away from being authority figures and instead step beside students as guides and partners in their learning.

Two of the chapters in this section explore opportunities for anti-racist community engagement. In Chapter 1, "'Dismantling the Machine': A Case Study of Cross-campus, Multi-institutional Efforts to Address Systemic Racism," Ava Brillat, Roxane Pickens, and Kelsa Bartley describe communal efforts to deconstruct systemic racism. A common reads program serves as a focal point for engaging instructors from area institutions in foundational conversations. Brillat, Pickens, and Bartley offer examples of actions taken to advance discourse and create awareness of anti-racist and critical pedagogy. They conclude with a reflection on their experience and discuss necessary steps to continue these efforts. Faith Bradham, in Chapter 2, "Actualizing Research Skills: Integrating Culturally Responsive Practices into Library Instruction," offers a reflection on her participation in her campus's Umoja Community. Umoja Communities are academic communities focused on culturally responsive pedagogy; the curriculum incorporates a variety of equitable teaching practices into a teaching framework. Bradham explores Umoja practices that are foundational to her pedagogy and professional practice. She encourages readers to consider the importance of continually adapting one's teaching while placing student needs at the forefront.

Incorporating anti-racist practices into one's teaching can be a daunting process. Three chapters share case studies that shine a light on the importance of instructional reflection and facilitating student-centered learning. In Chapter 3, "Civic Engagement in the Virtual Classroom: Using Dialogic Pedagogy to Create an Inclusive Space for Student Learning," Alicia G. Vaandering describes using dialogic pedagogy to intentionally create an inclusive learning environment. She outlines how she used online discussion forms to generate discourse among students and facilitate equity in a credit-bearing information literacy course that moved online at the beginning of the COVID-19 pandemic. Vaandering considers the importance of discussion-based learning as a tool for engendering student engagement, developing civic literacy, and amplifying student expertise. Kelleen Maluski, in Chapter 4, "The Impact of Oppression: Transforming Historical Database Instruction into Contemporary Discussion," outlines how she engaged with the scholarship of BIPOC (Black, Indigenous, and People of Color) library scholars to modify her teaching and create an activity centered on exploring inequities of information systems. An annual history lesson put on as a collaboration between a selective liberal arts college and an International Baccalaureate high school offered her an opportunity to deeply engage with critical pedagogy theory and construct a student-centered learning environment focused on the importance of elevating marginalized voices. Maluski describes the theory she used to develop the lesson, deconstructs its pedagogical elements, and offers examples of student experiences and reactions. In Chapter 5, "Unlearning: First Steps toward an Anti-oppressive Information Literacy," Scott R. Cowan and Selinda Adelle Berg introduce foundational concepts of anti-oppressive pedagogy. They describe a library instruction session focusing on the critical evaluation of curriculum kits. Throughout the session, students are guided to participate in a "culture of questioning" and reach a point at which they can begin unlearning their implicit biases. Handouts from the session provide guidance on how to structure an unlearning activity.

Three chapters focus on the importance of examining pedagogical practices. In Chapter 6, "Supporting Epistemic Justice in the Anti-racist Classroom," Maggie Clarke connects Miranda Fricker's framework of epistemic injustice to critical pedagogy practices in information literacy. Clarke argues librarians must work to dismantle the prevailing narrative of what sources are considered trustworthy and guide students to engage with a broader range of perspectives. She introduces foundational concepts from Fricker's scholarship and offers examples of what instructors can do to promote epistemic justice in an information literacy context. Melanie Sellar, in Chapter 7, "Algorithmic Literacy as Inclusive Pedagogy," proposes that librarians teach algorithmic literacy to facilitate inclusivity by incorporating tools that students are familiar with, moving away from the idea that there is one correct way to do research. She offers a portfolio of three lesson areas, each containing a rationale for its inclusiveness, learning goals, activities, and potential areas for extending the lesson further. Sellar discusses opportunities for scaling based on instructional constraints and concludes with an annotated list of resources for further study. Finally, in Chapter 8, "Oppressive Authority: Dismantling, Reexamining, and Reconstructing Notions of Authority in Information Literacy Instruction," Melissa Chomintra deconstructs the profession's contribution to the perpetuation of expertise concepts that are based in whiteness. She maintains that knowledge created by BIPOC scholars is delegitimatized and erased when librarians teach source evaluation as a neutral act. Chomintra examines how the "Authority Is Constructed and Contextual" frame codifies these instructional practices and offers actions librarians can take to implement anti-oppressive pedagogy.

Every instructor starts at a different point on their anti-racist journey, and there is no set path. Instead, we are called to reflect, retool, and engage with our campus communities to cultivate equitable and inclusive environments that benefit all of their members. I found inspiration in the ideas put forward by these authors and am excited to try out their practices at my institution. Whether you are just starting out on your anti-racist journey or come to this section with years of experience and a desire to freshen up your approach, I anticipate that you will leave with a sense of potential and a desire to critically reconsider your pedagogy.

CHAPTER 1

"Dismantling the Machine"

A Case Study of Cross-campus, Multi-institutional Efforts to Address Systemic Racism

Ava Brillat, Roxane Pickens, and Kelsa Bartley*

Introduction

> *Systemic racism is a machine that runs whether we pull the levers or not, and by just letting it be, we are responsible for what it produces. We have to actually dismantle the machine if we want to make change.*
>
> —Ijeoma Oluo, *So You Want to Talk About Race*[1]

---

* This case study focuses on anti-racist work in the university setting. Possible factors affecting the reading of this work include the racial identity and lived experiences of the authors. At least one author identifies as an able-bodied, white, cisgender female, and the other two identify as Black, able-bodied, cisgender females. Additionally, two authors are foreign-born US citizens with the third born and raised in the US South. At the time of writing, all authors are early-to-mid-career faculty librarians working at the University of Miami.

Dismantling the machinery of systemic racism in educational spaces is necessarily done in community, and the possibility of change depends on understanding the pernicious mechanisms at work and implementing new ways of teaching that are more inclusive and transformational. The inequities illuminated by the global pandemic of 2020, combined with an intensified spotlight on the nation's long-standing racial injustices, have been a clarion call for higher education, particularly regarding social justice in academia. With heightened levels of civic action around racial injustices that impact students, an all-hands-on-deck scenario emerged, compelling all university units—including libraries—to collaborate on addressing systemic racism in the learning environment. This chapter highlights one academic library's cross-campus collaborations to facilitate racial justice discussions and actions. Focusing on a common reads program at University of Miami (UM) in Florida, this case study outlines key library and campus partnerships and steps taken to promote dialogue and spearhead anti-racist and critical pedagogy awareness for instructors of record.

Literature Review

Organizational change of any type is difficult to usher in, particularly at large academic institutions. While change management is a well-studied niche of organizational research, the intersection of social justice and organizational change is a developing field without much in the way of established best practices.

Unfortunately, equity-focused change through academic leadership is an emerging field, particularly regarding actively anti-racist organizational change.[2] While top-down approaches to change may still be developing, consciousness-raising and grassroots approaches to anti-racist work have a long historical precedent, particularly in the Civil Rights movement of the 1960s–1970s in the United States. The embodied performance of protest, referred to by activists as "direct action," provided a citizen-level means by which to prompt political change regarding racial injustice,[3] as can still be seen in the 2020 Black Lives Matter movements. Grassroots or group activism often informs the evolution of legal and political changes, and discourse is the means by which to disrupt injustice and influence applicative justice.[4] Recent case studies, as outlined in Liera and Dowd, support the use of inquiry, discourse, and rhetoric to disrupt systemic racism.[5] Data alone is not enough to drive change, particularly at decision-making levels; discussion and inquiry are necessary to cement and nurture systemic change.[6] Engaging in discourse and inquiry, particularly for faculty, promotes and expands the knowledge and practice of anti-racist work through the act of boundary crossing that occurs when faculty of different disciplines and experiences purposefully engage with one another.[7]

Because of the historical precedent of direct action and the emerging case studies of the importance of inquiry and discussion to heighten the impact of anti-racist work, UM's One Book, One U program targeted instructors in order to create an environment for action. Through interdisciplinary discussion and the disruption of teaching silos, One Book, One U endeavored to promote grassroots conscious-ness-raising in order to support the long institutional evolution toward a more equi-table academic environment.

Merging best practices for change management with anti-racist pedagogies, particularly in a way that empowers faculty members and provides sustained energy to diversity practices, is of particular importance if systemic racism is to be addressed in higher education. Change management focused on anti-racist action is still devel-oping, particularly in regard to the development of best practices. The *Harvard Business Review* notes the need for vision and intent to bring about true anti-racist evolution in institutions.[8] Although this case study focuses on academic libraries, dismantling systemic racism must be cross-disciplinary and across all bodies of the American university in order for true change to occur.

Additionally, there is a need for sharing case studies, including practical aspects of anti-racist work in higher education. Variables such as policy changes, change management, training, cultural change, and restorative justice in higher education, especially those focused on anti-racist pedagogies, are needed in order to inspire change and provide institutions with examples to inspire their own iterations of anti-racist work. As each academic institution is unique, so too should anti-racist work reflect the distinct needs of each institution. Larger institutions, for example, will have different needs and approaches to anti-racist pedagogy than will smaller institutions. As a result, it is only by having both practical and theoretical informa-tion that any institution can even begin to dismantle, in earnest, systemic racism.

Case Study Background

The One Book, One U program at UM was founded in 2017 by an English and creative writing professor in the College of Arts and Sciences and a professor at the School of Law. Their goal was to help build campus-wide community through the shared reading of texts that deeply explore the human condition. The selection that year was Jennine Capó Crucet's novel *Make Your Home among Strangers*, and in courses and events during spring 2018—including a keynote presentation by the author—students, faculty, and staff joined in conversations about topics related to the text's main themes. The following years featured coursework, programming, and author keynotes for Patricia Engel's novel *Veins of the Ocean* in 2019 and Edwidge Danticat's memoir, *Brother, I'm Dying*, in 2020.

Always an interdisciplinary collaboration between academic and administra-tive units across the institution, the program is cosponsored by UM Libraries with increasing levels of librarian support. In the first two years, librarians served on the selection committee, helped promote events, and provided access to the book selections. In the third year, along with selection, book access, and promotions, two librarians also served on the program's coordinating committee and developed a research and instructors' guide to help faculty more easily incorporate the text into their courses. Additionally, UM Libraries had the honor of hosting Edwidge Danticat in its premier event space, the Kislak Center, and supplied copies of her book to students attending an intimate conversation that was held in its learning commons.

The success of the program in its third year and growing opportunities for collaboration between UM Libraries and key program partners such as the College of Arts and Sciences and the Center for the Humanities helped set the stage for the libraries to become the administrative home for One Book, One U. As the program readied for a new year with another book fostering the principles of dialogue, diversity, and inclusion—work that was complicated by having to make plans during the COVID-19 pandemic—a more urgent need arose: that of responding to the overwhelming call for justice in the wake of George Floyd's murder by a Minneapolis police officer in 2020 and subsequent Black Lives Matter demonstrations in the US and around the world. The program's coordinating committee called on the selection committee to reconvene and select a new text that would specifically address racial injustice in the country. The committee chose Ijeoma Oluo's *So You Want to Talk About Race* for 2020–21, inviting students and the entire university to deeply consider race, racism, and the ways in which our communities can become more equitable and just.

Instructor Reading Groups

In addition to supporting the program as in the past with a resource and teaching guide, print and digital copies of the book, and planning for events including the author keynote, three UM librarians worked with two university colleagues to co-facilitate two instructor reading groups aimed at helping faculty and staff incorporate the themes of Oluo's book into learning spaces. Functioning in the style of faculty learning communities and committed to inclusion, these reading groups were open to full-time, part-time, and graduate student instructors as well as staff working in student-facing capacities. Out of eighty registrants from nine schools and colleges, a total of sixty-five participants met for two series of three small-group conversations about *So You Want to Talk About Race*. Participants in the faculty reading groups mirrored the racial diversity of the larger university faculty population. The university faculty, however, do not reflect the diversity of the Miami-Dade County. Still, a broad range of backgrounds, disciplines, and teaching experiences were represented.

At the first meeting, a set of community agreements were discussed and established in order to facilitate discussion by establishing a community mindset. These agreed-upon practices were used to create avenues for conversation and to provide guidance for modeling openness and nonviolent communication. The presence of discussion facilitators, however, to actively support safe conversation, particularly for faculty members new to discussing issues of race, was key to enabling conversation to flow. The resulting conversations connected Oluo's text to such questions as "What are the systems of power that reinforce and reproduce racism in Miami? In Coral Gables? At UM? In our own classrooms?" and "How might we (or how do you already) affirm a commitment to classroom environments that promote and sustain diversity and acknowledge intersectionality? Any particular language you would include in your syllabi?"

Each of the facilitators, including the director of the Learning Innovation and Faculty Engagement instructional design team, the director of Special Projects in the Office of the Provost, an institutional culture consultant, and the three instructional librarians, had prior classroom teaching experience that emphasized equity, diversity, and inclusion. Thus, they were able to effectively lead discussions that prompted the group participants to new insights about how they might rethink their pedagogies. The reading groups helped build connections among a diverse community of colleagues—from anesthesiologists to biologists to law professors—in a novel way, and they prompted instructors and student-facing staff to collectively strategize about anti-racist engagement techniques. Additionally, participants explored ideas for engaging coworkers about race, racism, equity, and justice, even when work contexts (like clinical settings) could make these topics challenging to consider.

Participants in the instructor reading groups came from various levels of comfort and experience with discussing racially sensitive topics. In many cases, a facilitator acted as a model for how to engage in difficult conversation with empathy. For participants with little to no experience discussing race, seeing facilitators address seemingly hidden bias in generalizations made during conversation served as an inflection point for further scrutiny and reflection on racial bias. These experiences were critical to developing skills needed for guiding sensitive conversations in the classroom. For more experienced participants, it could be frustrating to engage in conversation with participants who were not as skilled at addressing racial bias, particularly in regard to self-reflection. It is difficult to arrange conversation groups in a way that meets the objectives of every participant. However, it is important to persist and to continue to offer opportunities for conversation in order to upskill instructors on how to engage in difficult conversations.

Anti-racist and Critical Pedagogy Reading Group

Several faculty participants were so interested in revising their teaching to be more inclusive and antiracist that they prompted the facilitators to develop and host a subsequent anti-racist and critical pedagogy reading group. A deeper dive into pedagogical theory and praxis, this reading group had fifty-five registrants who attended four sessions for discussions of essays by theorists such as bell hooks, Henry Giroux, Gloria Ladson-Billings, and Sara Ahmed. In an effort toward greater inclusion and collaborative potential, the facilitators opened participation to instructors from three South Florida institutions in addition to UM: Florida International University, Miami-Dade College, and Florida Atlantic University. This interinstitutional collaboration speaks to ACRL's *Roles and Strengths of Teaching Librarians*,[9] revealing how instructional designers and librarians together can leverage partnerships to provide inclusive and diverse student learning spaces.

In this more focused reading group, we explored anti-racist and critical pedagogical frameworks and vocabulary, as well as the necessary interrogation that both instructors and students would need to bring to an open dialogue. For example, one session considered redefining the concept of the "safe space," which implies an absence of productive discomfort, with a "brave space," which gives students opportunities to exercise vulnerability, responsibility to others, and commitment to learning and growth. We also considered sites of overlap and intersections of practice from our different disciplines (participants came from all parts of the educational spectrum) and across our different institutions.

We reflected on how to help students find language to articulate where they are in the learning process and get them closer to "the learning edge," or a space where they can encounter new material that may be discomforting and yet necessary for growth. We discussed how to have these kinds of conversations when instruction contact time is low, like during a thirty-minute meeting or a single class session. We exchanged ideas for facilitating in-class discussions among students, taking care, for example, to request names and pronouns before meeting and modeling ways of apologizing and recovering after difficult exchanges. We also talked about working with silences in the classroom and ways that empathetic and active listening might be deployed. The impact of these conversations among instructors—both faculty and educator staff—has been generative as participants found conversation partners among their colleagues both on and across our diverse campuses. Additionally, the relationships led to invitations for further discussion at subsequently scheduled reading groups hosted at the other campuses.

The 2021 One Book One U program and the anti-racist and critical pedagogy reading groups are related not only by content, but also by intention, and they are platforms for UM Libraries to practice critical librarianship from an anti-racist, decolonial perspective. While neoliberalism in academia calls for treating students as customers, deemphasizing community and upholding capitalistic ideals, decolonialism calls for the creation of an inclusive community that is actively anti-racist. Inclusivity creates space for all learners, including students who are traditionally overlooked or specifically excluded. With a challenge to the presumed neutrality of library spaces, the collaborations and learning communities that University of

Miami Libraries supports through these projects demonstrate the critical role that academic libraries play in promoting justice and equality in the educational context.

Reflections and Future Directions

The efforts and attempts of academic institutions to dismantle systemic racism by any means is of particular importance to document and share in order to inspire continued change. A pernicious effect of institutional racism is that it continues to be an active influence in the work of the academy, meaning that one will encounter resistance and efforts to thwart anti-racist pedagogies simply because of the nature of the academic environment. However, with continued sustained engagement, it is impossible for change not to occur. Academic institutions everywhere are beholden to engage in the messy struggle that is dismantling institutional racism, and there are lessons to be learned from any attempt at anti-racist pedagogies. As a result, it is of key importance that these experiences, both successful and unsuccessful, continue to be shared. It is by reflecting on all efforts that the way forward can be determined.

Related to anti-racist pedagogy work, research on the intersection of institutional change, anti-racism, and faculty empowerment must continue to expand. Best practices are sorely needed to guide and evaluate efforts and to usher in true systemic change. Although the road to shared understanding of best practices is long, academic institutions must continue to pursue anti-racist work with the same fervor as research into best educational practices. The more that educational goals and anti-racist work are aligned, the closer institutions can get to changing the inherently racist paradigm of higher education.

What we learned from both the One Book, One U instructor reading groups and the subsequent interinstitutional antiracist and critical pedagogy reading group is that instructors are eager for contexts in which they can reconsider their teaching with attention to inclusive, equitable, and specifically anti-racist practices in order to heighten the learning experiences of all their students. Because of the connections that instructional librarians already have with a diverse range of faculty, they stand to be natural collaborators with instructional designers and like-minded colleagues to host and facilitate teaching-related conversations and strategies.

We have also learned that instructors are on a spectrum in terms of implementation of anti-racist and critical pedagogy into their curriculums. Many instructors are ready to move beyond just talking and learning about systemic racism and are eager to start incorporating what they learned from both reading groups into their classroom activities. Some are even looking for better ways to improve or accelerate activities they have already been doing in their classrooms and beyond. At the other end of the spectrum, many instructors are either just beginning to engage in anti-racist work or are still continuing their learning journeys. Regardless of where they were in the process, at the end of reading groups, participants overwhelmingly called for advice and conversation on what the next steps should be for continuing the momentum of change. This encouragement from our colleagues has given us the impetus to continue growing our cross-campus and interinstitutional collaborations for dismantling the machine of institutional racism at University of Miami and other college campuses across the Miami community. We believe these community-led conversations that continue into our classrooms can have a broad impact in our goal of an anti-racist, inclusive, and equitable future for our students and the communities they will eventually lead.

Suggested Readings

The following readings are meant to be a blueprint for introductory-level readings on anti-racist pedagogies; however, any list of resources can quickly become outdated. Regardless, anti-racist work requires that one be active in seeking out new information and professional development opportunities. Consider searching for local diversity conferences, training, and discussion groups in order to develop and continue to finesse the skills of discussing racism and practicing anti-racist principles, both inside and outside of the classroom. One possible best practice may be to empower discussion group members to seek out anti-racist readings for discussion. What follows comes from the antiracist and critical pedagogy reading group reading list and can serve as a starting point for discussion.

Giroux, Henry A., and Susan Searls Giroux. "Challenging Neoliberalism's New World Order: The Promise of Critical Pedagogy." *Cultural Studies* ↔ *Critical Methodologies* 6, no. 1 (2006): 21–32. https://doi.org/10.1177/1532708605282810.

hooks, bell. "Embracing Change: Teaching in a Multicultural World." In *Teaching to Transgress: Education as the Practice of Freedom*, 35–44. New York: Routledge, 1994.

Kumashiro, Kevin K. "Toward a Theory of Anti-oppressive Education." *Review of Educational Research* 70, no. 1 (2000): 25–53. https://doi.org/10.3102/00346543070001025.

Ladson-Billings, Gloria. "Toward a Theory of Culturally Relevant Pedagogy." *American Educational Research Journal* 32, no. 3 (September 1995): 465–91. https://doi.org/10.3102/00028312032003465.

Paris, Django. "Culturally Sustaining Pedagogy: A Needed Change in Stance, Terminology, and Practice." *Educational Researcher* 41, no. 3 (April 2012): 93–97. https://doi.org/10.3102/0013189X12441244.

Ross, Sabrina N. "Critical Race Theory, Democratization, and the Public Good: Deploying Postmodern Understandings of Racial Identity in the Social Justice Classroom to Contest

Academic Capitalism." *Teaching in Higher Education* 14, no. 5 (2009), 517–28. https://doi.org/10.1080/13562510903186709.

Shrewsbury, Carolyn M. "What Is Feminist Pedagogy?" *Women's Studies Quarterly* 15, no. 3/4 (Fall–Winter 1987): 6–14. https://www.jstor.org/stable/40003432.

Tatum, Beverly. *Why Are All the Black Kids Sitting Together in the Cafeteria? And Other Conversations about Race*. New York: Basic Books, 2017.

Wagner, Anne E. "Unsettling the Academy: Working through the Challenges of Anti-racist Pedagogy." *Race Ethnicity and Education* 8, no. 3 (2005): 261–75. https://doi.org/10.1080/13613320500174333.

Yeager, David S., and Gregory M. Walton. "Social-Psychological Interventions in Education: They're Not Magic." *Review of Educational Research* 81, no. 2 (2011): 267–301. https://doi.org/10.3102/0034654311405999.

Notes

1. Oluo, Ijeoma, *So You Want to Talk About Race* (New York: Seal Press, 2019), 30.
2. Decoteau J. Irby, Coby V. Meyers, and Jason D. Salisbury, "Improving Schools by Strategically Connecting Equity Leadership and Organizational Improvement Perspectives: Introduction to Special Issue," *Journal of Education for Students Placed at Risk* 25, no. 2 (2020): 102, https://doi.org/10.1080/10824669.2019.1704628, ProQuest.
3. Randolph Hohle, *Black Citizenship and Authenticity in the Civil Rights Movement*, Routledge Research in Race and Ethnicity (New York: Routledge, 2013), 60.
4. Naomi Zack, *Applicative Justice* (Lanham, MD: Rowman & Littlefield, 2016), 66–67.
5. Román Liera and Alicia C. Dowd, "Faculty Learning at Boundaries to Broker Racial Equity," *Journal of Higher Education* 90, no. 3 (2019): 473–76, https://doi.org/10.1080/00221546.2018.1512805.
6. Alicia C. Dowd and Román Liera, "Sustaining Change towards Racial Equity through Cycles of Inquiry," *Education Policy Analysis Archives* 26 (May 21, 2018): 6, https://doi.org/10.14507/epaa.26.3274, ProQuest.
7. Amy R. Kline, "Faculty Motivation in Academic Program Assessment: An Instrumental Case Study on the Impact of an Inquiry-Based Process" (EdD diss, Northeastern University, 2020), 42–43, ProQuest Dissertations and Theses Global: Social Sciences (2393063509).
8. Evelyn R. Carter, "Restructure Your Organization to Actually Advance Racial Justice," *Harvard Business Review*, June 22, 2020, para. 4, https://hbr.org/2020/06/restructure-your-organization-to-actually-advance-racial-justice.
9. Association of College and Research Libraries, *Roles and Strengths of Teaching Librarians* (Chicago: Association of College and Research Libraries, 2017), https://www.ala.org/acrl/standards/teachinglibrarians.

Bibliography

Anthym, Myntha, and Franklin Tuitt. "When the Levees Break: The Cost of Vicarious Trauma, Microaggressions and Emotional Labor for Black Administrators and Faculty Engaging in Race Work at Traditionally White Institutions." *International Journal of Qualitative Studies in Education* 32, no. 9 (2019): 1072–93. https://doi.org/10.1080/09518398.2019.1645907.

Association of College and Research Libraries. *Roles and Strengths of Teaching Librarians.* Chicago: Association of College and Research Libraries, 2017. https://www.ala.org/acrl/standards/teachinglibrarians.

Carter, Evelyn R. "Restructure Your Organization to Actually Advance Racial Justice." *Harvard Business Review*, June 22, 2020. https://hbr.org/2020/06/restructure-your-organization-to-actually-advance-racial-justice.

Cole, Eddie R. "Race at the Top: Historical Insights on the College Presidency and Racial Inequities." *Change: The Magazine of Higher Learning* 52, no. 2 (2020): 17–21. https://doi.org/10.1080/00091383.2020.1732754.

Dadzie, Stella. *Toolkit for Tackling Racism in Schools.* Stoke-on-Trent, UK: Trentham Books, 2000. ProQuest.

Dowd, Alicia C., and Román Liera. "Sustaining Organizational Change towards Racial Equity through Cycles of Inquiry." *Education Policy Analysis Archives* 26 (May 21, 2018): 1–45. https://doi.org/10.1080/00221546.2018.1512805. ProQuest.

Gardner, Rachele, William M. Snyder, and Ayda Zuguy. "Amplifying Youth Voice and Cultivating Leadership through Participatory Action Research." *Education Policy Analysis Archives* 27, no. 54 (2019): 1–26. ProQuest.

Hohle, Randolph. *Black Citizenship and Authenticity in the Civil Rights Movement.* Routledge Research in Race and Ethnicity. New York: Routledge, 2013.

Irby, Decoteau J., Coby V. Meyers, and Jason D. Salisbury. "Improving Schools by Strategically Connecting Equity Leadership and Organizational Improvement Perspectives: Introduction to Special Issue." *Journal of Education for Students Placed at Risk* 25, no. 2 (2020): 101–6. https://doi.org/10.1080/10824669.2019.1704628. ProQuest.

King, Sabrina Hope, and Louis A. Castenell, eds. *Racism and Racial Inequality: Implications for Teacher Education.* Washington, DC: AACTE Publications, 2001. ProQuest.

Kline, Amy R. "Faculty Motivation in Academic Program Assessment: An Instrumental Case Study on the Impact of an Inquiry-Based Process." EdD diss., Northeastern University, 2020. ProQuest Dissertations and Theses Global: Social Sciences (2393063509).

Knaus, Christopher B. "Seeing What They Want to See: Racism and Leadership Development in Urban Schools." *Urban Review* 46, no. 3 (2014): 420–44. https://doi.org/10.1007/s11256-014-0299-0.

Lac, Van T., and Gwendolyn S. Baxley. "Race and Racism: How Does an Aspiring Social Justice Principal Support Black Student Leaders for Racial Equity among a Resistant White Staff." *Journal of Cases in Educational Leadership* 22, no. 1 (2019): 29–42. https://doi.org/10.1177/1555458918785655.

Lawrence, Sandra M., and Beverly Daniel Tatum. "Teachers in Transition: The Impact of Antiracist Professional Development on Classroom Practice." *Teachers College Record* 99, no. 1 (1997): 162–78. https://doi.org/10.1177/016146819709900101.

Lee, NTanya. "Thirty Years of Advocacy in San Francisco: Lessons Learned and the Next Generation of Leadership." *New Directions for Youth Development* 2008, no. 117 (Spring 2008): 61–75. https://doi.org/10.1002/yd.247.

Levine, David P. "The Birth of the Citizenship Schools: Entwining the Struggles for Literacy and Freedom." *History of Education Quarterly* 44, no. 3 (2004): 388–414. https://doi.org/10.1111/j.1748-5959.2004.tb00015.x.

Liera, Román, and Alicia C. Dowd. "Faculty Learning at Boundaries to Broker Racial Equity." *Journal of Higher Education* 90, no. 3 (2019): 462–85. https://doi.org/10.1080/00221546.2018.1512805.

Liera, Román. "Faculty Learning and Agency for Racial Equity." PhD diss., University of Southern California, 2018. ProQuest Dissertations and Theses Global: Social Sciences (2178744977).

Mangan, Katherine S. "Colleges Offer Cultural-Awareness Programs to Help Professors Understand Needs of Minority Students." *Chronicle of Higher Education* 37, no. 25 (March 6, 1991): A11–A12. ProQuest.

Moyer, Jeffrey S., Mark R. Warren, and Andrew R. King. "'Our Stories Are Powerful': The Use of Youth Storytelling in Policy Advocacy to Combat the School-to-Prison Pipeline." *Harvard Educational Review* 90, no. 2 (Summer 2020): 172–95. ProQuest.

Ocean, Mia, Damian Hawkins, and Kobitta Chopra. "Racial Disparities, Perceptions, and Evaluations: Counseling Model Choice and the Florida College System." *Community College Journal of Research and Practice* 38, no. 12 (2014): 1142–56. https://doi.org/10.1080/10668926.2012.752770.

Oluo, Ijeoma. *So You Want to Talk About Race*. New York: Seal Press, 2019.

Pour-Khorshid, Farima. "Cultivating Sacred Spaces: A Racial Affinity Group Approach to Support Critical Educators of Color." *Teaching Education* 29, no. 4 (2018): 318–29. https://doi.org/10.1080/10476210.2018.1512092.

Schoem, David, Linda Frankel, Ximena Zúñiga, and Edith A. Lewis, eds. *Multicultural Teaching in the University*. Westport, CT: Praeger, 1993. ProQuest.

Song, Samuel Y., Jacqueline M. Eddy, Heather M. Thompson, Brian Adams, and Jennifer Beskow. "Restorative Consultation in Schools: A Systematic Review and Call for Restorative Justice Science to Promote Anti-racism and Social Justice." *Journal of Educational and Psychological Consultation* 30, no. 4 (2020): 462–76. https://doi.org/10.1080/10474412.2020.1819298.

Tabb, Myrtis, and Christy Riddle Montesi. "A Model for Long-Term Leadership Development among Groups of Diverse Persons: The Delta Emerging Leaders Program." *Journal of the Community Development Society* 31, no. 2 (2000): 331–47. ProQuest.

Toure, Judith, and Dana Thompson Dorsey. "Stereotypes, Images, and Inclination to Discriminatory Action: The White Racial Frame in the Practice of School Leadership." *Teachers College Record* 120, no. 2 (2018). ProQuest.

Varghese, Rani. "Teaching to Transform? Addressing Race and Racism in the Teaching of Clinical Social Work Practice." *Journal of Social Work Education* 52 (2016): S134–S147. ProQuest.

Wilson, Camille, and Lauri Johnson. "Black Educational Activism for Community Empowerment: International Leadership Perspectives." *International Journal of Multicultural Education* 17, no. 1 (2015), 102–20. ProQuest.

Young, Evelyn Y. "The Four Personae of Racism: Educators' (Mis)Understanding of Individual vs. Systemic Racism." *Urban Education* 46, no. 6 (November 2011): 1433–60. https://doi.org/10.1177/0042085911413145.

Zack, Naomi. *Applicative Justice: A Pragmatic Empirical Approach to Racial Injustice*. Lanham, MD: Rowman & Littlefield, 2016.

CHAPTER 2

Actualizing Research Skills

Integrating Culturally Responsive Practices into Library Instruction

Faith Bradham

Introduction

As part of a profession that is over 80% white,[1] and in a country where "culture" is often used to imply "not white," academic librarians in the United States might seem wholly unsuited to integrating culturally responsive practices with their information literacy work. Some might wonder why I, as a white librarian myself, might grant myself the authority to dispense advice about culturally responsive teaching practices. These are valid critiques. However, I firmly believe that using culturally responsive pedagogy is not only possible for white librarians, it is imperative. If we, as those entrusted with giving students the skills to navigate the world of information, do not use culturally responsive practices, we are simply perpetuating the cycle of default white culture. By sticking to pedagogical practices that mirror what we already know and are comfortable with, our curricula will remain centered on whiteness and the white experience (and by extension, white supremacy culture).[2] This provides a disservice to every student we interact with, no matter their race or culture. Just as life is full of multiple cultures and experiences, so do our students deserve curricula that reflect this. How can we effectively prepare our students to

understand the full and rich tapestry of information if they can understand only a particular (singular-cultured) kind of information?[3]

This chapter acts as a case study of my own experience as a community college librarian working within one culturally responsive academic community, called the Umoja Community. While the practices emphasized in this chapter are based on Umoja's curriculum, these practices as a whole are not necessarily unique to Umoja—many have similarities with other established equitable teaching practices and philosophies, such as the work of Paulo Freire, Zaretta Hammond, and even universal design for learning.[4] As a result, the practices aren't groundbreaking on their own. Instead, Umoja offers these practices as a uniquely comprehensive framework for teaching. The practices I go over in this chapter are not bound to the library or to a classroom. Instead, they infuse all aspects of my librarianship and have caused me to rethink how I approach education and academia as a whole. My hope is to give you an example of how one person has incorporated one set of culturally responsive practices into librarianship so that you are able to draw inspiration for your own library environment.

What Is Umoja?

The Umoja Community is a California-based student success program that seeks to close the success gap for Black students in California community colleges through a curriculum responsive to the African and African American diasporas.[5] In Umoja programs, students of all races are welcome, but Black culture is centered, as is the success of Black students. There are Umoja programs at 58 of the 114 California community colleges, as well as at University of California, Riverside, and California State University, East Bay. The Umoja pedagogy is based on eighteen different practices, on which every program bases its curriculum.[6] Because Umoja seeks to be responsive to and inclusive of African American culture, the practices are not only pedagogical, but also incorporate elements of communication and culture.

When Bakersfield College's Umoja program began in 2016, the program coordinator, an English professor, approached the library about embedding library services into the program. The Bakersfield College Library offers a one-credit course called LIBR B1: Introduction to College Research, which many English professors encourage their students to take in conjunction with the English composition course at Bakersfield College. The program coordinator asked if the library would be interested in being part of a learning community made up of an Umoja section of LIBR B1 and the Umoja section of Bakersfield College's English composition course.

Because Umoja is a space for Black students, Umoja primarily seeks the inclusion of Black faculty in its programs. However, as is so common in librarianship,[7] there are no Black full-time librarians at the Bakersfield College Library, and so Bakersfield

College's Umoja program offered an open invitation to interested members of our all-white full-time library faculty. As someone passionate about equity, I accepted the invitation. To become "Umoja-fied"—as members of the Umoja community jokingly refer to faculty and staff trained in Umoja practices—I attended Umoja's annual faculty training institute. Six years ago, when I attended my first institute, I was one of a dozen or so white faculty and staff in a room of hundreds of Black faculty and staff. Although I spent much of the time plagued by shyness and imposter syndrome, I was grateful for the opportunity to sit and listen to the experiences and wisdom shared by the other Umoja practitioners at the institute (and I still am grateful for this opportunity when attending the institute currently). After my training, the Umoja English professor and I created a learning community consisting of the English composition course and the library research course. Our curricula are tied to each other so that whatever students learn in my course is immediately applicable to their research needs for their English course. Since then, Umoja at Bakersfield College has expanded to offer courses in many other disciplines.[8]

Since I became a part of the Umoja program on my campus and incorporated practices from Umoja pedagogy into my curriculum, my teaching practice has changed dramatically. Using Umoja's culturally responsive practices to inform my teaching has caused me to become a better instructor and a better librarian, not only for my Umoja students, but for all students on my campus. Yet getting to this point has not necessarily been simple. When I first joined Umoja, no other program had yet incorporated the library into its program as much as Bakersfield College's program had. This meant that I had to create my own blueprint for incorporating the eighteen Umoja practices into library instruction. This chapter shows the results of my work on this blueprint. While all of the Umoja practices are useful, there are five that have had the most impact on my teaching. The rest of this chapter will focus on how I integrate each of these five practices into the curriculum for my one-credit information literacy course as well as into my overall teaching practice for the library.

Incorporating Umoja Practices

The Porch

Umoja defines The Porch as "a place where our students can safely communicate and advocate for themselves"—in Umoja, we are charged to treat students as partners in learning with us, rather than as subordinates.[9] The Porch is about "real talk": just as you might gather with friends on the back porch to discuss something with them, your class might need to take a pause from learning to discuss an issue that might be disrupting their capacity to learn. This can mean that the instructor might call a Porch session during class to discuss real-world situations weighing heavily on students (such as the January 6, 2021, storming of the US Capitol, news of yet another police murder of a Black American, and so on). It can also mean calling a Porch session to hash out any interpersonal dynamics causing tension or unrest in the classroom, or using it as a space to let students know something personal about yourself. In an ideal classroom, students should also feel free to call a Porch during class.

As an educator who strives for a student-centered teaching philosophy, I have incorporated the concept of the Porch into my teaching in multiple ways. I intentionally call a Porch session on the very first day of my LIBR B1 class each semester in order to tell the students I'm white. Of course, they know I'm white—they can see it pretty clearly! However, it is important for me to acknowledge myself as a white professor in this Black-centered learning community. While Umoja is open to practitioners of all races, the Umoja program at my college intentionally seeks out Black faculty to teach within the program, as we want students to feel represented and understood by their Umoja faculty. Thus, I know that some students might feel put off by a white professor in their Black-centered Umoja program: they might be confused by or suspicious of my reasons for being part of the program. It's important for my students to trust me and know that my classroom is a safe space.

This initial Porch session is how I begin to establish trust with my students. During this session, I acknowledge my whiteness to the students, tell them why I've chosen to be involved with Umoja, and invite them to share any thoughts or concerns they have with me. I also make sure they know that they can get in touch with me one-on-one with any concerns they aren't comfortable stating in front of the whole class. The response to this varies. Sometimes, students want to talk about my motivations for joining Umoja and why I want to work with Black students. Other semesters, the students say "Oh, we already heard about you from other Umoja students, and we know you're OK." No matter the response, I want to give students space to process and feel like they are equal partners in the classroom with me. This process does take time, as students are often hesitant to give an authority figure their honest thoughts about a topic such as this on the first day of class. However, laying this groundwork in the first class meeting helps students understand that, although I am their professor, they will not be talked down to in this class and they will be able to make their voice heard.

In addition, I also make it clear throughout the semester that I or students are welcome to call a Porch during class time or in a one-on-one with me. Sometimes, class concepts are connected to a Porch session (for example, in a discussion about bias in research, a student might connect this to an experience they have encountered with bias), but other times, they aren't related to course content at all. One theme that has repeatedly come up over the years has been students wanting to discuss feelings and emotions related to interpersonal dynamics within the course (students in Umoja often take most or all of their courses together, so they are with each other every day of the week, which can of course occasionally lead to conflict). The first time a student called a Porch on this topic, I was hesitant to let it move forward, as it distracted from our class content. However, I realized that the tensions festering in the classroom were themselves distracting students from focusing on the course content. Hashing things out and getting everyone's feelings into the open in a respectful manner helps clear up these tensions, and we are able to move forward with a renewed focus. Of course, it can be quite difficult to let go of classroom control enough to allow for a Porch, but overall I find that students benefit from being able to be open and honest with me and their fellow students (and vice versa). The Porch allows students to feel like equal members of the classroom with me—they respect my authority as their professor, but they know that, in turn, I will respect them and the issues they need to bring up.

Although I don't use the language of The Porch explicitly in my teaching environments outside of Umoja (such as one-on-one interactions at the reference desk, one-shots, and research skills workshops), I continue to use the concepts of this practice in all of my teaching. For example, if a student (Umoja or not) is noticeably stressed or upset as I help them at the reference desk, I might pause to ask if they are OK and if they would like to go into my office to chat. Some students take me up on this, and some do not, but even this simple acknowledgement that I see them and am willing to hear them helps students feel safer in the library.

Manifesting

While the term "manifesting" might bring to mind New Age theory, in Umoja, Manifesting means giving students the ability to reproduce their newly learned skills with their community.[10] Someone incorporating this practice into their teaching seeks to give students the ability to actualize what they have learned and to connect their new skills to their community and to their culture. This practice comes very easily to librarianship, as library instruction focuses on very reproducible skills that students can immediately put into practice. However, it's important to think about students not only reproducing their skills for their academic and personal lives, but also with their friends, family, and wider community.

My teaching practice focuses on giving students functional, replicable skills that they can use to navigate information both in the academic world and in their personal lives. In this sense, Manifesting has simply given a name to a student-centered philosophy I already subscribe to. I continually encourage my students to share the information they learn in my class with their friends and family, and many of my assignments and class activities ask them how they will use these skills outside of my classroom. However, this practice has led to a few concrete changes in my class. Now, several assignments and discussions ask students to share how they plan to share and how they already have shared their skills with their friends and family. After learning about how information can become biased via algorithms, filter bubbles, and other distribution methods, one student shared with me that she had found this knowledge so useful that she had given a presentation to her fellow Army unit members about it and that it had been useful context for them in their Army trainings on radicalization via the internet. Students are also asked to reflect on how their understanding of information and of research has changed since the start of class.

In addition, I ask students to choose research topics that connect to their culture so that they can research topics throughout the semester that are immediately applicable to their interest in or curiosity about their culture. Recently, I've asked students to choose and narrow one of these umbrella topics: African American identity or systemic racism in America. Students have given me narrowed topics that include investigating how to fight systemic racism with the anti-racism movement in America and researching the effects of police brutality on the African American community. This gives students agency to research something that they might have a personal connection to and that might hold more meaning for them. The practice of Manifesting is a good reminder that, to be truly information literate, students should be able to understand how to use and understand information, not just focus on being able to find a couple of specific types of sources for a final exam.

Live Learning

Live Learning is a practice that can be both a liberating and a daunting practice for some practitioners. Live Learning asks the practitioner to "yield control of meaning and understanding in the classroom" by acknowledging that our students are intelligent and can learn in nontraditional ways.[11] Using this practice requires us as faculty to allow students agency in the classroom so that they may participate in their own learning process. In a Live Learning classroom, students work together to create knowledge and understanding of different concepts. For anyone who uses active learning and group work in the classroom, this practice might seem easy to incorporate. However, Live Learning means more than adding active learning components to a lesson plan. This practice encourages instructors to give up control of the learning process to the students in order to create new layers of meaning within the course material.

For instance, when I began teaching with Umoja, I assigned regular quizzes to students with the goal of assessing how well they were paying attention to my lectures. However, thinking about Live Learning made me reflect on the true purpose of these quizzes: was I assigning them because they actually benefited student learning and reflected meaningful data, or to make me feel a little more in control over the students? This reflection caused me to realize that although formative assessments can be useful, the ones I was assigning were not adding anything to my students' learning process. Instead of quizzes, I now assign in-class work where students can practice applying their new skills. Additionally, I began incorporating more reflection components into my major assignments.

For example, instead of a quiz on subject searching and Boolean operators, I might ask students to find sources and reflect on the search strategies they used to find those sources and how helpful the strategies may or may not have been. Students' reflection responses allow me to assess the same data (i.e., whether students understand how to use search strategies we covered in class), but they also give students much more freedom in how they will apply the knowledge they gained in class since, in this scenario, they can determine which search strategies they want to use and how they would like to use them. These reflection components not only allow me to learn whether students comprehend what I've taught, but I also learn which strategies my students find most useful and which they are likely to use again. This data helps me understand where my students are in the learning process, rather than if they can simply regurgitate a factoid I mentioned in class. In this way, Live Learning allows practitioners to become very purposeful with the choices they make in the classroom.

Mattering

Mattering is an intersectional practice: it means that the students matter, their learning experiences matter, and our choice of course content matters. It asks us to teach in a way that gives students agency, that takes their prior experiences and perspectives into account, and that acknowledges the racial disparities and inequalities inherent within instructional content.[12]

In my course, I practice Mattering by choosing course content that reminds students that they and their experiences matter, in addition to acknowledging the fact that racism is an inherent component of the information that makes up our world. This means decentering whiteness and colonialism from my course content. One of the simplest ways that I decenter whiteness or colonialism in my library instruction is that, in all resource demonstrations, citation examples, and so on, I do not use examples by white authors or that center whiteness. In my Umoja LIBR B1 course, I use only examples of Black scholarship. When teaching one-shots or research skills workshops, I also avoid using works by white authors or examples of white-focused scholarship in favor of using more diverse examples that are more reflective of my students. These changes might feel small, but in my experience, when students see themselves and their experiences represented in scholarship, they not only feel affirmed, but they also become much more invested in and excited by the learning process.

Another way I've incorporated Mattering is through the explicit acknowledge-ment and exploration of racist biases in research. Students may have encountered microaggressions (and more) within research before, or have noticed that there aren't as many sources for research topics that do not focus on the white experience. To explain why students may have had these experiences, I explicitly show students data on the overwhelming whiteness of academia and scholarly publishing so that students can see who is making the information they consume and thus can under-stand why they are seeing so little research and information about nonwhite experi-ences. I also show students examples of racist research that has been published, and we investigate the authors and publishers of this research in an attempt to understand how this research has been published. Students feel empowered by this knowledge: many have told me that learning about bias—in media, in search algorithms, and in peer-reviewed research itself—has completely changed how they view informa-tion and how they approach research. In class surveys, many have pinpointed this knowledge as the most impactful information they learned all semester.

Finally, part of Mattering is giving students agency. Empowering students through knowledge, as in the example above, is one way to do so. Another is to give students choice in their coursework. My course is structured to allow course assignments to be student-led: I might offer them some choices of research topic or assign a group project where the students discuss splitting up work among themselves democrat-ically (while monitoring to make sure that work is split up equitably, of course). Assignments also consistently include a reflection component that asks students to share their experiences and perspectives as they relate to course content. This reinforces to students that their thoughts and knowledge are worth hearing, that they matter.

Ethic of Love

The Ethic of Love asks practitioners to "humanize and make real the classroom": to share ourselves with our students so they see us as full humans, and vice versa.[13] While this does include sharing stories and our backgrounds with our students, humanizing teaching also carries a deeper implication. Humanizing library instruc-tion puts the burden on us as educators to remember that our students live full lives outside the vacuum of the library and the college campus. Bakersfield College is located in Kern County, California, which has a poverty rate of 19 percent. Each semester, I have students who are juggling parenting, full time jobs, and school at one time. Those who are not parents are often in charge of supervising their siblings or caring for other family members outside of class. In addition, students often struggle with housing and food insecurity. These issues take up a lot of headspace in these students, rightfully so! The Ethic of Love asks me as an instructor to be cognizant of all of the struggles my students are going through during their learning journey so that I can support them in their learning process rather than acting punitively toward them for having personal struggles outside of class.

The Ethic of Love infuses all of my interactions with my students. Although I always strive to make authentic connections with any student I come into contact with at the library, the Ethic of Love has challenged me to stretch myself. To implement this practice, I have had to remove the ego from instruction. Instead of assuming that students who fall behind in coursework are purposefully neglecting my class due to laziness, and so on, I have to remind myself that there are many, many reasons a student might not be able to complete an assignment or come to class one day (and even more so now in our post-COVID-19 world). Instead of sending these students an e-mail chastising them for falling behind, I might instead send an e-mail asking if they are OK, if anything is keeping them from doing coursework, and if I can help. These e-mails almost always get a response, as they are more approachable and affirming. Students tell me about the various difficulties they are having, we work through it together, and they learn that I am working within a framework of wanting them to succeed, not to fail. This establishes trust and accountability between us.

Just as with all of the practices, I use this practice in all of my library work, not just my for-credit course. However, this is the practice that challenges me the most on a day-to-day basis. It is the one that reminds me that just because I am tired of answering the same printing questions at the reference desk, or because students in my one-shot are unresponsive, does not mean they are purposefully trying to irritate me. Instead, I have to remember to approach students as real human beings who have never tried to print at the library before, or who are stressed out and not able to pay attention to a spiel on using library databases. Interacting with students through this lens has made students in all of my teaching environments more willing to communicate with me if there is something impeding them from completing coursework: showing students that I care makes them more willing to trust me and open up about anything they are going through. This allows me to make accommodations for students and connect them to resources on campus, which in turn leads to my students being more able to learn than if they were dealing with these struggles on their own.

Conclusion

As mentioned earlier, there are eighteen total practices that Umoja uses as the basis for its pedagogy. Umoja practitioners are encouraged to use all of them in a holistic manner throughout their education practices. Although the five practices mentioned in this chapter are the ones that have caused the greatest differences in my library instruction, I approach my library work through a holistic lens of all of the practices.

Incorporating the Umoja practices into my library instruction has not been a fast nor an easy process. Instead, it took me two to three years of steady implementation and refinement (and professional development through Umoja) to feel confident that I had been fully "Umoja-fied." After five years in the program, I am still making continual improvements and adjustments to my philosophy of librarianship through the Umoja lens. This is to say incorporating a culturally inclusive pedagogy into your librarianship is a process, not a one-time addition. In my case, meshing my teaching philosophy with Umoja as a white practitioner of this program required personal growth and a lot of (sometimes painful!) learning. I had to challenge internal biases and racism that I, with all of my liberal white privilege, was not aware existed within me. For anyone else wishing to use culturally inclusive pedagogy that reflects cultures that are not their own, I believe that this personal growing and learning process is absolutely essential in order not to cause harm through your practice of this type of pedagogy.

Committing to using culturally responsive practices in your librarianship often requires rethinking your framework for librarianship (and, often, for academia as whole). Becoming Umoja-fied made me take a keen look at my teaching philosophy and how I put that into practice. I've always had a student-centered teaching philosophy, but using Umoja's practices forced me to confront the fact that my student-centered philosophy didn't always translate into my day-to-day interactions with students at the library. Umoja's practices are student-centered in a way that focuses on student agency and on how the learning process can prove liberating for students. They have given me a better framework for how I approach student interactions, whether at the reference desk, in research workshops, in one-shots, in my Umoja class, or within campus as a whole. For example, once I began advocating for Umoja students in my committee work and other service to the college, I was able to become much more involved with equity work on campus. I believe that this is the natural extension of using an inclusive pedagogy for librarianship—if we truly want our information literacy work to become inclusive and equitable, we cannot limit our focus on inclusivity and equity to within the library. The students we interact with are not impacted only by the library, but by the entire campus and how welcoming or inclusive that campus is of our students' needs. If we are to fully incorporate culturally inclusive practices into our work, we must zoom out from the library and affix an equity lens onto our entire conception of academia and our position within it.

Notes

1.   US Bureau of Labor Statistics, "Employed Persons by Detailed Occupation, Sex, Race, and Hispanic or Latino Ethnicity," Current Population Survey, Household Data Annual Averages, table 11, last modified January 2020, https://www.bls.gov/cps/cpsaat11.pdf.

2. Dismantling Racism Works, "White Supremacy Culture," last modified April 2021, https://www.dismantlingracism.org/white-supremacy-culture.html.

3. Zaretta Hammond, *Culturally Responsive Teaching and the Brain* (Thousand Oaks, CA: Corwin, 2015).

4. Paulo Freire, *Pedagogy of the Oppressed*, 30th anniversary ed., trans. Myra Bergman Ramos (New York: Bloomsbury Academic, 2000); Hammond, *Culturally Responsive Teaching*, 21; CAST, "The Universal Design for Learning Guidelines," ver. 2.2, last modified 2018, https://udlguidelines.cast.org/.

5. Umoja Community, "Map of affiliated colleges and regions." Accessed May 18, 2021. https://umojacommunity.org/colleges-map.

6. Umoja Community, "Umoja Practices," accessed May 18, 2021, https://umojacommunity.org/umoja-practices.

7. US Bureau of Labor Statistics, "Employed Persons."

8. Bakersfield College, "Umoja Community ASTEP," accessed May 18, 2021, https://www.bakersfieldcollege.edu/student/aai/umoja.

9. Umoja Community, "Umoja Practices."

10. Umoja Community, "Umoja Practices."

11. Umoja Community, "Umoja Practices."

12. Umoja Community, "Umoja Practices."

13. Umoja Community, "Umoja Practices."

Bibliography

Bakersfield College. "Umoja Community ASTEP." Accessed May 18, 2021. https://www.bakersfield-college.edu/student/aai/umoja.

CAST. "The Universal Design for Learning Guidelines," ver. 2.2. Last modified 2018. https://udlguide-lines.cast.org/.

Dismantling Racism Works. "White Supremacy Culture." Last modified April 2021. https://www.dismantlingracism.org/white-supremacy-culture.html.

Freire, Paulo. *Pedagogy of the Oppressed*, 30th anniversary ed. Translated by Myra Bergman Ramos. New York: Bloomsbury Academic, 2000.

Hammond, Zaretta. *Culturally Responsive Teaching and the Brain: Promoting Authentic Engagement and Rigor among Culturally and Linguistically Diverse Students.* Thousand Oaks, CA: Corwin, 2015.

Umoja Community. "About Us." Accessed May 18, 2021. https://umojacommunity.org/about-us.

———. "Map of Affiliated Colleges and Regions." Accessed May 18, 2021. https://umojacommunity.org/colleges-map.

———. "Umoja Practices." Accessed May 18, 2021. https://umojacommunity.org/umoja-practices.

US Bureau of Labor Statistics. "Employed Persons by Detailed Occupation, Sex, Race, and Hispanic or Latino Ethnicity." Current Population Survey, Household Data Annual Averages, table 11. Last modified January 2020. https://www.bls.gov/cps/cpsaat11.pdf.

CHAPTER 3

Civic Engagement in the Virtual Classroom

Using Dialogic Pedagogy to Create an Inclusive Space for Student Learning

Alicia G. Vaandering[*]

Introduction

While engaging in equitable and inclusive teaching practices is a critical goal for many librarian educators, there is a parallel need to support communities in exploring and addressing civic issues.[1] For academic librarians who support students in exploring the intersection of civic issues and information literacy through instruction, the application of dialogic pedagogy, which encourages the critical examination and questioning of class content through open discourse, can provide opportunities for meaningful student discussion and reflection.[2] Dialogic pedagogy aims to democratize the classroom, empower students, explore varying perspectives, and apply knowledge and skills to real-world issues.[3] These goals align with many of those of civics education, in which dialogue has proven to be a critical component of

---

[*] Alicia G. Vaandering is a white, Pacific Northwest US–born, middle class, straight, cis, able-bodied woman. At the time of writing, she is an early career librarian employed in a tenure-track faculty position at the University of Rhode Island in Kingston, RI.

"fostering democratic living."[4] As Robin Alexander asserts, "Democracies need citizens who can argue, reason, challenge, question, present cases and evaluate them."[5] These shared goals make dialogic pedagogy a natural and highly useful approach to integrating civic literacy into the information literacy classroom.

Eliciting student participation in classroom discussions is often challenging in face-to-face classes, but COVID-19 and an increasing reliance on remote learning have exacerbated issues of student engagement.[6] This shift has required information literacy instructors to reimagine how to develop and sustain stimulating and inclusive discussions about civic issues, a challenge that is even more profound in the virtual classroom. The use of online platforms as a space for this work has become increasingly important for Generation Z students (born between the mid-to-late 1990s and early 2010s), who expect to engage with class content in a range of formats, including digital formats.[7]

This case study outlines the benefits and challenges of integrating dialogic pedagogy and civic learning in the college classroom and shares how these practices were implemented in a credit-bearing library course that was moved online in response to the COVID-19 pandemic. It also highlights how discussion-based learning can offer equitable and inclusive opportunities for students to engage with critical issues in traditional research processes and the broader information landscape.

Dialogic Pedagogy as a Teaching Practice

Dialogic pedagogy encourages students to meaningfully connect past experiences to new information and to explore potential real-world applications by centering discussion-based learning in the classroom. Snell and Lefstein explain that dialogic pedagogy creates an inclusive classroom environment that empowers students to share personal viewpoints, engage with multiple perspectives, and collaborate with peers and the instructor in the construction of knowledge and meaning.[8] Further research indicates that dialogic pedagogy plays an essential role in promoting student engagement and developing more open relationships between instructors and students.[9] When instructors provide a space for students to collaborate and question assumptions underlying theories and practices, they decentralize their roles as experts and create a more democratic classroom, particularly when discussions are meaningfully sequenced and student-led.[10] This type of learning empowers students, preparing them for active participation in a democratic society.

However, effectively integrating dialogic pedagogy in the classroom can be challenging. As Michael Fielding notes, students may be performative in their dialogue, which stifles genuine dialogue and undermines the empowerment of student voices.[11]

When students regulate their dialogue to meet instructor expectations, they lose the potential for a transformative and authentic learning experience. Furthermore, instructors' perceptions of a student's ability, particularly students perceived to be "low achievers," may result in lowered expectations of the student to critically engage with peers.[12] This can result in the creation of a less inclusive learning space in which instructors either fail to encourage all students to contribute or unilaterally exclude certain students from class discussions.

Civic Engagement and Undergraduate Students

Civic engagement and civil literacy are critical in higher education, as indicated in the American Association of Colleges and Universities (AAC&U) "Civic Engagement VALUE Rubric." The "Civic Engagement VALUE Rubric" outlines six outcomes for American colleges and universities: diversity of communities and culture, analysis of knowledge, civic identity and commitment, civic communication, civic action and reflection, and civic context/structures.[13] While the AAC&U encourages colleges and universities to adapt the language of the rubric to meet the needs of individual campuses, the rubric reflects a holistic approach to civic engagement that prioritizes the methods and modes of thinking that students should engage with in order to support healthy, thriving communities.

Just as the use of dialogic pedagogy in the classroom prepares students to participate in a democratic society, integrating civic learning in college coursework helps prepare students for their roles as informed citizens. Civic learning encompasses the range of ways that "citizens learn about collective social problems and make decisions about them that reflect the duties and responsibilities of citizenship."[14] Recent research indicates that integrating civic learning and engagement in the curriculum exposes students to social justice perspectives and supports the development of leadership skills.[15] First-year students, who are often living away from their families for the first time and experiencing their first opportunities to vote in local or national elections, in particular, benefit from this engagement. In a 2013 study, Ishitani and McKitrick found that engagement in civic issues through volunteer work and nonpartisan organizational activity correlated with greater civic engagement for students post-graduation.[16]

Engaging Generation Z students with civics education is a particularly pressing issue. Over the last several years, many members of Generation Z have become deeply engaged with social justice issues in response to national tragedies like the shooting at Stoneman Douglas High School in Parkland, Florida and the deaths of George Floyd and Breonna Taylor. However, as Seemiller and Grace indicate,

Generation Z continues to be mistrustful of the American political system.[17] This mistrust may exacerbate low voter turnout and disengagement with traditional political processes like donating to candidates, writing or calling in to local media outlets, and canvassing.[18] However, as Elizabeth Hollander and Nicholas V. Longo stress, while younger generations like millennials and Generation Z may eschew traditional political processes, they are often actively engaged with their communities in service work that is political in nature (e.g., outreach to immigrants).[19]

LIB 150: Search Strategies for the Information Age during the Pandemic

As a college of the University of Rhode Island, the University Libraries offers a series of three credit-bearing information literacy courses. These courses are typically taught by faculty librarians, although occasionally lecturers or adjunct professors teach additional sections. LIB 150: Search Strategies for the Information Age, the first in this series, provides an introduction to the exploration and practice of information literacy and library research concepts and skills. The course tends to primarily attract first-year students, although there are usually a few sophomores, juniors, and seniors in the class. The course supports two of the University of Rhode Island's General Education Course Outcomes: Communicate Effectively and Information Literacy.[20] LIB 150 has the following course objectives:

- Students will be able to navigate print and digital information research tools and use them for both college-level research and lifelong learning.
- Students will be able to differentiate information formats and quality and be able to apply these to college-level information research assignments.
- Students will be able to communicate their findings effectively to specific audiences.

While LIB 150 is traditionally taught face-to-face, due to the COVID-19 pandemic, the course transitioned to an online format starting in late spring 2020. During the 2020–21 year, I taught four online sections of the course, including both a summer session for URI's Talent Development program, which supports students from historically disadvantaged and marginalized backgrounds, and a section for Papuan students who were delayed in coming to campus as in-person international students because of COVID-19 travel restrictions.[21] I taught the course using a mix of synchronous class sessions and asynchronous work in the summer and fall, and then I moved to a fully synchronous model for the spring sections.

When I offer LIB 150 in person, I pair brief lectures with discussions and active-learning opportunities to support student learning, particularly for at-risk groups of students.[22] Students use discussion-based learning to question the deeper implications and real-life applications of the content that they are introduced to in course readings and lectures. These discussions play a critical role in creating an inclusive learning environment that encourages students to share perspectives and collaborate for mutual learning.

As I prepared to move my course online, two concerns overshadowed my preparations. First, I did not want to lose the opportunities for equitable and inclusive discourse that discussion-based learning presents. I knew that I needed to find a way to incorporate dialogic pedagogy into my virtual learning environment. Second, because 2020 was a pivotal election year, I also wanted to promote civic learning and engagement through activities that supported the LIB 150 course objectives. The corresponding changes that I made in my course became a critical part of my efforts to create and sustain an equitable and inclusive learning space.

A Framework for Integrating Dialogic Pedagogy in the Virtual LIB 150 Classroom

Applying dialogic pedagogy to the virtual classroom requires planning and foresight to ensure that discussions do not result in a small number of students dominating the conversation while others sit quietly on the sidelines, uncomfortable to join in and share their thoughts and perspectives. While breakout rooms offer a more intimate space for students to learn through discussion, they pose challenges for the solo instructor.[23] Limited to joining one room at a time, the instructor may miss opportunities to keep conversation flowing, stimulate deeper engagement, redirect conversations that have become inappropriate, and encourage each student to participate. To develop more equitable opportunities for students to engage each other in conversation about key topics in research and information seeking, I transitioned some discussions to an online discussion forum in Brightspace, the learning management system to which the University of Rhode Island had recently transitioned.

Beginning in a condensed five-week summer session, I piloted a series of weekly discussion forums that was expanded in the fall to include forums for seven of our thirteen weeks of class. Each weekly forum allowed students to engage with new content in the class through either reflection prompts or engage-and-reflect prompts.[24] In the reflection prompts, students reflected on course readings and their past research and information-seeking experiences. For example, in the

Plagiarism, Copyright, and Fair Use content module, one prompt asked students to describe the difference between plagiarism and copyright infringement in their own words and to pose a question they had after completing the course readings. Engage-and-reflect prompts asked students to read additional articles or complete an activity and then reflect upon the experience. For example, one engage-and-reflect prompt asked students to select a collection of physical or digital items and organize them by location, alphabet, time, category, or hierarchy in accordance with Richard Saul Wurman's LATCH system.[25] The students then reflected upon the process, identifying challenges and successes in employing their organizational schema.

Each week, students responded to two reflection prompts (a number that was reduced to one response during spring semester), one engage-and-reflect prompt, and the posts of two peers. Students had four to six prompts to choose from each week. Allowing students to choose from a variety of options provided multiple pathways to learning and engaging with course content, a key component to equitable pedagogy.[26] Students were able to engage in conversations that they found interesting and stimulating. In their peer responses, students composed substantive responses that asked follow-up questions or furthered the conversation by discussing similar or unique experiences, a practice that I modeled for the students in the early weeks of the semester by responding to students' posts myself. The expectations for discussion posts were also outlined early in the semester with examples of exemplary work and the provision of a rubric, which included criteria for discussion posts, that was used to grade student participation in the discussion forums.

The online format of the discussion forums created more equitable and inclusive opportunities for students to explore the application and implications of information creation, dissemination, and preservation. Due to the added pressures of the pandemic, students often struggled to regularly attend and participate in synchronous online class sessions. Many were working part- or full-time jobs, supporting their families by watching younger siblings or their own children, facing quarantine because they or a family member or friend had COVID, or struggling with increased anxiety or depression. Because the online discussion posts could be completed throughout the week, they offered students the flexibility to respond at a time that was conducive to their personal schedules. The online format also fostered broader participation in the discussions. Some students who rarely unmuted themselves in synchronous Zoom sessions wrote long, reflective posts and actively responded to their peers in the discussion forums. This was especially true for students from marginalized communities, particularly for the non-native English speakers in the class. In this way, students were offered an alternative method to becoming engaged learners, a critical step in establishing an inclusive classroom.[27]

Using Dialogic Pedagogy to Support Civic Learning and Engagement

As research has shown, dialogic pedagogy deepens learning by encouraging students to make real-world connections to the content they are introduced to in the classroom.[28] Civic learning and engagement complements this approach because it positions students to engage with their local, state, and national communities. The LIB 150 discussion forums integrated four major themes at the intersections of information literacy, media literacy, and civic literacy:

- being an informed citizen
- the impact of traditional processes of information creation, dissemination, and preservation on marginalized communities
- the power of student activism
- the role of academia and the media in civic issues

As I will explain below, by participating in discussions that explored civic learning and engagement, students completed work that also aligned with two of the AAC&U's "Civic Engagement VALUE Rubric" outcomes: analysis of knowledge, which requires students to connect knowledge from a study or discipline to civic engagement, and civic communication, which requires students to communicate information within a civic context.[29]

Discussion prompts that incorporated aspects of civic literacy provided authentic opportunities to explore, reflect upon, and discuss current topics.[30] In the summer session and fall semester, with the election on the horizon, one prompt asked students to find and share reliable resources for voter information. Another asked students to explore the intersection of information and social identity by examining how social identities impact what information is created, shared, and preserved. Students then reflected upon what role academia and the media should occupy in increasing the representation of marginalized voices and perspectives. Students were encouraged but not required to speak about their own personal experiences. Students responded with thought-provoking responses that questioned the whitewashing of history they had experienced in their education, highlighted the importance of increasing representation from marginalized communities in the media, and argued that universities have a responsibility to increase access to higher education.

While social inequalities in academia, the media, and American society can often feel insurmountable, the discussion forums aimed to empower LIB 150 students to question and reimagine the roles of students within these power structures. One prompt asked students to read a news article on the work of Dartmouth students

and librarians to change subject terms like "illegal alien" and "alien" to more inclusive terms like "unauthorized immigration" and "noncitizen" through a petition
to the Library of Congress. Students practiced summarizing and evaluating the
Dartmouth students' arguments and then posed follow-up questions. For another
prompt, students reached out to local and state representatives about a current issue
after locating, reading, and evaluating a reliable source on their issue. The students
shared their perspectives, called for action, or thanked their representatives for
previous actions taken. Because the purpose of the prompt was to practice finding,
applying, and communicating relevant, reliable information, I encouraged students
to focus on this process in their responses rather than the content, perspectives, or
arguments in the sources they used. This was also to ensure that students would feel
comfortable writing initial posts and responding to each other regardless of what
specific issues they addressed with their representative. In their responses, many
students said that this was their first time contacting a representative and reflected
upon their nervousness throughout the process. In peer responses, other students
shared that they had similar feelings of trepidation, forging conversations that helped
normalize these fears.

Class discussion prompts often provided explicit directions as to how students
could respond to their peers, although the prompts also made it clear that students
could allow their own questions and perspectives to guide them to respond in alter-
nate ways. Many posts, for example, encouraged students to answer questions their
peers had included in their posts *or* to pose their own follow-up questions. In the
prompt regarding Dartmouth students' petition to change Library of Congress subject
headings, students wrote original posts with questions about where the language of
"illegal alien" and "alien" originated and who should be responsible for changing
it. Some students responded by trying to answer those questions; however, others
chose to discuss their personal experiences with terms like "illegal alien." Allowing
this range of responses allowed students to engage in a way they felt comfortable
and confident, either relying upon their research to write more broadly about the
issue or leaning upon their own experiences to write a more personal response. In
a diversity statement included in the syllabus and in discussions in synchronous
class sessions, I stressed the value of sharing and exploring multiple perspectives
as we engaged with both new and familiar content, and the students were generally
respectful and curious when engaging with others who voiced different beliefs and
perspectives in the discussion forums.[31]

While I offered a variety of civics-related prompts, overall, these prompts did
seem less popular with the students than other prompts. In all four sections of LIB
150, the average number of responses to civics-related prompts lagged behind the
average number of responses to other prompts. Interestingly, my two classes with the
highest number of students from marginalized communities, my summer section
for the Talent Development program and my spring section of Papuan students, had

the smallest discrepancy in average responses, with an average of 10.3 responses to civics-related prompts and 12 responses to other prompts for students in the Talent Development program and an average of 5.2 and 7.9 for the Papuan students, respectively. My other sections had more dramatic differences, the widest gap being one section that averaged only 7.7 responses per civics-related prompt compared to 17.7 responses on other prompts. These differences might be the result of the different class sizes: the classes for the Talent Development program and the Papuan students were significantly smaller than my other classes (my class of Papuan students, in particular, had only nine students), so the students often knew each other well and were more comfortable exploring challenging topics together. However, this difference also suggests that the online discussion forums may have been seen as a more inclusive space to explore information, civic, and media literacies for students from marginalized communities. More research would need to be done, particularly in larger classes with a diverse student body, to test this correlation.

Despite the lower response rate, the discussions that explored information, media, and civic literacy showcased other successes. The responses to these prompts and to associated peers' responses often reflected critical thinking about current issues and modeled students' efforts to try to answer their own and their peers' questions. In their responses, students frequently incorporated knowledge that they had gained in other coursework, pulling in information from disciplines like history, political science, and philosophy. Additionally, students' responses demonstrated an eagerness to involve friends and family members in their coursework. One prompt asked students to informally poll their friends and family members to question the role of social media in fighting fake news, and many students responded enthusiastically to the prompt, writing at length about the responses they encountered. Furthermore, students eagerly responded to their peers, comparing differences and similarities between their poll responses and methods of polling. This enthusiasm suggests that dialogic pedagogy may offer further opportunities for students to critically engage with course content both inside and outside of the classroom.

Conclusion

The integration of dialogic pedagogy into the information literacy classroom offers librarians new and exciting opportunities to assist students in deepening their understanding of information literacy concepts and practices through questioning, discussion, and application, both in face-to-face and virtual classrooms. As research has shown, discussion-based learning heightens student engagement and can help democratize the classroom. This democratization of the classroom creates an inclusive space for students to engage with civic literacy as they analyze their roles as consumers and producers of information by questioning long-held assumptions and acknowledging different viewpoints. As many of my students remarked when they questioned the role of academia in the information landscape, universities are responsible for exposing students to multiple, diverse perspectives. Dialogic pedagogy provides a critical opportunity and approach for this work. Within information literacy instruction, in particular, dialogic pedagogy is a useful approach to explore the intersection of information, media, and civic literacies. By engaging with these practices and literacies, information literacy instructors can empower students' voices and provide more equitable and inclusive pathways to learning.

Notes

1. See Reneé Critcher Lyons, "A Rationale for Public Library Civics Instruction," *Public Library Quarterly* 35, no. 3 (July 2016): 255–56, https://doi.org/10.1080/01616846.2016.1210462; Mark Smith, "Making a Difference," *Public Libraries* 51, no. 4 (July 2012): 34, 39; Lesley S. J. Farmer, "Don't Get Faked Out by the News: Preparing Informed Citizens," *CSLA Journal* 41, no. 1 (Summer 2017): 12.
2. David R. Lankes points to the importance of conversation as an "iterative process" in knowledge building that is at the core of library interactions in his discussions of conversation theory (David R. Lankes, *The Atlas of New Librarianship* [Cambridge, MA: MIT Press, 2011], 31–33).
3. Julia Snell and Adam Lefstein, "'Low Ability,' Participation, and Identity in Dialogic Pedagogy," *American Educational Research Journal* 55, no. 1 (2018): 42, https://doi.org/10.3102/0002831217730010; Robert Sidelinger, "Dialogic Pedagogy in the College Classroom: Overcoming Students' Negative Perceptions of the Talkaholic Teacher," *Currents in Teaching and Learning* 10, no. 1 (Spring 2018): 22.
4. Bassel Akar, "Dialogic Pedagogies in Educational Settings for Active Citizenship, Social Cohesion and Peacebuilding in Lebanon," *Education, Citizenship and Social Justice* 11, no. 1 (March 2016): 44, https://doi.org/10.1177/1746197915626081.
5. Robin Alexander, *Essays on Pedagogy* (London: Routledge, 2008), 184.
6. Cora Orme, "A Visual Study of First-Generation College Students' Remote Learning Experiences during the COVID-19 Pandemic," *Journal of Higher Education Theory and Practice* 21, no. 5 (2021): 229–30, https://doi.org/10.33423/jhetp.v21i5.4283; Minsun Shin and Kasey Hickey, "Needs a Little TLC: Examining College Students' Emergency Remote Teaching and Learning Experiences during COVID-19," *Journal of Further and Higher Education* 45, no. 7 (September 2021): 982, https://doi.org/10.1080/0309877X.2020.1847261.
7. See Ivan Montiel et al., "New Ways of Teaching: Using Technology and Mobile Apps to Educate on Societal Grand Challenges," *Journal of Business Ethics* 161, no. 2 (2020): 245, https://doi.org/10.1007/s10551-019-04184-x; Anthony Turner, "Generation Z: Technology and Social Interest," *Journal of Individual Psychology* 71, no. 2 (Summer 2015): 105.
8. Snell and Lefstein, "'Low Ability,' Participation, and Identity," 42.
9. Sidelinger, "Dialogic Pedagogy"; Ester Ngan-Ling Chow et al., "Exploring Critical Feminist Pedagogy: Infusing Dialogue, Participation, and Experience in Teaching and Learning," *Teaching Sociology* 31, no. 3 (July 2003): 261–62, https://doi.org/10.2307/3211324.
10. Geoffrey Schneider, "Democratizing the Classroom: Sequencing Discussions and Assignments to Promote Student Ownership of the Course," *Review of Radical Political Economics* 42, no. 1 (2010): 101, 103–4, https://doi.org/10.1177/0486613409357185. Matusov, von Duyke, and Kayumova also explore the important role of agency that is developed through dialogic pedagogy.

For more, see Eugene Matusov, Katherine von Duyke, and Shakhnoza Kayumova, "Mapping Concepts of Agency in Educational Contexts," *Integrative Psychological and Behavioral Science* 50, no. 3 (2016): 425, https://doi.org/10.1007/s12124-015-9336-0.

11. Michael Fielding, "Transformative Approaches to Student Voice: Theoretical Underpinnings, Recalcitrant Realities," *British Educational Research Journal* 30, no. 2 (April 2004): 308–9, https://doi.org/10.1080/0141192042000195236.

12. Snell and Lefstein, "'Low Ability,' Participation, and Identity," 72–73. While Snell and Lefstein's study focused on students in upper elementary school classes, this study is worth noting for its emphasis on instructor behavior in response to student performance.

13. Association of American Colleges and Universities, "Civic Engagement VALUE Rubric," 2009, https://www.aacu.org/civic-engagement-value-rubric.

14. Bruce Jennings et al., "Civic Learning for a Democracy in Crisis," in "Democracy in Crisis: Civic Learning and the Reconstruction of Common Purpose," ed. Gregory E. Kaebnick et al., supplement, *Hastings Center Report* 51, no. S1 (January–February 2021): S3, https://doi.org/10.1002/hast.1221.

15. Amber Manning-Ouellette and Kevin M. Hemer, "Service-Learning and Civic Attitudes: A Mixed Methods Approach to Civic Engagement in the First Year of College," *Journal of Community Engagement and Higher Education* 11, no. 3 (2019): 10–11.

16. Terry T. Ishitani and Sean A. McKitrick, "The Effects of Academic Programs and Institutional Characteristics on Postgraduate Civic Engagement Behavior," *Journal of College Student Development* 54, no. 4 (July/August 2013): 392, https://doi.org/10.1353/csd.2013.0069.

17. Corey Seemiller and Meghan Grace, *Generation Z Goes to College* (San Francisco: Jossey Bass, 2016), 138.

18. Casey Anne Graham, "Attitudes and Perceptions about the Importance of Democratic Engagement among Generation Z Undergraduate Students" (PhD diss., University of Georgia, 2020), 104–5, ProQuest (2411036771).

19. Elizabeth Hollander and Nicholas V. Longo, "Student Political Engagement and the Renewal of Democracy," *Journal of College and Character* 10, no. 1 (2008): 2–3, https://doi.org/10.2202/1940-1639.1057.

20. The University of Rhode Island has four key objectives with twelve associated learning outcomes. For more information see University of Rhode Island, "Learning Outcomes," General Education, accessed June 3, 2021, https://web.uri.edu/general-education/students/learning-outcomes/.

21. For more about the Talent Development program, see University of Rhode Island, "About," Talent Development, accessed June 3, 2021, https://web.uri.edu/talentdevelopment/about/.

22. Eddy and Hogan found that classes with a moderate structure that incorporated more graded work and in-class activities made a disproportionately positive impact on the overall class performance of black and first-generation students. See Sarah L. Eddy and Kelly A. Hogan, "Getting under the Hood: How and for Whom Does Increasing Course Structure Work?" *Life Sciences Education* 13, no. 3 (2013): 463–64, https://doi.org/10.1187/cbe.14-03-0050.

23. Research has shown that an instructor's encouragement of discussion is a primary factor in setting the stage for productive classroom discussions. See Christopher H. Clark, "The Impact of Student Political Identity over the Course of an Online Controversial Issue Discussion," *Democracy and Education* 26, no. 2 (July 2018): 3.

24. During the other six weeks of the class, students focused on applying their developing skills and knowledge to group and individual projects.

25. Richard Saul Wurman, *Information Anxiety 2* (Indianapolis, IN: Que, 2001).

26. In a recent study, Goldman, Goodboy, and Weber found that offering more personalized learning for students can improve intrinsic motivations for learning. See Zachary W. Goldman, Alan

K. Goodboy, and Keith Weber, "College Students' Psychological Needs and Intrinsic Motivation to Learn: An Examination of Self-Determination Theory," *Communication Quarterly* 65 (2017): 186, https://doi.org/10.1080/01463373.2016.1215338.

27. As Mazer noted, engaged students are more likely to participate in learning activities in and outside of the classroom. See Joseph P. Mazer, "Associations among Teacher Communication Behaviors, Student Interest, and Engagement: A Validity Test," *Communication Education* 62, no. 1 (2013): 89, https://doi.org/10.1080/03634523.2012.731513.

28. Schneider, "Democratizing the Classroom, 103–4.

29. Association of American Colleges and Universities, "Civic Engagement VALUE Rubric," 2.

30. For more discussion on the importance of crafting authentic learning opportunities for online students, see Michelle Pacansky-Brock, Michael Smedshammer, and Kim Vincent-Layton, "Humanizing Online Teaching to Equitize Higher Education," *Current Issues in Education* 21, no. 2 (April 2020): 16.

31. Interestingly, Jonathan T. Cope points to the provision of a space for students to share varying perspectives as the best way to interrupt student intolerance. See Jonathan T. Cope, "The Reconquista Student: Critical Information Literacy, Civics, and Confronting Student Intolerance," *Communications in Information Literacy* 11, no. 2 (2017): 275, https://doi.org/10.15760/comminfolit.2017.11.2.2.

Bibliography

Akar, Bassel. "Dialogic Pedagogies in Educational Settings for Active Citizenship, Social Cohesion and Peacebuilding in Lebanon." *Education, Citizenship and Social Justice* 11, no. 1 (March 2016): 44–62. https://doi.org/10.1177/1746197915626081.

Alexander, Robin. *Essays on Pedagogy*. London: Routledge, 2008.

Association of American Colleges and Universities. "Civic Engagement VALUE Rubric." 2009. https://www.aacu.org/civic-engagement-value-rubric.

Chow, Esther Ngan-Ling, Chadwick Fleck, Gang-Hua Fan, Joshua Joseph, and Deanna M. Lyter. "Exploring Critical Feminist Pedagogy: Infusing Dialogue, Participation, and Experience in Teaching and Learning." *Teaching Sociology* 31, no. 3 (July 2003): 259–75. https://doi.org/10.2307/3211324.

Clark, Christopher H. "The Impact of Student Political Identity over the Course of an Online Controversial Issue Discussion." *Democracy and Education* 26, no. 2 (July 2018): 1–15.

Cope, Jonathan T. "The Reconquista Student: Critical Information Literacy, Civics, and Confronting Student Intolerance." *Communications in Information Literacy* 11, no. 2 (2017): 264–82. https://doi.org/10.15760/comminfolit.2017.11.2.2.

Critcher Lyons, Reneé. "A Rationale for Public Library Civics Instruction." *Public Library Quarterly* 35, no. 3 (July 2016): 254–57. https://doi.org/10.1080/01616846.2016.1210462.

Eddy, Sarah L., and Kelly A. Hogan, "Getting under the Hood: How and for Whom Does Increasing Course Structure Work?" *Life Sciences Education* 13, no. 3 (2013): 453–68. https://doi.org/10.1187/cbe.14-03-0050.

Farmer, Lesley S. J. "Don't Get Faked Out by the News: Preparing Informed Citizens." *CSLA Journal* 41, no. 1 (Summer 2017): 12–13.

Fielding, Michael. "Transformative Approaches to Student Voice: Theoretical Underpinnings, Recalcitrant Realities." *British Educational Research Journal* 30, no. 2 (April 2004): 295–311. https://doi.org/10.1080/0141192042000195236.

Goldman, Zachary W., Alan K. Goodboy, and Keith Weber. "College Students' Psychological Needs and Intrinsic Motivation to Learn: An Examination of Self-Determination Theory." *Communication Quarterly* 65 (2017): 167–91. https://doi.org/10.1080/01463373.2016.1215338.

Graham, Casey Anne. "Attitudes and Perceptions about the Importance of Democratic Engagement among Generation Z Undergraduate Students." PhD diss., University of Georgia, 2020. ProQuest (2411036771).

Hollander, Elizabeth, and Nicholas V. Longo. "Student Political Engagement and the Renewal of Democracy." *Journal of College and Character* 10, no. 1 (2008): 1–9. https://doi.org/10.2202/1940-1639.1057.

Ishitani, Terry T., and Sean A. McKitrick. "The Effects of Academic Programs and Institutional Characteristics on Postgraduate Civic Engagement Behavior." *Journal of College Student Development* 54, no. 4 (July/August 2013): 379–96. https://doi.org/10.1353/csd.2013.0069.

Jennings, Bruce, Michael K. Gusmano, Gregory E. Kaebnick, Carolyn P. Neuhaus, and Mildred Z. Solomon. "Civic Learning for a Democracy in Crisis." In "Democracy in Crisis: Civic Learning and the Reconstruction of Common Purpose," edited by Gregory E. Kaebnick, Michael Gusmano, Bruce Jennings, Carolyn P. Neuhaus, and Mildred Z. Solomon. Supplement, *Hastings Center Report* 51, no. S1 (January–February 2021): S2–S4. https://doi.org/10.1002/hast.1221.

Lankes, David R. *The Atlas of New Librarianship.* Cambridge, MA: MIT Press, 2011.

Manning-Ouellette, Amber, and Kevin M. Hemer. "Service-Learning and Civic Attitudes: A Mixed Methods Approach to Civic Engagement in the First Year of College." *Journal of Community Engagement and Higher Education* 11, no. 3 (2019): 5–18.

Matusov, Eugene, Katherine von Duyke, and Shakhnoza Kayumova. "Mapping Concepts of Agency in Educational Contexts." *Integrative Psychological and Behavioral Science* 50, no. 3 (2016): 420–46. https://doi.org/10.1007/s12124-015-9336-0.

Mazer, Joseph P. "Associations among Teacher Communication Behaviors, Student Interest, and Engagement: A Validity Test." *Communication Education* 62, no. 1 (2013): 86–96. https://doi.org/10.1080/03634523.2012.731513.

Montiel, Ivan, Javier Delgado-Ceballos, Natalia Ortiz-de-Mandojana, and Raquel Antolin-Lopez. "New Ways of Teaching: Using Technology and Mobile Apps to Educate on Societal Grand Challenges." *Journal of Business Ethics* 161, no. 2 (2020): 243–51. https://doi.org/10.1007/s10551-019-04184-x.

Orme, Cora. "A Visual Study of First-Generation College Students' Remote Learning Experiences during the COVID-19 Pandemic." *Journal of Higher Education Theory and Practice* 21, no. 5 (2021): 224–38. https://doi.org/10.33423/jhetp.v21i5.4283.

Pacansky-Brock, Michelle, Michael Smedshammer, and Kim Vincent-Layton. "Humanizing Online Teaching to Equitize Higher Education." *Current Issues in Education* 21, no. 2 (April 2020): 1–21.

Schneider, Geoffrey. "Democratizing the Classroom: Sequencing Discussions and Assignments to Promote Student Ownership of the Course." *Review of Radical Political Economics* 42, no. 1 (2010): 101–7. https://doi.org/10.1177/0486613409357185.

Seemiller, Corey, and Meghan Grace. *Generation Z Goes to College.* San Francisco: Jossey Bass, 2016.

Shin, Minsun, and Kasey Hickey. "Needs a Little TLC: Examining College Students' Emergency Remote Teaching and Learning Experiences during COVID-19." *Journal of Further and Higher Education* 45, no. 7 (September 2021): 973–86. https://doi.org/10.1080/0309877X.2020.1847261.

Sidelinger, Robert. "Dialogic Pedagogy in the College Classroom: Overcoming Students' Negative Perceptions of the Talkaholic Teacher." *Currents in Teaching and Learning* 10, no., 1 (Spring 2018): 19–31.

Smith, Mark. "Making a Difference." *Public Libraries* 51, no. 4 (July 2012): 34–39.

Snell, Julia, and Adam Lefstein. "'Low Ability,' Participation, and Identity in Dialogic Peda-
    gogy." *American Educational Research Journal* 55, no. 1 (2018): 40–78. https://doi.
    org/10.3102/0002831217730010.
Turner, Anthony. "Generation Z: Technology and Social Interest." *Journal of Individual Psychology* 71,
    no. 2 (Summer 2015): 103–13.
University of Rhode Island. "About." Talent Development. Accessed June 3, 2021. https://web.uri.edu/
    talentdevelopment/about/.
———. "Learning Outcomes." General Education. Accessed June 3, 2021. https://web.uri.edu/
    general-education/students/learning-outcomes/.
Wurman, Richard Saul. *Information Anxiety 2*. Indianapolis, IN: Que, 2001.

CHAPTER 4

The Impact of Oppression

Transforming Historical Database Instruction into Contemporary Discussion

*Kelleen Maluski**

> *...the most mainstream (e.g., white, heterosexual, Christian, middle-class) controlling regimes in society will privilege themselves and diminish or subdue all others in the organization of what constitutes legitimate knowledge. When we inherit privilege, it is based on a massive knowledge regime that foregrounds the structural inequalities of the past, buttressed by vast stores of texts, images, and sounds saved in archives, museums, and libraries.*

> — *Safiya Umoja Noble*[1]

* Kelleen Maluski is the student success and engagement librarian at the University of New Mexico Health Sciences Library and believes that her experience and knowledge are never more important than the learners she works with. Kelleen strives to learn and grow through every interaction and to center the voices and cultural wealth of all. She engages students with critical evaluation of the information landscape to more completely participate in the world around them through integration of social justice tenets. Kelleen's work as a student success librarian is always impacted by her current and changing position within society as a bisexual/pansexual cis white woman who was a first-generation student, speaks English as her primary language, and is a US-born US citizen, with the chronic health condition endometriosis (which leads to chronic pain and struggles with mental health). Her experiences within health care and adaptation to academic environments, and the privileges and roadblocks she has encountered through these journeys, are in large part why she is a health sciences librarian and grounds her work in holistic student success and the use of a feminist ethics of care framework.

Introduction

I, like all white female-identifying librarians, have to confront my own part in white supremacy culture, especially in spaces where my particular power and privilege can harm learners. It is vital work to decenter my voice, minimize the harm I cause, and make space for the lived experience and expertise of the learners I work with.[2] There have been movements within librarianship, such as critical librarianship, that call for facing up to power imbalances, but there have been valid criticisms of how these have been exclusionary in practice and explicitly ignored the need to engage with conversations around racism. Therefore, confronting my part in these structures is especially necessary in a system where "many librarians of color have already felt unwelcome because the movement regularly highlights the work of white librarians without recognizing that librarians of color have been doing this work without calling it 'theory.'"[3] While many times white persons in the profession are lauded for their work on what are often referred to as DEI (diversity, equity, and inclusion) initiatives, there is a valid tension because the BIPOC (Black, Indigenous, Persons of Color) librarians who shoulder much of this work are less frequently cited and acknowledged. While "discussion of race, sexuality, and gender within a theoretical framework and practice cannot solely be the responsibility of the few POC faculty and students," we must not use that as an open call to continue the pillaging and exploiting of our colleagues' work and our students' voices while asserting ourselves as "allies."[4]

This chapter will break down how I engaged with these needs and concerns for one specific class when tasked with teaching historical and academic database searching techniques to high school students conducting research for an historical essay on "slavery in the Americas." This lesson plan serves as an example of one way that I, as a white academic librarian, utilized the knowledge and expertise of BIPOC library scholars to adjust my teaching and create a comparison activity where we reviewed results for Susan B. Anthony versus Ida B. Wells to engage with the inequities and discrimination of information systems. I will review the critical pedagogy theory I employed when creating the lesson plan, break apart the lesson, and discuss the outcomes of this approach in terms of student engagement and participation.

Contextualizing within the Profession

Librarianship has built an image of itself as a noble profession, created to educate and bring knowledge to the public, but in reality our demographics and practices do not reflect the society we serve.[5] One indication of this disconnect is how we centralize traditional mechanisms of academic publishing that have been used to discriminate and exploit minoritized groups.[6] This builds a cycle of disenfranchising the voices of our students by further pushing an assimilation narrative to the future practitioners of various professions, including those who will produce scholarship. As "university and college students all over the nation commit to being tens of thousands of dollars in debt, it becomes a social justice issue that not only do they finish, but that they receive the best education possible."[7] We have a responsibility to our learners to challenge the false narrative of neutrality that upholds white supremacy.[8] For instance, teaching that a scholarly or peer-reviewed article (or the databases that they are housed in) is automatically more reputable than other sources is an oversimplified stance that discredits our learners' ability to engage with critical thinking and does a disservice to their education.

A refrain from white librarians is that having conversations that confront discriminatory practices, especially in the classroom, makes them uncomfortable. However, this stance itself shows how inequitable our teaching practices are because it assumes

- one, that we are owed comfort;
- two, that whiteness is central to our work and what we deem "accepted" knowledge;
- three, we have a right to opt out of doing the work that our colleagues who have been historically and systematically excluded don't have the option to opt out of.[9]

Choosing to not engage in conversations around the impact of systemic racism and discrimination within the information landscape inflicts harm on all learners and makes them less informed on the topics that we are supposed to be teaching. Not addressing the existence of these problems or pretending they don't exist reinforces the gaslighting of those learners who see the problems in our information systems.

Background

While I worked at a small liberal arts (SLA) college from 2015 to 2019, one responsibility of mine was to help organize one day each semester for a local International Baccalaureate high school to engage in college research practices while working on historical investigation papers.[10] We put this day together in collaboration with the high school's teachers and librarian, local public library librarians, and a few members of the SLA library team. The fall day took place in the public library with five sessions covering how to create a search strategy, search the library catalogs at the public library and the academic institution, search open access historical databases, search academic databases through the college subscriptions, edit their topics, and utilize print sources. While the students would be researching and writing two papers throughout the year with us, this was the first time they had all completed an essay for this program. It was therefore vital to convey the importance of each step of the research process and how to meet the needs of their assignment. For their essays, the students were required to use both print and online sources and at least one scholarly and one primary resource. The sessions were tight, with only thirty minutes each. Every session was taught by a different member of our collaborative group to make sure all of the roughly eighty students had appropriate attention. The days included time for the students to begin doing their own work while having access to the librarians and their teachers to ask questions. A research guide was also created to help build metacognitive skills and be a point of assistance when the students were working solo. The guide also included information on how to book a consultation with a librarian from the college.

In the fall of 2018 at our team meeting, the high school history professor indicated she was concerned that the students weren't really understanding the point of the historical investigation essay with the topic "slavery in the Americas." She wanted the assignment to be a way for them to confront current social injustices and how our history was not only impacting our present day but had led to it. Since the school had a predominately Black and Latinx population, the professor was even more concerned that the students should be able to engage with this conversation in an honest and meaningful way. We discussed the possibility of altering the assignment to build more on contemporary issues, but instead we decided to change how we were teaching the topic.

We decided to find a search example that would be used in every session to help build a cohesive thread to the day, and in the session on historical and scholarly database searching, we would discuss the discriminatory practices associated with our topic. Our objective was to engage students in a conversation about how what had occurred in the past was still a part of our present and that we need to work to shine light on this as opposed to creating a superlative mythos about present-day society.[11]

Planning

While we would need to convey very basic search strategy information in a short period of time, the subject matter warranted designing the lesson with extreme care. It was crucial to allow time to discuss the approach and lesson with colleagues so as to help break down any biases I might have been building into the lesson and to make sure the objectives were being appropriately met. If I had been creating this lesson today, another key element would have been to utilize trauma-informed care. While much of what we built into the lesson plan utilized concepts inherent to trauma-informed care, such as improving the "psychological and emotional well-being of patrons and staff accessing library services and using these spaces," this was not a theory I was as familiar with at the time.[12]

When crafting the lesson plan, we chose the search example of Wells and Anthony because it allowed us to integrate concepts that are perfectly outlined by Leung and López-McKnight:

> Center racialized examples and topics in your teaching and extend those further to disrupt ideas of what's appropriate or what counts, and what's valued, as legitimized knowledge. Challenge dominant information and knowledge-production processes that intentionally exclude BIPOC, showing its connectivity to White Supremacy's structural, historical, and contemporary realities. Recognize that even moments that may seem small and trivial are vitally important to the big picture, to the process that gets you to that larger impact. Trust the students to be worthwhile. Trust them to open our minds. Trust them to teach us.[13]

The lesson needed to not only make the correlation between past and present, but also break down traditional power dynamics in the classroom and build trust with students. The focus would be breaking the normalized hierarchy of white supremacy and utilizing the students' knowledge to frame our conversations, encouraging their agency through the sharing of their thoughts and voices.[14] With only thirty minutes and the students coming into a space they might not be familiar with to work with a new instructor who was from a discriminative profession, expectations needed to be tempered. This was about starting small to trust the students and have them trust themselves.

The groundwork for this lesson centered on a basic structure of questions and reflections to confront various damaging dominant academic practices (based in sexism, classism, and racism). We would work toward learning the searching techniques while critiquing the tools, societal beliefs, and practices that have led to a lack of representation. This meant building the lesson to be flexible enough to offer space for the students to share their thoughts, feelings, impressions, questions, and so on. We did not want to make assumptions about how the students saw their identities intersecting during the session, so we approached the subject from a place of cultural humility and with an ethic of care.

Central to the implementation of these pedagogies was how

> in a practice of cultural humility, we are open to the intersectionality of identities, but follow the lead of the patron in determining the importance of various aspects of their identities ...recognizing that what may be most salient from the librarian's perspective may or may not be significant to the interaction.[15]

Additionally, organizing our lesson with an ethic of care and critical race lens focused our praxis on relationship building and providing space for students to feel comfortable teaching each other rather than the typical praxis where the instructor wields the power in the classroom.[16] This pedagogical approach aligns with the ethos espoused in Safiya Umoja Noble's *Algorithms of Oppression* and critical race theory to examine how the library profession had actively contributed to the knowledge hierarchies and centering of white supremacy that created these structures.[17]

Selecting the Search Comparison Example

This lesson hinged completely on selecting a search example that could convey the fact that historical narratives are often skewed by the dominant culture and spoke to the myriad injustices at play when researching a topic like "slavery in the Americas." The hope was that the example would show how our information landscape continues to employ the discriminatory practices, such as lack of representation, that existed in the historical time periods the students would be researching and that issues of oppression permeate every facet of our society.[18] The example needed to be able to cover various areas of inequity within our society so that students could lead a conversation on what spoke to them most or review issues pertaining to intersectionality.[19] The example of Wells and Anthony spoke to each of these needs.

While the basis of why Wells and Anthony have been misrepresented in our historical discussions has much to do with racism, there are also many other issues at play, including classism and sexism.[20] With this example, students could explore intersectional injustices while also seeing how the discrimination and erasure that Wells experienced still happen in our current society. Women of color and especially Black women are consistently left out of the dialogues in which they have expertise.[21] This practice is founded in white supremacy and continues the cycle of pushing Black women out of academia. We wanted the students to be able to evaluate what stories get told and why, how our historical narrative is skewed by the elitism and deeply embedded white supremacy of academia. Furthermore, an end goal for their assignment was to have them realize that their voices mattered and they could help change the narrative. As Tressie McMillan Cottom says,

> When black writers are not read or black thinkers are not cited or black activists are not interviewed, we can say that it is just too hard for those who do not live, work, or learn near black people to find any.[22]

Considering this and understanding our time restraints, we decided to structure open-ended questions that could be answered in a verbal discussion (as opposed to a worksheet) to help learners connect the library materials and research with the historical injustices they were reviewing. To help show the primary resources and facilitate this discussion, we designed an activity where we compared results for Anthony and Wells in Chronicling America and JSTOR (through the college's subscription). These databases were chosen to fulfill the needs of the assignment and to show how the scholarship of today can be just as discriminatory as the publications of the time. Both elements could be addressed through the primary sources in Chronicling America and the representation of scholarly articles throughout the years in JSTOR. Facts about both Anthony and Wells were prepared in case the students weren't aware of who they were. This activity served as a way for the students to compare these two contemporaries and their statuses and how the historical record has impacted modern-day women writers, activists, and educators.

There also needed to be time for students to begin researching their own topics and to ask questions specific to them. At the end of the day, the students would have a larger amount of designated time for individual research, but we wanted each learner to begin working within the resource they discussed in each session. This is another reason it was useful to have a simple comparison with open-ended questions that were reflective in nature but didn't require written reflection. Open reflection further centered the students since they could focus more on their own work and navigating it than on a set activity that further centered the instructor's power in the classroom. With all of this in mind, I went about creating an outline (see appendix).

Teaching and Outcomes

Once in the classroom, after introductions and outlining objectives for the session, the class began by asking each group if they knew who Anthony was and then by asking if they knew of Wells. Most of the students raised their hands when asked about Anthony. From the entire day, of roughly eighty students, only one student indicated they knew of Wells. For the students who knew about Anthony, when asked who she was, they usually indicated things along the lines of her getting women the right to vote. The one student familiar with Wells knew she was a writer and activist but wasn't clear on all the details. With both examples, it was incredible to have the students start the class by sharing their knowledge and begin to break down the perception of college teachers as lecturers.

For both examples, since students were fuzzy on the details of who the women were, the previously prepared facts were shared with the students along with the question "Why do we think we know more about Susan B. Anthony than Ida B. Wells?" With every single group, there would be a semi-hesitant response of "Because Ida B. Wells is Black?" This statement was affirmed and encouraged as students were tasked with discussing more. With each group, after the students gave their responses, the dialogue around the ways in which these women's stories have been told and the perceived truth about our collective histories began. The body language of the students changed and the room became filled with side discussions. The students asked questions and other students participated in answering them.

From here, we could launch into looking at the databases and covering how more results for a person doesn't mean they are more important or more deserving. When we arrived at the portion of the lesson where we searched Chronicling America for both women, finding 869 results for Wells and 20,072 results for Anthony, there were actual gasps and boos. Here again, the students expressed their learning, their knowing, and their engagement with the materials. We made sure to cover trying alternative spellings, Boolean, and so on, but the biggest takeaway from the day was for them to trust themselves and to see how those who have the most privilege and power dictate our historical record. The impact of slavery in the Americas was not some distant concept that no longer had implications for our society or them. These historical essays were a chance for these students to change the dialogue.

From here, the students were then able to conduct their own work with time for questions that could be posted to all the educators. They were also encouraged to book appointments with librarians at the college and utilize the resources at the public library. While the evidence was anecdotal, all instructors felt that the individual research time led to more questions and edits to topics to make them more contemporary. Later, the history professor indicated that the papers did seem to improve in terms of topics connecting to student interest. The college librarians also saw a slight increase in the number of consultations booked. This was a step in the important direction of inviting the high school students to see that their research was worthwhile and that they were respected for their knowledge. The time that was taken to carefully plan the lesson and build in reflective, open-ended questions therefore met the objectives.

Conclusion

At the end of the day, the impact of acknowledging the truths that our students know about our society, accepting our role in that, and trusting the tools learners already have to change this narrative are critical. *Algorithms of Oppression* was a massively important text in updating this lesson, and the reasons for needing to unveil these truths cannot be stated better than the way Noble concluded:

> Arguably, if education is based in evidence-based research, and knowledge is a means of liberation in society, then the types of knowledge that widely circulate provide a crucial site of investigation. How oppressed people are represented, or misrepresented, is an important element of engaging in efforts to bring about social, political, and economic justice.[23]

Appendix: IB Research Lesson Plan, Fall 2018

Conducting Research in Databases Portion (half hour total)

Objective: Professor wants to make sure that this year we not only tackle how to do research but also convey to the students that the work they are doing on the historical investigation into the assignment "slavery in the Americas" is not just about history. Rather, the assignment represents contemporary issues as well. How have these practices impacted the development of these nations, and how are they still being implemented and the effects still felt?

Databases to Review
- Chronicling America (primary sources)
- JSTOR

Driving Frames to Map to from ACRL *Framework for Information Literacy*
- Authority Is Constructed and Contextual.
- Information Has Value.

Resource for Development of Lesson Plan
- *Algorithms of Oppression: How Search Engines Reinforce Racism* by Safiya Umoja Noble, https://nyupress.org/books/9781479837243/
- Susan B. Anthony quote: https://www.pbs.org/newshour/politics/hundreds-voted-stickers-left-susan-b-anthonys-grave

1. Introduce self
2. **Let students know we are going to discuss how to search databases, but we also want to start thinking about what stories get told and why. Who writes the history and scholarship? How can we layer our research to help expand our results to find credible evidence to back up our thesis? How can we add our voices to the conversation to help change the narrative?**
3. Explain that we will be discussing how to use databases for research, using
   a. Chronicling America **(as a way to find primary sources)**
      Display the guide again and show where they can learn more about primary sources and find this database.
   b. JSTOR **(a way to find scholarly articles)**
      Display the guide again and show where they can find the database.
   c. On the guide also show how they can get help with evaluating their resources.
   d. A little time for individual research and questions.
4. Before we start, who knows who Ida B. Wells is and who Susan B. Anthony is?

a. Facts on Ida: Journalist, educator, civil rights crusader, feminist. One of the founders of the NAACP. Born into slavery, fought against lynching, active in women's suffrage movement despite outspoken disapproval from other women in the movement who were white.

b. Facts on Susan: Reformer involved in the women's suffrage movement. Part of the antislavery movement, but once issues started arising with wanting to pass 15th Amendment (right of black MEN to vote), Anthony moved toward focusing only on the rights of women, literally wrote a history of the movement that credits her and Stanton with starting the movement and eliminates Black suffragists from the narrative. "I will cut off this right arm of mine before I will ever work or demand the ballot for the Negro and not the woman."

c. Why do we think we know more about Susan B. Anthony than Ida B. Wells?

d. Both women were important to equality in different ways, but issues arise when we start to look for information on their contributions and understanding how the narrative has been formed. **More results on a person does not mean they are more important.**

5. Review the databases

   a. Go into Chronicling America and do a search for "Ida B Wells"

     i. Ask if anyone knows why I used the quotation marks and discuss how this keeps a phrase together.

     ii. Show the guide and point out the **Boolean operators box**. Boolean operators *command* a database to refine my search to better find what I need.

These are for more advanced searching, and so you will want to refer to the guide and ask questions when you have a chance to try a database yourself.

     iii. Show how Chronicling America found newspaper articles from past time periods that discuss Ida B. Wells.

How many results do you think we will get for Ida B. Wells?

     iv. Now do the same search for "Susan B. Anthony."

How many results do you think we will get for Susan B. Anthony?

     v. **The differences in results—869 to 20,072—does this tell anyone anything?**

     vi. **Mention spelling names differently and also listing in other ways, like "Wells, Ida" or taking out the initials, though this could lead to false results.**

   b. Go into JSTOR and do the same searches.

    i.   Discuss how JSTOR is different from Chronicling America, looking for scholarly articles about a topic, not usually primary sources.

    ii.   Do a search for "Ida B Wells" AND "Susan B Anthony" to find things that might discuss the issues between their representation and within the movement.

    iii.   Explain that the AND is also a Boolean operator, and point this out on the guide. Explain that this allows me to find *both* concepts in the record.

    iv.   Point out subjects to filter with.

    v.   Remind students that research is iterative, though, so I might need to tweak and edit my search (using other synonyms or phrases) as I find more relevant results.

6. **As you move forward with your research, think about how slavery is still impacting the Americas, how the history has been written, and how you might think about changing the dialogue. Do we still see issues with the representation of Ida B. Wells vs. Susan B. Anthony? How can we change that narrative?**

7. Have 10 minutes for questions and individual research.

Notes

1. Safiya Umoja Noble, *Algorithms of Oppression* (New York: New York University Press, 2018), 140.

2. bell hooks, *Teaching to Transgress* (New York: Routledge, 1994); Diana Floegel and Lorin Jackson, "Recasting an Inclusive Narrative: Exploring Intersectional Theory," in *Recasting the Narrative: The Proceedings of the ACRL 2019 Conference, April 10–13, 2019, Cleveland, Ohio*, edited by Dawn M. Mueller (Chicago: Association of College and Research Libraries, 2019), 412–20, https://alair.ala.org/bitstream/handle/11213/17669/RecastinganInclusiveNarrative.pdf.

3. Jennifer Brown et al., "We Here: Speaking Our Truth," *Library Trends* 67, no. 1 (2018): 173, https://doi.org/10.1353/lib.2018.0031.

4. Brown et al., "We Here," 168.

5. Fobazi Ettarh, "Vocational Awe and Librarianship: The Lies We Tell Ourselves," *In the Library with the Lead Pipe*, January 10, 2018, http://www.inthelibrarywiththeleadpipe.org/2018/vocational-awe/; Kathy Rosa and Kelsey Henke, *2017 ALA Member Demographics Study* (Chicago: American Library Association Office of Research and Statistics, 2017), https://www.ala.org/tools/research/initiatives/membershipsurveys.

6. Stacie Williams, "Librarians in the 21st Century: It Is Becoming Impossible to Remain Neutral," *Literary Hub*, May 4, 2017, https://lithub.com/librarians-in-the-21st-century-it-is-becoming-impossible-to-remain-neutral/; Tara J. Yosso, "Whose Culture Has Capital? A Critical Race Theory Discussion of Community Cultural Wealth," *Race Ethnicity and Education* 8, no. 1 (March 2005): 69–91, https://doi.org/10.1080/1361332052000341006.

7. Symphony Bruce, "Teaching with Care: A Relational Approach to Individual Research Consultations," *In the Library with the Lead Pipe*, February 5, 2020. http://www.inthelibrarywiththe-

leadpipe.org/2020/teaching-with-care/.

8. Ettarh, "Vocational Awe and Librarianship"; Sofia Leung and Jorge López-McKnight, "Dreaming Revolutionary Futures: Critical Race's Centrality to Ending White Supremacy," *Communications in Information Literacy* 14, no. 1 (2020): 12–26, https://doi.org/10.15760/comminfolit.2020.14.1.2; Sofia Leung and Jorge López-McKnight, eds., *Knowledge Justice* (Cambridge, MA: MIT Press, 2021), https://doi.org/10.7551/mitpress/11969.001.0001; Williams, "Librarians in the 21st Century"; Noble, *Algorithms of Oppression*; Floegel and Jackson, "Recasting an Inclusive Narrative"; nina de jesus, "Locating the Library in Institutional Oppression," *In the Library with the Lead Pipe*, September 24, 2014, http://www.inthelibrarywiththeleadpipe.org/2014/locating-the-library-in-institutional-oppression/.

9. Skyller Walkes, "More Than Words: Without Action, It's Just Musical Acronyms" (presentation, UNM Pharmacy Practice and Administrative Sciences Meeting, Albuquerque, NM, May 19, 2021); Desiree Adaway, Jessica Fish, and Ericka Hines, "Whiteness at Work" (class, June 2020), https://courses.equityatwork.us/p/whiteness-at-work/ (web page discontinued); McKensie Mack, "Shifting the Center: Transforming Academic Libraries through Generous Accountability" (presentation, ACRL Together Wherever [virtual event], June 10, 2020), YouTube video, 1:28:19, https://www.youtube.com/watch?v=P2pnoUcF_o4; Tressie McMillan Cottom, *Thick and Other Essays* (New York: New Press, 2019); Yosso, "Whose Culture Has Capital?"

10. International Baccalaureate, "Education Programmes," accessed July 27, 2021, https://www.ibo.org/programmes/.

11. Noble, *Algorithms of Oppression*, 141.

12. Monte-Angel Richardson et al., "Bringing Trauma-Informed Practices to Underserved Patrons at University Libraries," in *Underserved Patrons in University Libraries: Assisting Students Facing Trauma, Abuse, and Discrimination*, ed. Julia C. Skinner and Melissa Gross (Santa Barbara, CA: Libraries Unlimited, 2021), 93.

13. Leung and López-McKnight, "Dreaming Revolutionary Futures," 21.

14. hooks, *Teaching to Transgress*, 84.

15. David A. Hurley, Sarah R. Kostelecky, and Lori Townsend, "Cultural Humility in Libraries," *Reference Services Review* 47, no. 4 (2019): 551, https://doi.org/10.1108/RSR-06-2019-0042.

16. Veronica Arellano Douglas, "Moving from Critical Assessment to Assessment as Care," *Communications in Information Literacy* 14, no. 1 (June 2020): 46–65, https://doi.org/10.15760/comminfolit.2020.14.1.4; hooks, *Teaching to Transgress*; Floegel and Jackson, "Recasting an Inclusive Narrative"; Maria T. Accardi, *The Feminist Reference Desk* (Sacramento, CA: Litwin Books, 2017); Richard Delgado, Jean Stefancic, and Angela Harris, *Critical Race Theory*, 3rd ed. (New York: New York University Press, 2017).

17. Noble, *Algorithms of Oppression*, 137.

18. Noble, *Algorithms of Oppression*; Ibram X. Kendi, *Stamped from the Beginning* (New York: Nation Books, 2016); Yosso, "Whose Culture Has Capital?"; Delgado, Stefancic, and Harris, *Critical Race Theory*.

19. Kimberlé Crenshaw, "Mapping the Margins: Intersectionality, Identity Politics, and Violence against Women of Color," in *Critical Race Theory: The Key Writings That Formed the Movement*, ed. Kimberlé Crenshaw, Neil Gotanda, Gary Peller, and Kendall Thomas (New York: New Press, 1995), 357–83; Kimberlé Crenshaw, "Demarginalizing the Intersection of Race and Sex: A Black Feminist Critique of Antidiscrimination Doctrine, Feminist Theory and Antiracist Politics," *University of Chicago Legal Forum* 1989, no. 1 (1989): article 8; Audre Lorde and Roxane Gay, *The Selected Works of Audre Lorde* (New York: W. W. Norton, 2020).

20. Paula Giddings, *Ida* (New York: Amistad, 2008), 7.

21. McMillan Cottom, *Thick and Other Essays*; Lorde and Gay, *Selected Works of Audre Lorde*; hooks, *Teaching to Transgress*; Brown et al., "We Here"; Yosso, "Whose Culture Has Capital?"; Kendi,

Stamped from the Beginning; Mikki Kendall, *Hood Feminism* (New York: Viking, 2020); Cite
   Black Women home page, accessed May 21, 2021, https://www.citeblackwomencollective.org/.
22.   McMillan Cottom, *Thick and Other Essays*, 216.
23.   Noble, *Algorithms of Oppression*, 141.

Bibliography

Accardi, Maria T. *The Feminist Reference Desk: Concepts, Critiques, and Conversations.* Sacramento,
   CA: Litwin Books, 2017.
Adaway, Desiree, Jessica Fish, and Ericka Hines. "Whiteness at Work." Class, June 2020. https://white-
   nessatwork.com/.
Arellano Douglas, Veronica. "Moving from Critical Assessment to Assessment as Care." *Commu-
   nications in Information Literacy* 14, no. 1 (June 2020): 46–65. https://doi.org/10.15760/
   comminfolit.2020.14.1.4.
Brown, Jennifer, Jennifer A. Ferretti, Sofia Leung, and Marisa Méndez-Brady. "We Here: Speaking
   Our Truth." *Library Trends* 67, no. 1 (2018): 163–81. https://doi.org/10.1353/lib.2018.0031.
Bruce, Symphony. "Teaching with Care: A Relational Approach to Individual Research Consulta-
   tions." *In the Library with the Lead Pipe*, February 5, 2020. http://www.inthelibrarywiththelead-
   pipe.org/2020/teaching-with-care/.
Cite Black Women home page. Accessed May 21, 2021. https://www.citeblackwomencollective.org/.
Crenshaw, Kimberlé. "Demarginalizing the Intersection of Race and Sex: A Black Feminist Critique
   of Antidiscrimination Doctrine, Feminist Theory and Antiracist Politics." *University of Chicago
   Legal Forum* 1989, no. 1 (1989): article 8.
———. "Mapping the Margins: Intersectionality, Identity Politics, and Violence Against Women of
   Color." In *Critical Race Theory: The Key Writings That Formed the Movement*, edited by Kimberlé
   Crenshaw, Neil Gotanda, Gary Peller, and Kendall Thomas, 357–83. New York: New Press, 1995.
de jesus, nina. "Locating the Library in Institutional Oppression." *In the Library with the
   Lead Pipe*, September 24, 2014. http://www.inthelibrarywiththeleadpipe.org/2014/
   locating-the-library-in-institutional-oppression/.
Delgado, Richard, Jean Stefancic, and Angela Harris. *Critical Race Theory: An Introduction*, 3rd ed.
   New York: New York University Press, 2017.
Ettarh, Fobazi. "Vocational Awe and Librarianship: The Lies We Tell Ourselves." *In the Library
   with the Lead Pipe*, January 10, 2018. http://www.inthelibrarywiththeleadpipe.org/2018/
   vocational-awe/.
Floegel, Diana, and Lorin Jackson. "Recasting an Inclusive Narrative: Exploring Intersectional
   Theory." In *Recasting the Narrative: The Proceedings of the ACRL 2019 Conference, April 10–13,
   2019, Cleveland, Ohio*, edited by Dawn M. Mueller, 412–20. Chicago: Association of College and
   Research Libraries, 2019. https://alair.ala.org/bitstream/handle/11213/17669/RecastinganInclu-
   siveNarrative.pdf.
Giddings, Paula. *Ida: A Sword among Lions: Ida B. Wells and the Campaign against Lynching.* New
   York: Amistad, 2008.
hooks, bell. *Teaching to Transgress: Education as the Practice of Freedom.* New York: Routledge, 1994.
Hurley, David A., Sarah R. Kostelecky, and Lori Townsend. "Cultural Humility in Libraries." *Reference
   Services Review* 47, no. 4 (2019): 544–55. https://doi.org/10.1108/RSR-06-2019-0042.
International Baccalaureate. "Education Programmes." Accessed July 27, 2021. https://www.ibo.org/
   programmes/.
Kendall, Mikki. *Hood Feminism: Notes from the Women That a Movement Forgot.* New York: Viking,
   2020.

Kendi, Ibram X. *Stamped from the Beginning: The Definitive History of Racist Ideas in America*. New York: Nation Books, 2016.

Leung, Sofia, and Jorge López-McKnight. "Dreaming Revolutionary Futures: Critical Race's Centrality to Ending White Supremacy." *Communications in Information Literacy* 14, no. 1 (2020): 12–26. https://doi.org/10.15760/comminfolit.2020.14.1.2.

———, eds. *Knowledge Justice: Disrupting Library and Information Studies through Critical Race Theory*. Cambridge, MA: MIT Press, 2021. https://doi.org/10.7551/mitpress/11969.001.0001.

Lorde, Audre, and Roxane Gay. *The Selected Works of Audre Lorde*. New York: W. W. Norton, 2020.

Mack, McKensie. "Shifting the Center: Transforming Academic Libraries through Generous Accountability." Presentation, ACRL Together Wherever (virtual event), June 10, 2020. YouTube video, 1:28:19. https://www.youtube.com/watch?v=P2pnoUcF_o4.

McMillan Cottom, Tressie. *Thick and Other Essays*. New York: New Press, 2019.

Noble, Safiya Umoja. *Algorithms of Oppression: How Search Engines Reinforce Racism*. New York: New York University Press, 2018.

Richardson, Monte-Angel, Stephanie Rosen, Marna M. Clowney-Rosen, and Danica San Juan. "Bringing Trauma-Informed Practices to Underserved Patrons at University Libraries." In *Underserved Patrons in University Libraries: Assisting Students Facing Trauma, Abuse, and Discrimination*, edited by Julia C. Skinner and Melissa Gross, 91–108. Santa Barbara, CA: Libraries Unlimited, 2021.

Rosa, Kathy, and Kelsey Henke. *2017 ALA Member Demographics Study*. Chicago: American Library Association Office of Research and Statistics, 2017. https://www.ala.org/tools/research/initiatives/membershipsurveys.

Walkes, Skyller. "More Than Words: Without Action, It's Just Musical Acronyms." Presentation, UNM Pharmacy Practice and Administrative Sciences Meeting, Albuquerque, NM, May 19, 2021.

Williams, Stacie. "Librarians in the 21st Century: It Is Becoming Impossible to Remain Neutral." Literary Hub, May 4, 2017. https://lithub.com/librarians-in-the-21st-century-it-is-becoming-impossible-to-remain-neutral/.

Yosso, Tara J. "Whose Culture Has Capital? A Critical Race Theory Discussion of Community Cultural Wealth." *Race Ethnicity and Education* 8, no. 1 (March 2005): 69–91. https://doi.org/10.1080/1361332052000341006.

CHAPTER 5

Unlearning
First Steps toward an Anti-oppressive Information Literacy

Scott R. Cowan and Selinda Adelle Berg

> *You can't say you respect people and not respect their experiences.*
>
> —*Horton and Freire*[1]

Anti-oppressive pedagogy acknowledges that there are inequities and oppressive hegemonic structures within classrooms and aims to minimize the effects of these structures. Applying anti-oppressive pedagogy requires the acknowledgement that students are unique individuals and that the manifestation of oppression such as racism, sexism, homophobia, ableism, and other forms of oppression are also unique to the individual. As a result, the anti-oppressive classroom must be flexible and responsive. Unlearning is a key element of anti-oppressive pedagogy. This chapter explores the complicated process of unlearning in anti-oppressive pedagogy by providing an example of librarians' implementation of this concept in their instruction. In a traditional one-shot" library session transformed into a workshop, students within a faculty of education critically examined the biases and prejudices within the curriculum and library resources, as well as their own unintentional biases in selecting the *best* resources for curricula. Through this process, the students became aware of the multiple oppressive structures at play when designing a simple lesson and the curriculum at large.

Anti-oppressive Pedagogy

Teaching with an anti-oppressive pedagogy consists of several complex elements. While unable to take up all aspects, this chapter will focus on one example, which

addresses identifying, understanding, and starting the process of unlearning. Unlearning is the process of recognizing and addressing the fact that white, patriarchal, capitalist, colonial systems of privilege permeate all of our systems as well as our experiences within those systems. Through unlearning we challenge and destabilize the dominant values around us.

The application of anti-oppressive pedagogy acknowledges that manifestations of oppression such as racism, classism, sexism, heterosexism, homophobia, and ableism are not a singular occurrence or experience applicable to all members of one particular social group.[2] Oppression is intersectional. It is a congregation of multiple, overlapping personal experiences of prejudice and power that is deeply contextual and suffered differently by each person.[3] Anti-oppressive pedagogy calls for educators to acknowledge these experiences and the different ways in how two individuals can experience oppression.[4] By way of personal example, we are members of the LGBTQ2S+ community and work in the same Canadian academic library: Selinda is a cisgender, white, queer female who grew up in a more rural and predominantly conservative region of Canada; Scott, a former middle school and high school teacher, is a cisgender, white gay male who grew up in a more urban and liberal part of the country. While we recognize we have both experienced oppression and bigotry in our lives, we know that the events and consequences differ. This understanding is also reflected in our professional practice. In particular, we aim to take an anti-oppressive pedagogical approach to our teaching. A key starting point in anti-oppressive pedagogy is an understanding that each student is unique and an acknowledgement that their relationship to and experience of inequity and oppression is also unique. Anti-oppressive pedagogy emphasizes that individual experiences of oppression or marginalization—that of being something other than the "norm" of social power—permeates and influences the experiences, and in turn interactions, for each person differently.

Anti-oppressive pedagogy seeks to actively challenge systems of oppression and create an environment where students can develop what Freire refers to as *conscientization*, a critical consciousness that will empower them to enact change within and against oppressive systems.[5] A key element in this process is that of "unlearning" for both teacher and student. Students and teachers must put aside and discard what they have "previously learned as 'normal' or normative."[6] Teachers and students are asked to disrupt those ideas that perpetuate white, heteronormative, patriarchal, and colonial systems of privilege as normal. Going through this unlearning, or "awakening" to oppression and injustice,[7] is challenging and can lead students to feel guilty, defensive, or helpless as they acknowledge past behaviours and confront their privileges.[8] This point of discomfort is complex and is not a quick process. Creating time and space for students to work through this unlearning is crucial.

For librarians, who are often limited in the time that they spend with students in the classroom, finding ways to critically engage students with an anti-oppressive pedagogy can be challenging. Faced with time restrictions, skills-based point-and-click sessions focused on information retrieval can become a default.[9] However, this default approach reinforces the power structure of *instructor-as-expert*, where instructors simply disseminate information to students, erasing the students' understanding and experiences and creating a one-sided conversation. Additionally, students are not given the opportunity to critically engage with and reflect on the information sources. In contrast, anti-oppressive pedagogy seeks to create an environment where students and teachers explore their understandings, biases, and behaviours together to move beyond their current understanding of power, privilege, and oppression. This approach encourages a *culture of questioning*, where students and instructor work together to acknowledge and question the environment in which they exist.[10] In turn, adopting an anti-oppressive pedagogy approach could move librarians closer to a "praxis that promotes critical engagement with information sources, considers students collaborators in knowledge production practices (and creators in their own right), recognizes the affective dimensions of research, and (in some cases) has liberatory aims."[11] Moving toward a structure where students are fellow collaborators requires a change in *how* we teach critical information literacy, not just *what* we teach.

These changes include the instructor acknowledging students as whole beings with complex lives and experiences and validating those stories and experiences as truth.[12] Students and instructors must acknowledge their own power and privilege and acknowledge that the experiences of others are different and equally valid. This recognition that every individual, and every class, is unique negates the ability to teach every class in the same way or to expect every class to be similar. Attempting to teach all classes with the same approach or expecting all classes to be similar ignores the intersectional and overlapping nature of oppression.[13] There is no singular, cookie-cutter, or "correct" method for developing a critical consciousness in students; rather, it requires the instructor to be responsive to the experiences and reactions of the class. This need for flexibility, openness, and responsiveness is reinforced within a classroom where the hegemonic structures that situate the instructor-as-expert are broken down. The classroom transforms into a community of learners, including the instructor, who listen, respond, and grow with and from one another. Any expectation that one can duplicate a classroom experience or standardize an approach reverts the classroom back to the hegemonic structure that reinforces the "banking concept" of education,[14] in which students are empty vessels to be filled with the knowledge of the instructor and repeat it back; an input-output approach without any critical thinking.

In summary, anti-oppressive pedagogy can be challenging to instructors because it requires instructors to acknowledge their own biases and to be vulnerable. It also requires instructors to carefully balance planning with the ability to change or modify the lesson on the go. Anti-oppressive pedagogy calls upon the instructor to actively engage with the content and the students as means to developing a *culture of questioning*[15]—an environment where students and instructors work together to take notice of and to question the ideologies, messages, and representations they encounter. In turn, students move toward developing a critical consciousness in which they become aware of, and enact change within, systems of power.

A Library Classroom Example

Librarians may be restricted in time and space with students, but we still have the ability to engage classes meaningfully using an anti-oppressive pedagogy. Presented here is a snapshot of one way in which the principles of anti-oppressive pedagogy can be integrated in the library classroom. The following is an example of a two-hour workshop/instruction session I (Scott) had with a group of students within the Faculty of Education at our university.

A faculty member from the Faculty of Education asked me to work with her students/teacher candidates, in the English Methodologies course, a course designed to teach approaches to teaching English language arts in middle school and high school. I was allotted two out of the three hours of the weekly scheduled class. The faculty member asked for a demonstration of the ready-made lesson plan resources and accompanying curriculum kits or manipulatives in our Curriculum Resource Centre and to discuss some basics of implementing one of the lessons during student practicum placements. Knowing that some of the resources were older and generic, I proposed an approach that would help the teacher candidates develop more critically based lessons and classrooms that they could continue to implement as teachers in their future classrooms. The faculty member enthusiastically agreed.

In Ontario, the bachelor of education is a consecutive or concurrent degree. As such, all of these teacher-candidates would have had, or would be currently working on, a previous or separate undergraduate degree. I did not know each teacher-candidate's understanding of oppression, bias, racism, classism, sexism, homophobia, or ableism, but I presumed that they were aware of the existence of or definitions of these concepts. I focused on the process of understanding and unlearning personal, implicit bias in the classroom. This learning would also assist them in their own future classrooms, which will be composed of students from various social groups who experience forms of oppression. In consideration of the time restrictions, I decided to place the resources, not the individuals, at the center of critique to help each teacher-candidate draw parallels to society before they reflected on themselves.

Setting the Groundwork

To start the session, I introduced myself, shared a brief overview of our time together, spoke about the importance of inclusivity in the classroom, and shared my own experience as a student and former teacher. I made sure to include some of my successes and failures as a teacher. I included the failures to illustrate that we all face difficult moments and to illustrate ways I could have made the situation better. I then shared a well-known quote widely attributed to Maya Angelou: "Do the best you can until you know better. Then, when you know better, do better."[16] I hoped that sharing these experiences would demonstrate my openness to learning from others, including the students.

Some time was spent talking about some of the principles underlying oppression and inclusiveness. Students were encouraged to come from a place of curiosity and honesty; to be willing to hear, accept, and believe others; to treat everyone respectfully. They were encouraged to acknowledge, apologize, and move on from mistakes rather than dwell on them and feel guilty. I emphasized that I, too, as someone who focuses on issues of diversity, equity, inclusion, and accessibility, make mistakes. I explained that I may make an error when speaking or may use an outdated term at times, and I encouraged them to correct me if I did; we were to act as a community of learners where we all learn from each other. I gave the example that as a cisgender gay man, I consciously, and for particular reasons, use the word *Queer* to refer to the LGBTQ2S+ community; however, some people within the LGBTQ2S+ community do not like the use of that term. I encouraged them to ask why I use the term if they wanted to discuss it or needed clarification but also said that if the use of that term made someone uncomfortable, they could let me know, publicly or privately, and I would use the term they preferred for the rest of our session. Students were also encouraged to push themselves to the boundaries of their own comfort zone as a means to feed their curiosity, ask questions, while avoiding shutting down, blocking out, or becoming unwilling to listen to or try new ideas. I recommended every student allow this class to be a judgment-free community where it is safe to try new ideas, make mistakes, and learn from others. Students who were nervous to speak in front of the class or ask specific questions were welcome to have a discussion with me privately. Finally, I reassured students that I would not judge.

It is difficult for students to trust that the librarian in front of them, someone they are possibly meeting for the first time, will not judge them. I hoped that providing information about myself and demonstrating my willingness to be corrected and change my language would help ease the students and lay some groundwork for creating a community for the rest of our time together. To help encourage questions, I then shared a quote attributed to John Abbott: "'How do you know so much about everything?' was asked of a very wise and intelligent man; and the answer was 'By never being afraid or ashamed to ask questions as to anything of which I was ignorant.'" I followed up by giving a short explanation about why I love questions and the importance of questions in our learning about oppression and inclusiveness.

Identifying Power and Privilege

The teacher-candidates were then divided into small groups of two or three and asked to examine two ready-made lesson plans from the resources, one physical and one electronic. They were asked to fill out a handout (appendix A) based on Swanson's questions to challenge implicit and explicit biases[17] and walk-through questions such as these: Whose voice is most present/represented? Whose voice or knowledge gets left out? Does this lesson require knowledge of specific cultural references (e.g., a fairy tale or an analogy/metaphor)? What are the physical require-ments to complete this lesson (do students have to move around a lot)? This part of the lesson was intended to underline the prevalence of power and privilege in these resources and lead to a discussion about implicit bias.

As the teacher-candidates worked through the handout, I walked among the groups to help answer questions and provide guidance. Approximately ten minutes was allotted for the handout, but the flow of the class was taken into account to begin a full class discussion once most of the students were finished. During the full class discussion, students quickly identified that most lesson plans were geared toward white, middle-class children with English as a first language. The missing voices and representation of racialized and queer communities were also called out. However, the biggest surprise for me was that, in a class where the vast majority of students were women, no one mentioned the missing representation of women. There was a definitive stunned silence when I pointed this out. Several women were visibly taken aback and responded with quiet comments of "oh" or "whoa." This stunned silence provided an opportunity to ask why the students thought they didn't realize that women's voices and representation were missing. Comments from female students included "I guess I'm just used to it," "It was the same literature I remember learn-ing from," and "This literature is just what we teach—they're classics." As a cisgen-der male, I asked some women to elaborate on their experiences as women and of having their voices omitted. I then asked students to elaborate on their experiences studying literature in the middle school, high school, and university classrooms. In particular I asked what materials they studied by women and whether this mattered. Some cisgender heterosexual male students questioned whether it was their job, and worth the extra work, to provide such material in the classroom. They suggested that this was "protecting the classics." In response, one student identified themselves as part of the Queer community and spoke of their frustration not seeing themselves represented in their classrooms or curriculum.

The discussion led to an exciting and unplanned discussion around Emily Style's notion that the curriculum should be a *window and mirror*,[18] where students are able to see themselves reflected back at themselves and also see what's possible in their future. I let this discussion go on with minimal intervention so I could also learn from the experiences and knowledge of the teacher-candidates. My original lesson plan was designed with different prompt questions in case of minimal or sparse discussion. However, based on the students' robust and in-depth discussion and participation, I decided to ignore my prepared prompts and let the students lead us in a different direction. This responsiveness, as noted, is critical when taking an anti-oppressive pedagogical approach.

Identifying Implicit Bias in Ourselves

The teacher-candidates were then asked to take the learning objectives of the lesson plan they had chosen and imagine how they may re-create the lesson to be more inclusive—ensuring objectives were met but adjusting the approach, or *how* they taught the lesson, to match students in two different classrooms. To assist them, the teacher-candidates received a second handout that included a scenario of a realistic classroom. In this scenario, the school and classroom were identified as racially, culturally, and religiously diverse and the makeup of the students in each class changed (appendix B).

Shortly after the teacher-candidates started the second worksheet, they became frustrated. Based on the discussion that came from the previous exercise, I decided to start a full-class discussion instead of continuing with the handout and furthering students' frustration. I expected the frustrations from the teacher-candidates to be centered around perceptions that the assignment was unrealistic. In contrast, the frustration arose from implicit biases and assumptions about students, behaviours, and societal norms. For example, one student remarked that those afraid to take risks "just have to learn to step out of their comfort zone" or students had to "pick themselves up by the bootstraps/suck it up and do the assignment as asked." It was unnecessary for me to point out the bias embedded in the statement because another student did so by identifying themselves as "one of those high school students" and explaining why the comment was inaccurate. These comments led to a conversation among the teacher-candidates around introverts, extroverts, cultural differences, understanding expectations and cultural references, meeting teacher and family expectations, and challenging power and authority. With subtle facilitation, students started to make the connection between our first activity and their own implicit bias.

Beginning the Process of Unlearning

At this point, a few of the teacher-candidates started to reach what Kumashiro refers to as *crisis*,[19] where feelings of guilt, embarrassment, and helplessness emerge as they acknowledge their privilege or past behaviours. This place of crisis "can lead in one of many directions—such as liberating change, or toward more entrenched resistance."[20]

This was a crucial moment of unlearning for the teacher-candidates. I recognized that I had limited time with them and wanted to avoid anyone feeling like they were on display and directed the conversation back to the resources and how we may improve upon them, knowing what we know now and after learning from each other. The students continued to demonstrate their learning by recognizing how they could use the resources as a starting point to incorporate ideas they learned from each other during our discussions, address the missing voices, and make the lesson relevant to the students directly in their class. We discussed how they could do this while still infusing their own experiences and personality and meeting the needs of their students. Through the large-group discussion, it was clear that the teacher-candidates started to understand that individuals—student and teachers alike—had unique experiences, understandings, or expectations. The teacher-candidates also recognized that the lesson plan that they were creating was more about the students as whole people, rather than as empty vessels waiting for the teacher to fill with their knowledge.[21] We were able to wrap up the discussion with ideas for finding more information and resources to integrate the experiences of racialized and marginalized communities. It is noteworthy that many great resources were suggested by the teacher-candidates themselves, and I wrote down the suggestions for purchase by the library—again, more opportunity for me to learn, grow, and demonstrate the process through the experience.

As a wrap-up, or what is referred to as an "exit slip," I often end my class by asking students to share five things they learned or will take away from our time together. In this instance, the takeaways included "Our teaching should be a mirror and window," "Everyone is different and brings something different to our classroom; we can't just teach cookie-cutter lessons," and my favourite one that I will never forget, "It's not about me." These comments, especially the last one, underscored that the teacher-candidates were starting to understand the importance of critically examining the resources they use in their classroom and thinking about how the resources may or may not reflect the diversity of identities and experiences within the classroom. They started to see the potential pitfalls, assumptions, and biases of a ready-made lesson and recognize that there are better ways to meet the disparate needs of a diverse classroom. Overall, the teacher-candidates expressed an appreciation for recognizing the uniqueness of individuals and their experiences.

Anti-oppressive Pedagogy in the Library Classroom

Becoming aware of one's unconscious bias is paramount to starting the process of unlearning, but it also takes time and often requires repetition. Instructors will not necessarily see or know of any immediate or lasting impact of their teaching. The acceptance, and understanding, of unconscious bias, power, and privilege can take time to settle in or "click." Unlearning and challenging forms of oppression takes time and supportive spaces to make mistakes. Librarians are able to build a safe learning community that allows for the critical examination of resources and information sources and to identify oppressive and biased components within these resources. This exercise can help facilitate the acknowledgement of learners' own privileges and implicit bias, as well as consideration of their role in systemic forms of oppression.

With the example used in this chapter, although students experienced feelings of discomfort and defensiveness when facing their own privilege and bias, placing the resources at the fore of the critique, and not the person, helped navigate students through their discomfort by allowing them to make connections to their own life. The students made their own connections and applied the work and discussions to their understanding of oppression and their role in or contribution to systems that perpetuate oppression, rather than an accusatory approach where students may have become defensive or disconnected because they felt they already knew the information, knew more than the instructor, or felt the instructor did not understand their experiences.

The example presented here was within a context of a workshop, where the faculty member was flexible with the content and generous with time allotment. There are ways to integrate some of the principles presented here in more rigid settings. In the library classroom, librarians can use examples that generate conversations around the experiences within the classroom and be responsive and flexible to those experiences. Librarians who reject the instructor-as-expert approach can also give students opportunity to share, to teach, and to engage differently. Moving the power from the instructor, especially when exploring bias and oppressive structures, can prevent students rejecting the content, shutting down, and becoming defensive. An anti-oppressive approach to pedagogy sets up the classroom as a community of learners and collaborators. In even the most time-restricted classroom, one can explore "whose voices are missing" by exploring *manels,* or male-dominated panels (see https://allmalepanels.tumblr.com/). In addition to critiquing academic panels with the lens of (binary) gender, one can explore the overall homogeneity of academic panels. It is a way in which we can underline the absence of the voices of people of colour, people with disabilities, people representing the range of sexual and gender diversity. The exploration of manels can be integrated into classroom conversations with approaches as simple as a *Far Side* cartoon and still have significant impact.

By understanding and applying the principles of anti-oppressive pedagogy, librarians recognize that each individual is unique. Librarians overtly acknowledge that there is not one common experience of inequity or oppression. Librarians are flexible in their approach within the classroom and respond to student experiences, knowledge, and expertise. The library classroom becomes a community of learners, where there is an openness by all to learn from one another. Through this work, the library classroom can emerge as a place for learning and unlearning.

Appendix A: Critical Evaluation of Resources Handout 1, English Methodologies

Typical "canned" resources for teachers ostensibly seem to be ideologically neutral. Yet every text (hard copy or online) represents certain ideological stances. In this exercise, we will be thinking about how to critically evaluate resources to consider how they shape the discourse of English studies at the intermediate/senior level.

Name of Resource:
Evaluative Questions:
(a) In scanning through this resource, what type of knowledge gets left out or marginalized? Whose voice is most prevalent? Whose voice(s) is/are missing? Who, and what culture(s), is mostly represented? Who, and what culture(s), is not represented?
(b) What are the most effective components of this resource? What would you do to adapt it, if anything?

(c) What are some of the implicit assumptions about literacy in this
     resource?

(d) Does this text foster multiple perspectives? Does it encourage a
     political focus regarding language and/or literary representations in a
     societal context? If so, in what ways? If not, imagining that you were
     the textbook editor, how would you suggest the author(s) improve the
     resource in this sense?

(e) Does this lesson require knowledge of specific cultural references?
     What are the physical requirements to complete this lesson (e.g., think/
     pair/share, moving to different stations, technological requirements)?

Appendix B: Critical Evaluation of Resources Handout 2, English Methodologies

Imagine you are teaching in a school with a large and culturally/religiously diverse student population. Create learning objectives that would match the resource(s) you have been looking at.

Objectives:

How would you utilize the resource(s) to meet your objectives with the following class?

- The majority of students are enthusiastic.
- Some of the students are strong leaders and happy to take learning risks.
- A small group of students are constantly challenging the purpose/reason for doing things.
- Students are comfortable asking questions when they do not know what to do or understand the material.
- One student is in a wheelchair.

Now, your period 2 class arrives, same grade, but with the following makeup of students:

- Two new students that arrived from another country several weeks ago.
- Several students have English as a second or additional language.
- Students are afraid to take risks; many of the students want to know exactly what the teacher expects and how he/she/they want things done or are unwilling to try unless they know they will be successful.

How do you approach this class in a manner that will still meet the same objectives? What changes would be implemented to differentiate from the other class to ensure all students are still learning/meeting stated objectives?

Notes

1. Myles Horton and Paulo Freire, *We Make the Road by Walking* (Philadelphia: Temple University Press, 1990), 178.
2. Kevin K. Kumashiro, "Toward a Theory of Anti-oppressive Education," *Review of Educational Research* 70, no. 1 (Spring 2000): 25–53; Kevin K. Kumashiro, "Teaching and Learning through Desire, Crisis, and Difference: Perverted Reflections on Anti-oppressive Education." *Radical Teacher* 58 (Fall 2000): 6–11.

3. Paula S. Rothenberg, *Racism and Sexism* (New York: St. Martin's Press, 1988); Stacy Collins, "Anti-Oppression and Research Guides with Stacy Collins - part 1," interview by Allison Jones and Karen Ng, *Organizing Ideas*, podcast, January 8, 2021,

4. Brandy Humes, "Moving toward a Liberatory Pedagogy for All Species: Mapping the Need for Dialogue between Humane and Anti-oppressive Education," *Green Theory and Praxis: The Journal of Ecopedagogy*, 4, no. 1 (April 2008): 65–85; Lance T. McCready, "Understanding the Marginalization of Gay and Gender Non-conforming Black Male Students," *Theory into Practice* 43, no. 2 (Spring 2004): 136–43; Iris Marion Young, "Five Faces of Oppression," in *Readings for Diversity and Social Justice*, 4th ed., ed. Maurianne Adams, Warren J. Blumenfeld, D. Chase J. Catalano, Keri Dejong, Heather W. Hackman, Larissa E. Hopkins, Barbara Love, Madeline L. Peters, Davey Shlasko, and Xiema Zuniga (New York: Routledge, 2018), 35–49.

5. Paulo Freire, "Cultural Action and Conscientization," *Harvard Educational Review* 68, no. 4 (Winter 1998): 499–521.

6. Kumashiro, "Toward a Theory," 37.

7. Morton Deutsch and Janice M. Steil, "Awakening the Sense of Injustice," *Social Justice Research*, no. 1 (1988): 3–23.

8. Kumashiro, "Teaching and Learning."

9. Brian M. Kopp and Kim Olson-Kopp, "Depositories of Knowledge: Library Instruction and the Development of Critical Consciousness," in *Critical Library Instruction: Theories and Methods*, ed. Maria Accardi, Emily Drabinski, and Alana Kumbier (Duluth, MN: Library Juice Press, 2010), 55–67.

10. Henry A. Giroux and Susan Searls Giroux, *Take Back Higher Education* (New York: Palgrave Macmillan, 2004).

11. Maria T. Accardi, Emily Drabinski, and Alana Kumbier, Introduction to *Critical Library Instruction: Theories and Methods*, ed. Maria T. Accardi, Emily Drabinski, and Alana Kumbier (Duluth, MN: Library Juice Press, 2010), xii.

12. Jennifer A. Ferretti, "Building a Critical Culture: How Critical Librarianship Falls Short in the Workplace," *Communications in Information Literacy* 15, no. 1 (2020): 134–52; bell hooks, *Teaching to Transgress* (New York: Routledge, 1994).

13. Melissa Villa-Nicholas, "Teaching Intersectionality: Pedagogical Approaches for Lasting Impact," *Education for Information* 34, no. 2 (October 2018), 121–33.

14. Paulo Freire, *Pedagogy of the Oppressed*, 50th anniversary ed., trans. Myra Bergman Ramos (New York: Bloomsbury Academic, 2018).

15. Giroux and Giroux, *Take Back Higher Education*.

16. Although the quote is widely used and attributed to Maya Angelou in various forms, no original source can be identified.

17. Troy A. Swanson, "Information Is Personal: Critical Information Literacy and Personal Epistemology," in *Critical Library Instruction: Theories and Methods*, ed. Maria T. Accardi, Emily Drabinski, and Alana Kumbier (Duluth, MN: Library Juice Press, 2010), 265–78.

18. Emily Style, "Curriculum as Window and Mirror," *Social Science Record*, Fall 1996: 35–42.

19. Kumashiro, "Teaching and Learning," 6.

20. Kumashiro, "Teaching and Learning," 7.

21. Freire, *Pedagogy of the Oppressed*.

Bibliography

Accardi, Maria T., Emily Drabinski, and Alana Kumbier. Introduction to *Critical Library Instruction: Theories and Methods*, edited by Maria T. Accardi, Emily Drabinski, and Alana Kumbier, ix–xiv. Duluth, MN: Library Juice Press, 2010.

Collins, Stacy. "Anti-Oppression and Research Guides with Stacy Collins – Part 1." Interview by Allison Jones and Karen Ng. *Organizing Ideas* podcast, episode 34, January 8, 2021. https://anchor.fm/organizing-ideas/episodes/ Ep-34---Anti-Oppression-and-Research-Guides-with-Stacy-Collins---part-1-emikuk

Deutsch, Morton, and Janice M. Steil. "Awakening the Sense of Injustice." *Social Justice Research,* no. 1 (1988): 3–23.

Ferretti, Jennifer A. "Building a Critical Culture: How Critical Librarianship Falls Short in the Workplace." *Communications in Information Literacy* 15, no. 1 (2020): 134–52.

Freire, Paulo. "Cultural Action and Conscientization." *Harvard Educational Review* 68, no 4 (Winter 1998): 499–521.

———. *Pedagogy of the Oppressed*, 50th anniversary ed. Translated by Myra Bergman Ramos. New York: Bloomsbury Academic, 2018.

Giroux, Henry A., and Susan Searls Giroux. *Take Back Higher Education: Race, Youth, and the Crisis of Democracy in the Post–Civil Rights Era.* New York: Palgrave Macmillan, 2004.

hooks, bell. *Teaching to Transgress: Education as the Practice of Freedom.* New York: Routledge, 1994.

Horton, Myles, and Paulo Freire. *We Make the Road by Walking: Conversations on Education and Social Change* (Philadelphia: Temple University Press, 1990).

Humes, Brandy. "Moving toward a Liberatory Pedagogy for All Species: Mapping the Need for Dialogue between Humane and Anti-oppressive Education." *Green Theory and Praxis: The Journal of Ecopedagogy* 4, no. 1 (April 2008): 65–85.

Kopp, Brian M., and Kim Olson-Kopp. "Depositories of Knowledge: Library Instruction and the Development of Critical Consciousness." In *Critical Library Instruction: Theories and Methods,* edited by Maria Accardi, Emily Drabinski, and Alana Kumbier, 55–67. Duluth, MN: Library Juice Press, 2010.

Kumashiro, Kevin K. "Teaching and Learning through Desire, Crisis, and Difference: Perverted Reflections on Anti-oppressive Education." *Radical Teacher,* no. 58 (Fall 2000): 6–11.

———. "Toward a Theory of Anti-oppressive Education." *Review of Educational Research* 70, no. 1 (Spring 2000): 25–53.

McCready, Lance T. "Understanding the Marginalization of Gay and Gender Non-conforming Black Male Students." *Theory into Practice* 43, no. 2 (Spring 2004): 136–43.

Rothenberg, Paula S. *Racism and Sexism: An Integrated Study.* New York: St. Martin's Press, 1988.

Style, Emily. "Curriculum as Window and Mirror." *Social Science Record,* Fall 1996: 35–42.

Swanson, Troy A. "Information Is Personal: Critical Information Literacy and Personal Epistemology." In *Critical Library Instruction: Theories and Methods,* edited by Maria T. Accardi, Emily Drabinski, and Alana Kumbier, 265–78. Duluth, MN: Library Juice Press, 2010.

Tumblr. "Congrats, you have an all male panel!" https://allmalepanels.tumblr.com/.

Villa-Nicholas, Melissa. "Teaching Intersectionality: Pedagogical Approaches for Lasting Impact." *Education for Information* 34, no. 2 (October 2018): 121–33.

Young, Iris Marion. "Five Faces of Oppression." In *Readings for Diversity and Social Justice,* 4th ed., edited by Maurianne Adams, Warren J. Blumenfeld, D. Chase J. Catalano, Keri Dejong, Heather W. Hackman, Larissa E. Hopkins, Barbara Love, Madeline L. Peters, Davey Shlasko, and Xiema Zuniga, 35–49. New York: Routledge, 2018.

CHAPTER 6

Supporting Epistemic Justice in the Anti-racist Classroom

Maggie Clarke

Introduction

Since the publication of her 2007 monograph *Epistemic Injustice,* Miranda Fricker's conceptual framework of epistemic injustice has been widely discussed across disciplines as a useful lens through which we can explore how humans relate to one another as both knowers and seekers of knowledge. It has not, however, yet been widely discussed within the context of libraries and librarianship. Given the growing conversation in our field surrounding our role in communicating the importance of truth and the potential pitfalls of unchecked or unacknowledged bias, particularly in the context of academic information literacy instruction, this is a timely moment for librarians and information professionals to interrogate how we communicate about facts and the potential biases within our practice that may be supporting structural inequity.

In a time and space of increased focus on equipping students with the tools and dispositions necessary to critically evaluate information, it is important to reflect not only on detecting misinformation but also on considering who or what students *can* trust. In academic settings conversations about high-quality information have largely centered on scholarly articles published in peer-reviewed journals. While this is essential for student success, instruction that focuses narrowly on scholarly

communication fails to address the narrow (white, Western, cisgender, male) perspectives that have been and continue to be privileged in academia.[1]

Though this paper is by no means the first to consider how privilege, power, and prejudice operate in the information literacy classroom, by mapping Fricker's notion of epistemic injustice onto critical pedagogical practices in information literacy, I hope to present a novel lens with which instruction librarians can consider how they address issues of authority in both their curriculum and pedagogy.

Epistemic Injustice

Considering the term *epistemic injustice,* it would seem that there are numerous potential definitions for such a phenomenon. Injustice could take the form of unequal access to knowledge due to educational, institutional, financial, or legal barriers or of a system in which knowledge is willfully kept from certain people in order to oppress them. While these forms of injustice are both real and important, what makes Fricker's *epistemic injustice* a highly relevant frame for librarians to consider is that it goes beyond addressing distributive injustices of unequal knowledge resources or access to information and addresses instances of injustice that are specifically epistemic in nature.[2] That is to say, rather than describing incidents where lack of access to knowledge is an incidental effect of another form of inequity, epistemic injustice is a discrete phenomenon related directly to how we conceptualize and communicate knowledge.[3]

With its roots in feminist epistemology and critical race studies, epistemic injustice gives us a vocabulary to discuss injustices that the hegemonic limitations of our knowledge production and communication practices have previously excluded from the conversation—those injustices perpetrated against individuals and groups as knowers or possessors of knowledge. In doing so, this theory acknowledges the social injustices that are not always best illustrated by the distribution of goods or opportunities but exist in the (often tacit) knowledge of individuals and groups of their relative position in society. This awareness, acknowledged or not, contributes to both *incidental injustices,* which occur between individuals, and *structural injustices,* which "'track' the subject through different dimensions of social activity."[4]

Fricker further separates the forms of epistemic injustices into two categories: *testimonial injustice* and *hermeneutical injustice.* Testimonial injustice, as the name perhaps implies, refers to an instance of epistemic injustice in which the subject's testimony is discredited, ignored, or invalidated due to negative stereotypes associated with their social identity or identities. A hypothetical example from an academic context is an indigenous scholar's work describing their own experiences of indigenous culture being rejected by a white editor on the basis of lack of objectivity or bias. In this situation, the white editor is choosing not to accept or take seriously the testimony of their indigenous colleague as a knower of their own experience. Rather than being seen as a source of knowledge about their experiences, the indigenous scholar, by virtue of their indigeneity, is assumed to be only a subject of other's knowledge. Testimonial injustices manifest as both incidental and structural injustices that erase the subjects of oppression from conversations about their own experiences.

In my experience, once you become aware of a phenomenon, you begin to see it everywhere. From overweight adults being denied medical care,[5] to Black Lives Matter activists being labeled as irrational instigators who exaggerate their accounts of the violence they experience,[6] to trans people being dismissed as merely "confused" about their own gender identity,[7] it does not take much looking to see that marginalized people are routinely discredited when it comes to knowing the reality of their own lived experiences. The flip side of this *credibility deficit* that is so routinely applied to marginalized groups and individuals is the *credibility surplus* that is applied to privileged observers of marginalized groups—the white, heterosexual, cisgender, able-bodied, thin, and/or neurotypical (to name a few) commentators whose "knowledge" about the lives of oppressed people is so often taken more seriously than the accounts of the marginalized themselves. This positions those at a credibility deficit not as knowers in their own right but merely subjects of knowledge held by those on whom the privilege of credibility is bestowed.[8]

This is not to suggest that individual testimony can always be accepted as complete truth, or used as a reliable basis to make sweeping judgements about the experiences of all members of a group. However, the fact that all humans are capable of misrepresenting, either intentionally or unintentionally, their experiences does not account for the credibility differential that falls so clearly along lines of privilege and marginalization. Such a state of affairs points to ingrained prejudice in our epistemic judgements that goes beyond that which most people are probably consciously aware of, or, as Anderson phrases it, "testimonial exclusion becomes structural when institutions are set up to exclude people without anyone having to decide to do so."[9] Decisions, traditions, and ways of doing that seem so ingrained, so fundamental, as to never be questioned are the locus of ongoing injustice.

On the other hand, *hermeneutical injustice* describes "a gap in collective interpretative resources [that] puts someone at an unfair disadvantage when it comes to making sense of their social experiences."[10] Building upon our previous example to illustrate hermeneutical injustice, we can imagine the same hypothetical indigenous scholar attempting to conduct research addressing indigenous land stewardship within a discipline that does not accept understandings of non-Western forms of property ownership. As Goetze notes, indigenous knowledge gives those who are familiar with it unique hermeneutical tools to interpret their experiences, while simultaneously making these interpretations difficult to understand for those without these interpretive tools.[11] Without a term with an accepted definition for the practices and dispositions they are researching, the scholar is shut out of communicating their lived knowledge in a way their audience of non-indigenous academics can receive. In this instance the scholar has been "wronged in their capacity as a subject of social understanding."[12] This dearth of hermeneutical resources available to them is the result of systematic exclusion of those who share their identity from the processes by which social understanding is created. Though such injustice can be illuminated by the experiences of individuals, hermeneutical injustice is inherently structural and reflects hegemonic societal prejudice rather than individual prejudice.

For librarians, confronting such pervasive injustice may seem, at best, daunting and, at worst, completely insurmountable. As I will discuss below, admitting the extent to which we, as individuals and as a profession, have contributed to the erasure or suppression of marginalized voices begets some uncomfortable questions about the role prejudice plays in our professional practice. If, as Morales, Knowles, and Bourg suggest, "Academic librarians are …uniquely equipped and empowered to define and redefine systems of knowledge that convey 'truths' about what we know about the world and how that knowledge is organized and evaluated," then it is incumbent upon academic librarians to consider critically how to employ this power and our role in ameliorating past and present injustices.[13] The established positions many academic librarians hold in the knowledge landscape of their institutions—as gatekeepers, arbiters, custodians, and distributors of knowledge—engender a particular responsibility to confront and oppose injustices surrounding knowledge. The entrenched whiteness of our field both reflects, and is reflected in, our current failure to meaningfully address injustice in our work.

Epistemic Injustice in Information Literacy Instruction

In terms of my work as an instruction librarian, one thing that immediately drew me to epistemic injustice is its natural synergy with the values found in the ACRL *Framework*, specifically the frames "Authority Is Constructed and Contextual" and "Information Creation as a Process."[14] Exploring the oppression that comes with being wronged as a knower, and the credibility deficits and excesses that underpin this phenomenon, requires not just an acknowledgement that authority is constructed, but a critical exploration as to how and why this construction has and continues to develop. Epistemic injustice contextualizes the information creation process within an epistemic landscape that systematically disenfranchises individuals and groups based on prejudicial stereotypes about their identities. Beyond the epistemic barriers confronted by marginalized knowers in all areas of society, I argue that academic and scholarly communication that is often most highlighted in information literacy instruction presents further challenges to epistemic justice.

By approaching information literacy instruction with the perspectives of epistemic injustice, specifically testimonial injustice, instructors have a useful mode for empowering students as knowers and encouraging critical engagement with evaluating resources. Because epistemic injustice has been explored and applied by scholars to many disciplines, it can also provide a useful shared language for contextualizing critical library instruction for faculty partners who may have a narrower understanding of what to expect from a one-shot instruction session.

Many scholars have explored the pervasive whiteness of scholarly epistemology, methodology, and research practices. The hegemonic domination of epistemologies of whiteness and ways of knowing rooted in whiteness are rooted in pervasive white-supremacist and settler-colonizer attitudes within academia.[15] Others have explored the epistemological barriers faced by nonwhite people inherent to existence in spaces, such as academia and scholarly publishing, that consistently devalue and deny ways of knowing of people of color.[16] These barriers place scholars and students of color at a persistent disadvantage for participation in scholarly communication through citation bias, obfuscated criteria for publication and tenure that mask racial bias in selection decisions, and the perception that research that uses "nontraditional methods" or centers the perspectives of people of color is less legitimate than more "objective" methodologies, to name a few.[17]

Fricker herself situates epistemic injustice in a similar environment of structural social injustice, noting, "But our predicament as hearers is that even if we are personally innocent of prejudicial beliefs, still the social atmosphere in which we must judge speakers' credibility is one in which there are, inevitably, many stray residual prejudices which threaten to influence our credibility judgements."[18] Therefore, essential to examining how epistemic injustice operates in the library context is the willingness to confront how oppression on a systemic level and an individual level manifests in academic libraries.

As purveyors, creators, and arbiters of both scholarly knowledge and knowledge about the process of academic information creation and dissemination, university libraries and librarians are certainly complicit in maintaining this structural epistemic whiteness. The pervasive whiteness of librarianship as a profession is certainly implicated here as a circumstance that contributes to a lack of institutional and professional motivation to question what many of us perceive as accepted ways of knowing. Patricia Hill Collins notes that oppressed people, by virtue of their oppression, create unique knowledge that privileged individuals and groups cannot create on their own.[19] In this way the racial privilege afforded to white librarians in a system rooted in white supremacy may make it difficult or impossible for white librarians to accurately perceive the racial injustice in our epistemic practices. Despite this, scholars of librarianship, led by the work of BIPOC scholars, have long identified and condemned libraries' role in consistently centering white ways of knowing while failing to meaningfully address the legacies of racism, anti-Blackness, and anti-indigeneity—not to mention sexism, queerphobia, and ableism—that under-pin the systems of knowledge production common in academia.[20] This can be seen across LIS praxis from cataloging schemata that center the importance of Western, European, white knowledge and our professional failure to meaningfully address government surveillance of communities of color to common attitudes that assume an inherent neutrality to libraries and librarians without critical consideration of our professional roots in settler-colonialism, assimilation, and racism.[21] Within the context of information literacy instruction, presenting information literacy concepts without situating them in the context of a system of information production, orga-nization, and dissemination that is structurally racist contributes to continued white supremacy.[22] I argue that by virtue of the role libraries and librarians have played in reifying epistemic injustices, it is essential that we prioritize mitigating this harm by committing to dismantling epistemic injustice in our practices and dispositions.

Toward Epistemically Just Information Literacy

In considering what movement toward epistemic justice as an anti-racist practice may look like in information literacy education, I examine two areas: librarians' dispositions toward students and our dispositions toward information.

Dispositions toward Learners

As education scholar Casey Rebecca Johnson notes, part of the role of the educator is not only to practice epistemic justice themselves, but also to train students as epistemic agents in their own right.[23] I argue that this is particularly true in the infor-mation literacy classroom where how students find, access, and evaluate information is often the explicit focus of the class. In line with critical pedagogical practices that situate students as autonomous individuals who each bring their own experiences, understandings, and knowledge to the classroom, a pedagogy of epistemic justice recognizes that students enter the classroom as unique epistemic agents who already have significant experience in creating, communicating, and making judgments about knowledge.

With these understandings of our students as knowers, creators, and dissemi-nators of knowledge in place, how might this translate into praxis? I have found the most significant challenge in this area is not in developing my own disposition toward students, but in encouraging students to see themselves as knowers, even potential experts, by virtue of their previous experiences. In my own experience, for students used to receiving expertise from others, viewing themselves, or others like them, as knowers and creators of knowledge can be a challenge, particularly in a classroom setting in which students are expecting to learn about the highly rarefied sources of information created and used by scholars. If we understand one of the mechanisms by which racism and other forms of oppression function to be gaslighting the oppressed to ensure that they constantly question their experiences of oppression, it makes sense that nonwhite students or those who are otherwise oppressed may struggle to recognize the knowledge they have created through their experiences.[24]

One way I address this is by beginning discussions about authority by posing a series of questions:

- What is something that you know more about than most people?
- How did you learn about this?
- Do you consider yourself an expert on this topic?

Depending on the classroom context, these questions can be posed verbally or via a paper or digital form. I am privileged to work in a library with a dedicated classroom with computers for library instruction and, particularly for larger classes, that allows for opportunities to compile and share student answers using tools like Google Forms or Padlet. However, in most classrooms on my campus, digital tools are extremely limited and I have had positive experiences simply writing these prompts on a whiteboard and using that to guide a conversation. If the class is small, I may encourage students to share their answers out loud. If that is not possible, I review their answers and may share anonymized responses in our discussion. My goal in posing these questions is to situate authority within the process by which knowledge is gained, rather than tying it to an identity or job title (such as doctor, professor, or teacher). I acknowledge that, while we will be focusing on information situated in an academic context in class, formal education is not the only, or even the most important, way for knowledge to be developed and that every student is already a creator of knowledge, an expert on something, and thereby empowered to participate in our collective knowledge practices.

While the accompanying discussion will, of course, flow according to student responses and observations, typical themes include self-education, finding information online or through personal experience, and what it means to be an expert in something. For students resistant to identifying themselves as having expertise on any topic, I will often bring the conversation back to their own experiences—if nothing else, they are the ultimate authority on their own experiences, thoughts, and feelings. If it does not emerge on its own from student observations, I will wrap up the conversation by observing that just as everyone in the classroom is an expert on something, there are also things we are not experts on, which is why we are here. No one is an expert on everything. I will often use myself as an example and explain that while I'm an expert on libraries and finding and evaluating information, I am not necessarily an expert on the topics students are interested in exploring, so we will be collaborating with our different knowledge to help them succeed in their research projects. In separating these knowledge domains, my goal is to problematize the credibility surpluses afforded to the often highly privileged people undertaking academic research (myself included) and support students in centering themselves within the process of knowledge creation. In this way students are empowered to make their own nuanced judgements about the credibility of information sources.

Dispositions toward Information

Much of the criticism around academic libraries' role in reinforcing and perpetuating white supremacy describes practices and dispositions that center whiteness and white ways of knowing.[25] Even within existing literature on critical information literacy, scholars have identified problematic overreliance of European theory and a bias toward European ways of thinking that color critical conversations about information in our field.[26] Perhaps the most essential move instruction librarians can make toward epistemic justice is personally and institutionally engaging with these criticisms and examining how accepted understandings of authority systematically disenfranchise nonwhite people and other groups.

Returning to the ACRL frames discussed previously—working with students to explore the construction of authority and dissemination of academic or scholarly information provides numerous opportunities for frank discussion about the epistemic oppression inherent in academia's epistemic norms, including the historical and continued practices that exclude scholars who are not white men from study and publication and that reify positivist notions of objectivity in research that present white male perspectives as neutral.[27] For example, when discussing the research process and how scholars build upon the works of other researchers by citing and engaging with research from the past, I mention that throughout the history of most academic disciplines, most people, including people of color, women, and those working outside academic centers in the global north, have been excluded from scholarly conversations and that academic publishing is still dominated by white men in many fields. I also note the expense associated with accessing scholarly articles and how inaccessible this type of information is for those outside of well-funded academic and research contexts.

An activity that I find useful for practicing these concepts is to guide students through comparing two information sources on the same topic, one academic and one testimonial (for example a YouTube video or social media post). In comparing these sources I ask students to consider what information can be gleaned from each, who created this information, and why they are sharing it. Rather than comparing different sources on the same topic in order to illuminate qualities that are often framed as deficits in nonscholarly information sources—for example, personal bias, lack of evidence, or being created by someone without an advanced education—I instead hope to examine how different knowledge sources can provide researchers with a variety of pieces of information that may be valuable to the researcher and to validate that scholarly and popular sources are not in competition but rather complement one another. Rather than framing students' existing knowledge and knowledge practices as somehow flawed or in need of remediation, or implying that the purpose of our time together is for me to impart instructions for the "right" way to find information, I seek to integrate and validate existing ways of knowing while offering options to increase students' confidence in accessing and analyzing scholarly sources of information.

Challenges and Conclusion

I'm sure by this point that seasoned instruction librarians have identified the primary challenge to this type of work—that we must often contend with the tension inherent in collaborating with faculty whose disciplinary or personal dispositions toward academic research may differ from our own. Beyond this, there are expectations from both faculty partners and students that specific skills and information will be transmitted during most information literacy instruction sessions. It is not difficult to imagine that a crash course in epistemic injustice is not what many instructors expect from a library one-shot.

In closing, this chapter advocates for librarian instructors to consider what responsibility we bear for the values we espouse as teachers and as information professionals. If readers take away nothing else from this chapter, I hope it is clear that epistemic injustice is part of a vast web of intersecting oppressions that marginalize nonwhite people and other groups across multiple facets of existence. Epistemic injustice can be dismantled, but it requires the most privileged of us (particularly the majority of academic librarians who are white), to commit to opposing the structures of oppression where we can. This may require us to be challenging, uncomfortable, but it can't be ignored.

Notes

1.   Ray Delgado, "The Imperial Scholar: Reflections on a Review of Civil Rights Literature," *University of Pennsylvania Law Review* 132, no. 3 (1984): 561–78, https://doi.org/10.2307/3311882; Aileen Moreton-Robinson, "Whiteness, Epistemology, and Indigenous Representation," In *Whit-*

ening Race: Essays in Social and Cultural Criticism, ed. Aileen Moreton-Robinson (Canberra: Aboriginal Studies Press, 2000), 75–88; Vincent Larivière et al., "Bibliometrics: Global Gender Disparities in Science," *Nature* 504, no. 211 (2013): 211–13, https://doi.org/10.1038/504211a; Lilia D. Monzó and Suzanne SooHoo, "Translating the Academy: Learning the Racialized Languages of Academia," *Journal of Diversity in Higher Education* 7, no. 3 (2014): 147–65, https://doi.org/10.1037/a0037400; Salvador Vidal-Ortiz, "Dismantling Whiteness in Academe," Inside Higher Ed, November 10, 2017, https://www.insidehighered.com/advice/2017/11/10/how-whiteness-structuring-interactions-higher-education-essay; Victor Ray, "The Racial Politics of Citation," Inside Higher Ed, April 27. 2018, https://www.insidehighered.com/advice/2018/04/27/racial-exclusions-scholarly-citations-opinion; National Center for Education Statistics, "Characteristics of Postsecondary Faculty," in *The Condition of Education 2020*, NCES 2020-144, ed. Thomas Nachazel, Megan Barnett, and Stephen Purcell (Washington DC: National Center for Education Statistics, Institute of Education Statistics, US Department of Education, 2020), https://nces.ed.gov/programs/coe/pdf/coe_csc.pdf.

2. Miranda Fricker, *Epistemic Injustice* (Oxford: Oxford University Press, 2007), 1.

3. Fricker, *Epistemic Injustice*, 7.

4. Fricker, *Epistemic Injustice*, 27.

5. Rebecca Puhl and Kelly D. Brownell, "Bias, Discrimination, and Obesity," *Obesity Research* 9, no. 12 (December 2001): 788–805, https://doi.org/10.1038/oby.2001.108: Hilary Offman, "The Otherness of Fat: An Intersectional Enactment of Epic Proportions," *Psychoanalytic Perspectives* 17, no. 3 (2020): 342–65, https://doi.org/10.1080/1551806X.2020.1801050.

6. Alia E. Dastagir, "After Eric Garner, Twitter Unconvinced #Blacklivesmatter," *USA Today*, December 4, 2014, https://www.usatoday.com/story/news/nation/2014/12/03/eric-garner-reactions/19851535/; Jelani Ince, Fabio Rojas, and Clayton A. Davis, "The Social Media Response to Black Lives Matter: How Twitter Users Interact with Black Lives Matter through Hashtag Use," *Ethnic and Racial Studies* 40, no. 11 (2017): 1814–30, https://doi.org/10.1080/01419870.2017.1334931.

7. Amanda Kennedy, "Because We Say So: The Unfortunate Denial of Rights to Transgender Minors Regarding Transitions," *Hastings Women's Law Journal* 19, no. 2 (2008): 281–302, https://repository.uchastings.edu/hwlj/vol19/iss2/5; Rachel M. Schmitz and Kimberly A. Tyler, "The Complexity of Family Reactions to Identity among Homeless and College Lesbian, Gay, Bisexual, Transgender, and Queer Young Adults," *Archives of Sexual Behavior* 47 (2018): 1195–207, https://doi.org/10.1007/s10508-017-1014-5.

8. Fricker, *Epistemic Injustice*, 17–19.

9. Elizabeth Anderson, "Epistemic Justice as a Virtue of Social Institutions," *Social Epistemology* 26, no. 2 (2012): 166, https://doi.org/10.1080/02691728.2011.652211.

10. Fricker, *Epistemic Injustice*, 1.

11. Trystan S. Goetze, "Hermeneutical Dissent and the Species of Hermeneutical Injustice," *Hypatia* 33, no. 1 (2017): 73–90, https://doi.org/10.1111/hypa.12384.

12. Fricker, *Epistemic Injustice*, 7.

13. Myrna Morales E., Em Claire Knowles, and Chris Bourg, "Diversity, Social Justice, and the Future of Libraries," *portal: Libraries and the Academy* 17, no. 3 (July 2017): 445, https://doi.org/10.1353/pla.2014.0017.

14. Association of College and Research Libraries, *Framework for Information Literacy for Higher Education* (Chicago: Association of College and Research Libraries, 2016), https://www.ala.org/acrl/standards/ilframework.

15. Moreton-Robinson, "Whiteness, Epistemology, and Indigenous Representation"; Owen J. Dwyer and John Paul Jones III, "White Socio-spatial Epistemology," *Social and Cultural Geography* 1, no. 2 (2000): 209–22, https://doi.org/10.1080/14649360020010211; Cheryl E. Matias and Peter

M. Newlove, "Better the Devil You See, Than the One You Don't: Bearing Witness to Emboldened En-whitening Epistemology in the Trump Era," *International Journal of Qualitative Studies in Education* 30, no. 10 (2017): 920–28, https://doi.org/10.1080/09518398.2017.1312590: Ryuko Kubota, "Confronting Epistemological Racism, Decolonizing Scholarly Knowledge: Race and Gender in Applied Linguistics," *Applied Linguistics* 41, no. 5 (2019): 712–32, https://doi.org/10.1093/applin/amz033.

16. Shannon Sullivan and Nancy Tuana, "Introduction," in *Race and Epistemologies of Ignorance*, ed. Shannon Sullivan and Nancy Tuana (New York: SUNY Press, 2007), 1–10; Linda Tuhiwai Smith, *Decolonizing Methodologies* (London: Zed Books, 1999), 101–2.

17. Delgado, "Imperial Scholar"; Ray, "Racial Politics of Citation"; Patricia A. Matthew, "Introduction: Written/Unwritten: The Gap between Theory and Practice," in *Written/Unwritten: Diversity and the Hidden Truths of Tenure*, ed. Patricia A. Matthew (Chapel Hill: University of North Carolina Press, 2016), 1–15; Rebecca A. Reid and Todd A. Curry, "The White Man Template and Academic Bias," Inside Higher Ed, April 12, 2019, https://www.insidehighered.com/advice/2019/04/12/how-white-male-template-produces-barriers-minority-scholars-through-out-their.

18. Fricker, *Epistemic Injustice*, 5.

19. Patricia Hill Collins, "Intersectionality and Epistemic Injustice," in *The Routledge Handbook of Epistemic Injustice*, ed. Ian James Kidd, José Medina, and Gaile Pohlhaus, Jr. (London: Routledge, 2017), 115–24.

20. Zita Cristina Nunes, "Cataloging Black Knowledge: How Dorothy Porter Assembled and Organized a Premier Africana Research Collection," *Perspectives on History*, December 2018, https://www.historians.org/publications-and-directories/perspectives-on-history/december-2018/cataloging-black-knowledge-how-dorothy-porter-assembled-and-organized-a-premier-africana-research-collection; Jody Natasha Warner, "Moving beyond Whiteness in North American Academic Libraries," *Libri* 51 (2007): 167–72, https://doi.org/10.1515/LIBR.2001.167; nina de jesus, "Locating the Library in Institutional Oppression," *In the Library with the Lead Pipe*, September 24, 2014, http://www.inthelibrarywiththeleadpipe.org/2014/locating-the-library-in-institutional-oppression/; Michelle Gohr, "Ethnic and Racial Diversity in Libraries: How White Allies Can Support Arguments for Decolonization," *Journal of Radical Librarianship* 3 (2017): 42–58, https://core.ac.uk/download/pdf/290491674.pdf; Sofia Y. Leung and Jorge R. López-McKnight, "Dreaming Revolutionary Futures: Critical Race's Centrality to Ending White Supremacy," *Communications in Information Literacy* 14, no. 1 (2020): 12–26, https://doi.org/10.15760/comminfolit.2020.14.1.2; Jack Anderson, "Information Criticism: Where Is It?" in *Questioning Library Neutrality*, ed. Alison Lewis (Sacramento, CA: Library Juice Press, 2008), 97–108.

21. Grace Lo, "'Aliens' vs. Catalogers: Bias in the Library of Congress Subject Heading," *Legal Reference Services Quarterly* 38, no. 4 (2019): 170–96, https://doi.org/10.1080/027031 9X.2019.1696069; Robert Jensen, "The Myth of the Neutral Professional," in *Questioning Library Neutrality*, ed. Alison Lewis (Sacramento, CA: Library Juice Press, 2008), 89–96; Myrna E. Morales and Stacie Williams, "Moving towards Transformative Librarianship: Naming and Identifying Epistemic Supremacy," in *Knowledge Justice: Disrupting Library and Information Studies through Critical Race Theory*, ed. Sofia Y. Leung and Jorge R. López-McKnight, (Boston: MIT Press, 2021), 73–93.

22. Angela Pashia, "Examining Structural Oppression as a Component of Information Literacy: A Call for Librarians to Support #BlackLivesMatter through our Teaching," *Journal of Information Literacy* 11, no. 2 (2017): 86–104, https://doi.org/10.11645/11.2.2245.

23. Casey Rebecca Johnson, "Teaching as Epistemic Care," in *Overcoming Epistemic Injustice: Social and Psychological Perspectives*, ed. Benjamin R. Sherman and Stacey Goguen (Washington DC: Rowman & Littlefield, 2019), 255–66.

24. Angelique M. Davis and Rose Ernst, "Racial Gaslighting," *Politics, Groups, and Identities* 7, no. 4 (2019): 761–74.
25. Morales and Williams, "Moving towards Transformative Librarianship."
26. Michael Flierl and Clarence Maybee, "Refining Information Literacy Practice: Examining the Foundations of Information Literacy Theory," *IFLA Journal* 46, no. 2 (2020): 124–32, https://doi.org/10.1177/0340035219886615.
27. Satya P. Mohanty, "Epilogue. Colonial Legacies, Multicultural Futures: Relativism, Objectivity, and the Challenge of Otherness," *PMLA* 110, no. 1 (January 1995): 108–18, https://www.jstor.org/stable/463198.

Bibliography

Anderson, Elizabeth. "Epistemic Justice as a Virtue of Social Institutions." *Social Epistemology* 26, no. 2 (2012): 163–73. https://doi.org/10.1080/02691728.2011.652211.

Anderson, Jack. "Information Criticism: Where Is It?" In *Questioning Library Neutrality*, edited by Alison Lewis, 97–108. Sacramento, CA: Library Juice Press, 2008.

Association of College and Research Libraries. *Framework for Information Literacy for Higher Education*. Chicago: Association of College and Research Libraries, 2016. https://www.ala.org/acrl/standards/ilframework.

Dastagir, Alia E. "After Eric Garner, Twitter Unconvinced #Blacklivesmatter." *USA Today*, December 4, 2014. http://www.usatoday.com/story/news/nation/2014/12/03/eric-garner-reactions/19851535/.

Davis, Angelique M., and Rose Ernst. "Racial Gaslighting." *Politics, Groups, and Identities* 7, no. 4 (2019): 761–74. https://doi.org/10.1080/21565503.2017.1403934.

de jesus, nina. "Locating the Library in Institutional Oppression." *In the Library with the Lead Pipe,* September 24, 2014. http://www.inthelibrarywiththeleadpipe.org/2014/locating-the-library-in-institutional-oppression/.

Delgado, Ray. "The Imperial Scholar: Reflections on a Review of Civil Rights Literature." *University of Pennsylvania Law Review* 132, no. 3 (1984): 561–78. https://doi.org/10.2307/3311882.

Dwyer, Owen J., and John Paul Jones III. "White Socio-spatial Epistemology." *Social and Cultural Geography* 1, no. 2 (2000): 209–22. https://doi.org/10.1080/14649360020010211.

Flierl, Michael, and Clarence Maybee. "Refining Information Literacy Practice: Examining the Foundations of Information Literacy Theory." *IFLA Journal* 46, no. 2 (2020): 124–32. https://doi.org/10.1177/0340035219886615.

Fricker, Miranda. *Epistemic Injustice: Power and the Ethics of Knowing.* Oxford: Oxford University Press, 2007.

Goetz, Trystan S. "Hermeneutical Dissent and the Species of Hermeneutical Injustice." *Hypatia* 33, no. 1 (2017): 73–90. https://doi.org/10.1111/hypa.12384.

Gohr, Michelle. "Ethnic and Racial Diversity in Libraries: How White Allies Can Support Arguments for Decolonization." *Journal of Radical Librarianship* 3 (2017): 42–58. https://core.ac.uk/download/pdf/290491674.pdf.

Hill Collins, Patricia. "Intersectionality and Epistemic Injustice." In *The Routledge Handbook of Epistemic Injustice*, edited by Ian James Kidd, José Medina, and Gaile Pohlhaus, Jr., 115–24. London: Routledge, 2017.

Ince, Jelani, Fabio Rojas, and Clayton A. Davis. "The Social Media Response to Black Lives Matter: How Twitter Users Interact with Black Lives Matter through Hashtag Use." *Ethnic and Racial Studies* 40, no. 11 (2017): 1814–30. https://doi.org/10.1080/01419870.2017.1334931.

Jensen, Robert. "Myth of the Neutral Professional?" In *Questioning Library Neutrality*, edited by Alison Lewis, 89–96. Sacramento, CA: Library Juice Press, 2008.

Johnson, Casey Rebecca. "Teaching as Epistemic Care." In *Overcoming Epistemic Injustice: Social and Psychological Perspectives*, edited by Benjamin R. Sherman and Stacey Goguen, 255–66. Washington DC: Rowman & Littlefield, 2019.

Kennedy, Amanda. "Because We Say So: The Unfortunate Denial of Rights to Transgender Minors Regarding Transitions." *Hastings Women's Law Journal* 19, no. 2 (2008): 281–302. https://repository.uchastings.edu/hwlj/vol19/iss2/5.

Kubota, Ryuko. "Confronting Epistemological Racism, Decolonizing Scholarly Knowledge: Race and Gender in Applied Linguistics." *Applied Linguistics* 41, no. 5 (2019): 712–32. https://doi.org/10.1093/applin/amz033.

Larivière, Vincent, Choaquin Ni, Yves Gingras, Blaise Cronin, and Cassidy R. Sugimoto. "Bibliometrics: Global Gender Disparities in Science." *Nature* 504 (2013): 211–13. https://doi.org/10.1038/504211a.

Leung, Sofia Y., and Jorge R. López-McKnight. "Dreaming Revolutionary Futures: Critical Race's Centrality to Ending White Supremacy." *Communications in Information Literacy* 14, no. 1 (2020): 12–26. https://doi.org/ 10.15760/comminfolit.2020.14.1.2.

Lo, Grace. "'Aliens' vs. Catalogers: Bias in the Library of Congress Subject Heading." *Legal Reference Services Quarterly* 38, no. 4 (2019): 170–96. https://doi.org/10.1080/0270319X.2019.1696069.

Matias, Cheryl E., and Peter M. Newlove. "Better the Devil You See, Than the One You Don't: Bearing Witness to Emboldened En-whitening Epistemology in the Trump Era." *International Journal of Qualitative Studies in Education* 30, no. 10 (2017): 920–28. https://doi.org/10.1080/09518398.2017.1312590.

Matthew, Patricia A. "Introduction: Written/Unwritten: The Gap between Theory and Practice." In *Written/Unwritten: Diversity and the Hidden Truths of Tenure*, edited by Patricia A. Matthew, 1–26. Chapel Hill: University of North Carolina Press, 2016.

Mohanty, Satya P. "Epilogue. Colonial Legacies, Multicultural Futures: Relativism, Objectivity, and the Challenge of Otherness." *PMLA* 110, no. 1 (January 1995): 108–18. https://www.jstor.org/stable/463198.

Monzó, Lilia D., and Suzanne SooHoo. "Translating the Academy: Learning the Racialized Languages of Academia." *Journal of Diversity in Higher Education* 7, no. 3 (2014): 147–65. https://doi.org/10.1037/a0037400.

Morales, Myrna E., Em Claire Knowles, and Chris Bourg. "Diversity, Social Justice, and the Future of Libraries." *portal: Libraries and the Academy* 17, no. 3 (July 2014): 439–51. https://doi.org/10.1353/pla.2014.0017.

Morales, Myrna E., and Stacie Williams. "Moving towards Transformative Librarianship: Naming and Identifying Epistemic Supremacy." In *Knowledge Justice: Disrupting Library and Information Studies through Critical Race Theory*, edited by Sofia Y. Leung and Jorge R. López-McKnight, 73–93. Boston: MIT Press, 2021.

Moreton-Robinson, Aileen. "Whiteness, Epistemology, and Indigenous Representation." In *Whitening Race: Essays in Social and Cultural Criticism*, edited by Aileen Moreton-Robinson, 75–88. Canberra: Aboriginal Studies Press, 2000.

National Center for Education Statistics. "Characteristics of Postsecondary Faculty." In *The Condition of Education 2020*, NCES 2020-144, edited by Thomas Nachazel, Megan Barnett, and Stephen Purcell, 150–53. Washington DC: National Center for Education Statistics, Institute of Education Statistics, US Department of Education, 2020. https://nces.ed.gov/programs/coe/pdf/coe_csc.pdf.

Nunes, Zita Cristina. "Cataloging Black Knowledge: How Dorothy Porter Assembled and Organized a Premier Africana Research Collection." *Perspectives on History*, December 2018. https://www.historians.org/publications-and-directories/perspectives-on-history/december-2018/cataloging-black-knowledge-how-dorothy-porter-assembled-and-organized-a-premier-africana-research-collection.

Offman, Hilary. "The Otherness of Fat: An Intersectional Enactment of Epic Proportions." *Psychoanalytic Perspectives* 17, no. 3 (2020): 342–65. https://doi.org/10.1080/1551806X.2020.1801050.

Pashia, Angela. "Examining Structural Oppression as a Component of Information Literacy: A Call for Librarians to Support #BlackLivesMatter through Our Teaching." *Journal of Information Literacy* 11, no. 2 (2017): 86–104. https://doi.org/10.11645/11.2.2245.

Puhl, Rebecca, and Kelly D. Brownell. "Bias, Discrimination, and Obesity." *Obesity Research* 9, no. 12 (December 2001): 788–805. https://doi.org/10.1038/oby.2001.108.

Ray, Victor. "The Racial Politics of Citation." Inside Higher Ed, April 27, 2018. https://www.insidehighered.com/advice/2018/04/27/racial-exclusions-scholarly-citations-opinion.

Reid, Rebecca A., and Todd A. Curry. "The White Man Template and Academic Bias." Inside Higher Ed, April 12, 2019. https://www.insidehighered.com/advice/2019/04/12/how-white-male-template-produces-barriers-minority-scholars-throughout-their.

Schmitz, Rachel M., and Kimberly A. Tyler. "The Complexity of Family Reactions to Identity among Homeless and College Lesbian, Gay, Bisexual, Transgender, and Queer Young Adults." *Archives of Sexual Behavior* 47 (2018): 1195–207. https://doi.org/10.1007/s10508-017-1014-5.

Smith, Lina Tuhiwai. *Decolonizing Methodologies: Research and Indigenous People.* London: Zed Books, 1999.

Sullivan, Shannon, and Nancy Tuana. "Introduction." In *Race and Epistemologies of Ignorance*, edited by Shannon Sullivan and Nancy Tuana, 1–10. New York: SUNY Press, 2007.

Vidal-Ortiz, Salvador. "Dismantling Whiteness in Academe." Inside Higher Ed, November 10, 2017. https://www.insidehighered.com/advice/2017/11/10/how-whiteness-structuring-interactions-higher-education-essay.

Warner, Jody Natasha. "Moving beyond Whiteness in North American Academic Libraries." *Libri* 51 (2007): 167–72. https://doi.org/10.1515/LIBR.2001.167.

CHAPTER 7

Algorithmic Literacy as Inclusive Pedagogy

Melanie Sellar

Acknowledging the Algorithmic Elephant in Library Instruction

Early in my career as an instruction librarian, I sensed something was missing in my workshops. It seemed I was doing everything right. I followed best practices for designing and delivering engaging sessions and made sure to tightly align my instruction with course assignments. Then I came to a realization: we were prioritizing subscription library databases and neglecting student use of Google. If we did talk about Google (and similar tools), we quickly dismissed it as inferior, characterized the information as unreliable, and positioned library databases as the best and only way to succeed on course assignments.

At my next institution, where I helped to directly shape the library's information literacy curriculum, we opened up discussions around Google in first-year composition courses and created a research narrative assignment to elicit student thinking. By centering student voice, we became more certain of the need to include search engines in first-year instruction. When we listened to what students wrote in their narratives, it was evident that they felt their experiences were marginalized, even looked down upon, as articulated by one student:

> I eventually gave up on my search for scholarly articles. Using good ol'
> Google, I typed in the exact phrase I used when searching in the databases.
> And if those librarians say otherwise about my proficiency in research and
> quote citing, I have other papers that I would be happy to show to prove
> them wrong.

This reluctance to engage with nonacademic sources was reflective of the time. Project Information Literacy surfaced the culture of research assignments in a 2010 study, finding that faculty were most likely to point students to traditional library sources in their assignment directions.[1] Search engines, websites, Wikipedia, and blogs were the least likely to be mentioned as possible, permissible sources.[2] Within this culture it seemed difficult for librarians to find room in workshops to advocate for and lead discussions around how to use nontraditional sources. Nevertheless, many librarians began to initiate those discussions and see some traction. For example, Nelson and Jacobs describe their faculty-librarian partnership leading a semester-long Wikipedia project in an undergraduate history course.[3]

As the decade wore on, our students and faculty came to use and rely upon an ever-increasing set of information tools, including YouTube, Twitter, Facebook, Instagram, and Snapchat. Each platform wrestles enormous sets of data into ordered results lists. When Netflix launched a one million dollar prize for the first entrant who could improve its recommendation algorithm's predictions by 10 percent, it was an acknowledgement that tailoring results to be more precise and appealing keeps users happy and subscribing.[4] People generally like algorithms, value the shortcuts they offer, and place a high degree of trust in the algorithmically driven tools used in their daily lives. In its 2020 study, Project Information Literacy mused that "the lack of trust in traditional authority figures meant trust was placed in Google as the arbiter of truth, sometimes to a ridiculous extent."[5] Algorithms hook us and keep us using.

The increase in these platforms also ushered in growing concern about the invisible influence they wield over how we interpret the world and create new knowledge. At the 2021 ACRL conference, librarian Ian O'Hara observed that "search results have the power to structure knowledge and create an alternative material reality. Google search is an inflection point for an epistemic crisis."[6] These algorithms operate entirely behind closed, proprietary walls; they are not easily open to critique; and they change constantly. A Google employee and former search engineer shared that key intellectual property like search engine algorithms is not open to all employees; instead, Google has an internal hierarchy of access levels that involve nondisclosure agreements and other clearances.[7] What we know of how these algorithms operate is entirely based upon what limited information the companies share and what we can observe about the algorithms through use.

We are now seeing academics spanning the fields of philosophy, ethics, education, and social sciences begin to study the societal impacts of algorithms, and a new field of critical algorithm studies being forged.[8] We are asking questions about what the public and our students know and do not know about how algorithms operate.[9] In librarianship we too are awakening to the role we can play in facilitating student awareness and critical discussion of algorithms. We may give particular credit to Safiya Noble's keynote "Searching for Girls: Identity for Sale in the Age of Google" at the 2015 American Library Association conference and her 2018 book *Algorithms of Oppression* for igniting our professional interest and demonstrating how algorithmic profiling can cause social harm.[10] The *Framework for Information Literacy for Higher Education* released in 2016 also gives us space to take on these overarching information literacy issues.[11] Many of our colleagues have started doing important work in piloting lessons and curricula, some of which is highlighted in this chapter. Teaching algorithmic literacy, I argue next, is an inclusive teaching practice that we should adopt as a profession.

Connecting Inclusive Pedagogy with Algorithmic Literacy

The inclusive education movement has its roots in K–12 special education over twenty years ago. Parents and teachers began to reject the segregation of children with disabilities from the mainstream classroom; instead, they called for inclusive spaces that could support all differently abled students.[12] This idea broadened its focus over time to advocate for the full inclusion of students from all cultural, ethnic, linguistic, racial, and academic backgrounds. Teachers were encouraged to embrace and build upon the prior knowledge and experiences of their students, not to disregard or diminish their lived experiences and identities. Fundamentally the goal was to value the unique experiences of each student and avoid their marginalization within the classroom.

This call for inclusive education has now captured the wide interest of academics, including information literacy practitioners. There is no authoritative guidebook on how to enact inclusivity; rather, we are building that guidebook through our teaching itself and then sharing our practices in publications such as this one, following the established approach of the K–12 field.[13]

As our profession begins to develop a repertoire of inclusive teaching approaches, I propose that we include support of algorithmic literacy as one focus for how we enact and embrace inclusive education. Algorithmic literacy, a relatively new concept, refers to an understanding of what algorithms are, how they are used, and how they can positively and negatively impact individuals and groups. Koenig goes so far as to suggest that "the next phase in technological literacy is to incorporate the role of algorithms."[14] Faculty across academia believe that algorithmic literacy should be intentionally cultivated in college, but rarely discuss it, preferring instead that "someone else took the lead."[15]

As information literacy practitioners, we could take this lead. By facilitating student awareness and critical discussion of algorithms, we can enact these inclusive teaching goals in our teaching contexts:

- highlight and center the experiences and voices of all students and communities;
- value the authentic, daily, and lifelong research needs of our students; and
- inculcate dispositions and skills for seeking and finding the voices of diverse communities.

Our students enter our classrooms as complex humans with varied backgrounds, opinions, and ideas. They also bring positive and negative research experiences using varied tools outside of the library. When we ignore these academic and everyday research experiences they bring into college and lament their reliance on search tools like Google, we invalidate their experiences, elevate one privileged academic notion of research, and miss an opportunity to connect with them. Even worse, we allow the biases (racial, gender, political, geographical, to name a few) in algorithms to go uncritiqued and undetected, inadvertently sending the message that these tools are neutral and do not merit examination.

Getting Started with Algorithmic Literacy as Inclusive Pedagogy

To bring this proposal into greater clarity, it's helpful to look at what shape this work could take in a few contexts. I have sketched three lesson areas that could be incorporated into a lower division course, as one or two embedded sessions. Within each area I have highlighted some inclusive practices, informed partly by the Association of College and University Educators' "Inclusive Teaching for Equitable Learning" curriculum crosswalk."[16] The areas also suggest a range of activities that librarians could adapt in their own instruction. Where they are inspired by materials in the resources section, I have indicated so.

Deconstructing Google Searches

Inclusion rationale: Search engines like Google are central to how students search for information.

While many students have some basic understanding of how those search algorithms function, that is not uniformly true and, more importantly, it is usually unaccompanied by a critical perspective.[17] Given that students (and the public at large) normally consult just the first page of search results, they yield a lot of decision-making power to Google without being given the space and skills needed to ask about the impact of Google's decisions on topic narratives.

Learning goals: Students typically begin (and often end) their research using Google. This lesson area acknowledges this student preference and supports them in becoming more critical users of it. Goals include being able to articulate some understanding of how Google's ranking algorithm works, to identify some limitations of relying on top ranked results, and to identify more sophisticated strategies for or alternatives to searching Google.

Inclusion-oriented activities: The workshop content itself is inclusive because of its focus on students' authentic experiences, on lifelong research skills, and on developing alternative ways of searching to bring in more diverse perspectives. I often kick off this kind of session with an assessment as a way to foreground student voice and experience; it could take the form of asking students to reflect on a question like "How does Google work?" using an anonymous tool such as Jamboard. Videos or textual materials on Google's ranking algorithm could be explored in class or offered beforehand via a module in the learning management system. Students can work in pairs or small groups to discuss and refine their understanding, using a provided worksheet around a common search to guide their exploration. For example, they can be prompted to note the nature of the top publishers, proportion and placement of ads, observed top level domains, and geographic locations of results. Most importantly, students should be asked to reflect on why they think the top results are structured in this way, what the potential implications are not just for their own information seeking but also for their community or society at large, and what they might be missing. This not only gives them space to comment descriptively on what they are seeing, but also supports them in developing more critical perspectives. It also gives instructors an important window into student thinking, allowing us to adjust our instruction and identify new areas of potential support.

Extensions: There are many variations and extensions to this lesson area. Students could pick a different search platform (of their choice or a common one) to learn about and deconstruct, such as YouTube or Twitter, and then comment on the implications of their findings for their own search practices. There are also a number of materials in this chapter's list of resources that provide excellent extension activities, including Berg's "Googling Google: Search Engines as Market Actors," Masunaga's "Evaluating Online Sources with Lateral Reading" and "Exploring Google Scholar with a Summer Bridge Program." and Caffrey Gardner's "Analyzing Search Engines: What Narrative Is Told through the Algorithm."[18] An interesting lesson centered on the representation of authority in Instagram is offered by Andrews, Pho and Roh.[19]

Surfacing Bias in Search Results

Inclusion rationale: The issue of greatest concern and study in the last five years related to algorithms is that of bias. Scholars and advocates have been exposing and critiquing the range of harmful ways that algorithms reinforce bias and systems of privilege relating to race, gender, class, and ethnicity.[20] When bias in information tools is left unacknowledged, librarians risk exacerbating this problem and inadvertently creating learning environments open to misrepresentation of diverse groups.

Learning goals: Lessons in this area seek to surface biases in search tools and expose them to critique. Students will explore how information production is not neutral but rather can reinforce stereotypes and traditional power structures. They should connect that knowledge not only to their college research assignments, but also, more importantly, to their larger communities and society.

Inclusion-oriented activities: The workshop content itself is inclusive because of its focus on students' authentic and everyday search experiences, with an emphasis on surfacing and critically analyzing the biases encountered in those tools. Moving the discussion into how to seek and elevate alternative perspectives and narratives helps center the voices of diverse communities and helps inculcate lifelong dispositions needed to seek out and advocate not only for those perspectives but also for better tools. I have adopted Davis's lesson "Bias in Your Search Results" into a first-year composition course with great student engagement.[21] Students work in small groups to read articles about bias in a tool, source type, or system and answer questions to share with the larger class. If students were surveyed beforehand about the preferred tools they use, the articles could also be customized to align with those preferences. To help create a safe space for dialogue around biases, establishing some discussion guidelines beforehand will be important.

Extensions: This lesson area can be varied and extended in many ways. Caffrey Gardner's "Analyzing Search Engines" workshop provides a good activity centered on bias in Google images.[22] The University of California, Merced, similarly has Google images and Google auto-complete exercises in its LibGuide "Algorithm Bias and Gaming."[23] Schubert, Wiley, and Young have an adaptable and interactive LibWizard tutorial.[24] The University of Louisville's lesson on algorithms at play in academic disciplines is a useful activity for introducing and identifying issues of bias in those realms.[25]

Navigating Algorithms in News Platforms

Inclusion rationale: Digital platforms are widely used as sources for news information, as documented by a 2021 Pew Research report.[26] When I asked first-year composition students where they got their news from, the majority indeed told me

YouTube, Twitter, Instagram, Apple News, Snapchat, and TikTok. One student noted, "I get literally all my news from Twitter."[27] While librarians have done good work in recent years supporting the critical evaluation of news sources, we have yet to widely extend our pedagogy to embrace examining how algorithms serve up those news sources into the platforms we use.

Learning goals: We know that students already get news from an array of different sources. This lesson area builds upon that foundation, guiding them to reflect upon the platforms they are using, highlighting the role of algorithms in those platforms, and then identifying strategies for adding more diverse news outlets to their following.

Inclusion-oriented activities: The workshop content itself is inclusive because of its focus on students' authentic experiences and on incorporating additional news search strategies to bring in more diverse voices. As a diagnostic assessment, I foreground student voice by asking them to share where they get their news from using an anonymous tool like Jamboard. Another helpful activity to kick off the lesson would be to ask students what they know about news platforms and what they'd like to learn. Using the learning management system, I typically ask students to watch videos on social media news platforms and engage with simulations like TheirTube or "Can You Spot the Deceptive Facebook Post?"[28] Students can be grouped in think-share or small discussion forum groups to share thoughts as they explore the materials.

Extensions: With more faculty collaboration, you could ask students to track a news issue on social media over time, and then write an essay discussing how platforms differed in their portrayal and coverage of it. Students could also be introduced to AllSides and Pew's "Political Typology Quiz" as a way to explore different political ideologies in news sources and implications for how that shapes their perceptions of stories.[29]

Scaling Algorithmic Literacy Up and Down

When we can't secure the space for an entire session devoted to algorithmic literacy, we could choose one learning outcome, one small activity, or one formative assessment. As Carolyn Caffrey Gardner shared, "We always joke in my library that no one's really ever asked for a one-shot session on algorithmic bias, ...so it's really about finding that space whether it's one-on-one or in those one-shots where you are given more freedom."[30] If aiming for an entire lesson feels challenging, try to find spaces in an existing lesson where you might draw student attention to algorithms. For example, Caffrey Gardner often adds a question like "How do you think this search algorithm is ordering results?" in a database session.[31] That can begin to open up bigger conversations with faculty. In line with Caffrey Gardener's approach, Lloyd suggests that we should regularly incorporate and demonstrate a mindset of questioning results and automated decisions into our regular instruction.[32] For those wanting to imagine what algorithmic literacy might look like at a multicourse or programmatic level, consult Koenig and Caffrey Gardner for learning outcome approaches.[33]

It's clear that algorithmically driven platforms underpin everything our students do in their lives. They are ubiquitous, and their influence is growing. By adopting algorithmic literacy as an inclusive pedagogy, we can assert that we will honor, be attentive to, and discuss the information tools that they use every day in their lives, not just the scholarly ones used for an assignment immediately before them. As Heidi Jacobs wrote in her call to include broader and more critical approaches to information literacy: "When we limit the kinds of questions we ask our students and ask ourselves about information…, we limit the ways in which we can be informed, critical, and engaged."[34] Let's acknowledge and address the algorithms at play in our students' lives and, by doing so, push our information literacy work to be far more critical and inclusive.

An Annotated List of Resources

Community of Online Research Assignments (CORA)–Hosted

CORA is an open educational resource for librarians, faculty, and other educators hosted by Loyola Marymount University. Search it for lesson plans on algorithms, algorithmic bias, and so on. Some are profiled below.

- "Analyzing Search Engines: What Narrative Is Told through the Algorithm," Caffrey Gardner.
  Learning outcomes: Students will identify advertisements within a list of search results, discuss the role advertising plays in how search results are ordered, and describe how search results are impacted by human biases in their ranking algorithms.
- "Bias in Your Search Results," Davis
  Learning outcome: Students will be able to recognize that search tools and systems reflect power structures of race, gender, sexuality, class, and so on.
- "Evaluating Online Sources with Lateral Reading," Masunaga
  Learning outcomes: Students will use lateral reading to identify potential biases or controversies associated with an organization publishing online

sources using resources found on Google. They will consider if they would recommend the sources they evaluate to the community at large.

- "Exploring Algorithmic Bias with a Summer Bridge Program," Acosta
  Learning outcomes: Students will discuss the effects of algorithm bias in order to articulate how some individuals or groups of individuals may be misrepresented or systematically marginalized in search engine results. They will also develop an attitude of informed skepticism in order to critically evaluate Google search results.
- "Exploring Google Scholar with a Summer Bridge Program," Masunaga
  Learning outcomes: Students will be able to search Google Scholar in order to find scholarly and discipline-specific sources for their information needs. Students will understand Google Scholar's limitations and biases in order to critically evaluate their search results.
- "Googling Google: Search Engines as Market Actors" Berg
  Learning outcomes: Students will articulate clearly how algorithms such as PageRank influence information-seeking behavior and search results; explain Google's data security and privacy issues; and create searches that show critical thinking and awareness of how Google works.
- "What's behind a Web Search? Bias and Algorithms," Schubert, Wiley, and Young
  Learning outcomes: Students will define a broader context for algorithms, analyze Google results for algorithmic bias, and identify actions for countering algorithmic bias. The lesson includes an excellent LibWizard tutorial.

LibGuides or Google Docs–Hosted

- "Algorithm Bias and Gaming," University of California, Merced, https://libguides.ucmerced.edu/algorithmic-bias
  Learning outcomes: Define algorithmic bias. Recognize how algorithms may perpetuate bias or misrepresent certain people or groups. Understand how algorithms may be altered or gamed for certain purposes. Brainstorm strategies to minimize algorithm bias.
- "Algorithmic Literacy," University of Louisville, https://library.louisville.edu/citizen-literacy/algorithmic
  Learning outcomes: Explore the impact of unseen algorithms on the online content we see and the ramifications on privacy, discrimination, and political polarization.
- "Media Literacy," University of North Carolina at Charlotte, https://guides.library.uncc.edu/c.php?g=995102&p=7709547

This LibGuide provides links to various resources and digital learning objects which library instructors could use in teaching algorithmic literacy.

- "Example Muscat Scholars 2020: Critical Information Literacy Activity," University of San Francisco, https://docs.google.com/document/d/1D0_QT9BWbkI7LSjEzoeIUYhMcfe9Hiwtg7DrALqXZzM/edit

  This Google Doc describes a summer workshop for first-generation students. The focus is on critically exploring Instagram influencers for authority and authenticity.

Open Textbooks

- *Introduction to College Research,* Butler, Sargent, and Smith, https://introto-collegeresearch.pressbooks.com/part/the-age-of-algorithms/

  The chapter "Age of Algorithms" explores algorithms and their pervasiveness, identifies key concerns around algorithmic bias, and discusses the psychology and sociological effects of algorithms.
- *Humans R Social Media,* Daly, https://opentextbooks.library.arizona.edu/hrsm/

  Of particular relevance is chapter 4: "Algorithms: Invisible, Irreversible, and Infinite."
- *Digital Survival Skills: My Media Environment,* Krouse and Lee, https://www.oercommons.org/courseware/lesson/63817

  There are activities that could be adapted to lower division undergraduate students.

Journals to Follow

- *Big Data and Society*
- *Journal of Media Literacy Education*

Search Terms to Get Started Reading and Learning

- Algorithmic justice
- Algorithmic literacy
- Recommendation engines
- Collaborative filtering

- Critical algorithm studies
- Critical data studies

Other Sources

- *Masked by Trust: Bias in Library Discovery* (Reidsma)
- *The Age of Surveillance Capitalism* (Zuboff)

Notes

1. Alison Head and Michael Eisenberg, "Assigning Inquiry: How Handouts for Research Assign-ments Guide Today's College Students," progress report, Project Information Literacy Research Institute, July 12, 2010, https://projectinfolit.org/pubs/research-handouts-study/pil_re-search-handouts_2010-07-13.pdf.
2. Head and Eisenberg, "Assigning Inquiry."
3. Robert L. Nelson and Heidi L. M. Jacobs, "History, Play, and the Public: Wikipedia in the University Classroom," *History Teacher* 50, no.4 (August 2017): 483–500, https://www.jstor.org/stable/44507270.
4. Blake Hallinan and Ted Striphas, "Recommended for You: The Netflix Prize and the Produc-tion of Algorithmic Culture," *New Media and Society* 18, no. 1 (2016): 117–37, https://doi.org/10.1177/1461444814538646.
5. Alison Head, Barbara Fister, and Margy MacMillan, *Information Literacy in the Age of Algo-rithms* (Santa Rosa, CA: Project Information Literacy Research Institute, January 15, 2020), 22, https://projectinfolit.org/pubs/algorithm-study/pil_algorithm-study_2020-01-15.pdf.
6. Ian O'Hara, "If… Then… Else: Algorithmic Systems and Epistemic Crises," in *Ascending into an Open Future: Proceedings of the ACRL 2021 Virtual Conference, April 13–16, 2021,* ed. Dawn M. Mueller (Chicago: Association of College and Research Libraries, 2021), 102, https://www.ala.org/acrl/sites/ala.org.acrl/files/content/conferences/confsandpreconfs/2021/IfThenElse.pdf; J. Michael Peterson, "Inclusive Schooling," in *Family and Society,* ed. Michael Shally-Jenson, vol. 3 of *Encyclopedia of Contemporary American Social Issues* (Santa Barbara, CA: ABC-CLIO, 2011), 1040–48, Gale.
7. E-mail communication with anonymous Google engineer, June 2021.
8. Tarleton Gillespie and Nick Seaver, "Critical Algorithm Studies: A Reading List," Social Media Collective, last updated December 15, 2016, https://socialmediacollective.org/reading-lists/criti-cal-algorithm-studies/.
9. Chris D. Ham, "Why Is This First? Understanding and Analyzing Internet Search Results," *Journal of Educational Research and Practice* 9, no. 1 (2019): 400–12, https://doi.org/10.5590/JERAP.2019.09.1.28; Abby Koenig, "The Algorithms Know Me and I Know Them: Using Student Journals to Uncover Algorithmic Literacy Awareness," *Computers and Composition* 58 (December 2020): 102611, https://doi.org/10.1016/j.compcom.2020.102611.
10. Safiya Umoja Noble, *Algorithms of Oppression* (New York: New York University Press, 2018).
11. Association of College and Research Libraries, *Framework for Information Literacy for Higher Education* (Chicago: Association of College and Research Libraries, 2016), https://www.ala.org/acrl/standards/ilframework.
12. Peterson, "Inclusive Schooling."

13. For example: Lani Florian and Kristine Black-Hawkins, "Exploring Inclusive Pedagogy," *British Educational Research Journal* 37, no. 5 (2011): 813–28, https://doi.org/10.1080/01411926.2010.501096; Jennifer Spratt and Lani Florian, "Inclusive Pedagogy: From Learning to Action; Supporting Each Individual in the Context of 'Everybody,'" *Teaching and Teacher Education* 49 (July 2015): 89–96, https://doi.org/10.1016/j.tate.2015.03.006.

14. Koenig, "Algorithms Know Me."

15. Head, Fister, and MacMillan, *Information Literacy*, 23.

16. Association of College and University Educators, "Inclusive Teaching for Equitable Learning," curriculum crosswalk, 2020, https://acue.org/?acue_courses=inclusive-teaching-for-equitable-learning.

17. Koenig, "Algorithms Know Me"; Head, Fister, and MacMillan, *Information Literacy*.

18. Jacob Berg, "Googling Google: Search Engines as Market Actors," CORA (Community of Online Research Assignments), November 4, 2016, https://www.projectcora.org/assignment/googling-google-search-engines-market-actors; Jennifer Masunaga, "Evaluating Online Sources with Lateral Reading," CORA (Community of Online Research Assignments), February 15, 2021, https://www.projectcora.org/assignment/evaluating-online-sources-lateral-reading; Jennifer Masunaga, "Exploring Google Scholar with a Summer Bridge Program," CORA (Community of Online Research Assignments), November 7, 2018, https://www.projectcora.org/assignment/exploring-google-scholar-summer-bridge-program; Carolyn Caffrey Gardner, "Analyzing Search Engines: What Narrative Is Told through the Algorithm," CORA (Community of Online Research Assignments), December 10, 2018, https://www.projectcora.org/assignment/analyzing-search-engines-what-narrative-told-through-algorithm.

19. Nicola Andrews, Annie Pho, and Charlotte Roh, "Muscat Scholars 2020: Critical Information Literacy Activity," Google Docs, accessed September 2021, https://docs.google.com/document/d/1D0_QT9BWbkI7LSjEzoeIUYhMcfe9Hiwtg7DrALqXZzM/edit.

20. Caffrey Gardner, "Analyzing Search Engines."

21. Lindsay Davis, "Bias in Your Search Results," CORA (Community of Online Research Assignments), July 12, 2019, https://www.projectcora.org/assignment/bias-your-search-results.

22. Caffrey Gardner, "Analyzing Search Engines."

23. University of California, Merced, Library, "Algorithm Bias and Gaming," LibGuide, last updated October 29, 2020, https://libguides.ucmerced.edu/algorithmic-bias.

24. Carolyn Schubert, Malia Wiley, and Alyssa Young, "What's Behind a Web Search? Bias and Algorithms," CORA (Community of Online Research Assignments), May 6, 2021, https://www.projectcora.org/assignment/what%E2%80%99s-behind-web-search-bias-and-algorithms.

25. University of Louisville Libraries, "Algorithmic Literacy," last updated October 7, 2020, https://library.louisville.edu/citizen-literacy/algorithmic.

26. Mason Walker and Katerina Eva Matsa, "News Consumption across Social Media in 2021," Pew Research Center, September 20, 2021, https://www.pewresearch.org/journalism/2021/09/20/news-consumption-across-social-media-in-2021/.

27. Jamboard post in author's workshop, Spring 2021.

28. Tomo Kihara, TheirTube home page, accessed September 2021, https://www.their.tube/; Keith Collins and Sheera Frenkel, "Can You Spot the Deceptive Facebook Post?" *New York Times*, September 4, 2018, https://www.nytimes.com/interactive/2018/09/04/technology/facebook-influence-campaigns-quiz.html.

29. AllSides home page, accessed September 2021, https://www.allsides.com/; Pew Research Center, "Political Typology Quiz," October 14, 2017, https://www.pewresearch.org/politics/quiz/political-typology/.

30. Carolyn Caffrey Gardner, "Teaching about Algorithms," interview by Amanda Piekart and Jessica Kiebler, *The Librarian's Guide to Teaching*, podcast audio, February 9, 2021, https://librariansguidetoteaching.weebly.com/episodes/episode-33-teaching-about-algorithms.

31. Caffrey Gardner, "Teaching about Algorithms."
32. Annemaree Lloyd, "Chasing Frankenstein's Monster: Information Literacy in the Black Box Society," *Journal of Documentation* 75, no. 6 (2019): 1475–85, https://doi.org/10.1108/JD-02-2019-0035.
33. Koenig, "Algorithms Know Me"; Carolyn Caffrey Gardner, "Teaching Algorithmic Bias in a Credit-Bearing Course," *International Information and Library Review* 5, no. 4 (2019): 321–27, https://doi.org/10.1080/10572317.2019.1669937.
34. Heidi L.M. Jacobs, "Pedagogies of Possibility within the Disciplines," *Communications in Information Literacy* 8, no. 2 (2014): 192–207, https://doi.org/10.15760/comminfolit.2014.8.2.166.

Bibliography

Acosta, Elisa. "Exploring Algorithmic Bias with a Summer Bridge Program." CORA (Community of Online Research Assignments), October 28, 2018. https://www.projectcora.org/assignment/exploring-algorithmic-bias-summer-bridge-program.

AllSides home page. Accessed September 2021. https://www.allsides.com/.

Andrews, Nicola, Annie Pho, and Charlotte Roh. "Muscat Scholars 2020: Critical Information Literacy Activity." Google Docs. Accessed September 2021. https://docs.google.com/document/d/1D0_QT9BWbkI7LSjEzoeIUYhMcfe9Hiwtg7DrALqXZzM/edit.

Association of College and Research Libraries. *Framework for Information Literacy for Higher Education*. Chicago: Association of College and Research Libraries, 2016. https://www.ala.org/acrl/standards/ilframework.

Association of College and University Educators. "Inclusive Teaching for Equitable Learning." Curriculum crosswalk, 2020. https://acue.org/?acue_courses=inclusive-teaching-for-equitable-learning.

Berg, Jacob. "Googling Google: Search Engines as Market Actors." CORA (Community of Online Research Assignments), November 4, 2016. https://www.projectcora.org/assignment/googling-google-search-engines-market-actors.

Butler, Walter D., Aloha Sargent, and Kelsey Smith. *Introduction to College Research*, edited by Cynthia M. Cohen. Press Books, 2021. https://introtocollegeresearch.pressbooks.com/.

Caffrey Gardner, Carolyn. "Analyzing Search Engines: What Narrative Is Told through the Algorithm." CORA (Community of Online Research Assignments), December 10, 2018. https://www.projectcora.org/assignment/analyzing-search-engines-what-narrative-told-through-algorithm.

———. "Teaching about Algorithms." Interview by Amanda Piekart and Jessica Kiebler. *The Librarian's Guide to Teaching*. Podcast audio, February 9, 2021. https://librariansguidetoteaching.weebly.com/episodes/episode-33-teaching-about-algorithms.

———. "Teaching Algorithmic Bias in a Credit-Bearing Course." *International Information and Library Review* 5, no. 4 (2019): 321–27. https://doi.org/10.1080/10572317.2019.1669937.

Daly, Diana, ed. *Humans R Social Media*, 3rd ed. Tucson: University of Arizona Center for University Education Scholarship, 2021. https://opentextbooks.library.arizona.edu/hrsm/.

Davis, Lindsay. "Bias in Your Search Results." CORA (Community of Online Research Assignments), July 12, 2019. https://www.projectcora.org/assignment/bias-your-search-results.

Detmering, Robert, Amber Willenborg, and Terri Holtze. University of Louisville Libraries. "Algorithmic Literacy." Last updated October 7, 2020. https://library.louisville.edu/citizen-literacy/algorithmic.

Florian, Lani, and Kristine Black-Hawkins. "Exploring Inclusive Pedagogy." *British Educational Research Journal* 37, no. 5 (2011): 813–28. https://doi.org/10.1080/01411926.2010.501096.

Gillespie, Tarleton, and Nick Seaver. "Critical Algorithm Studies: A Reading List." Social Media Collective. Last updated December 15, 2016. https://socialmediacollective.org/reading-lists/critical-algorithm-studies/.

Hallinan, Blake and Ted Striphas. "Recommended for You: The Netflix Prize and the Production of Algorithmic Culture." *New Media and Society* 18, no. 1 (2016): 117–37. https://doi. org/10.1177/1461444814538646.

Ham, Chris D. "Why Is This First? Understanding and Analyzing Internet Search Results." *Journal of Educational Research and Practice* 9, no. 1 (2019): 400–12. https://doi.org/10.5590/ JERAP.2019.09.1.28.

Head, Alison, and Michael Eisenberg. "Assigning Inquiry: How Handouts for Research Assignments Guide Today's College Students." Progress report. Project Information Literacy Research Institute, July 12, 2010. https://projectinfolit.org/pubs/research-handouts-study/pil_research-handouts_2010-07-13.pdf.

Head, Alison, Barbara Fister, and Margy MacMillan. *Information Literacy in the Age of Algorithms: Student Experiences with New and Information, and the Need for Change.* Santa Rosa, CA: Project Information Literacy Research Institute, January 15, 2020. https://projectinfolit.org/pubs/algorithm-study/pil_algorithm-study_2020-01-15.pdf.

J. Murrey Atkins Library. "Media Literacy." Research guide. University of North Carolina at Charlotte. Last updated October 27, 2021. https://guides.library.uncc.edu/c.php?g=995102&p=7709547.

Jacobs, Heidi L. M. "Pedagogies of Possibility within the Disciplines." *Communications in Information Literacy* 8, no. 2 (2014): 192–207. https://doi.org/10.15760/comminfolit.2014.8.2.166.

Kihara, Tomo. TheirTube home page. Accessed September 2021. https://www.their.tube.

Koenig, Abby. "The Algorithms Know Me and I Know Them: Using Student Journals to Uncover Algorithmic Literacy Awareness." *Computers and Composition* 58 (December 2020): 102611. https://doi.org/10.1016/j.compcom.2020.102611.

Lloyd, Annemaree. "Chasing Frankenstein's Monster: Information Literacy in the Black Box Society." *Journal of Documentation* 75, no. 6 (2019): 1475–85. https://doi.org/10.1108/JD-02-2019-0035.

Masunaga, Jennifer. "Evaluating Online Sources with Lateral Reading." CORA (Community of Online Research Assignments), February 15, 2021. https://www.projectcora.org/assignment/ evaluating-online-sources-lateral-reading.

———. "Exploring Google Scholar with a Summer Bridge Program." CORA (Community of Online Research Assignments), November 7, 2018. https://www.projectcora.org/assignment/ exploring-google-scholar-summer-bridge-program.

Nelson, Robert L., and Heidi L. M. Jacobs. "History, Play, and the Public: Wikipedia in the University Classroom." *History Teacher* 50, no. 4 (August 2017): 483–500. https://www.jstor.org/ stable/44507270.

Noble, Safiya Umoja. *Algorithms of Oppression: How Search Engines Reinforce Racism.* New York: New York University Press, 2018.

O'Hara, Ian. I..Ihen… Else: Algorithmic Systems and Epistemic Crises." In *Ascending into an Open Future: Proceedings of the ACRL 2021 Virtual Conference, April 13–16, 2021,* edited by Dawn M. Mueller, 98–106. Chicago: Association of College and Research Libraries, 2021. https://www.ala. org/acrl/sites/ala.org.acrl/files/content/conferences/confsandpreconfs/2021/IfThenElse.pdf.

Peterson, J. Michael. "Inclusive Schooling." In *Family and Society,* edited by Michael Shally-Jensen, 1040–48. Vol. 3 of *Encyclopedia of Contemporary American Social Issues.* Santa Barbara, CA: ABC-CLIO, 2011. Gale.

Pew Research Center. "Political Typology Quiz." November 9, 2021. https://www.pewresearch.org/ politics/quiz/political-typology/.

Reidsma, Matthew. *Masked by Trust: Bias in Library Discovery.* Sacramento, CA: Litwin Books, 2019.

Schubert, Carolyn, Malia Wiley, and Alyssa Young. "What's Behind a Web Search? Bias and Algorithms." CORA (Community of Online Research Assignments), May 6, 2021. https://www. projectcora.org/assignment/what%E2%80%99s-behind-web-search-bias-and-algorithms.

Spratt, Jennifer, and Lani Florian. "Inclusive Pedagogy: From Learning to Action; Supporting Each Individual in the Context of 'Everybody.'" *Teaching and Teacher Education* 49 (July 2015): 89–96. https://doi.org/10.1016/j.tate.2015.03.006.

University of California, Merced, Library. "Algorithm Bias and Gaming." LibGuide. Last updated October 29, 2020. https://libguides.ucmerced.edu/algorithmic-bias.

Walker, Mason, and Katerina Eva Matsa. "News Consumption across Social Media in 2021." Pew Research Center, September 20, 2021. https://www.pewresearch.org/journalism/2021/09/20/news-consumption-across-social-media-in-2021/.

Zuboff, Shoshana. *The Age of Surveillance Capitalism*. New York: PublicAffairs, 2019.

CHAPTER 8

Oppressive Authority

Dismantling, Reexamining, and Reconstructing Notions of Authority in Information Literacy Instruction

*Melissa Chomintra**

Introduction

A core tenet of information literacy instruction is to teach students how to evaluate information for authority and credibility. However, evaluation is political, and the ways in which we have traditionally defined authority have been framed by structures that privilege homogenous knowledge and intellectual production.

Library and information science as a profession, structure, and institution has contributed and continues to contribute to the determination of what is and isn't considered knowledge.[1] Knowledge created by Black, Indigenous, and People of

---

* Melissa Chomintra is a white first-generation college graduate. She was raised in Las Vegas in a multigenerational working poor family. Her research is viewed through a feminist lens and is shaped by her lived experience in and outside of the academy. She is working toward a better understanding of how gender, class, and race participate in and intersect in the academy and the classroom and uses her teaching as a site of resistance. She fully understands that she is operating and participating within the same systems that she criticizes and that her own privilege and position are problematic and contribute to upholding the many things that she critiques. She also acknowledges the genealogy of radical scholarship that has come before that allowed this chapter to be accepted. Thank you.

Color (BIPOC) has been historically invalidated by long-standing societal authority structures, hierarchies, and power dynamics that are replicated in academia. These structures and institutions exist as thinly veiled white supremacy working to silence, exclude, and erase the voices, experiences, and knowledge created by those they are committed to systemically oppressing.

As librarians we must scrutinize the ways in which our work enacts pervasive ideologies of racial power, and more specifically, white supremacy and white privilege within our professional structures, policies, and practices.[2] For these reasons, it is important to challenge traditional ways of conducting information literacy instruction, to recognize the systems of oppression in academia, and to develop new teaching techniques that help dismantle those systems and reduce harm.

In this chapter I examine ways knowledge authority structures can be oppressive in relation to information literacy instruction and discuss how librarians can implement equitable and inclusive pedagogy in their library instruction by dismantling, reexamining, and reconstructing notions of authority. Finally, I propose a reframing of the Association of College and Research Libraries (ACRL) *Framework for Information Literacy for Higher Education* and its concept that "Authority Is Constructed and Contextual."

Oppressive Authority

ACRL adopted the *Framework for Information Literacy for Higher Education* in January 2016 with the intended purpose of serving as a set of core ideas to guide teaching librarians.[3] The six frames outline a concept deemed critical to information literacy.

This particular way of approaching teaching and learning is referred to as threshold concept theory. First introduced in 2003 by Meyer and Land, threshold concept theory posits that there are discipline-specific core ideas and processes in student learning that must be achieved before students are able to progress or grasp more advanced concepts.[4] In conversation about the ACRL *Framework*, Beilin analyzes critiques from a critical information literacy perspective employing threshold concept theory. He concludes that while the intention of threshold concepts is to align information literacy goals with the way that knowledge functions in our existing information system, they may reinforce disciplinary boundaries and institutional hierarchies.[5] Librarians wanting to implement critical information literacy instruction will need to spend time intentionally reexamining and reinterpreting the frames.[6]

The frame Authority Is Constructed and Contextual acknowledges that

> information resources reflect their creators' expertise and credibility, and
> are evaluated based on the information need and the context in which the

information will be used. Authority is constructed, in that various communities may recognize different types of authority. It is contextual in that the information need may help to determine the level of authority required.[7]

While at first glance the language seems innocuous, further examination reveals its problematic underpinnings and applications. Authority is constructed insofar as it is an *achieved status*, though not one that is earned solely by operating in traditional, disciplinary modes of knowledge production—it is also influenced by power dynamics along the lines of race, class, and gender. The frame's definition is imprecise and can be interpreted as apolitical, while authority and knowledge are always political. By not explicitly acknowledging the existence of this dynamic, ACRL is presenting information literacy as apolitical instead of a product of the environment it is created in. It would be misguided to think that the racism, sexism, homophobia, and other forms of oppression that are perpetuated by the dominant culture disappear once we walk into the library classroom—instead, they are replicated.[8] Neutrality cannot exist in a political space, nor can a political space create a neutral structure or framework.

The frame implies an ideological hierarchy that materializes in library classrooms in ways that align with the expectations of the faculty creating the curriculum and assignment requirements. For example, librarians often cater to assignment requirements containing stipulations about the types of information qualified to be included in students' research papers. Because our profession has a long history of trying to prove ourselves and our worth, we fall prey to appeasing to maintain relationships even if they uphold hierarchies and white supremacy.

Recontextualizing authority would eliminate the reliance on privilege and expand our definitions of scholarship. We can then begin to reframe how we engage with knowledge production and its creators and eliminate yet another unnecessary power structure. Academia has a long history of bolstering theories and practices designed to "set up unnecessary and competing hierarchies of thought which reinscribe the politics of domination by designating work as either inferior, superior, or more or less worthy of attention."[9] I argue that this frame reinforces these histories.

What roles do librarians play in creating, maintaining, and uplifting cultures of inequality in information literacy instruction? Four key (not exhaustive) oppressive authority practices will guide this chapter.

Political Positionality of Libraries and Librarians

As librarians, we exist within multiple sustained systems and structures that work to restrict our ability to immerse ourselves in liberatory teaching practices. Before discussing anti-oppressive knowledge authority practices, I want to start with a conversation about the positionality of the profession of academic librarians that presents itself as its own interconnected system of power, oppression, and authority—one that is often exploitative, repressive, and neoliberal. This positionality is represented by three dominant structural bedrocks of librarianship linked to subordination: historical connections to structures of social dominance, gender power dynamics, and neutrality.[10]

First, as outlined by Eino Sierpe, librarianship has a history of being subordinate to power structures committed to white supremacy, sexism, classism, and other structures of social dominance.[11] Second, librarianship and librarians perform within systems of subordination through gender power dynamics. Librarianship is a gendered profession. Academic libraries consist predominantly of white (81.3%) women (82.1%), and they work within institutions of higher education that consist of predominantly white men (40%).[12] This fosters an environment earmarked by misogyny and gendered frameworks resulting in librarians being seen as care workers, babysitters, and assistants, not as true partners, professionals, or knowledge creators.[13] The third way in which libraries and librarianship are subordinate is through their core value of neutrality.[14] By definition, neutrality means to take a neutral position. Neutrality denies librarians the opportunity to challenge misinformation, teach honest histories, or confront the systemic arrangement. Submitting to this professional ethic, librarians are actively harming marginalized communities through silence while simultaneously touting it as a professional strength.

These three forms of subordination create a dynamic of extreme precarity and professional championing and upholding of white supremacy. It is this structure that creates the opportunity for subordinate legacies to evolve, compound, and prevail. We need to identify and be critical of the ways we respond to the pervasive ideologies of racism and sexism, how they present themselves in the classroom, and how they are interconnected to professional structures, policies, and practices.

Oppressive Authority Practices

The following examples of knowledge authority practices serve as pillars of reinforcement of oppression in the academy. Citations, knowledge production, popular and scholarly sources, and experiential authority are places prime for interrogation because of their attachment to power and privilege. These practices are of particular concern for librarians as they are tethered to information literacy instruction concepts and learning outcomes. It is important that librarians be able to recognize the ways in which oppressive authority practices present themselves in order to make intentional strides to dismantle them.

Politics of Citation

Societal white supremacy is reinscribed in academia through scholarly communication and publishing. The primary way that knowledge is validated and added to the information landscape is through the work created within academic institutions.[15] The academy creates the population of authors, editors, and reviewers that gatekeep the knowledge production and voices allowed to participate in the scholarly arena.[16] As a result, citations and citational practices are influenced by the long—and continuing—history of unequal racial power in the academy, making them highly political. The effects of their politics are far-reaching and present themselves in many ways throughout academia.

The lack of citations of scholars of color furthers racial dominance and forecloses potentially valuable avenues of intellectual inquiry.[17] This creates warped and inaccurate representations of the past and future alike. By over-citing white male authors we are drawing from a very shallow set of experiences and continuing to support cultures of exclusion.

Knowledge Production Co-opting

Knowledge production co-optation occurs when theories, ideas, or terms created outside of the traditional academic literature are not properly cited by scholars. For example, the terms *BIPOC* and *women of color* were coined outside of the academic literature, but are consistently used by scholars without proper citation.[18] Feminist theory and acumen have been victim to co-opting of knowledge production—specifically white women's co-optation of black knowledge production.[19]

Moya Bailey and Trudy had significant roles in the creation and proliferation of the term *misogynoir*. *Misogynoir* describes the anti-Black racist misogyny that Black women experience. Since the term was coined, there have been many instances of erasure and plagiarism of *misogynoir*.[20] These occurrences substantiate the definition of the term itself and serve as an example of the societal predisposition to question the intelligence and the validity of a concept that centers how Black women experience misogyny.[21] This is referred to as opportunistic plagiarism and punitive plagiarism. Opportunistic plagiarists use writing and tweets without citation to meet journalistic and academic deadlines, whether for pay, social status, or a combination. Punitive plagiarists want the opportunities they can gain through exploitation and erasing academic labor. For example someone could refer to Moya coining the term *misogynoir*, but then in turn plagiarize the theory it was gleaned from.[22]

Scholars diminish the value of knowledge outside of the academy and are quick to co-opt it and use it to advance their scholarly pursuits. This is a direct result of yet another oppressive system rooted in white supremacy, capitalism, and misogyny: tenure and the commodification of education. Feminist theory produced within the hierar-chical structures of academia enables women, most often white women, to plagiarize work of less visible scholars.[23] While hooks is specifically talking about the co-opting of feminist knowledge production, the structures and systems that allow this to perpetuate exist throughout all disciplines and are not unique to feminist theory and women. This is the result of the compounded vulnerability created by being left out of or erased by the systemic arrangement; the fact that you have been left out makes you vulnerable.

Devaluing of Popular Sources

Bias against the value and adequacy of popular sources, in the form of devalu-ing, discrediting, penalizing, or restricting their use, serves to uphold the author-ity and position of scholars. While the ACRL frame Authority Is Constructed and Contextual states that the authority of a resource matters within the context in which the information is used, assignment guidelines often include a caveat that popu-lar sources or nonscholarly sources do not count toward the minimum number of sources required for a sufficiently researched paper. This practice contributes to further othering of nonacademic work, devaluing its authority and place in research while also signaling to students that these sources are lesser than.

The practice of ranking knowledge makes assumptions about positionality and who can know what and limits ways of knowing and knowledge creation to academic affiliation and traditional educational experiences. This eliminates the opportunity for breadth and depth of knowledge because "most of the traditional disciplines are grounded in cultural worldviews which are either antagonistic to other belief systems or have no methodology for dealing with other knowledge systems."[24] The ways that academia defines, engages with, and places emphasis on "reliable" sources discredits other ways of knowing, partic-ularly ways of knowing experienced by Black, Indigenous, and People of Color.

Erasure of Experiential Authority

Librarianship participates in a power structure that disregards and dismisses the reality of students' and faculty lived experiences. The erasure of and the devaluing of experiential authority is a consequence of the historical structure of academia that allows faculty to be seen as experts on a given research topic without the requirement of firsthand experience. Because of this power structure, "they make careers out of examining experiences they have themselves never had; consuming knowledge obtained in marginalized communities,"[25] subsequently using an ethnocentric or androcentric gaze to publish and profit. Faculty then reinforce these politics in the classroom and their participation in the academic milieu.

If authority were reconstructed, it would be both an admission and acknowledgement that there are other ways of knowing, in turn dismantling the power dynamic created by Western ideologies. Fear of displacement and defrauding makes academics feel threatened and invaluable. They must continue to push the same narratives of authority so that their position of power is not challenged. If pushed to criticize and challenge the dominant academic structure, obvious fissures would be exposed in the professorial identity, consequently dismantling the idea of a "professor" and permanently changing its societal status.[26]

Without realigning our praxis to uplift experiential and lived experience, we contribute to the further erasure of knowledge production outside of the academy as well as belittling any form of knowing that is not tied to an institution of higher education. This compounds the lack of representation that would allow new approaches and understandings to be added into the scholarly conversation and classroom, which often include those on race and feminism,[27] and teaches our students that their experiences and histories hold little value in educational settings.[28]

Incorporating Anti-oppressive Authority Practices into Instruction

On paper (such as in policies and mission/vision/value statements), many academic libraries have a commitment to diversity, equity, and inclusion (DEI), often coinciding with a larger institutional commitment.[29] Can an institution commit to DEI without a tandem commitment to critical pedagogies? I think our work starts by having organizational conversations about committing to instructional practices that champion liberation. If your institution, library, or instruction program is committed to DEI, shouldn't support be extended to teaching practices? Theatrical optics and appeasement tactics create contradictions and reveal true commitment to contentment in upholding white supremacy. Below I have outlined a sampling of anti-oppressive authority practices, from both my own experience and those identified in the literature and work of others, in an effort to provide a foundation of resistance for librarians wishing to engage in this work.

Position Yourself in Your Praxis

Identify your own positionality as a librarian engaging in critical pedagogy. When engaging with faculty, staff, students, community practitioners, and other collaborators, intentionally communicate your commitment to critical pedagogy and that you engage in conversations about race, oppression, white supremacy, privilege, and power dynamics. It is not enough to inwardly commit to this work. We must also commit outwardly: drawing attention to its existence and its importance in the work we do in the classroom. Below is a draft of an e-mail response to a faculty member requesting instruction that explicitly states my commitment to my praxis and how it presents itself in the concepts and content I present in the classroom. I find that when I engage with faculty in this way, it helps to break down the power dynamic that can exist between faculty and librarian, as many of us do not have faculty status, and allows me to create agency and establish my position as a collaborator. This creates a space for dialogue around the learning experience.

> Hi Colleague,
>
> Thank you for reaching out about a library instruction session for your Intro-duction to Gender and Sexualities studies course. Before we schedule a date I want to communicate a few things about my praxis and what you can expect from me in the classroom. I teach from a critical pedagogy and critical infor-mation literacy philosophy in order to encourage students to push beyond just finding and using information to thinking critically about and critiquing the structures of power and oppression as they exist in research, scholarship, and the larger information ecosystem.
>
> I look forward to working together to create a critical and powerful learning experience. If you have any questions please reach out to me. I am always happy to engage in conversation about transgressive teaching practices!
>
> Warmly,
>
> Librarian

Liberatory LibGuides

LibGuides are a form of digital publication that is a direct representation of your own positions on authority. Many academic librarians utilize LibGuides as a digital learning object to connect students with information resources on myriad topics. LibGuides can be extremely library-centric, and it is common practice to structure them entirely around peer-reviewed, textual library sources.[30] Be intentional about the voice you give your LibGuides, and be systematic about the collective message you are communicating to users. You have the agency to uplift knowledge creators who have not traditionally been included in the systemic arrangement of the academy.

By not privileging one type of information or a homogenous pool of creators, you are working to shift the practices that contribute to upholding oppressive authority frameworks constructed to devalue popular sources, experiential knowledge, and other ways of knowing. The following are guidelines you can follow as you create and revise your own LibGuides:

- Ensure that the content included and displayed strikes a balance of sources of knowledge production inside and outside of the academy.
- Promote marginalized knowledge creators and intellectuals.
- Eliminate jargon.
- Use inclusive language.
- Give social context and nuance to the content you are including.
- Avoid gatekeeping by including sources that exist behind paywalls. Guides are publicly discoverable.[31]
- Include a discussion of citational politics. Can you have a conversation about citational practices and styles without also discussing their politics?
- Make your LibGuides available in multiple languages.
- Check your LibGuides for accessibility.

Figure 8.1 is an example of a guide created and revised according to these guidelines.

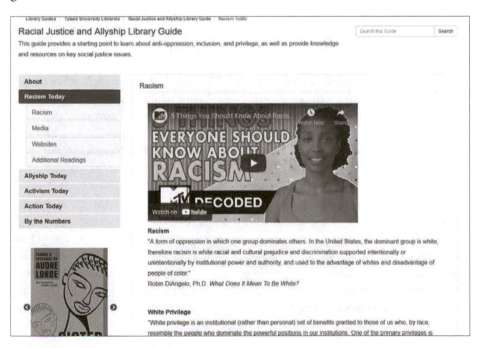

Figure 8.1
Screen capture of Racial Justice and Allyship LibGuide

At the time of writing, I learned of the amazing work taking place at CalPoly: the Robert E. Kennedy Library's Open LibGuide Review Sessions (LORDS) project.[32] The project was created to provide space for critique, discussion, and criticality with the goal of implementing anti-racist practices into their LibGuides using critical race theory. The project works toward implementing an open review system to ensure that LibGuides contain the criticality required to dismantle the idea that neutrality exists within knowledge organizations. The LORDS rubric includes criteria to evaluate your guides for accessibility, critical race theory application, content contextualization, and the positionality of the guide's author.[33]

Positionality of Knowing

During instruction sessions, have your students write an information positionality statement. What lenses do they view information through? What informs their ways of knowing? Power dynamics are embedded in every step of the research process. Identifying how their positionality intersects with ways of knowing can help to reframe, disrupt, and contextualize the instruction session by shaping students' lived experience as authoritative and opening up discourse about the breadth and depth of ways of knowing. Ask students to think about their major, their previous access to information, their experience with research, their class/race/gender identities, and other intersectionalities. An example student response is below.

> I am an environmental biology major. I attended a private high school and had access to a well-resourced library. I am a white, cisgendered male, who grew up in an upper middle class neighborhood in the northeast in a two-parent household. My primary ways of knowing and interacting with information come from TV news, my parents watched Fox News a lot, and internet news sites.

After students have written their positionality statements, discuss how certain positionalities present and interact with the larger information ecosystem. These statements serve as an activity that encourages students to start thinking about how they interact with and seek information. It allows students to recognize their own lenses, biases, positionalities, and privileges and to frame how and where they receive information in the larger context. This shapes our conversations moving forward. Students have the language and conceptual understanding to confront and identify their relationships with positionality and knowing.

Decenter the Academic Database

Decentering the academic database creates space for discourse and learning around the politics of citation and how those politics contribute to devaluing and othering knowledge creators outside of the academy. For example, demonstrating a variety of information sources during instruction can work to shift the narrative surrounding the use of information sources created by an authority without an institutional affiliation.

Databases outside of the academy, blogs, zines, podcasts, social media, and oral histories are all examples of content and scholarship that can add value and depth to research. Think about what information sources you are privileging in the classroom: How are you demonstrating that other ways of knowing are valuable? We can demonstrate that these aren't "other" ways of knowing; they are just ways of knowing. Period. Many academic databases champion the capitalistic neoliberal bedrock of publishing. Incorporate nonacademic affiliated sources of intellectual generation into your instruction session and teach students how to locate and navigate these resources. The appendix includes a list of sources to get you started.

Citation Counting Activity

In order to demonstrate the interplay of the politics of citation and the imbalance in the quantity of scholarship produced and cited by white male faculty, have students conduct a search on any given topic in a library database. Repeat the same search in Google Scholar and Google search. Have students conduct a Google search of the authors of the first five results of each individual search and tally by race. Demonstrate how to do some additional digging to determine if an author has a public positionality statement. Searching an institution's web page and locating a faculty bio or social media account are all really great places to start. While it can be challenging and problematic to make assumptions about authors' identities, I encourage students to also read for clues of the place from which the author is writing: What is their relationship to the subject? How does the author self-identify (e.g., in terms of gender, race, ability, nationality, sexuality, ethnicity, etc.)? How might these identities impact the author's perspective and approach? Does the author primarily employ a particular theoretical framework or perspective?

The tally acknowledges the existence of white supremacy in scholarship and in the larger information landscape. While it is not a perfect tool, it teaches students how to engage with the backgrounds of the scholars and scholarship they are including in their research and understand that positionality matters.

Additional Suggestions for Your Faculty

I highly recommend the suggestions contained in "Teaching Antiracist Citational Politics as a Project of Transformation: Lessons from the Cite Black Women Movement for White Feminist Anthropologists" by Christa Craven.[34] Here are my favorite:

- Look at whose books and articles you assign, and ask yourself: What would a visual representation reveal?
- Be explicit that citing Black women is not an add-on.
- Engage with the ideas of Black women, not just the most-often-repeated things they have said or written.
- Read promiscuously.

Conclusion

> *The crisis is everywhere, massive, massive, massive. And we are small. But emergence notices the way small actions and connections create complex systems, patterns that become ecosystems and societies. Emergence is our inheritance as a part of this universe; it is how we change. Emergent strategy is how we intentionally change in ways that grow our capacity to embody the just and liberated worlds we long for.*
>
> —*adrienne maree brown, Emergent Strategy: Shaping Change, Changing Worlds*[35]

As librarians we should always think critically about our teaching practices and be reflexive. Those working to transform the curriculum to address and prevent biases or challenge systems of dominance are individuals willing to take the risks that engaged pedagogy requires and see their teaching praxis as a site of resistance.[36]

My experience implementing these practices has been eye-opening, sometimes restorative, and other times defeating. It is encouraging when entire departments that have long been estranged from the library become collaborators in response to the shift in pedagogy. Conversely, others are more content with continuing to dictate how and what I teach, actively redirecting instruction away from critical practices and reinforcing just how deeply embedded white supremacy is in the classroom.

The anti-oppressive authority practices suggested in this chapter are just the beginning. They are small actions riddled with imperfection, but they are an attempt at disruptions to stillness. I fully understand that I am operating and participating within the same systems that I criticize and that my own privilege and position are problematic and contribute to upholding the many things that I critique.

Systematic change is needed to address systemic oppression because the institutions and systems we learn and work in are problematic. Criticalness can and should influence our research, teaching, and practice, so I encourage you to share, remix, and critique the ideas and suggestions I put forth in this chapter.

Appendix

Cite Black Authors (https://citeblackauthors.com/listings/) seeks "to enhance recognition and citation of Black academic voices." Its approach "requires a shift from traditional citation practices that are passive and white-centric to active citation practices that both quantify and equilibrate racial representation."[37]

Black Women Radicals (https://www.blackwomenradicals.com/database) "is a Black feminist advocacy organization dedicated to uplifting and centering Black women and gender expansive people's radical political activism. Rooted in intersectional and transnational Black feminisms and Womanisms, we are committed to empowering Black transgender, queer, and cisgender radical women and gender expansive activists by centering their political, intellectual, and cultural contributions to the field of Black Politics across time, space, and place in Africa and the African Diaspora."[38]

The African American Intellectual History Society's *Black Perspectives* blog (https://www.aaihs.org/black-perspectives/) is dedicated to "producing and disseminating cutting-edge research that is accessible to the public and is oriented towards advancing the lives of people of African descent and humanity."[39]

HistSex (https://histsex.org/) is "a freely-available, peer-reviewed, and open-source resource by sex educators, historians, and librarians active in sexuality fields."[40] It contains bibliographies, research collections and archives, digital projects, and time lines on the history of sexuality.

"Latinx Voices of Southern Nevada" (https://www.library.unlv.edu/latinx) "preserv[es] and shar[es] the life stories of Southern Nevada's Latinx residents...by collecting and preserving ...oral histories" to ensure that "the perspectives of [the] region's Latinx residents are reflected in [its] collections so that present and future generations can learn and study more about their achievements, aspirations, and experiences."[41]

The Twitter account @QueerFaculty (https://twitter.com/QueerFaculty) "follow[s] and highlight[s] LGBTQ+ faculty from all fields & any part of the globe to inspire students, & future queer faculty."[42]

Notes

1. Sofia Y. Leung and Jorge R. López-McKnight, eds., *Knowledge Justice* (Cambridge, MA: MIT Press, 2021).
2. Eino Sierpe, "The Election of Donald Trump to the Presidency and the Crisis of Liberalism in Librarianship: The Need to Reconsider the Social Function of the Library and Its Role in Critical Information Literacy and Political Education in Response to the Rise of Alt-right Fascism in the United States," *Journal of Radical Librarianship* 3 (2017): 65–75.
3. Association of College and Research Libraries, *Framework for Information Literacy for Higher*

Education (Chicago: Association of College and Research Libraries, 2016), https://www.ala.org/acrl/standards/ilframework.

4. Jan Meyer and Ray Land, *Threshold Concepts and Troublesome Knowledge* (Edinburgh: University of Edinburgh, 2003).
5. Ian Beilin, "Beyond the Threshold: Conformity, Resistance, and the ACRL Information Literacy Framework for Higher Education," *In the Library with the Lead Pipe*, February 25, 2015, https://www.inthelibrarywiththeleadpipe.org/2015/beyond-the-threshold-conformity-resistance-and-the-aclr-information-literacy-framework-for-higher-education/.
6. Beilin, "Beyond the Threshold."
7. Association of College and Research Libraries, *Framework.*
8. Maria T. Accardi, *Feminist Pedagogy for Library Instruction* (Sacramento, CA: Library Juice Press, 2013).
9. bell hooks, *Teaching to Transgress* (New York: Routledge, 1994), 64.
10. Sierpe, "Election of Donald Trump."
11. Sierpe, "Election of Donald Trump," 66.
12. National Center for Education Statistics, "Characteristics of Postsecondary Faculty," in *The Condition of Education 2020*, NCES 2020-144, ed. Thomas Nachazel, Megan Barnett, and Stephen Purcell (Washington, DC: National Center for Education Statistics, Institute of Education Statistics, US Department of Education, 2020), 150–53, https://nces.ed.gov/programs/coe/indicator_csc.asp.
13. Veronica Arellano Douglas and Joanna Gadsby, "Gendered Labor and Library Instruction Coordinators: The Undervaluing of Feminized Work," in *At the Helm: Leading Transformation: The Proceedings of the ACRL 2017 Conference, March 22-25, 2017, Baltimore, Maryland*, ed. Dawn M. Mueller (Chicago: Association of College and Research Libraries, 2017), 266–74.
14. Stephen Macdonald and Briony Birdi, "The Concept of Neutrality: A New Approach," *Journal of Documentation* 76, no. 1 (2020): 333–53.
15. Harrison W. Inefuku, "Relegated to the Margins: Faculty of Color, the Scholarly Record, and the Necessity of Antiracist Library Disruptions," in *Knowledge Justice: Disrupting Library and Information Studies through Critical Race Theory*, ed. Sofia Y. Leung and Jorge R. López-McKnight (Cambridge, MA: MIT Press, 2021), 197–216.
16. Inefuku, "Relegated to the Margins."
17. Victor Ray, "The Racial Politics of Citation," Inside Higher Ed, April 27, 2018, https://www.insidehighered.com/advice/2018/04/27/racial-exclusions-scholarly-citations-opinion.
18. Sandra E. Garcia, "Where Did BIPOC Come From?" *New York Times*, June 17, 2020, https://www.nytimes.com/article/what-is-bipoc.html; Loretta Ross, "Here's a Much-Needed History Lesson on the Origins of the Term 'Women of Color,'" Everyday Feminism, March 10, 2015, https://everydayfeminism.com/2015/03/origin-of-term-woc/.
19. hooks, *Teaching to Transgress.*
20. Moya Bailey, "On Misogynoir: Citation, Erasure, and Plagiarism," *Feminist Media Studies* 18, no. 4 (2018): 762–68.
21. Bailey, "On Misogynoir," 764.
22. Bailey, "On Misogynoir," 765–66.
23. hooks, *Teaching to Transgress.*
24. Linda Tuhiwai Smith, *Decolonizing Methodologies: Research and Indigenous Peoples*, 2nd ed. (London: Zed Books, 2012), 68.
25. Clelia O. Rodríguez, *Decolonizing Academia* (Black Point, NS: Fernwood, 2018), 19.
26. hooks, *Teaching to Transgress*, 140.
27. hooks, *Teaching to Transgress*, 105.
28. Stacy D. Saathoff, "Healing Systemic Fragmentation in Education through Multicultural Educa-

tion," *Multicultural Education* 25, no. 1 (Fall 2017): 2–8.

29. Alice M. Cruz, "Intentional Integration of Diversity Ideals in Academic Libraries: A Literature Review," *Journal of Academic Librarianship* 45, no. 3 (2019): 220–27.

30. Alison Hicks, "LibGuides: Pedagogy to Oppress?" *Hybrid Pedagogy*, April 15, 2015, https://hybridpedagogy.org/libguides-pedagogy-to-oppress/.

31. Amanda Meeks, "Feminist LibGuides: Towards Inclusive Practices in Guide Creation, Use, and Reference Interactions," in *The Feminist Reference Desk: Concepts, Critiques, and Conversations*, edited by Maria T. Accardi. Series on Gender and Sexuality in Information Studies (Sacramento, CA: Litwin Books, 2017), 294-295.

32. California Polytechnic State University, "Open LibGuide Review," last updated April 22, 2022, https://guides.lib.calpoly.edu/c.php?g=1052808&p=8173550.

33. California State University, "CSU Rubrics," December 2, 2020, https://docs.google.com/spreadsheets/d/13kORPNd69A0JSCFv2yHUGYrWH5EVRcBVkpcoZLOpATA/edit#gid=479275756.

34. Christa Craven, "Teaching Antiracist Citational Politics as a Project of Transformation: Lessons from the Cite Black Women Movement for White Feminist Anthropologists," *Feminist Anthropology* 2, no. 1 (2021): 120–29.

35. adrienne maree brown, *Emergent Strategy* (Edinburgh: AK Press, 2017), 3, ProQuest Ebook Central.

36. hooks, *Teaching to Transgress*.

37. Cite Black Authors, "Mission and Vision," https://citeblackauthors.com/mission-and-vision/.

38. Black Women Radicals, "About: Black Women Radicals," https://www.blackwomenradicals.com/database.

39. African American Intellectual History Society, "About," *Black Perspectives* (blog), https://www.aaihs.org/about-black-perspectives/.

40. This Is the History of Sexuality home page, https://histsex.org/.

41. University of Nevada, Las Vegas, "Latinx Voices of Southern Nevada," https://www.library.unlv.edu/latinx.

42. "The Queer Faculty Project" (@QueerFaculty), Twitter, https://twitter.com/QueerFaculty.

Bibliography

Accardi, Maria T. *Feminist Pedagogy for Library Instruction* Sacramento, CA: Library Juice Press, 2013.

African American Intellectual History Society. "About." *Black Perspectives* (blog). https://www.aaihs.org/about-black-perspectives/.

Association of College and Research Libraries. *Framework for Information Literacy for Higher Education*. Chicago: Association of College and Research Libraries. http://www.ala.org/acrl/standards/ilframework.

Bailey, Moya. "On Misogynoir: Citation, Erasure, and Plagiarism." *Feminist Media Studies* 18, no. 4 (2018): 762–68.

Beilin, Ian. "Beyond the Threshold: Conformity, Resistance, and the ACRL Information Literacy Framework for Higher Education." *In the Library with the Lead Pipe*, February 25, 2015. https://www.inthelibrarywiththeleadpipe.org/2015/beyond-the-threshold-conformity-resistance-and-the-aclr-information-literacy-framework-for-higher-education/.

Black Women Radicals. "About: Black Women Radicals." https://www.blackwomenradicals.com/database.

brown, adrienne maree. *Emergent Strategy: Shaping Change, Changing Worlds.* Edinburgh: AK Press, 2017. ProQuest Ebook Central.

California Polytechnic State University. "Open LibGuide Review." Last updated April 22, 2022. https://guides.lib.calpoly.edu/c.php?g=1052808&p=8173550.

California State University. "CSU Rubrics." December 2, 2020. https://docs.google.com/spreadsheets/d/13kORPNd69A0JSCFv2yHUGYrWH5EVRcBVkpcoZLOpATA/edit#gid=479275756

Cite Black Authors. "Mission and Vision." https://citeblackauthors.com/mission-and-vision/.

Craven, Christa. "Teaching Antiracist Citational Politics as a Project of Transformation: Lessons from the Cite Black Women Movement for White Feminist Anthropologists." *Feminist Anthropology* 2, no. 1 (2021): 120–29.

Cruz, Alice M. "Intentional Integration of Diversity Ideals in Academic Libraries: A Literature Review." *Journal of Academic Librarianship* 45, no. 3 (2019): 220–27.

Douglas, Veronica Arellano, and Joanna Gadsby. "Gendered Labor and Library Instruction Coordinators: The Undervaluing of Feminized Work." In *At the Helm: Leading Transformation: The Proceedings of the ACRL 2017 Conference, March 22–25, 2017, Baltimore, Maryland*, edited by Dawn M. Mueller, 266–74. Chicago: Association of College and Research Libraries, 2017.

Garcia, Sandra E. "Where Did BIPOC Come From?" *New York Times*, June 17, 2020. https://www.nytimes.com/article/what-is-bipoc.html

Hicks, Alison. "LibGuides: Pedagogy to Oppress?" *Hybrid Pedagogy*, April 15, 2015. https://hybridpedagogy.org/libguides-pedagogy-to-oppress/.

hooks, bell. *Teaching to Transgress: Education as the Practice of Freedom.* New York: Routledge, 1994.

Inefuku, Harrison W. "Relegated to the Margins: Faculty of Color, the Scholarly Record, and the Necessity of Antiracist Library Disruptions." In *Knowledge Justice: Disrupting Library and Information Studies through Critical Race Theory*, edited by Sofia Y. Leung, Jorge R. López-McKnight, 197–216. Cambridge, MA: MIT Press, 2021.

Leung, Sofia Y., and Jorge R. López-McKnight, eds. *Knowledge Justice: Disrupting Library and Information Studies through Critical Race Theory.* Cambridge, MA: MIT Press, 2021.

Macdonald, Stephen, and Briony Birdi. "The Concept of Neutrality: A New Approach." *Journal of Documentation* 76, no. 1 (2020): 333–53.

Meeks, Amanda. "Feminist LibGuides: Towards Inclusive Practices in Guide Creation, Use, and Reference Interactions." In *The Feminist Reference Desk: Concepts, Critiques, and Conversations*, edited by Maria T. Accardi, 294–295. Series on Gender and Sexuality in Information Studies. Sacramento, CA: Litwin Books, 2017.

Meyer, Jan, and Ray Land. *Threshold Concepts and Troublesome Knowledge: Linkages to Ways of Thinking and Practising within the Disciplines.* Edinburgh: University of Edinburgh, 2003.

National Center for Education Statistics. "Characteristics of Postsecondary Faculty." In *The Condition of Education 2020*, NCES 2020-144, edited by Thomas Nachazel, Megan Barnett, and Stephen Purcell, 150–53. Washington, DC: National Center for Education Statistics, Institute of Education Statistics, US Department of Education, 2020. https://nces.ed.gov/programs/coe/indicator_csc.asp.

"Queer Faculty Project" (@QueerFaculty). Twitter. https://twitter.com/QueerFaculty.

Ray, Victor. "The Racial Politics of Citation." Inside Higher Ed, April 27, 2018. https://www.insidehighered.com/advice/2018/04/27/racial-exclusions-scholarly-citations-opinion.

Rodríguez, Clelia O. *Decolonizing Academia: Poverty, Oppression and Pain.* Black Point, NS: Fernwood, 2018.

Ross, Loretta. "Here's a Much-Needed History Lesson on the Origins of the Term 'Women of Color.'" Everyday Feminism, March 10, 2015. https://everydayfeminism.com/2015/03/origin-of-term-woc/.

Saathoff, Stacy D. "Healing Systemic Fragmentation in Education through Multicultural Education." *Multicultural Education* 25, no. 1 (Fall 2017): 2–8.

Sierpe, Eino. "The Election of Donald Trump to the Presidency and the Crisis of Liberalism in Librarianship: The Need to Reconsider the Social Function of the Library and Its Role in Critical Information Literacy and Political Education in Response to the Rise of Alt-right Fascism in the United States." *Journal of Radical Librarianship* 3 (2017): 65–75.

Smith, Linda Tuhiwai. *Decolonizing Methodologies: Research and Indigenous Peoples*, 2nd ed. London: Zed Books, 2012.

This Is the History of Sexuality home page. https://histsex.org/.

University of Nevada, Las Vegas. "Latinx Voices of Southern Nevada." https://www.library.unlv.edu/latinx.

Intentional Information Literacy

Introduction

Maura Seale

The thread that runs through each of the chapters in this section is a willingness to reflect, revise, reframe, and, above all, experiment with instruction across the library. Three of the chapters concern traditional realms of library instruction—information literacy, legal research, and primary sources—and describe how authors rethought them in order to be more inclusive. In Chapter 9, "The Feminist First-Year Seminar: Using Critical Pedagogy to Design a Mandatory Information Literacy Course," Heather Campbell describes how she used feminist pedagogy to develop a mandatory first-year seminar. The seminar was intended to teach traditional information literacy and academic research, but to also address competencies specific to the Ursuline values of the college and to its position as a women's college. Campbell outlines the inclusive and collaborative approach to developing a seminar focused on personal growth and fostering commitment to social justice that incorporated but did not solely focus on information literacy. She also offers a clear-eyed analysis of the benefits and drawbacks of such an approach, particularly in regard to the labor of creating and teaching the course.

Clanitra Stewart Nejdl, in Chapter 10, "Better Learning through Legal Research: Increasing Law Students' Cultural Competency and Awareness of Diversity, Equity, Inclusion, and Accessibility Using Legal Research Instruction," offers an overview of legal research education that might be unfamiliar to many instruction librarians. She outlines the very real importance of cultural competence and understanding of diversity, equity, inclusion, and accessibility (DEIA) for law students and suggests that the law library classroom offers an excellent opportunity to explicitly incorporate them. Research is the first step of working with cases, and legal research education typically focuses on detailed exercises that necessitate in-depth research. Because these exercises are based on historical or possible cases, it is easy and important to incorporate equity and inclusion. Stewart Nejdl's chapter includes a guide to how to plan for instruction, including developing the exercises and moderating discussion, that will be of interest to any instruction librarian. Finally, Glenn Koelling, in Chapter 11, "Digital Archive Kits: Accessibility and Flexibility," describes creating a digital archive kit in order to engage more students in work with archival sources, both because working with physical archives is only so scalable and because physical archives can often feel exclusionary. She outlines the process she used to create her digital archive kit and considerations for making it inclusive in terms of content and also technically accessible. Her chapter ends with a lesson plan and worksheet for working with digital archive kits and information about how to make your own kit.

Three chapters in this section turn to critical information literacy and critical library pedagogy, but also to other theories and frameworks that complicate and extend both. Tierney Steelberg primarily teaches single sessions focused on technology tools, and in Chapter 12, "Teaching Technology Inclusively: One Librarian's Critical Digital Pedagogy Approach to One-Shot Instruction Sessions," she brings together critical digital pedagogy and critical library pedagogy. She identifies three elements that foreground inclusivity—building community, creating space for practice and collaboration, and taking time for reflection—and describes the specific strategies she uses to develop each element in the classroom. Although she focuses on teaching technology, these strategies will be of interest to any instruction librarians who primarily teach one-shots. In Chapter 13, "Theories of Motivation as Inclusive Pedagogy: Strategies for Engaging and Equitable Instruction," Francesca Marineo Munk turns to the disciplines of education and educational psychology and their theorizations of motivation. She argues that understanding motivation can help promote inclusive pedagogy, specifically through a consideration of the concepts of autonomy and value. Autonomy can be incorporated into library instruction by facilitating choices and practicing transparency, while value can be emphasized by fostering relevance and decentering the classroom. Marineo Munk notes that these ideas intersect with other inclusive forms of pedagogy such as universal design for learning (UDL) and provides examples applicable to many forms of library instruction. Similarly, Debbie Krahmer brings the principles of intergroup dialogue to bear on both ACRL's *Framework for Information Literacy for Higher Education* and critical information literacy in Chapter 14, "Facilitating Critical Information Literacy: Using Intergroup Dialogue to Engage with the *Framework*." D begins with a helpful overview of intergroup dialogue, suggests several ways library instructors might incorporate it in their sessions generally, and then turns to how D uses it specifically when teaching sessions on visual literacy and in reference consultations. The many examples D provides—and indeed, the many examples provided by all of these authors—will undoubtedly inspire those of us who are constantly reflecting on and revising our instructional practices.

The final two chapters in this section offer food for thought for improving library instruction, but also seek to destabilize how we understand and teach academic research practices. Kari D. Weaver, Frances Brady, and Alissa Droog, in Chapter 15, "Drawing to Conceptualize Research, Reduce Implicit Bias, and Establish Researcher Positionality in the Graduate Classroom," offer individual reflections on how they have experienced drawing in instruction and how they now incorporate drawing in their own library instruction sessions focused on academic research with graduate students. They use drawing to help graduate students grapple with affective elements of their research; to think about their own identities, subjectivities, and experiences as researchers and in relation to their research; to destabilize dominant white, Western notions of what research "should" be; and to reveal implicit biases. The chapter concludes with a lesson plan based on drawing. In Chapter 16, "Examining the Information Literacy Dreamfield: Applying a Sentipensante Pedagogy to Library Research Consultations," Sheila García Mazari and Samantha Minnis argue that library instruction must consider the broader context of the learning environment. Higher education and information literacy might be understood as Dreamfields that are rooted in particular values that are often implicit but are not universal. Intellectualism and an emphasis on thinking rather than allowing for intuition and emotion is one such value of the Dreamfields of higher education and information literacy as embodied by the *Framework for Information Literacy for Higher Education*. They argue instead for a Sentipensante pedagogy that allows for intuition and emotion, acknowledges research can be violent or disempowering, and is grounded in both an ethics of care and trauma-informed pedagogy. The authors conclude with individual reflections on how they have employed Sentipensante pedagogy in research consultations.

As a mid-career librarian whose positions have always included instruction, and as a researcher of critical information literacy and critical library pedagogy, I found each chapter touched on something I had not truly considered before in my own thinking or practices. Each chapter made me reflect on and reconsider what I do when I teach, from the epistemology that academic research takes as natural, to the way I work with individual students in the classroom, at the reference desk, and in my office for individual consultations. I hope you experience the same.

CHAPTER 9

The Feminist First-Year Seminar

Using Critical Pedagogy to Design a Mandatory Information Literacy Course

Heather Campbell

Introduction and Context

This chapter describes a feminist approach to creating a mandatory first-year seminar at Brescia University College, Canada's only remaining women's university. Brescia is a small, Catholic, primarily undergraduate university with approximately 1,500 students. It was founded in 1919 by the Ursuline Sisters, a Roman Catholic teaching order "committed to social justice, community service, and the development of women."[1] Today, it is a beautiful and welcoming campus affiliated with a large research institution of over 40,000 students.[2]

As early as 2009, librarians and faculty at Brescia were interested in creating an introductory research course for all incoming first-year students. At first, this was inspired by changing staff and faculty workloads:

> An increasing number of Brescia students between 2006 and 2009 reported
> feeling overwhelmed and anxious over the demands of academic research.
> More students requested one-on-one, intensive research assistance from
> library staff during this period, while faculty reported an anecdotal increase
> in plagiarism.[3]

This was corroborated by a research study I conducted, where students' self-reported information literacy knowledge and confidence were much lower than their instructors' expectations: "The majority of survey respondents reported having regular difficulties with academic research …a result all the more meaningful since these survey respondents also self-identified as regular library users."[4]

There was considerable support for a mandatory first-year course among Brescia faculty and staff, but many felt students needed an introduction to all of Brescia's degree-level learning outcomes, not just information literacy. Developed from the mission and values statements, these outcomes –called the Brescia Competencies– included common academic learning outcomes such as communication, critical thinking, inquiry, and analysis, along with three values embodying an Ursuline philosophy of education:

1. *Self-Awareness and Development*: Learn to know yourself and your unique contributions to the world.
2. *Social Awareness and Engagement*: Love others and help them to recognize their own individual strengths. Work with them to build a shared vision in pursuit of social justice.
3. *Valuing*: Reconcile your actions with your values or beliefs, taking responsibility for your choices.[5]

To balance our Ursuline foundations with the demands of academic research in the digital age,[6] Brescia's first-year course needed to be different. This chapter, then, explores our use of feminist pedagogy to create a student-centered, values-based information literacy course.

The Pilot

Brescia first delivered an academic first-year seminar in 2017–18.[7] Overall, the course goal was to introduce students to the Brescia Competencies by examining a complex question or problem from an interdisciplinary perspective. The course's assignments and learning activities focused particularly on academic research skills and included a wide range of inclusive pedagogies: small-group discussions, where students were encouraged to share lived experience; reflective journaling and self-exploration exercises; active learning and opportunities for hands-on Competency practice; guest lectures; and a scaffolded essay assignment with opportunities for personalized feedback and peer review. There were no course tests or exams.

As many studies on first-year seminars have found,[8] following "best practices" does not guarantee success for every context or every student. For example, while students received multiple information literacy lessons and personalized feedback from both librarians and their instructors, most participants in a follow-up study did not feel better prepared to complete assignments in other courses. The course development team felt confident we followed inclusive first-year seminar curriculum design, but some students struggled to see how course topics related from week to week. Respondents who felt dissatisfied with the course also reported feeling disconnected from course content and topics. When asked what the course should do differently, students commented on the noticeable lack of attention paid to women and gender issues, significant given Brescia's place as Canada's only women's university. My final report on the pilot therefore recommended that the course "integrate women's learning more directly.... This would require that course instructors be familiar and comfortable using and describing pedagogical methods that benefit women learners."[9]

Educating Women

The course development team experienced a threshold moment when Brescia librarian Jennifer Foley encouraged us to explore feminist pedagogy. Building on critical theory,[10] feminist pedagogy's connection to our course goals and institutional values was immediately (even embarrassingly) obvious. The goal of feminist pedagogy, as influenced by key writers such as bell hooks and Maralee Mayberry,[11] is to "create a more hospitable place for all students, but especially women."[12] Each student's unique gifts, perspectives, and experiences are honoured through a holistic, community-driven teaching approach. Many feminist instructors incorporate skills-based instruction into their teaching, but they do so within the broader context of dismantling systems of oppression and privilege.[13] A common element in feminist classrooms, similar to an Ursuline approach, is fostering students' commitment to social justice. As Crawley, Lewis, and Mayberry explain: "all feminist work should focus on positive social change."[14]

Despite being a women's university, Brescia had never formally adopted a feminist identity: Women and Gender Studies is offered at the larger, affiliated institution, and there is little to no literature connecting Ursuline philosophy to a feminist approach. The parallels, though, are striking, and worthy of further exploration: the Ursulines explain that the purpose of education is to support students' awakening to their place in society and in the universe, achieved by trusting "that there is an inner guide helping [students] to grow to [their] full potential."[15] Educators, therefore, must foster students' abilities to observe: "to see as others see, and therefore respect differences."[16] Feminist pedagogy, meanwhile, focuses on creating engaged classrooms:

> Engaged with self in a continuing reflective process; engaged actively with the material being studied; engaged with others in a struggle to get beyond our ...destructive hatreds and work together in order to know more; engaged with community and with movements for social change.[17]

The course design team for Brescia's first-year seminar immediately committed to using a feminist approach to curriculum design, but had some unique considerations before moving forward. Feminist pedagogy is more often described as a teaching philosophy than an institutional value, let alone a strategic initiative. There is evidence to suggest that common first-year experiences are beneficial to fostering students' feeling of belonging,[18] but the strength of feminist pedagogy is in the community and personal relationships formed in each classroom. We wanted to create a course that was intersectional and welcoming of all learners—with their unique backgrounds, identities, values, and perspectives—but on an institutional scale that resulted in logistical restrictions. We could not, for example, ask every instructor or stakeholder involved to adopt feminist values. There were important human resources considerations, as well: given Brescia's size, we had only one teaching librarian supporting the course as it scaled up to become mandatory for all incoming students.

Inclusive Classrooms through Feminist Design

We addressed these concerns by carefully creating a cross-institutional curriculum team (see team membership and individual responsibilities in table 9.A.1 in the appendix). As an educational developer and associate director of Brescia's teaching and learning centre by this point, I served as an unofficial course coordinator, helping to bring together and communicate with the team. A feminist disruption of traditional power structures was reflected in our team functioning, as each member provided leadership in their area of expertise (noted in tables 9.A.1 and 9.A.2 in the appendix with "train-the-trainer" responsibility). While ultimate responsibilities for course delivery and assessment remained with the two faculty instructors, all team members were invited to contribute reading, lesson, and learning activity ideas.

We coordinated our large team through weekly meetings, held nearly year-round. Meetings used the following format:

1. Identifying and resolving immediate problems or concerns with the current week of the course.
2. Reviewing course content for the upcoming week(s).
3. Training for future lessons and activities (provided by campus experts).

The tables in the appendix list the type of training each campus expert provided: in my capacity as educational developer, for example, I delivered professional development on feminist pedagogy and the Brescia Competencies, while my librarian colleague offered information literacy training (discussed in more detail below). Weekly meetings were always attended by course instructors, seminar leaders, the educational developer (me), and usually the librarian; other members of the larger course team would attend on an as-needed basis (see also table 9.A.2). Academic advisors, for example, would liaise with course instructors about students at risk, while student experience professionals trained the team each summer on first-year or international students' common transitionary needs. Students registered in the course, though, were largely unaware of this team-based approach. To maintain classroom community, they saw the same course instructors each week in their seminar discussions, outside of the occasional guest lecture.

Weekly meetings at the end of term shifted to course assessment when I collected feedback from all parties. This assessment included interviews and group discussions with the instructors, as well as focus groups and surveys with students. Students were asked for feedback on course content and logistics, as well as broad-sweeping questions about women's learning and their experiences attending an all-women's university. Instructors, meanwhile, reflected on the course week by week, identifying any pedagogies or logistical decisions that may require future adjustment. Any acutely problematic elements with the course were addressed between the fall and winter terms. During the summer months, more extensive reflection took place so that course planning for the next year could commence. We would review the course learning outcomes, determine whether the course theme or pedagogies needed adjusting, and analyze available survey and focus group data. New rounds of professional development and training were arranged for the later parts of the summer, particularly as new course instructors and other staff members came and went.

The Feminist First-Year Seminar

By using a feminist approach, the final version of our first-year seminar centred on supporting students' personal growth and fostering their commitment to social justice. Information literacy was still an important component, but it took on a critical approach as students explored the realities of change making. Knowing that students are more engaged when they feel personally connected to their learning, a loose course theme was chosen to allow for flexibility and student input;[19] the revised pilot's theme, for example, was "Living in a Fractured World." Course content was firm during the first three weeks while students settled into university: we introduced students to the Brescia Competencies, provided a history of Brescia and the Ursuline philosophy of education, and asked them to complete community and team-building exercises and self-exploration activities. At the same time, students suggested different social justice fractures to explore for the rest of the course, such as the climate crisis, racial discrimination, food insecurity, or gender equality. Each fracture, though, would inevitably take an interdisciplinary approach,[20] with students encouraged to link class discussions to previous readings, discussions, their self-reflections, and lived experience.

The next seven weeks of class explored the fractures themselves, selected by course instructors from student suggestions. Through seminar discussions, students explored how change happens in each fracture, who holds power and who does not, and the role of academic research and researchers within those structures. We were able to anticipate many of these fractures in advance, so instructors were not left scrambling to create content at the last minute; if needed, the course design team was ready to step in with ideas and lesson plans during our weekly meetings. Since the theme of the course naturally questioned authority and expertise, course content and readings went beyond academic sources to include TED Talk and YouTube videos, government policy, not-for-profit white papers, and poetry. Guest lectures and community mentors, including alumnae and Ursuline representatives, were invited to share their expertise, and we hope that senior peer students can lead discussions in future terms.

Throughout weeks 4 through 11, students worked on scaffolded team projects. After receiving training in teamwork, communication, and group accountability in weeks 1 through 3, students worked together to identify where they, as a group, could address the fracture given their new identities as university students. Groups were encouraged to incorporate academic and other forms of knowledge into their reasoning. At the end of the course, teams presented their recommended approach for the fracture to the rest of their first-year cohort, with a prize going to the top presentation as selected by their peers.

Flexibility and choice are key elements of feminist pedagogy, so Brescia's first-year seminar is a pass/fail course with no grades assigned unless requested. This caused anxiety for some students, but as the course went on most were able to relax into the freedom and creativity this approach provided. The team projects were scaffolded throughout the term, with small elements due periodically, and 'due-by' dates assigned to allow groups to work ahead should they desire. Students were provided with rubrics to understand what constituted a pass, but if they did not pass an assignment, they were also given feedback from instructors and encouraged to resubmit. To allow for individual assessment opportunities, students completed journaling exercises throughout the term. These reflections connected course readings and discussions to students' lived experiences or personal values, or they asked students to practice finding and using academic research relevant to that week's fracture.

Analysis
The Feminist Institution

As mentioned above, Brescia's first-year seminar is a unique case study in feminist pedagogy, given our scale in application. The design team certainly experienced growing pains when expanding the pilot into a mandatory course for all incoming students.

From my perspective as course coordinator, using a large course design team requires an incredible amount of trust, communication, emotional regulation, and organization; last-minute changes or pivots made pedagogical sense but could be stressful with so many moving parts. The power structures in the university didn't disappear overnight either, so while feminist pedagogy aims to address and reduce oppressive power structures, there were still tensions to be navigated. For example, the course instructors of the full-scale version also served as dean and associate dean—and were therefore the direct supervisors for most of us on the design team. Since these instructors were responsible for final decisions on course content and assessments, it took conscious effort from each team member to learn when and how to voice opinions. I also observed that using a feminist course design does not equate to feminist teaching philosophies: with all members of the team relatively new to using this approach, weekly meetings demonstrated how we each identified with feminism pedagogy differently, and therefore approached course design differently, as well.

Lessons in humility were an inevitable result of this project. The flip side of working collaboratively, of course, is that no one person is most right, more important, or gets what they want. For example, the librarians involved (including me) were forced to re-examine our relationship with information literacy: instituting a mandatory, information-literacy-based course felt like a huge victory, but students in the pilot struggled to identify with the social-justice elements of information literacy and to see how their newfound skills applied to different assignments or other contexts. Expanding our definition of information literacy was a key first step to addressing this dissonance: if information literacy really is about teaching students to become lifelong learners,[21] feminist writers tell us that course planning must be holistic, interdisciplinary, and collaborative.[22] I needed to be humble: the information literacy components of the course were not more important than the broader goals, despite my long history in actualizing the course. Information literacy is a discipline rooted in Eurocentrism, after all, so focusing our information literacy teaching on "academic skills development" simply did not fit our feminist design.[23] In Brescia's context, taking a feminist approach meant elevating students' lived experience as authorities and knowledgeable experts to an equal place to academic research.[24] The focal point of information literacy instruction shifted accordingly, from the mechanics of searching to introducing—and sometimes critiquing—the place of academic research in a global society. Students were still taught about databases and keywords, but within much broader discussions of authority, expertise, and social justice.

Student Experience

As much as the curriculum team was an essential component of Brescia's feminist approach, we needed to understand the impacts of our redesign on students. I studied two cohorts of Brescia's first-year seminar: (1) the revised pilot delivered in winter, 2019, and (2) the full rollout of the course to all incoming first-year students in the 2019–20 academic year. The study used a mixed-methods approach, including coding and analysis of student reflection and journaling assignments, student interviews and focus groups, and a student survey. Like most things in 2020, though, data collection was disrupted by the COVID-19 pandemic. We had to pivot to put the course online after only one term and then redesigned it again for the 2020–21 academic year.

Analysis and coding of student assignments from this initial data indicated that most participants (83%) in the 2019 pilot articulated an increased personal commitment to making social change. All (100%) pilot study participants demonstrated the three Ursuline learning outcomes in their assignments by the end of the course, as well. Pilot study participants articulated these outcomes in interviews with me, attributing their success directly to the feminist pedagogies used in the course:

> I found the fact I got to choose what we talked about as a class …was a big thing for me, compared to my other classes. Which made me be motivated to go to class, since even if a topic wasn't something I chose, I knew it was important to someone else in the class.

> I think that's very important to feel connected. To feel you're a part of something…. I was a little worried about being a very mature student with kids the same age as first-year students, but nobody is bothered.

> I have learned a lot about myself…. I thought talking about sensitive topics I did not have any background knowledge on would be challenging for me. I actually really enjoyed looking at these issues because it helped me understand what others are experiencing and I believe I became more empathetic.

Focus-group participants from the 2019–20 cohort described discussion sections as "safe spaces" that helped to "open up our way of thinking into other people's ways." The meaningful topics discussed in class resonated with students, as they had during the 2019 pilot, with 2020 focus-group participants reporting that it is "important to discuss controversial topics with no 'right' answer in class" and to "feel a personal connection with what we're learning."

Negative feedback on the course was largely related to scheduling and technical hiccups, as well as resistance to the pass/fail model. When we first offered the course to every incoming student in 2019–20, we used a brand-new building that experienced technical glitches during the first three weeks of class; some students' course registration was disrupted by a separate error. Given the importance of grounding students during those first three weeks, as described above, it was easy to see how some students felt disconnected from the course.

Even though a significant portion of the course focused on information literacy, and students demonstrated information literacy learning in nearly all of their course assignments, very few study participants mentioned or acknowledged the library's role in the course. Nearly all participants from both cohorts improved their ability to identify and locate a peer-reviewed, academic source and then integrate it into their reflective writing and team projects: of a total sample size of 61, only one student did not pass this element of the course. Yet only two focus-group participants (and zero survey respondents) mentioned the library at all: one named the librarian in-class workshops as helpful, while another, a returning student, found library presentations repetitive from her previous degree.

Discussion and Conclusion

There is a lot of value in Brescia's first-year seminar, particularly from an information literacy perspective. Reflecting on our team-based approach has me questioning who information literacy learners are, or who librarians actually teach. On the surface, it looked as if we followed the traditional one-shot information literacy approach in this course, as my librarian colleague conducted two in-class sessions as a guest lecturer. Few students identified the role librarians played in course learning. But behind the scenes, our librarian trained course instructors on library search techniques, counselled them on bottlenecks that students commonly experience during information literacy learning,[25] designed lesson plans, and gave feedback on assignment design. Knowing how important it is to build a learning cohort between the students and their instructors, oftentimes librarians were *not* the ones teaching information literacy concepts; instructors and seminar leaders did, instead. Just as much information literacy teaching happened during our weekly team meetings, I would argue, as during the two in-class lessons. Sara Crawley, Jennifer Lewis, and Maralee Mayberry explain that using a feminist approach means understanding how we fit into the system and asking how our choices enable others to understand their own places and power.[26] Committing to a feminist, lifelong-learning approach for Brescia's information literacy program meant incorporating feminist values into all aspects of our teaching. If the teaching and learning was happening, if students were acquiring new information literacy knowledge, did it matter who delivered the lessons? We needed to *become* feminist pedagogues, personally, to successfully deliver this feminist course.

That said, it is not clear whether everyone involved with the course similarly adopted a feminist teaching philosophy: it would be valuable to formally investigate instructors' experience in teaching a collaborative, team-based course like this. Similarly, our course demonstrates that feminist curriculum design does not automatically result in intersectional teaching, despite good intentions: the course will continue to evolve as Brescia explores decolonizing and Indigenizing its curriculum and pedagogy. The year 2020 made it clear we need to better understand the impacts of a feminist approach on marginalized populations beyond women;[27] racialized students opted out of my studies more often than not, which needs immediate and careful attention.

For now, it seems that study participants responded positively to the increased flexibility and choice available to them in our feminist redesign. I remain hopeful that holistic, inclusive, and intersectional teaching is possible even in scaled-up and strategic initiatives like common first-year courses. But we need more student voices to know for certain. Fortunately, we planned for students-as-partners work in our original course design and Brescia will have second-year students serving as peer mentors (and curriculum consultants) in future cohorts. Through their contributions, I hope we can better understand the impact of our feminist first-year seminar on students' confidence and ability to effect real, systemic change.

Acknowledgements

Many loving hands went into creating this course. In this space, I want to acknowledge my library colleagues' contributions—this course was a long time in the making, with a community of powerful librarian voices involved behind the scenes. Thank you especially to Jennifer Foley, Caroline Whippey, Adrienne Co-Dyre, and Colleen Sharen (our honourary librarian), for your ideas, commitment, honesty, and friendship.

Appendix

Table 9.A.1. Course Development Team

Member	Department	Responsibilities
Course instructors	Faculty (2)	• Course content, pedagogy and instruction, LMS maintenance • Student feedback and assessment • Train-the-trainer area: course theme, readings, final lesson plans for each week
Seminar leaders	Faculty (2)	• Seminar facilitation • Train-the-trainer area: student seminar discussions and feedback
Educational developer (chapter author)	Teaching and Learning Centre	• Course assessment, creation of course LMS • Coordination of weekly team meetings • Train-the-trainer area: feminist pedagogy, degree-level outcomes, first-year seminar "practices"
Learning and curriculum support librarian	Library	• Information literacy lesson plans and delivery • Train-the-trainer area: information literacy teaching and assessment
Manager of experiential learning	Student Affairs	• Coordination of community partners (e.g., guest lectures; mentorship opportunities)
All		• Course reading, activity, and assessment suggestions

Table 9.A.2. Additional Campus Consultants

Member	Department	Responsibilities
International student coordinator	Registrar's Office	Train-the-trainer area: cultural competence; needs of international students
Student experience coordinator	Student Affairs	Train-the-trainer area: student transition and needs of first-year students
Director of campus ministry	Campus Ministry	Train-the-trainer area: Ursuline philosophy of education; history of Brescia

Table 9.A.2. Additional Campus Consultants

Member	Department	Responsibilities
Academic advisors	Registrar's Office	Support for students identified as "at risk"
Course registrants	First-Year Students	Identification of course topics or subthemes (aspect of feminist course design)
Senior peer leaders	Second-Year Students*	*Planned for future cohorts only:* Peer mentors, curriculum advisors

Notes

1. Brescia University College, "Who We Are," accessed May 7, 2021, https://brescia.uwo.ca/about/who_we_are/index.php.
2. Western University, "Facts and Figures 2019–2020," accessed June 14, 2021, https://www.uwo.ca/about/whoweare/facts.html (information for 2019–2020 removed from web page).
3. Heather Campbell, "Millennials Project: Final Results" (master's thesis, University of Western Ontario, 2010), 5.
4. Campbell, "Millennials Project," 74.
5. Brescia University College, "Competency Based Learning," accessed June 14, 2021, https://brescia.uwo.ca/about/competency_based_learning/index.php.
6. Marie de St. Jean Martin, *Ursuline Method of Education* (Rahway, NJ: Quinn and Boden, 1946).
7. George D. Kuh, *High-Impact Educational Practices* (Washington, DC: AAC&U Publishing, 2008); Jennifer R. Keup et al., *The First-Year Seminar* (Columbia: National Resource Center, First-Year Experience and Students in Transition, University of South Carolina, 2011).
8. Dallin George Young, *2012–2013 National Survey of First-Year Seminars*, Research Reports on College Transitions, No. 4 (Columbia: National Resource Center, First-Year Experience and Student in Transition, University of South Carolina, 2014); Keup et al., *First-Year Seminar*.
9. Heather Campbell and Stephanie Horsley, "Brescia ONE Recommendations," report in the author's possession, 2015.
10. Paolo Freire, *Pedagogy of the Oppressed*, trans. Myra Bergman Ramos (New York: Bloomsbury, 1970); bell hooks, *Feminist Theory* (New York: Routledge, 2015).
11. bell hooks, *Teaching to Transgress* (New York: Routledge, 1994); Maralee Mayberry and Ellen Cronan Rose, eds. *Meeting the Challenge* (New York: Routledge, 1999).
12. Catherine Hurt Middlecamp, "What Is Feminist Pedagogy? Useful Ideas for Teaching Chemistry," *Journal of Chemical Education* 76, no. 4 (1999): 520.
13. Danielle M. Currier, "Feminist Pedagogy," in *Companion to Feminist Studies*, ed. Nancy A. Naples (New York: Wiley, 2021): 345–51.
14. Sara. L. Crawley, Jennifer E. Lewis, and Maralee Mayberry, "Introduction—Feminist Pedagogies in Action: Teaching beyond Disciplines," *Feminist Teacher* 19, no. 1 (2008): 5.
15. *Ursuline Education: Handing on the Torch/Passer Le Flambeau*, accessed June 14, 2021, 11, https://www.osu.pl/uploadfiles/materialy/ursuline_education_1.pdf.
16. *Ursuline Education*, 11.
17. Carolyn M Shrewsbury, "What Is Feminist Pedagogy?" *Women's Studies Quarterly* 15, no. 1/2 (1997): 16.
18. Lauren Chism Schmidt, Janine Graziano, and National Resource Center for the First-Year Experience and Students in Transition, *Building Synergy for High-Impact Educational Initiative*

(Columbia: National Resource Center, First-Year Experience & Students in Transition, University of South Carolina, 2016).

19. Keonya Booker, "Connection and Commitment: How Sense of Belonging and Classroom Community Influence Degree Persistence for African American Undergraduate Women," *International Journal of Teaching and Learning in Higher Education* 28, no. 2 (2016): 224; Crawley, Lewis and Mayberry, "Introduction," 5.

20. Kimberlé Crenshaw, "Mapping the Margins: Intersectionality, Identity Politics, and Violence against Women of Color," *Stanford Law Review* 43, no. 6 (1991 1990): 1244.

21. Eamon Tewell, "A Decade of Critical Information Literacy: A Review of the Literature," *Communications in Information Literacy* 9, no. 1 (2015): 29, http://pdxscholar.library.pdx.edu/comminfolit/vol9/iss1/2.

22. hooks, *Teaching to Transgress*, 13–22; Maralee Mayberry, "Reproductive and Resistant Pedagogies: The Comparative Roles of Collaborative Learning and Feminist Pedagogy in Science Education," in *Meeting the Challenge: Innovative Feminist Pedagogies in Action*, ed. Maralee Mayberry and Ellen Cronan Rose (New York: Routledge, 1999), 9.

23. Todd Honma, "Trippin' over the Color Line: The Invisibility of Race in Library and Information Science," *InterActions: UCLA Journal of Education and Information Studies* 1, no. 2 (2005): 16, https://doi.org/10.5070/D412000540.

24. Brenda Leibowitz, "Cognitive Justice and the Higher Education Curriculum," *Journal of Education*, no. 68 (2017): 100, http://joe.ukzn.ac.za/index.php/joe/issue/view/22.

25. Joan Middendorf and Andrea Bear, "Bottlenecks of Information Literacy," in *Building Teaching and Learning Communities: Creating Shared Meaning and Purpose*, ed. Craig Gibson and Sharon Mader (Chicago: Association of College and Research Libraries): 53.

26. Crawley, Lewis and Mayberry, "Introduction," 3.

27. King's and Brescia Joint Presidents' Anti-Racism Working Group, *"They Think You Are Exaggerating"* (London, ON: Brescia University College and King's University College, November 2021), https://brescia.uwo.ca/president/docs/kbarwg_campus_racial_climate.pdf.

Bibliography

Booker, Keonya. "Connection and Commitment: How Sense of Belonging and Classroom Community Influence Degree Persistence for African American Undergraduate Women." *International Journal of Teaching and Learning in Higher Education* 28, no. 2 (2016): 218–29.

Brescia University College. "Competency Based Learning." Accessed June 14, 2021. https://brescia.uwo.ca/about/competency_based_learning/index.php.

———. "Who We Are." Accessed May 7, 2021. https://brescia.uwo.ca/about/who_we_are/index.php.

Campbell, Heather. "Millennials Project: Final Results." Master's thesis, University of Western Ontario, 2010.

Crawley, Sara. L., Jennifer E. Lewis, and Maralee Mayberry. "Introduction—Feminist Pedagogies in Action: Teaching beyond Disciplines." *Feminist Teacher* 19, no. 1 (2008): 1–12.

Crenshaw, Kimberlé. "Mapping the Margins: Intersectionality, Identity Politics, and Violence against Women of Color." *Stanford Law Review* 43, no. 6 (1991 1990): 1241–1300.

Currier, Danielle M. "Feminist Pedagogy." In *Companion to Feminist Studies*, edited by Nancy A. Naples, 345–51. New York: Wiley, 2021.

Freire, Paolo. *Pedagogy of the Oppressed*. Translated by Myra Bergman Ramos. New York: Bloomsbury, 1970.

Honma, Todd. "Trippin' over the Color Line: The Invisibility of Race in Library and Information Science." *InterActions: UCLA Journal of Education and Information Studies* 1, no. 2 (2005). https://doi.org/10.5070/D412000540.

hooks, bell. *Feminist Theory: From Margins to Center*. New York: Routledge, 2015.

———. *Teaching to Transgress: Education as the Practice of Freedom*. New York: Routledge, 1994.

Keup, Jennifer R., Mary Stuart Hunter, James E. Groccia, Brad Garner, Jennifer A. Latino, Michelle Ashcraft, Dan Friedman, Joni Webb Petschauer, and National Resource Center for the First-Year Experience and Students in Transition. *The First-Year Seminar: Designing, Implementing, and Assessing Courses to Support Student Learning and Success*. Columbia: National Resource Center, First-Year Experience and Students in Transition, University of South Carolina, 2011.

King's and Brescia Joint Presidents' Anti-racism Working Group. *"They Think You Are Exaggerating": A Report on Campus Racial Climate at King's and Brescia*. London, ON: Brescia University College and King's University College, November 2021. https://brescia.uwo.ca/president/docs/kbarwg_campus_racial_climate.pdf.

Kuh, George D. *High-Impact Educational Practices: What Are They, Who Has Access to Them, and Why They Matter*. Washington, DC: AAC&U Publishing, 2008.

Leibowitz, Brenda. "Cognitive Justice and the Higher Education Curriculum." *Journal of Education*, no. 68 (2017): 93–111. https://journals.ukzn.ac.za/index.php/joe/issue/view/22.

Martin, Marie de St. Jean. *Ursuline Method of Education*. Rahway, NJ: Quinn and Boden, 1946.

Mayberry, Maralee. "Reproductive and Resistant Pedagogies: The Comparative Roles of Collaborative Learning and Feminist Pedagogy in Science Education." In *Meeting the Challenge: Innovative Feminist Pedagogies in Action*, edited by Maralee Mayberry and Ellen Cronan Rose, 1–22. New York: Routledge, 1999.

Mayberry, Maralee, and Ellen Cronan Rose, eds. *Meeting the Challenge: Innovative Feminist Pedagogies in Action*. New York: Routledge, 1999.

Middendorf, Joan, and Andrea Bear. "Bottlenecks of Information Literacy." In *Building Teaching and Learning Communities: Creating Shared Meaning and Purpose*, edited by Craig Gibson and Sharon Mader, 51–68. Chicago: Association of College and Research Libraries, 2019.

Middlecamp, Catherine Hurt. "What Is Feminist Pedagogy? Useful Ideas for Teaching Chemistry." *Journal of Chemical Education* 76, no. 4 (1999): 520–25.

Schmidt, Lauren Chism, Janine Graziano, and National Resource Center for the First-Year Experience and Students in Transition. *Building Synergy for High-Impact Educational Initiatives: First-Year Seminars and Learning Communities*. Columbia: National Resource Center, First-Year Experience and Students in Transition, University of South Carolina, 2016.

Shrewsbury, Carolyn M. "What Is Feminist Pedagogy?" *Women's Studies Quarterly* 15, no. 1/2 (1997): 8–16.

Tewell, Eamon. "A Decade of Critical Information Literacy: A Review of the Literature." *Communications in Information Literacy* 9, no. 1 (2015): 24–43. https://pdxscholar.library.pdx.edu/comminfolit/vol9/iss1/2.

Ursuline Education: Handing on the Torch/Passer Le Flambeau. Accessed June 14, 2021. https://www.osu.pl/uploadfiles/materialy/ursuline_education_1.pdf.

Western University. "Facts and Figures 2019–2020." Accessed June 14, 2021. https://www.uwo.ca/about/whoweare/facts.html (information for 2019–2020 removed from web page).

Young, Dallin George. *2012–2013 National Survey of First-Year Seminars: Exploring High-Impact Practices in the First College Year*. Research Reports on College Transitions, No. 4. Columbia: National Resource Center, First-Year Experience and Students in Transition, University of South Carolina, 2014.

CHAPTER 10

Better Learning through Legal Research

Increasing Law Students' Cultural Competency and Awareness of Diversity, Equity, Inclusion, and Accessibility Using Legal Research Instruction

Clanitra Stewart Nejdl

As future attorneys, law students must acquire the skills to effectively interview, advise, and represent clients from diverse races, ethnicities, cultures, and backgrounds, all of whom also have diverse experiences and expectations.[1] As the practice of law becomes more global, effective and ethical representation of a client in a legal issue will hinge on effective communication as well as understanding cultural norms and differences that affect the choices a client makes.[2] Attorneys must be able to recognize how the laws, procedures, and other circumstances associated with a legal issue may be biased or otherwise unfair to their clients given those clients' backgrounds or experiences.[3] Only through training in cultural competence and only with a strong understanding of how issues related to diversity, equity, inclusion, and accessibility (DEIA) can affect their clients' experiences (and the outcomes of their

legal matters) can attorneys be expected to successfully handle their responsibilities in these matters. This chapter explores how legal research instruction can contribute toward the transformation of law students into capable attorneys who are culturally competent and who understand how DEIA affects their clients' legal matters.

Legal Research as Part of Legal Education

Legal research instruction is just one area of legal education through which law students are trained to become attorneys. However, it is usually the area of legal education in which academic law librarians are most closely involved. Academic law librarians, who typically hold both a master's degree in library science and a law degree (i.e., a Juris Doctor degree), play a very distinct role within a law school by serving the research needs of law students and law faculty. Academic law librarians may also instruct law students in the core skill of legal research. This instruction could occur in either a formal or an informal manner.

Formal legal research instruction can consist of teaching classes that are part of the law school curriculum. These may be stand-alone classes or combined classes in which the students also learn the separate, but related skill of legal writing. Formal legal research instruction, which includes legal research classes for first-year law students and advanced or specialized research classes for second-year or third-year law students, may last for just a few sessions or for one or more semesters. Informal research instruction, on the other hand, may consist of periodic research workshops, research talks in doctrinal law classes, or single research instruction sessions. Notably, legal research instruction is included as part of the American Bar Association's *Standards and Rules of Procedure for Approval of Law Schools* ("ABA *Standards and Rules*"). The American Bar Association (ABA), the accrediting body for US law schools,[4] specifically includes legal research as a skill in which law students must be competent.[5] Regardless of the extent of the legal research instruction they provide, however, academic law librarians have the unique opportunity to use their instruction time with law students to not only teach them the key principles of and effective methods for legal research, but also to help them develop their skills related to cultural competency and DEIA awareness.[*]

---

[*] It is important to note that legal research instruction should not be the sole area of the law school curriculum in which such training occurs. Ideally, all classes in the law school curriculum would be designed to contribute toward teaching students to be culturally competent and to recognize DEIA issues relevant to their clients' legal matters.

Cultural Competence and DEIA Awareness for Law Students

Cultural competence has been referred to in scholarship by a variety of terms, including *cross-cultural awareness*, *cultural intelligence*, and *intercultural communications*.[6] Definitions of cultural competence vary depending on the discipline involved,[†] but in general the concept involves the "awareness of differences based on one's race/ethnicity, religion, sexual orientation, socioeconomic class, etc."[7] It is "a set of academic and personal skills that allow [individuals] to increase [their] understanding and appreciation of cultural differences between groups."[8] In terms of the attorney-client relationship, it more specifically means "having the capacity to provide effective legal assistance that is grounded in an awareness of and sensitivity to the diverse culture[s]"[9] and requires "the provision of services that are appropriate and accessible to a diverse range of clients, as well as work that addresses issues of equality and access to justice."[10] At its essence, cultural competency for attorneys is "driven [...] by *client preferred choices*, not by culturally blind or culturally-free interventions,"[11] as well as "the implementation of a trust-promoting method of inquiry, advice, and counsel."[12]

DEIA is related to cultural competence in multiple ways, but one of the ways most important to the attorney-client relationship relates to appropriate training in cultural competence during law school. Such training helps attorneys to be better prepared to represent diverse clients and to recognize when those clients' legal matters stem from or are affected by issues related to equity and inclusion (or a lack thereof). At a bare minimum, an attorney should be able to identify when a client's race, ethnicity, religion, sexual orientation, or other characteristic may be the cause of or related to the client's legal issue. For example, to properly represent a client in an employment discrimination claim, an attorney must be able to recognize the factors at the heart of the discrimination, which would inherently require the attorney to be aware of and to be able to identify the aspects of the case related to DEIA.

Although the ABA has not yet explicitly included a requirement in the ABA *Standards and Rules* that law schools teach law students to be culturally competent, the

---

† One of the earliest and most prominent definitions of cultural competence was proposed in the health-care field in 1989 by Terry L. Cross, Barbara J. Bazron, Karl W. Dennis, and Mareasa R. Isaacs from the Georgetown University Child Development Center. Their definition includes five crucial elements for cultural competence: valuing diversity, having the capacity for cultural self-assessment, being conscious of the dynamics inherent when cultures interact, having institutionalized cultural knowledge, and having developed adaptations to diversity (Terry L. Cross et al., *Toward a Culturally Competent System of Care: A Monograph on Effective Services for Minority Children Who Are Severely Emotionally Disturbed* [Washington, DC: CASSP Technical Assistance Center, Georgetown University Child Development Center, 1989], 28).

Council of the Section of Legal Education and Admissions to the Bar recently made a final recommendation that the ABA *Standards and Rules* be amended to require law schools to provide "education to law students on bias, cross-cultural competency, and racism" both at the beginning of law school and again before graduation from law school.[13] This recommendation will soon be considered by the ABA House of Delegates.[14] Currently, however, cultural competency is still a professional skill recognized by the ABA.[15] It is clear, then, that cultural competence is a professional skill envisioned as a potential part of the law school curriculum and one which a law school is free to emphasize, even absent express requirements.[16]

Even beyond the ABA *Standards and Rules*, there is strong indication that cultural competency and an awareness of DEIA issues is needed by attorneys. The ABA Model Rules of Professional Conduct (Model Rules)[*][17] guide attorneys on many of the professional responsibilities that they must meet and how they must conduct themselves as attorneys.[18] The Model Rules address conduct such as competence, diligence, and advising clients,[19] all of which are affected by an attorney's cultural competence and awareness of DEIA issues.[20] For example, Rule 2.1 of the Model Rules states that "[i]n rendering advice, a lawyer may refer not only to law but to other considerations such as moral, economic, social and political factors, that may be relevant to the client's situation."[21] It would be quite difficult, if not impossible, for an attorney who is not culturally competent or able to recognize the presence of DEIA issues to fully and effectively evaluate the moral, economic, social, or political factors that may be relevant to a client's situation when that client differs from the attorney in ways such as religion, gender, sexual orientation, race, ethnicity, or socioeconomic status.[22]

Pairing Legal Research Instruction with Cultural Competence and DEIA Awareness

As academic law librarians, we can play our part in teaching law students to be culturally competent and aware of DEIA concerns that may affect their clients by incorporating issues related to cultural competence and DEIA into our legal research instruction. There are many arguments to be made in favor of legal research

---

* Each jurisdiction has its own Rules of Professional Conduct for attorneys licensed in that jurisdiction, but the ABA Model Rules of Professional Conduct provide an example of the language that may be included in such rules.

instruction that promotes cultural competence and DEIA awareness. To some extent, these arguments can generally be traced back to scholarship that emphasizes the importance of using the general law school curriculum to teach law students to be culturally competent attorneys and of incorporating DEIA issues into the curriculum.[23] This line of scholarship has focused primarily on incorporating these issues into doctrinal law classes, including Torts, Corporate Law, and Contracts; into legal clinics in law schools; and into legal writing classes.[24] Legal research instruction, however limited in duration it may be, is no less suited for such an endeavor than other law school classes. In fact, in many ways, the legal research classroom is better suited for such an endeavor than many other law school classes.

The legal research classroom "presents the perfect opportunity to introduce students to concepts of diversity contextualized with the framework of learning how to be a lawyer."[25] Unlike doctrinal law school classes in the US, which traditionally emphasize the Socratic method of teaching,[26] the experiential nature of legal research instruction provides students with the opportunity to practice and learn the skills needed by a culturally competent lawyer in an interactive setting.[†] Additionally, unlike in doctrinal classes, legal research instruction provides for more direct interaction with the instructor on a regular basis as well as substantial feedback to the students at multiple points during the instruction. Legal research instruction also requires students to identify actual laws and legal resources that are applicable in various jurisdictions, to analyze those laws and resources, and to determine whether they are applicable in a specific situation. Although legal research instruction does not involve interviewing actual clients with legal matters, the use of detailed research exercises involving hypothetical clients facing realistic legal problems provides students with the opportunity to learn how to research and analyze legal matters like those their future clients may have.[27] Because conducting legal research is one of the earliest steps in the process of representing a client (occurring before drafting legal memos or briefs and long before accompanying a client to court), it makes sense to begin to consider if there are any relevant DEIA issues at this early stage in the process. Indeed, one of the first questions an attorney might ask herself after meeting with a potential new client to discuss a legal issue is "What law is applicable in this matter?" Finally, because law students conduct legal research on a variety of substantive law issues, legal research instruction provides a

---

† Johanna K. P. Dennis notes that "though the Socratic Method in legal education calls for a discussion between the professor and the student, this falls short of an authentic assessment or the intended purpose of an assessment in a multicultural education. While the Socratic Method certainly permits the teacher the ability to determine whether a student knows the concepts and is essentially asking the students the same questions as would be on a pop quiz or a test, the missing step is the authentic assessment, such as an analytic paper, research exercise, or other presentation, which calls for the students to manipulate the knowledge in a critical way beyond a spontaneous response to a hypothetical [emphasis added]." (Johanna K. P. Dennis, "Ensuring a Multicultural Educational Experience in Legal Education: Start with the Legal Writing Classroom," *Texas Wesleyan Law Review* 16, no. 4 [2010]: 623.)

wide choice of topics through which to promote cultural competency and awareness of DEIA issues, as opposed to a doctrinal class, which typically focuses on just one substantive area of law.

Key Considerations for Planning Your Instruction

In my experience as an academic law librarian who provides formal legal research instruction to first-year law students and formal advanced legal research instruction to second-year and third-year law students, it is more common that academic law librarians teach only a few class sessions with their first-year students (either as part of legal writing or separately) as opposed to a full semester of class time or more. Designing effective legal research instruction that lasts just a few sessions requires extremely careful consideration of the desired objectives and outcomes as well as acknowledgement that only a limited amount of information can be conveyed in such a short time. However, this should not dissuade anyone from also designing legal research instruction that promotes cultural competence and DEIA awareness. To be sure, the most critical learning outcomes for legal research instruction are those that create future attorneys who are proficient legal researchers. However, there is no reason that cultural competence and DEIA awareness cannot be additional objectives. With careful planning, all of these goals can be achieved as part of legal research instruction.

There are a few key considerations when determining how to ensure that your legal research instruction is effective and also promotes cultural competency and DEIA awareness.

1. Determine the extent to which you will integrate cultural competency and DEIA awareness into your legal research instruction
    Including cultural competency training and DEIA awareness as part of legal research instruction will require planning. Because there are multiple training models that have been used to successfully teach law students to be culturally competent,[28] it is worth taking the time to review these models to determine which might be best suited for your legal research instruction. For example, Susan Bryant and Jean Koh Peters's well-known chapter "Five Habits for Cross-Cultural Lawyering" is frequently referred to in considering how to teach law students to be culturally competent through promoting self-awareness and introspection.[29] The "Five Habits" require lawyers to "identify the similarities and differences between themselves and their clients,"[30] examine the potential "effects of the similarities and differences that exist between the client, the legal decisionmaker, and

the lawyer,"[31] "explore alternative explanations for clients' behaviors by thinking of multiple interpretations or 'parallel universes,'"[32] exercise effective "cross-cultural communication" as part of "the process of lawyer-client communication,"[33] and engage in "self-reflection" and consideration of their own cultural biases.[34] Other models of cultural competency and DEIA awareness training include those that focus on anti-racism and diversity-based issues,[35] on the "culture and demographics of specific ethno-cultural groups,"[36] and on "equality-based cultural competence."[37] An examination of each of these models will help you consider which are best suited for the nature, extent, and content of the legal research instruction you have planned.

2. Create session guidelines or a course syllabus.

    Regardless of the length of instruction, providing the students with session guidelines, or a full syllabus for legal research instruction that will last for multiple sessions or more, will help the students to understand more fully what the objectives and outcomes of the instruction sessions will be. This also means including in the guidelines or syllabus objectives or outcomes that explicitly reference cultural competence and DEIA awareness as key aspects of the instruction along with the more typical learning outcomes and objectives related to becoming a proficient legal researcher. Further, it is worth considering the inclusion of a diversity statement that "communicate[s] your commitment to an inclusive, supportive learning environment."[38] It is also appropriate to include an explanation of the rules and expectations related to class discussion, especially discussion related to sensitive issues.[39] Transparency regarding all of these aspects of instruction will help the students better understand how cultural competency and DEIA awareness improve their legal education and how they tie into legal research.[40]

3. "Diversify" your legal research exercises and assignments.

    Anyone who has drafted exercises and assignments for research instruction knows it can be a time-consuming process. For academic law librarians, writing salient law-related hypotheticals and tying them to the most appropriate legal research tasks to create a realistic legal research experience for a law student takes a tremendous amount of thought and effort to do well. While undergoing the process of drafting exercises and assignments that will best help students to learn how to conduct legal research, however, it is worth drafting with an eye toward the additional goals of promoting cultural competency and DEIA awareness. Approaching the drafting process with these goals in mind can significantly help with the drafting process, as many causes of action that might be used in a legal research exercise are tied to DEIA awareness.

Some tips for creating legal research exercises and assignments that promote cultural competency and DEIA awareness are as follows:

- As a starting point, draft exercises and assignments that reflect the real-life diversity in everyday individuals. For example, use names for individuals in your materials that show ethnic or cultural diversity, as well as that are gender-neutral to help students identify their potential biases.[41] Also practice gender pronoun awareness when drafting your exercises and assignments.[42]
- Include "diverse contexts"[43] in your legal research hypotheticals to accurately reflect the many ways in which issues related to DEIA can manifest themselves in legal disputes. Examples of diverse contexts in law-related hypotheticals have included a contractual dispute related to quinceañera dresses;[44] employment discrimination disputes related to race, gender, religion, or sexual orientation;[45] disputes related to Native American tribal communities;[46] immigration disputes where language barriers are involved;[47] and court cases stemming from police shootings.[48]
- Consider the variety of legal research activities that could promote DEIA awareness and help law students become more culturally competent. For example, an exercise on court docket research can be designed to require an analysis of court documents in a specific case in which DEIA issues are prominent.[49] Similarly, an exercise on identifying search terms to find relevant cases on a legal issue might include a discussion of the evolution of the specific search terms used to refer to diverse populations, including terms used to refer to Native Americans, African Americans, or other racial minorities, terms used to refer to members of the LGBTQIA community, and terms used to refer to individuals with physical or mental disabilities.[50] Further, an exercise on locating statutes can be drafted so that the students must locate statutes on a DEIA-related topic such as discrimination or sexual harassment, while an exercise on locating regulations can be drafted to require students to locate and analyze regulations about issues like fair housing or immigration.
- Use or modify the facts from real cases* and items from the news involving aspects of DEIA to create the fact patterns for your legal

---

* Two useful resources for locating real-life discrimination cases are the US Equal Employment Opportunity Commission's E-RACE Initiative website (https://www.eeoc.gov/initiatives/e-race/e-race-initiativeeradicating-racism-and-colorism-employment), which includes "Significant EEOC Race/Color Cases Covering Private and Federal Sectors," and the US Department of Justice Civil Rights Division's Cases and Matters Search (https://www.justice.gov/crt/search-cases-and-matters), which includes cases about employment litigation, immigrant rights, voting, and other relevant topics.

research hypotheticals.[51] Students often respond positively to learning that the research exercises and assignments they must complete are tied to real-life problems. You might even create an exercise in which the students try to locate the actual case on which your legal research hypothetical was based, which would require students to use the case-finding tools they have learned about in class.

4. Class discussion.

It is critical to be prepared for the discussions that might arise in a legal research instruction session or class when cultural competency and DEIA awareness are incorporated.[52] It is also necessary to prepare your students for these discussions,[53] including acknowledging that you do not have all of the answers on DEIA-related topics.[54] In addition to including your expectations in the session guidelines or syllabus as noted above, this should also be reiterated in person. Doing so both in writing and verbally allows you to clearly "define the parameters of the class discussion by limiting the topic under discussion and encouraging students to express their views in a professional manner [...]."[55] Given the relatively limited context in which these issues will be discussed (i.e., in the context of a legal research exercise or assignment), the session or class need not be dominated by DEIA-related discussions, and incivility in discussing these issues may be less likely.† However, making room for discussing the DEIA-related aspects of the legal issue being researched allows students the opportunity to practice critical thinking about the same DEIA-related issues that they will certainly be expected to identify and discuss as attorneys.

5. Feedback from students.

Finally, I recommend including a mechanism for receiving feedback on your session or class from your students. For example, you might provide an online questionnaire for students to anonymously fill out after the session. If you are teaching multiple legal research instruction sessions or a full-semester course, you might ask the students to complete an evaluation (even if one is not required by your institution). This will allow you to determine what went well during the session or class and what did not, especially for the aspects of the class related to cultural competency and DEIA awareness. It will also help you revise your instruction materials for future sessions or classes.[56]

---

† Bonny L. Tavares provides an insightful discussion of dealing with student resistance and classroom incivility in the law school classroom when having cross-cultural conversations. (Bonny L. Tavares, "Changing the Construct: Promoting Cross-Cultural Conversations in the Law School Classroom," *Journal of Legal Education* 67, no. 1 [2017]: 234–41).

Administrative Buy-In

Any attempt to promote cultural competency and DEIA awareness into the legal research curriculum should be preceded by one or more substantial discussions with the administrative stakeholders at your institution. Depending upon your institution, this may include the law library director, the law school's academic affairs office, the law school's student affairs office, and other appropriate administrative stakeholders.[57] Having these discussions can alert you to any concerns specific to your institution that you may not have considered. They can also result in helpful feedback on your legal research instruction materials that increases your odds of success in meeting your class objectives. At institutions in which multiple academic law librarians teach legal research instruction sessions or classes, it may also lead to the opportunity to coordinate with your colleagues so that there is consistency in achieving these objectives across the legal research curriculum.[58]

Conclusion

As legal research instructors, academic law librarians can play a substantial role in ensuring that law students become attorneys who are "equipped with knowledge, skills and attitudes to effectively represent clients whose personal and professional matters will extend beyond local, state and national borders" and who can "communicate with individuals whose cultural background, identity and experience may be radically different from the lawyers' own."[59] To this end, like others who provide legal education, we should incorporate cultural competency and DEIA awareness into our instruction, thereby helping our law students become such attorneys.

Notes

1. Shamika Dalton and Clanitra Stewart Nejdl, "Developing a Culturally Competent Legal Research Curriculum," *AALL Spectrum* 23, no. 4 (2019): 18–21; Mary Lynch, "The Importance of Experiential Learning for Development of Essential Skills in Cross-Cultural and Intercultural Effectiveness," *Journal of Experiential Learning* 1, no. 1 (2014): 129–47.
2. Heidi Frostestad Kuehl, "Resources for Becoming Culturally Competent in a Multijurisdictional Practice: G20 Nations and Associated Legal Traditions," *International Journal of Legal Information* 44, no. 2 (2016): 83–115; Lynch, "Importance of Experiential Learning," 135–38; Serena Patel, "Cultural Competency Training: Preparing Law Students for Practice in Our Multicultural World," *UCLA Law Review Discourse* 62 (2014): 140–56.
3. Irene Oritseweyinmi Joe, "Regulating Implicit Bias in the Federal Criminal Process," *California Law Review* 108, no. 3 (2020): 965–88; Fatma E. Marouf, "Implicit Bias and Immigration Courts," *New England Law Review* 45, no. 2 (2011): 417–48; Anona Su, "A Proposal to Properly Address Implicit Bias in the Jury," *Hastings Women's Law Journal* 31, no. 1 (2020): 79–100.

4.   American Bar Association, "ABA-Approved Law Schools," 2021, https://perma.cc/7APM-5YAR.

5.   American Bar Association, *Standards and Rules of Procedure for Approval of Law Schools 2021–2022* (Chicago: American Bar Association, 2021), https://perma.cc/U7X6-647W.

6.   Annette Demers, "Cultural Competence and the Legal Profession: An Annotated Bibliography of Materials Published between 2000 and 2011," *International Journal of Legal Information* 39, no. 1 (2011): 23.

7.   Shamika Dalton, "Teaching Cultural Competency through Legal Research Instruction," in *Integrating Doctrine and Diversity: Inclusion and Equity in the Law School Classroom*, ed. Nicole P. Dyslewski, Raquel J. Gabriel, Suzanne Harrington-Steppen, Anna Russell, and Genevieve B. Tung (Durham, NC: Carolina Academic Press, 2021), 280.

8.   Cynthia M. Ward and Nelson P. Miller, "The Role of Law Schools in Shaping Culturally Competent Lawyers," *Michigan Bar Journal* 89, no. 1 (2010): 16.

9.   American Bar Association, "Standard 2.4 on Cultural Competence," Standards for the Provision of Civil Legal Aid, accessed June 2, 2021, https://perma.cc/6S5H-MKUL.

10. Cynthia Pay, "Teaching Cultural Competency in Legal Clinics," *Journal of Law and Social Policy* 23 (2014): 190–92.

11. Aastha Madaan, "Cultural Competency and the Practice of Law in the 21st Century," *ABA Probate and Property Magazine*, March 1, 2017. https://perma.cc/LQE8-JXSP.

12. Ward and Miller, "Role of Law Schools," 17.

13. American Bar Association Section of Legal Education and Admissions to the Bar, "Final Recommendations: Standards 205, 303, 507, and 508," memo, August 16, 2021, https://perma.cc/BH3T-23A7.

14. American Bar Association Section of Legal Education and Admissions to the Bar, "Final Recommendations."

15. American Bar Association, "Chapter 3: Program of Legal Education," in *Standards and Rules of Procedure for Approval of Law Schools 2021–2022* (Chicago: American Bar Association, 2021), https://perma.cc/R8K5-WDLG.

16. Dalton and Nejdl, "Culturally Competent Legal Research Curriculum," 19; Lynch, "Importance of Experiential Learning," 138-40; Bonny L. Tavares, "Changing the Construct: Promoting Cross-Cultural Conversations in the Law School Classroom," *Journal of Legal Education* 67, no. 1 (2017): 216.

17. American Bar Association, "Model Rules of Professional Conduct: Table of Contents," 2020, https://perma.cc/KWP5-KJP5.

18. Debra Chopp, "Addressing Cultural Bias in the Legal Profession," *NYU Review of Law and Social Change* 41, no. 3 (2017): 388-401; American Bar Association, "Model Rules of Professional Conduct: Preamble and Scope," 2020, https://perma.cc/K5V9-D8DH.

19. American Bar Association, "Rule 1.1: Competence," Model Rules of Professional Conduct, 2020, https://perma.cc/7Q5E-PBGS; American Bar Association, "Rule 1.1 Competence—Comment," Model Rules of Professional Conduct, 2020, https://perma.cc/3XM5-YN5U; American Bar Association, "Rule 1.3: Diligence," Model Rules of Professional Conduct, 2020, https://perma.cc/47MH-AVUW; American Bar Association, "Rule 1.3 Diligence—Comment," Model Rules of Professional Conduct, 2020, https://perma.cc/9RSD-46QC; American Bar Association, "Rule 2.1: Advisor," Model Rules of Professional Conduct, 2020, https://perma.cc/GSZ4-XW8G; American Bar Association, "Rule 2.1: Advisor—Comment," Model Rules of Professional Conduct, 2020, https://perma.cc/2JNY-TD5T.

20. Chopp, "Addressing Cultural Bias," 388-401.

21. American Bar Association, "Rule 2.1"; Chopp, "Addressing Cultural Bias," 395-97.

22. Dalton and Nejdl, "Culturally Competent Legal Research Curriculum," 19.

23. Charles R. Calleros, "Training a Diverse Student Body for a Multicultural Society," *La Raza*

Law Journal 8, no. 2 (1995): 140–65; Chopp. "Addressing Cultural Bias"; Ederlina Co, "Teaching Cultural Competence as a Fundamental Lawyering Skill," *Journal of the Legal Writing Institute* 23 (2019): 4–6; Lynch, "Importance of Experiential Learning"; Patel, "Cultural Competency Training"; Julie M. Spanbauer and Katerina P. Lewinbuk, "Embracing Diversity through a Multicultural Approach to Legal Education," *Charlotte Law Review* 1, no. 2 (2009): 223–51; Tavares, "Changing the Construct"; L. Danielle Tully, "The Cultural (Re)Turn: The Case for Teaching Culturally Responsive Lawyering," *Stanford Journal of Civil Rights and Civil Liberties* 16, no. 2 (2020): 201–58.

24. Okianer Christian Dark, "Incorporating Issues of Race, Gender, Class, Sexual Orientation, and Disability into Law School Teaching," *Willamette Law Review* 32, no. 3 (Summer 1996): 541–76; Cheryl L. Wade, "Attempting to Discuss Race in Business and Corporate Law Courses and Seminars," *St. John's Law Review* 77, no. 4 (2003): 901–18; Deborah Zalesne, "Racial Inequality in Contracting: Teaching Race as a Core Value," *Columbia Journal of Race and Law* 3, no. 1 (2013): 23–48; Pay, "Teaching Cultural Competency"; Paul R. Tremblay, "Interviewing and Counseling across Cultures: Heuristics and Biases," *Clinical Law Review* 9, no. 1 (2002): 373–416; Lorraine Bannai and Anne Enquist, "(Un)Examined Assumptions and (Un)Intended Messages: Teaching Students to Recognize Bias in Legal Analysis and Language," *Seattle University Law Review* 27, no. 1 (2003): 1–40; Co, "Teaching Cultural Competence"; Sha-Shana Crichton, "Incorporating Social Justice into the 1L Legal Writing Course: A Tool for Empowering Students of Color and of Historically Marginalized Groups and Improving Learning," *Michigan Journal of Race and Law* 24, no. 2 (2019): 251–98; Johanna K. P. Dennis, "Ensuring a Multicultural Educational Experience in Legal Education: Start with the Legal Writing Classroom," *Texas Wesleyan Law Review* 16, no. 4 (2010): 613–44.

25. Raquel J. Gabriel, "Integrating Diversity into Legal Research: Building an Essential Skill for Law Students," in *Integrating Doctrine and Diversity: Inclusion and Equity in the Law School Classroom*, ed. Nicole P. Dyslewski, Raquel J. Gabriel, Suzanne Harrington-Steppen, Anna Russell, and Genevieve B. Tung (Durham, NC: Carolina Academic Press, 2021), 267.

26. Dennis, "Ensuring a Multicultural Educational Experience," 623; Matt Hlinak, "The Socratic Method 2.0," *Journal of Legal Studies Education* 31, no. 1 (2014): 1–20.

27. Patel, "Cultural Competency Training," 151–52.

28. Susan Bryant and Jean Koh Peters, "Five Habits for Cross-Cultural Lawyering," in *Race, Culture, Psychology, and Law*, ed. Kimberly Holt Barrett and William H. George (Thousand Oaks, CA: Sage, 2005), 47–62; Pay, "Teaching Cultural Competency."

29. Bryant and Peters, "Five Habits"; Pay, "Teaching Cultural Competency," 205–8.

30. Bryant and Peters, "Five Habits"; Patel, "Cultural Competency Training," 146.

31. Bryant and Peters, "Five Habits"; Patel, "Cultural Competency Training," 147.

32. Bryant and Peters, "Five Habits"; Patel, "Cultural Competency Training," 147.

33. Bryant and Peters, "Five Habits"; Patel, "Cultural Competency Training," 148.

34. Bryant and Peters, "Five Habits"; Patel, "Cultural Competency Training," 149.

35. Pay, "Teaching Cultural Competency," 208–15.

36. Pay, "Teaching Cultural Competency," 199–205.

37. Pay, "Teaching Cultural Competency," 215–18.

38. Dalton, "Teaching Cultural Competency," 281.

39. Dalton, "Teaching Cultural Competency," 281–82; Dalton and Nejdl, "Culturally Competent Legal Research Curriculum," 21.

40. Gabriel, "Integrating Diversity," 271–72.

41. Dalton and Nejdl, "Culturally Competent Legal Research Curriculum," 21; Gabriel, "Integrating Diversity," 271–73; Gabriel, "Integrating Diversity," 271–73.

42. Calleros, "Training a Diverse Student Body," 150–51.

43.   Calleros, "Training a Diverse Student Body," 151–53; Tavares, "Changing the Construct," 233–34.
44.   Calleros, "Training a Diverse Student Body," 151–52.
45.   Dalton, "Teaching Cultural Competency," 283–84.
46.   Calleros, "Training a Diverse Student Body," 151–52.
47.   Calleros, "Training a Diverse Student Body," 146.
48.   Crichton, "Incorporating Social Justice," 252–54.
49.   Dalton, "Teaching Cultural Competency," 285–86.
50.   Dalton, "Teaching Cultural Competency," 282–83.
51.   Clanitra Stewart Nejdl, "This Really Happened: Incorporating Legal News Items and Current Events into Legal Research Courses," *Second Draft* 30, no. 2 (Fall 2017): 46–49; Gabriel, "Integrating Diversity," 275.
52.   Tavares, "Changing the Construct," 223–25.
53.   Tavares, "Changing the Construct," 220–23.
54.   Tavares, "Changing the Construct," 227–28.
55.   Calleros, "Training a Diverse Student Body," 161.
56.   Gabriel, "Integrating Diversity," 269–70.
57.   Gabriel, "Integrating Diversity," 272–73.
58.   Shamika Dalton, "Incorporating Race into Your Legal Research Class," *Law Library Journal* 109, no. 4 (2017): 705–6.
59.   Lynch. "Importance of Experiential Learning," 136.

Bibliography

American Bar Association. "ABA-Approved Law Schools." 2021. https://perma.cc/7APM-5YAR.

———. "Chapter 3: Program of Legal Education." In *Standards and Rules of Procedure for Approval of Law Schools 2021–2022*. Chicago: American Bar Association, 2021. https://perma.cc/2NPA-KFRN.

———. "Model Rules of Professional Conduct: Preamble and Scope." 2020. https://perma.cc/K5V9-D8DH.

———. "Model Rules of Professional Conduct: Table of Contents." 2020. https://perma.cc/KWP5-KJP5.

———. "Rule 1.1: Competence." Model Rules of Professional Conduct. 2020. https://perma.cc/7Q5E-PBGS.

———. "Rule 1.1: Competence—Comment." Model Rules of Professional Conduct. 2020. https://perma.cc/3XM5-YN5U.

———. "Rule 1.3: Diligence." Model Rules of Professional Conduct. 2020. https://perma.cc/47MH-AVUW.

———. "Rule 1.3: Diligence—Comment." Model Rules of Professional Conduct. 2020. https://perma.cc/9RSD-46QC.

———. "Rule 2.1: Advisor." Model Rules of Professional Conduct. 2020. https://perma.cc/GSZ4-XW8G.

———. "Rule 2.1: Advisor—Comment." Model Rules of Professional Conduct. 2020. https://perma.cc/2JNY-TD5T.

———. "Standard 2.4 on Cultural Competence." Standards for the Provision of Civil Legal Aid. Accessed on June 2, 2021. https://perma.cc/6S5H-MKUL.

———. *Standards and Rules of Procedure for Approval of Law Schools 2021–2022*. Chicago: American Bar Association. 2021. https://perma.cc/U7X6-647W.

American Bar Association Section of Legal Education and Admissions to the Bar. "Final Recommendations: Standards 205, 303, 507, and 508." Memo, August 16, 2021. https://perma.cc/BH3T-23A7.

Bannai, Lorraine, and Anne Enquist, "(Un)Examined Assumptions and (Un)Intended Messages: Teaching Students to Recognize Bias in Legal Analysis and Language." *Seattle University Law Review* 27, no. 1 (2003): 1–40.

Bryant, Susan, and Jean Koh Peters. "Five Habits for Cross-Cultural Lawyering." In *Race, Culture, Psychology, and Law,* edited by Kimberly Holt Barrett and William H. George, 47–62, Thousand Oaks, CA: Sage, 2005.

Calleros, Charles R. "Training a Diverse Student Body for a Multicultural Society." *La Raza Law Journal* 8, no. 2 (1995): 140–65.

Chopp, Debra. "Addressing Cultural Bias in the Legal Profession." *NYU Review of Law and Social Change* 41, no. 3 (2017): 364–402.

Co, Ederlina. "Teaching Cultural Competence as a Fundamental Lawyering Skill." *Journal of the Legal Writing Institute* 23 (2019): 4–6.

Crichton, Sha-Shana. "Incorporating Social Justice into the 1L Legal Writing Course: A Tool for Empowering Students of Color and of Historically Marginalized Groups and Improving Learning." *Michigan Journal of Race and Law* 24, no. 2 (2019): 251–98.

Cross, Terry L., Barbara J. Bazron, Karl W. Dennis, and Mareasa R. Isaacs. *Toward a Culturally Competent System of Care: A Monograph on Effective Services for Minority Children Who Are Severely Emotionally Disturbed.* Washington, DC: CASSP Technical Assistance Center, Georgetown University Child Development Center, 1989.

Dalton, Shamika. "Incorporating Race into Your Legal Research Class." *Law Library Journal* 109, no. 4 (2017): 703–10.

———. "Teaching Cultural Competency through Legal Research Instruction." In *Integrating Doctrine and Diversity: Inclusion and Equity in the Law School Classroom,* edited by Nicole P. Dyslewski, Raquel J. Gabriel, Suzanne Harrington-Steppen, Anna Russell, and Genevieve B. Tung, 279–86. Durham, NC: Carolina Academic Press, 2021.

Dalton, Shamika, and Clanitra Stewart Nejdl. "Developing a Culturally Competent Legal Research Curriculum." *AALL Spectrum* 23, no. 4 (2019): 18–21.

Dark, Okianer Christian. "Incorporating Issues of Race, Gender, Class, Sexual Orientation, and Disability into Law School Teaching." *Willamette Law Review* 32, no. 3 (Summer 1996): 541–76.

Demers, Annette. "Cultural Competence and the Legal Profession: An Annotated Bibliography of Materials Published between 2000 and 2011." *International Journal of Legal Information* 39, no. 1 (2011): 22–50.

Dennis, Johanna K. P. "Ensuring a Multicultural Educational Experience in Legal Education: Start with the Legal Writing Classroom." *Texas Wesleyan Law Review* 16, no. 4 (2010): 613–44.

Gabriel, Raquel J. "Integrating Diversity into Legal Research: Building an Essential Skill for Law Students." In *Integrating Doctrine and Diversity: Inclusion and Equity in the Law School Classroom,* edited by Nicole P. Dyslewski, Raquel J. Gabriel, Suzanne Harrington-Steppen, Anna Russell, and Genevieve B. Tung, 267–78. Durham, NC: Carolina Academic Press, 2021.

Hlinak, Matt. "The Socratic Method 2.0." *Journal of Legal Studies Education* 31, no. 1 (2014): 1–20.

Joe, Irene Oritseweyinmi. "Regulating Implicit Bias in the Federal Criminal Process." *California Law Review* 108, no. 3 (2020): 965–88.

Kuehl, Heidi Frostestad. "Resources for Becoming Culturally Competent in a Multijurisdictional Practice: G20 Nations and Associated Legal Traditions." *International Journal of Legal Information* 44, no. 2 (2016): 83–115

Lynch, Mary. "The Importance of Experiential Learning for Development of Essential Skills in Cross-Cultural and Intercultural Effectiveness." *Journal of Experiential Learning* 1, no. 1 (2014): 129–47.

Madaan, Aastha. "Cultural Competency and the Practice of Law in the 21st Century." *ABA Probate and Property Magazine*, March 1, 2017. https://perma.cc/LQE8-JXSP.

Marouf, Fatma E. "Implicit Bias and Immigration Courts." *New England Law Review* 45, no. 2 (2011): 417–48.

Nejdl, Clanitra Stewart. "This Really Happened: Incorporating Legal News Items and Current Events into Legal Research Courses." *Second Draft* 30, no. 2 (Fall 2017): 46–49.

Patel, Serena. "Cultural Competency Training: Preparing Law Students for Practice in Our Multicultural World." *UCLA Law Review Discourse* 62 (2014): 139–56.

Pay, Cynthia. "Teaching Cultural Competency in Legal Clinics." *Journal of Law and Social Policy* 23 (2014): 188–219.

Spanbauer, Julie M., and Katerina P. Lewinbuk. "Embracing Diversity through a Multicultural Approach to Legal Education." *Charlotte Law Review* 1, no. 2 (2009): 223–51.

Su, Anona. "A Proposal to Properly Address Implicit Bias in the Jury." *Hastings Women's Law Journal* 31, no. 1 (2020): 79–100.

Tavares, Bonny L. "Changing the Construct: Promoting Cross-Cultural Conversations in the Law School Classroom." *Journal of Legal Education* 67, no. 1 (2017): 211–41.

Tremblay, Paul R. "Interviewing and Counseling across Cultures: Heuristics and Biases," *Clinical Law Review* 9, no. 1 (2002): 373–416.

Tully, L. Danielle. "The Cultural (Re)Turn: The Case for Teaching Culturally Responsive Lawyering." *Stanford Journal of Civil Rights and Civil Liberties* 16, no. 2 (2020): 201–58.

Wade, Cheryl L. "Attempting to Discuss Race in Business and Corporate Law Courses and Seminars." *St. John's Law Review* 77, no. 4 (2003): 901–18.

Ward, Cynthia M., and Nelson P. Miller. "The Role of Law Schools in Shaping Culturally Competent Lawyers." *Michigan Bar Journal* 89, no 1. (2010): 16–21.

Zalesne, Deborah. "Racial Inequality in Contracting: Teaching Race as a Core Value." *Columbia Journal of Race and Law* 3, no. 1 (2013): 23–48.

CHAPTER 11

Digital Archive Kits
Accessibility and Flexibility

Glenn Koelling

It's easy to get students excited about physical archival items. All a librarian has to do is place items on the table and the materiality and rarity make them irresistible to students. As the English liaison of the University Libraries at the University of New Mexico (UNM), I encourage instructors working with early undergraduates to come into the archives so students can get hands-on work with primary sources. But that's not always possible for a variety of reasons, and moreover, archival one-shots are often limited by time.

Digital archives, conversely, can simultaneously over- and underwhelm students; the computer's flattening effect of the items, the emphasis on content over form, and unfamiliar or unwieldy interfaces are barriers to creating genuine learning opportunities using digital archival material.[1] Yet digital archives have undeniable benefits—the most prominent being ease of access.

In 2018, a colleague and I began a project that introduced early undergraduate literature students to work in the archives. Students learned how to handle fragile books while closely examining them in preparation for an essay where they compared two editions of the same novel and hypothesized about the significance of the differences. From that collaboration, we theorized that physical archives create an embodied learning experience that lends itself well to certain information literacy concepts so instructors should not treat digital and physical archives as pedagogically identical.[2] Thanks to this collaboration, I was inspired to try to provide a better pedagogical experience with digital archives. As Lindquist and Long concluded from their study about educational digital archives platforms, above all the technology "should be easy for students and faculty to use and save their time."[3] But more than that, digital archives used for teaching should be accessible for all users, regardless of physical ability. In this chapter, I use the Web Accessibility Initiative's definition of accessibility ("Web accessibility means that people with disabilities can equally

perceive, understand, navigate, and interact with websites and tools") as well as its definition of inclusivity ("Inclusion: is about diversity, and ensuring involvement of *everyone* [emphasis mine] to the greatest extent possible.")[4] How could I create an inclusive digital archives experience designed for our population in an accessible, online environment using my limited technical know-how and resources?

Archive Kit as Pedagogical Resource

As an answer, I created the Archive Kit (https://digitalrepository.unm.edu/oer_letters/) using our Bepress institutional repository in spring 2020. In brief, the Archive Kit is a collection of thirteen digitized letter files from our special collections, a worksheet, and a lesson plan—all hosted in our repository as PDFs. The Archive Kit is designed to be accessible, flexible, and easy to set up. UNM is Carnegie classified as having Very High Research Activity. There is a heavy research emphasis at all levels, but it skews toward STEM fields at the undergrad level. The Archive Kit was initially intended to support English instructors who may not be able to come into the archives but who wanted their students to have experience working with primary sources. Our library instruction program provides a lot of support for English instructors at the 1000 level, and the Archive Kit was a nice opportunity to provide a digital learning object for instructors at the 2000 level. It was quickly apparent, however, that the Archive Kit was not limited to English; the worksheet guides students through a mini original research project rooted in their curiosity about the letters, which would be appropriate for any subject that uses archival research. This chapter is divided into two main parts: (1) an explanation of the purpose and pedagogy of the Archive Kit and (2) the process of creating one.

Inclusivity

University archives can be unwelcoming or intimidating places—especially to undergraduates and people of color.[5] UNM is a Hispanic-serving institution with a large Native student population, and most of our students come from New Mexico. As a result, UNM has a wonderfully diverse student body with strong ties to the state, and the digital learning objects we create need to represent this diversity. While digital archives remove some of the physical barriers of the archives, who is included and excluded in that content still speaks volumes.[6] The Archive Kit was an opportunity for students to see some of New Mexico's diversity reflected in the letters.

To this end, I included many letters with clear New Mexico connections that covered a wide range of topics from a variety of perspectives, time periods, and languages. Among the voices, there is a New Mexican teacher writing to the constitutional governor of Tabasco about Mexican sex ed, a jailed kidnapper writing (quite distressed) to his parents, a Japanese fan writing to Katherine Otero Stinson (a famous New Mexican pilot), and the governor of Zuni Pueblo advocating for better representation. In terms of topics and times, the letters range from an exchange negotiating marriage in the 1860s to a complaint against a state police officer in 1997 (included in an LGBT collection). There is one Spanish language letter.

Inclusivity is more than representation,[7] so each letter is fully and richly accessible in this digital landscape, meaning that all users can access the content regardless of ability. The World Wide Web Consortium created the Web Content Accessibility Guidelines (WCAG) 2.1, which lay out the standards for online accessibility, including for images like those in the Archive Kit.[8] Since the Archive Kit relies primarily on digitized images of text, I applied several accessibility features to the PDFs: alternative text for images, headings for document structure and navigation, and optical character recognition (OCR) to make text in images readable for a computer. These features are key for users who have poor vision or who rely on assistive software like screen readers and can be added using software like Adobe Acrobat Pro. Those letters that could not be OCRed have a transcript. All letters have a short, physical description of the item at the end, for example: "One page of yellowed paper, written on front and back, creases showing it had been folded in quarters. Discolored, grey upper corner and sides of back. Messy handwriting, written in pencil, uneven lines." Accessibility is a place where digital archives can even the playing field if done properly; all students can have access both to the intellectual content and to descriptions of the physical content.

Archive Kit's Purpose and Pedagogy

The lesson plan and worksheet are situated in the Association of College and Research Libraries' frame "Research as Inquiry"[9] and guide instructors and students through a miniature original research project using the letters. This exercise offers a soft introduction to working with primary sources. The main point of the lesson plan is to help students develop their ability to ask questions about something unfamiliar that they then try to answer—a skill that will be useful in academia and beyond—rather than becoming proficient at interpreting primary sources. However, the Archive Kit lays the groundwork to support more advanced primary source instruction because students ask questions, summarize content, and learn about the letter's context.[10]

The lesson plan (see appendix A) walks instructors through the exercise, giving learning objectives, explaining the preparation work necessary for the instructor, and providing guidance about grading. There are three learning objectives: (1) students will examine primary materials (letters) in order to draft research questions about them, (2) students will use their research questions in order to focus their secondary research efforts, and (3) students will synthesize their observations and findings in order to present an explanation of their letter. The lesson plan also identifies modifications and areas students may get stuck (primarily doing secondary research) and suggests solutions. The lesson plan is clear that "this exercise focuses on asking questions about primary materials and answering them using research, not source evaluation or citations." It is perhaps tempting to use this exercise as a way to practice citations, but to reduce cognitive load and to focus more narrowly on the research process, I suggest that instructors use this as a way to scaffold learning, focusing on citations in a separate assignment.

Inspired by the Right Question Institute's Question Formulation Technique's emphasis on asking questions,[11] the worksheet (see appendix B) guides students through their mini original research project. It demonstrates to students, in a short, manageable way, what original research looks like at the most basic level of asking and trying to answer questions. It is comprised of six parts and designed to take about one and a half hours. Part 1 asks students to browse letters and choose one. In part 2, students set a timer for five minutes to get to know their letter; they are prompted to think about both the content and the appearance. For part 3, students brainstorm twelve questions with the emphasis on quantity rather than getting hung up on quality. The goal is to get students to practice asking questions—to stretch their curiosity and creativity. There are no right or wrong questions, and the student can go in whichever direction makes sense to them. Then in part 4, students choose their top three questions with an explanation as to why they chose each question. This part is designed for students to identify and explain what makes a question interesting. Part 5 asks students to try to answer those three questions. Students have a lot of freedom in answering their questions—the worksheet acknowledges that they may not be able to answer their specific questions so they may need to get creative in finding a link to investigate. The important thing is that they identify something about their item to research using secondary sources, even if it diverges from their questions. For instance, a student might wonder who the letter writer was and try to find information about them, while another student might wonder what the political climate of New Mexico was in the 1990s. The worksheet also gives guidance about how to start finding information like this, including directing students to look at their letter's finding aid as well as linking to useful library resources like historical newspapers or encyclopedias. Students also list citation information in this part to what they find. Finally, the last part is a summary of their findings. The worksheet ends by tying this practice to other forms of research they're likely to encounter: "You can use this same process for other research projects: (1) get to know your topic by figuring out what you already know, (2) ask some questions about it, and (3) see if you can answer those questions using research."

Flexibility

While I have provided a lesson plan and worksheet, the Archive Kit's flexibility means it can be tailored to a variety of different classes, depending on class goals and student needs. The lack of metadata or detailed descriptions of the letters enables different instructors to use it in different ways. For example, while the lesson plan and worksheet offer a taste of original research, a composition class could use the letters for genre or rhetorical analysis. A history class could use them as objects for historical analysis. A class in archives or museum studies could use them to practice metadata. Since it is hosted in our institutional repository, it would be easy to add other lesson plans or worksheets.

In my own instruction, I teach an upper division, three-credit course called Managing Information for Professionals for the Organization, Information, and Learning Sciences department, which is in the same college as UNM Libraries. As part of this class, we talk about how information structures (like databases) work. I used the Archive Kit's letters for an assignment where students drafted a simple database schema. This is an example where having vague metadata was useful as the students created their own fields and decided on their own vocabulary.

Creating the Archive Kit

The process for creating the Archive Kit was not hard. It required some tools and software that we already had, but none of them were particularly unique. I collaborated with several UNM colleagues on this project who helped make this a success, but this shouldn't dissuade solo librarians or archivists—it might take longer, but an Archive Kit could be done on one's own. UNM's Center for Southwest Research (CSWR) has an abundant archive, but even that isn't necessary. Old documents might hold a certain appeal, but this project would work equally well with modern documents since the emphasis is on asking questions and finding answers.

Selecting Items

While an Archive Kit could be made of any collection of primary materials, I chose letters in part because they rely on the written word, which is easier to make accessible, as opposed to photographs, where a lot of description would be necessary for people with vision impairments. Letters are also a familiar format to students—while the content may change, letters share commonalities of structure. For example, there is a sender and receiver, there is a location, they are one-sided, and so on.

I identified potential letters from looking at finding aids, and CSWR staff pointed me in the direction of other letters of interest. Variety and intrigue were two of my top considerations when choosing letters, and almost all letters had a New Mexico connection. I especially looked for typed letters that could take optical character recognition in order to reduce the number of them that would need transcripts. All letters needed to have something that could spark students' curiosity—enough to pull them in but not be prohibitively long. Since so many of them offered glimpses into fascinating stories, I often included response letters when available to give more context.

Digitizing and Hosting

We chose our institutional Bepress repository to host since I could upload and manage content with minimal training, and it is easily accessible by students and instructors. Our repository is managed by our Digital Initiatives and Scholarly Communication (DISC) department, so student employees from the CSWR digitized my selections as high-resolution preservation copies and put them into a shared drive where a DISC colleague converted them to a lower resolution PDF appropriate for the repository. This process took about three weeks, during which I transcribed and described letters. The only metadata included was the title, author, and date of the letter, with a brief description of content and link to the CSWR's finding aid.

The repository also offered the needed functionality to protect materials under copyright. Many of the letters are out of copyright, but not all. We were unable to get permission to publicly share one of the letters. Since it is a relatively recent letter (1997) about policing and civil liberties in New Mexico, I wanted to keep it because the language is more familiar (unlike the conventions of the 1860s letters) and because it relates to current issues of policing. Instead, we restricted access only to the UNM community, and anyone interested in viewing the letters must enter their UNM credentials. Unfortunately, we could not do this on a letter-by-letter basis, so the entire Archive Kit requires authentication. As an additional protection, since these are high quality images, each letter got a CSWR watermark.

Making the Kit Accessible

Archival work is more than just accessing the intellectual content of the letters; it is also an experience working with the physical properties of the items.[12] While digital archives do not lend themselves to all our senses as physical archives do, we can still add what sensory descriptions we can not only as a way of being inclusive for folks with visual impairments but also as a way of enriching the digital document for all users. Any associated items like envelopes or family transcriptions were also included in the digitization. I used Adobe Acrobat Pro to recognize the text, correct the OCR, and merge PDFs into one file. Some letters—usually written on a typewriter or handwritten—could not take OCR nicely and needed a transcript to ensure screen reader access. Each letter starts with the image and is followed by a description and transcript if needed in one file.

As someone who doesn't use a screen reader, I wasn't sure how the experience would be for someone who uses one. A colleague at UNM's Accessibility Resource Center agreed to review the files using her screen reader and gave me feedback. This step took several iterations as I learned more about the limits of OCR using Adobe; for example, words that appeared normal to me would actually be squished together or broken apart oddly for the screen reader. It was for this reason I used more transcripts than I originally had anticipated. My colleague also suggested language to help students navigate the collection at the outset: "Please note that in order to read these letters with all accessibility features intact, you will need to save the document to your PC and then open it using Acrobat Reader DC, rather than using a browser extension like the Adobe Acrobat Extension for Google Chrome."

Assessment

In a stroke of good timing, this project was finished during spring of 2020, right when COVID had moved all courses remote. As instructors scrambled to move online, we were able to offer the Archive Kit as a pedagogical resource—lesson plan already done. Feedback from one instructor who beta tested it was positive. A few of their students agreed to share their worksheets with me, and I was amazed at the range of questions they asked and the lines of inquiry they followed, many of which had never occurred to me. As of November 2022, Archive Kit files have been downloaded over 560 times. One student from a recent class that used the Archive Kit reflected: "One thing that surprised me about archival research is that it wasn't boring." I am delighted by this feedback because it indicates sincere engagement with the research process. While it's hard to know exactly how these letters are being used and by whom, it's heartening to see the steady click of usage. In an ideal world, I would know which classes this is being used in and how students are applying skills they learned in this activity to other contexts. Embedded or co-teaching librarians would have better access to assessments like these. Instructors could use this activity as a scaffold to asking and answering questions in disciplinary-specific activities (applying this process to a topic instead of letters, for instance).

Conclusion and Future Directions

Archives kits are not hard to put together with a few standard tools and a little time, and I hope other librarians and archivists feel inspired to create their own kits, tailored for their communities. They're a great way to make collections accessible and to get students working with primary materials while providing support for instructors at the same time. As for UNM's Archive Kit, I hope to include other lesson plans and other types of primary resources that would speak to this time and this location and that would spark students' curiosity—all richly described and accessible.

Appendix A: Archive Kit Online Lesson Plan

This lesson plan uses digitized letters scanned from UNM's Center for Southwest Research and a worksheet to guide students through a mini original research project. In this activity, students will choose a letter to work with. They'll examine it, ask questions about it, and then use those questions to do research about some aspect of their letter.

Time: At least 1.5 hours
Materials: Archive Kit—Letters: https://digitalrepository.unm.edu/oer_letters/ & Student Analysis Worksheet

Objectives

- Objective 1: Students will examine primary materials (letters) in order to draft research questions about them.
- Objective 2: Students will use their research questions in order to focus secondary research efforts.
- Objective 3: Students will synthesize their observations and findings in order to present an explanation of their letter.

Overview

PREWORK

Instructor should review letters and worksheet to familiarize themselves with the activity. Ideally, connect this activity with what's being done in class. How does this activity complement the course? For example, explain that this is an exercise in doing original research or that this exercise mirrors the research process students will be doing for a research paper.

Post the link to the Archive Kit in the class with directions, and let them know how many points are associated with the exercise and where they should turn in their worksheet. The worksheet may be assigned all at once or may be broken into different components; parts 1–3 could be due earlier and parts 4–6 due later. The instructor may also want to download the worksheet and post in class (although the worksheet is also available in the Archive Kit). The instructor may also wish to modify the worksheet. For example the analysis in part 6 has no instructions for length or formality of writing. But remember, this exercise focuses on asking questions about primary materials and answering them using research, not source evaluation or citations.

Directions (Modify as Needed)

You will be completing a worksheet using digitized letters from UNM's archives. This worksheet has six parts and will walk you through your analysis. Please do the parts in the order they appear on the worksheet. Enter your responses on the worksheet and turn it in to the proper assignment link. Worksheets are due:

ACTIVE WORK FOR STUDENTS

The worksheet will guide students through the activity. The instructor or a librarian may be needed to help students with secondary research.

REVIEWING COMPLETED WORKSHEETS

If grading this assignment, there are no right answers. This exercise focuses on asking questions about primary materials and answering them using research (which is an abbreviated version of the research cycle), so the assessment should focus on these aspects. The emphasis of this exercise is not source evaluation or proper citation technique, so those requirements should be very loose.

Appendix B: Archive Kit—Letters: Student Analysis Worksheet

Directions: This worksheet has six parts and will walk you through your analysis. Please do the parts in the order they appear on this worksheet. Enter your responses on this worksheet.

Part 1: Browse through the letters in the Archive Kit. There are transcriptions for handwritten ones, but you might want to see what you can read on your own. Choose one that you want to work with.

- Enter the title of your chosen letter here:

Part 2: Now that you've chosen your letter, spend some time with it (just your letter please—hold off on googling/researching for now). Set a timer for at least 5 minutes (but take as much time as your need), and get to know your document. Remember, these letters have appearances as well as content. If you're stuck, think about who, what, when, where, why, and how.

- What details seem important about your document? Write them down here:

Part 3: Now that you've reviewed your letter, what questions do you have about it or parts of it? What are you curious about? What do you wish you knew? Write down 12 questions (or more) about the letter—these can be big or small questions! Right now, we're going for quantity over quality.

- Q1:
- Q2:
- Q3:
- Q4:
- Q5:
- Q6:
- Q7:
- Q8:
- Q9:
- Q10:
- Q11:
- Q12:

Part 4: Look back over your questions and highlight your favorite 3 questions. Below, write a sentence or two for each question about why you chose it.

- Write your reasoning for each question here:

Part 5: Now we're going to take these questions and use them as a starting point to get into doing some research on your letter. Can you answer any of your questions? You may be able to answer them. You may not. Either way that's fine. You have a lot of freedom here—you just have to be able to connect your research to your letter. You may need to get creative. For example, maybe you research names or locations or an aspect of the era—you decide. Here are some resources to get you started (you may use others):

- Look at the link to the item in your letter's description—this will have more information about where the letter came from.
- Wikipedia
- ProQuest Historical Newspapers (need your UNM NetID & password if off-campus)
- Gale Encyclopedias (need your UNM NetID & password if off-campus)
- UNM library or ebooks (Use the main Catalog search box. You can filter by "Source Type" to "ebooks")
- Library databases (Click on "Database" tab, then you can use the drop-downs to look for databases by subject—like History—or by type.)

What did you find?

- Enter an informal citation for your research here. Citation should include author, title, date, & URL (if these are available—if not, just do your best):

Part 6: Last but not least! Write up a summary of your letter and what you found with your research about the letter (or some aspect of it). Imagine you are explaining it to someone who is unfamiliar with the letter.

- Enter your analysis here:

Congratulations! You've just finished a mini original research project! You can use this same process for other research projects: (1) get to know your topic by figuring out what you already know, (2) ask some questions about it, and (3) see if you can answer those questions using research.

Notes

1. Peter Lester, "Of Mind and Matter: The Archive as Object," *Archives and Records* 39, no. 1, (2018): 75, https://doi.org/10.1080/23257962.2017.1407748; Thea Lindquist and Holley Long, "How Can Educational Technology Facilitate Student Engagement with Online Primary Sources? A User Needs Assessment," *Library Hi Tech* 29, no. 2 (2011): 227–28, https://doi.org/10.1108/07378831111138152.
2. Amy Gore and Glenn Koelling, "Embodied Learning in a Digital Age: Collaborative Undergraduate Instruction in Material Archives and Special Collections," *Pedagogy* 20, no. 3 (October 2020): 453–72, https://muse.jhu.edu/article/765008.
3. Lindquist and Long, "How Can," 236.
4. W3C Web Accessibility Initiative, "Accessibility, Usability, and Inclusion," last updated May 6, 2016, https://www.w3.org/WAI/fundamentals/accessibility-usability-inclusion/.
5. Meredith E. Torre, "Why Should Not They Benefit from Rare Books? Special Collections and

Shaping the Learning Experience in Higher Education," *Library Review* 57, no. 1 (2008): 37, https://doi.org/10.1108/00242530810845044; Ashley Farmer, "Archiving While Black," *Chronicle of Higher Education*, July 22, 2018, https://www.chronicle.com/article/archiving-while-black/.

6. S. L. Ziegler, "Digitization Selection Criteria as Anti-racist Action," *Code4Lib Journal* 45 (August 9, 2019), https://journal.code4lib.org/articles/14667.

7. W3C Web Accessibility Initiative, "Accessibility."

8. W3C, *Web Content Accessibility Guidelines (WCAG) 2.1*, ed. Andrew Kirkpatrick, Joshue O Connor, Alastair Campbell, and Michael Cooper, June 5, 2018, https://www.w3.org/TR/WCAG21/; W3C, "Perceivable," *Web Content Accessibility Guidelines (WCAG) 2.1*, ed. Andrew Kirkpatrick, Joshue O Connor, Alastair Campbell, and Michael Cooper, June 5, 2018, https://www.w3.org/TR/WCAG21/#perceivable.

9. Association of College and Research Libraries, *Framework for Information Literacy for Higher Education* (Chicago: Association of College and Research Libraries, 2016), https://www.ala.org/acrl/standards/ilframework.

10. ACRL RBMS–SAA Joint Task Force on the Development of Guidelines for Primary Source Literacy, *Guidelines for Primary Source Literacy*, Summer 2017, 4–5, https://www2.archivists.org/sites/all/files/Guidelines%20for%20Primary%20Souce%20Literacy%20-%20FinalVersion%20-%20Summer2017_0.pdf.

11. Right Question Institute, "What Is the QFT?," accessed May 20, 2021, https://rightquestion.org/what-is-the-qft/.

12. Lester, "Of Mind," 77.

Bibliography

ACRL RBMS–SAA Joint Task Force on the Development of Guidelines for Primary Source Literacy. *Guidelines for Primary Source Literacy*. Summer 2017. https://www2.archivists.org/sites/all/files/Guidelines%20for%20Primary%20Souce%20Literacy%20-%20FinalVersion%20-%20Summer2017_0.pdf.

Association of College and Research Libraries. *Framework for Information Literacy for Higher Education*. Chicago: Association of College and Research Libraries, 2016. https://www.ala.org/acrl/standards/ilframework.

Farmer, Ashley. "Archiving While Black." *Chronicle of Higher Education*, July 22, 2018. https://www.chronicle.com/article/archiving-while-black/.

Gore, Amy, and Glenn Koelling. "Embodied Learning in a Digital Age: Collaborative Undergraduate Instruction in Material Archives and Special Collections." *Pedagogy* 20, no. 3 (October 2020): 453–72. https://muse.jhu.edu/article/765008.

Lester, Peter. "Of Mind and Matter: The Archive as Object." *Archives and Records* 39, no. 1 (2018): 73–87. https://doi.org/10.1080/23257962.2017.1407748.

Lindquist, Thea, and Holley Long. "How Can Educational Technology Facilitate Student Engagement with Online Primary Sources? A User Needs Assessment." *Library Hi Tech* 29, no. 2 (2011): 224–41. https://doi.org/10.1108/07378831111138152.

Right Question Institute. "What Is the QFT?" Accessed May 20, 2021. https://rightquestion.org/what-is-the-qft/.

Torre, Meredith E. "Why Should Not They Benefit from Rare Books? Special Collections and Shaping the Learning Experience in Higher Education." *Library Review* 57, no. 1 (2008): 36–41. https://doi.org/10.1108/00242530810845044.

W3C. *Web Content Accessibility Guidelines (WCAG) 2.1*, edited by Andrew Kirkpatrick, Joshue O Connor, Alastair Campbell, and Michael Cooper. June 5, 2018. https://www.w3.org/TR/WCAG21/.

———. "Perceivable." *Web Content Accessibility Guidelines (WCAG) 2.1*, edited by Andrew Kirkpatrick, Joshue O Connor, Alastair Campbell, and Michael Cooper. June 5, 2018. https://www.w3.org/TR/WCAG21/#perceivable.

W3C Web Accessibility Initiative. "Accessibility, Usability, and Inclusion." Last updated May 6, 2016. https://www.w3.org/WAI/fundamentals/accessibility-usability-inclusion/.

Ziegler, S. L. "Digitization Selection Criteria as Anti-racist Action." *Code4Lib Journal*, no. 45 (August 9, 2019). https://journal.code4lib.org/articles/14667.

CHAPTER 12

Teaching Technology Inclusively

One Librarian's Critical Digital Pedagogy Approach to One-Shot Instruction Sessions

Tierney Steelberg

In Between: Critical Digital Pedagogy and the One-Shot Library Session

As a librarian teaching one-shot technology sessions embedded within semester-long classes taught by faculty colleagues, I have found myself in an in-between space in considering my pedagogy. The vast majority of the literature on critical digital pedagogy focuses on or is written from the perspective of teachers of semester-long classes, and the vast majority of the literature on critical pedagogy in library teaching focuses on teaching information literacy: where, then, can I find myself as a teacher?

In true librarian spirit, I have found my answer through research and community. I ground my pedagogical approach in the work of Paulo Freire and bell hooks, and other teachers who work to envision and outline education as a liberatory practice through critical pedagogy. And going beyond this foundational

171

work, I owe a debt to the many teachers writing, presenting, sharing, and tweeting about their engagement with critical digital pedagogy and critical library pedagogy, whose work has taught me so much about possibilities for my own practice. I used to worry that one-shot technology teaching, which so often requires explicit step-by-step instruction, was incompatible with critical pedagogy: reading chapters by so many others in Pagowsky and McElroy's *Critical Library Pedagogy Handbook* was a revelation to me, in considering how the power that I hold in the classroom could be wielded "in a way that is authoritative ...rather than authoritarian"[1] and in helping me both validate and critique my own approach to teaching with the inclusion of technology-focused lesson plans.[2] Learning from other teachers and thinking creatively about connections to my own practice, I can make space for the one-shot library session within the context of critical digital pedagogy's focus on the semester-long class, while also making space for critical library pedagogy within the context of teaching technology rather than information literacy.

My critical digital pedagogy approach to teaching one-shot instruction sessions across technology topics as varied as digital mapping, web design, or digital citation management revolves around three central tenets: building community in the one-shot classroom, creating space (and providing scaffolding) for hands-on practice and collaboration, and taking time for reflection. A critical and inclusive approach to teaching technology feels necessary in our current moment. In her foreword to *Critical Digital Pedagogy: A Collection*, Ruha Benjamin writes, "I am convinced that without a deep engagement with critical digital pedagogy, as individuals and institutions, we will almost certainly drag outmoded ways of thinking and doing things with us."[3] The lens of critical digital pedagogy provides a framework for inclusive teaching and centers humans, rather than technology tools:[4] at its core, critical pedagogy envisions the classroom as a space for problem posing, for mutual creation, for deep reflection, and for challenging norms and systems of power and oppression—all of which can happen, when approached with thoughtfulness and care, within the confines of the one-shot session.

Building Community in the One-Shot Classroom

My approach to inclusive critical digital pedagogy begins with laying the foundations of community building within the confines of the one-shot classroom: these approaches help build an inclusive classroom environment that engages all students by building on the bedrock of their prior knowledge.

Meeting Students Where They're At, Explicitly

After introducing myself and the topic, I open each session by asking students what experience they might have had, if any, with this tool or application or others like it, making connections between their prior experience and the topic at hand and going beyond validating their experiences to actually engaging with them.[5] Have they used a maps app to get from one place to another? Then they have experience with the basics of digital mapping. Have they posted updates on social media? Then they have a starting point for posting on the class blog. This is an inclusive practice that welcomes students into the topic, helping them make connections and envision it as an extension of their prior knowledge. Students share these experiences with me and with the rest of the class, and we use these shared experiences and expertise as our collective starting point. Through our work together, we become Freire's "teacher-student with students-teachers," each of us learning from the others.[6]

This sharing also allows me to tailor my session to the students' needs and desires and create a shared learning experience that is unique, rather than a cookie-cutter template. I am explicit about the underpinnings of my teaching and my plans for the session: I make sure the class knows that, while I have a general plan for the session, that plan is completely malleable depending upon their expertise, their interests, and what they feel like they need to learn to be successful.

Incorporating Their Experience and Expertise

As I lay the groundwork for learning about an application that may be new to many or even all of the students in the class, I build in additional opportunities beyond the initial check-in to incorporate students' own experience and expertise into our session. I create all resources for a session using collaborative editing programs that allow me to change things around and add the content we cocreate as a class in real time. This willingness to be flexible and to work together to cocreate a session that accomplishes our shared goals is invaluable in building community with the students during our shared time together.

I continue to build in opportunities for students to share prior knowledge and experiences. For example, in a session on web development, I help them make the move from web consumers to creators by asking them to critique websites they visit regularly, considering what makes a "good" website (a consideration we problematize together), what features are necessary or helpful, what features might be useful within one context but not others, what features or styling are dependent on one's audience. We consider these questions together, generating responses as a group, and I act as a notetaker for our conversation, building a shared repository of ideas and recommendations that students can refer to as they work on their own.

Having established the basics together, we can harken back to this conversation and these ideas throughout the rest of the session. In discussing web accessibility, I refer to students' own ideas and examples that relate directly to accessibility concerns (such as using a legible font or ensuring appropriate color contrast) to showcase the universality of web accessibility, and these then become a starting point to consider additional principles of web accessibility with which students may not yet be familiar (such as the conventions for properly nesting headings). Making these connections explicitly helps students unearth their own expertise, embedded within opinions and experience they already have, and urges them to consider how they can make use of this existing knowledge in our session and in their work.

Making Connections

Community and collaboration are at the heart of critical digital pedagogy.[7] Beyond making sure students get hands-on practice with the tool at hand, I work to ensure that students make connections—not only with the material but also with me, as their instructor for this one-shot session, and with each other. I try to build this connection using humor and a lighthearted approach, often including relevant memes and GIFs in my slides (welcoming any good-natured teasing about references I make that may be less than current) and asking students to share relevant examples of their own as well. I also work to pull in current events, when applicable, and use illustrative examples of topics at hand (such as the perils of image hot-linking, as illustrated by a major publication) to help make things tangible, again inviting students to share their own examples as well. I make sure to externalize as much as possible my thought processes, approaches, and even feelings as I am working through questions and issues with technology, keeping in mind bell hooks and the need to "practice being vulnerable in the classroom":[8] not only does this help students connect with me on a human level, but it also helps model for them possible approaches to troubleshooting or recovering from getting stuck, which can be an emotionally fraught experience when it comes to working with technologies that can seem opaque and unforgiving.

It is incredibly important to me to work to build community with students in a way that reaches beyond the confines of the classroom, building trust and building a relationship with them so that they know I am available as a resource for them as they encounter questions and issues in their exploration of technology beyond this time-limited one-shot session. I do this with an awareness of my positionality within the classroom: as a person who is white, nondisabled, queer, middle class, in possession of a graduate degree, and as a guest invited into the classroom of the instructor who has requested this session, I cannot lose sight of the impact of my identity and the students' identities on our experience of the classroom together. I hold authority in the classroom even as I may try to relinquish it and must work to overcome my own biases and help students overcome theirs as I invite them to bring themselves as fully as they would like into the space of our session. Above all, I need to trust the students, and build trust with them—this trust is at the heart of a critical pedagogy approach, digital or not.[9]

The connections students build with each other over the course of this session are also incredibly important: facilitating those is an important piece of my role as a guest instructor. I create opportunities for collaborative work throughout, inviting students to work together in different permutations (small groups, sharing in pairs) in ways that are scaffolded and inclusive of different needs. Whenever possible, I end class by explicitly turning the session over to the students and tasking them with teaching each other now that they have experience with the application at hand. They share what they have learned and what may not have worked well, what features they have discovered that their classmates might find useful, and how they might critique the tool we have considered together. In this way, students can further their own learning with a head start that I am able to help structure, and they build community by teaching each other. Their learning about the tool at hand is amplified by the connections and community we are able to create together, and they also know they have an entire classroom community's worth of fellow teachers and learners at the ready to help with the questions, issues, glitches, and the like that invariably arise when working with technology.

Creating Space (and Providing Scaffolding) for Hands-On Practice—and Collaboration

The most important component of any technology teaching session is giving students the time and space (and necessary scaffolding) for hands-on practice with the application at hand—and, as an equitable teaching practice, supporting students with the time and space to collaborate and learn with one another in the ways that are most fruitful for them.

Building In Structure

Providing clear structure for students is an inclusive teaching practice, especially when it comes to teaching technology, as long as that structure is flexible and approachable, able to meet students where they are at. In order to make space for each individual student's learning style, comfort level, prior experience, current emotional headspace, and the like, I offer students as much structure as possible and explicitly let them pick and choose what they need from a detailed accompanying handout that provides a step-by-step overview of the lesson. This includes not only clearly labeled walk-throughs of the tool broken down by task, but also any central questions and points of discussion clearly written out, to give students advance notice. I share not only my contact information, but also links to other related resources for documentation and further learning, for any students who might prefer to seek out additional support on their own. Creating detailed, modular support resources helps scaffold the lesson, providing multiple entry points for students depending on their prior experience and level of comfort, who can focus on learning what is new to them without needing to worry about following a narrow, predetermined lesson plan.

In keeping with one of universal design for learning's central guidelines, providing multiple means of representation, I try to ensure that students are supported in their hands-on practice by this structure in order to provide inclusive entry points for as many learning or processing styles as I can. Rather than provide accommodations only upon request, I try to anticipate needs in advance and build this in: as Catherine Denial writes in her consideration of a pedagogy of kindness, "my job, as I see it now, is to make my classroom accessible to everyone."[10] I provide clear instructions in the detailed handouts I create, I build walk-throughs with screenshots, and I do live demonstrations of the most important functions of the tool at hand. As we begin our time together, I make sure that students know that they are welcome to engage with these resources in whatever ways are most helpful for them as individual learners and that they can return to cocreated resources afterward as needed.

I scaffold the hands-on portion of a session into small, approachable chunks or components, as dictated by the necessary tasks of a given tool or application. This helps ensure that no one falls behind before we move forward together, while still allowing students with prior familiarity to work ahead without getting bored. This structure provides students with space for exploration, discovery, curiosity—without throwing them into the deep end before they even know how to use a given tool. Breaking up a technology-focused lesson into chunks also ensures that there is time for reflection, discussion, collaboration, and critical thinking throughout, in an iterative approach.

Encouraging Collaboration

This modular approach to hands-on work allows for different configurations throughout, leading to collaboration and critical thinking. Whether students are working on projects in groups or individually, they get both individual and collaborative hands-on work time. I try to vary opportunities for collaboration so that these are scaffolded and adapted in ways that are equitable for different learning styles, making sure that students can articulate their thoughts in small groups before being asked to share with the class as a whole.

As part of thoughtful hands-on practice, I try to model for students a collaborative approach to solving issues and finding work-arounds. As I encounter issues with a tool, or make mistakes, or am confronted with questions whose answer I do not yet know, I externalize this thought process and pull the entire class in to help solve this issue collaboratively, asking students for their help and tapping into their prior knowledge and expertise. When we encounter questions we cannot answer collectively, we use a given tool's documentation or user forums, or even conduct a quick web search, in order to work through an issue or a question so that students learn to incorporate these approaches to getting unstuck into their own hands-on work.

Taking Time for Reflection

Taking time for reflection is important whenever learning is taking place—and it is especially important within the context of inclusive teaching, as well as the context of teaching and learning about technology, as it can often get lost in the tight timing of a one-shot session.

Reflecting Throughout

Similar to my approach to hands-on practice, my approach to engaging in an inclusive practice of reflection revolves around providing structure for students to reflect individually, in the ways that best suit them, and then move into sharing more widely. Throughout the session, I often crowdsource responses to reflection questions using tools that allow us to view (anonymized) responses together so that students know others in the class may feel similarly and so we can all answer questions that may come up. As a session wraps up, students reflect individually on what they have learned, then pair up to share what they have created with another student: they showcase not only their end result but also their process, and then give each other feedback and suggestions. This small-group approach ensures every student gets feedback on their work and is also helpful for students who might have some difficulty sharing in a wider setting. I even use my one-shot teaching assessment survey as an opportunity for reflection, as well as an opportunity to get feedback from students, asking them to share what they feel was the most important thing they learned in this session and what they still have questions about. This also allows me to follow up with the class after the session as needed with further resources.

Validating Emotions

As we work together, I try to model how to embrace reflection throughout the learning process. Being able to tackle a mistake, an issue, a gap in knowledge is an important piece of working with technology—and being able to work through this honestly and collaboratively is an important piece of critical pedagogy. There is an emotional element there that is not always acknowledged, and that I think needs to be named and worked through when it comes to teaching technology inclusively and critically. When I make a mistake or encounter a glitch, I get students' feed-back on troubleshooting and walk them through my own approach, as needed. I find this approach to be helpful in soothing anxieties and frustrations students may feel around technology, especially for students who may be coming in with a preconceived notion of themselves as "not a tech person." Throughout a session I take regular temperature checks and ask students not only about whether things are working but also about how they are feeling: it's important to validate any negative emotions they may be experiencing while also helping them work through these feelings to the best of the class's collective ability. This care is a critical aspect of critical digital pedagogy.[11] The community we have built together as a class helps us move through these difficulties together when they arise, allowing us to bring our full selves into the classroom.

Technology can often activate feelings of fear or anxiety, and I find it important to consider a reflective and inclusive approach to moving through these feelings: what can one do when stuck or in need of help, and what can one do when a tool or application (invariably) breaks down? This happens regularly in sessions with students, and how I respond—with humor, with an attempt to validate very real frustrations without being consumed by them, and with practical reflection on how to get things back on track—helps set a tone for the class and for how students subse-quently approach a tool. This affective dimension of teaching technology connects again to bell hooks's teachings on vulnerability and the importance of honoring our emotional responses:[12] honoring, naming, and explicitly working through these vulnerable emotions, while also leaving space for both the pains and joys of the learning process, makes for a more inclusive classroom.

Encouraging Critical Thinking

As we work to reflect together, I try to help students hone their reflective lens, build-ing in more critical thinking throughout the session. Inspired by the work of others in critical digital pedagogy, I encourage students to connect their hands-on practice with a more critical approach toward the tools that they are using. Who created this tool, and who is its target audience? Who is missing from this approach? Who benefits from this tool? What has the tool left unsaid or implicit, especially around concerns of data usage, security, privacy, and the like? These considerations can be raised at the beginning, when a tool is introduced, to spark dialogue, but conversations can and should continue throughout. Critical digital pedagogy necessitates critical thinking around digital tools.

In "A Guide for Resisting Edtech: The Case against Turnitin," Morris and Stommel share an exercise they have created for critically evaluating digital tools that revolves around asking similar questions and subsequently thoroughly researching tools: they bill this exercise as "a critical thinking exercise aimed at asking critical questions, empowering critical relationships, encouraging new digital literacies."[13] While there may not be space for this in-depth research in the span of a one-shot session, relevant considerations can be raised, like questions of consent around digital technologies, problematic algorithms, or Gilliard's concept of digital redlining.[14] Asking these kinds of questions opens those conversations and homes in on many critical considerations that students are already thinking about. Explicitly scaffolding this thinking around technology allows them to continue the critical work of this session, broadening their critical lens and extending it to other arenas, especially around the technologies they use every day. How do these technologies "re-inscribe" inequities?[15] Together we build and reinforce these reflective and critical habits, working to uncover and name biases within tools and considerations that are left implicit, knowing that no tool is neutral as we make more informed choices in our selection and use. This ongoing collaborative reflection and dialogue is at the heart of critical digital pedagogy.

Conclusion

My approach to critical digital pedagogy in the library classroom as a guest instructor relies on the central tenets of building community, engaging students in hands-on practice, and embracing reflection—throughout the session, interwoven with one another, and with an emphasis as much as possible on collaboration and critical thinking. These practices inform and build off of each other, and I use this approach for any session on teaching technology, no matter the audience (from one-shots for students to faculty development sessions) and no matter the length. This approach is iterative and can be used to scaffold a session into smaller chunks that then build on each other and create more space for discovery, exploration, and playfulness as students feel increasingly comfortable with the basics of an application. Together, these practices form the foundation of an inclusive pedagogical approach, creating a welcoming and supportive environment for learners and furthering their learning in flexible ways that best fit their needs—in addition to an inclusive approach to the session's content through critical consideration of the very technologies being taught in the session.

If you are teaching technology in a thoughtful and active way and are hoping to incorporate more of critical digital pedagogy into your approach, I hope you find this helpful in getting started. Know that you can take so much of what you are already doing to address community, practice, and reflection and build this in with more intention and purpose and thus participate in cocreating, even within the limitations of the one-shot, an experience with students that engages them inclusively, thoughtfully, meaningfully as learners and as teachers.

Notes

1. Nicole Pagowsky and Kelly McElroy, "Introduction," in *Critical Library Pedagogy Handbook*, vol. 1, ed. Nicole Pagowsky and Kelly McElroy (Chicago: Association of College and Research Libraries, 2016), xvii.
2. Joshua F. Beatty, "Zotero: A Tool for Constructionist Learning in Critical Information Literacy," in *Critical Library Pedagogy Handbook*, vol. 2, ed. Nicole Pagowsky and Kelly McElroy (Chicago: Association of College and Research Libraries, 2016), 215–21.
3. Ruha Benjamin, "A Foreword to Critical Digital Pedagogy," in *Critical Digital Pedagogy: A Collection*, ed. Jesse Stommel, Chris Friend, and Sean Michael Morris (Washington, DC: Hybrid Pedagogy, 2020), https://cdpcollection.pressbooks.com/front-matter/foreword/.
4. Jesse Stommel, "Critical Digital Pedagogy: A Definition," *Hybrid Pedagogy*, November 17, 2014, https://hybridpedagogy.org/critical-digital-pedagogy-definition/.
5. Heidi LM Jacobs, "Falling Out of Praxis: Reflection on a Pedagogical Habit of Mind," in *Critical Library Pedagogy Handbook*, vol. 1, ed. Nicole Pagowsky and Kelly McElroy (Chicago: Association of College and Research Libraries, 2016), 4.
6. Paulo Freire, *Pedagogy of the Oppressed*, 30th anniversary ed., trans. Myra Bergman Ramos (New York: Continuum, 2000), 80.
7. Stommel, "Critical Digital Pedagogy."
8. bell hooks, *Teaching to Transgress* (New York: Routledge, 1994), 21.
9. Amy Hasinoff, "Do You Trust Your Students?" *Hybrid Pedagogy*, August 22, 2018, https://hybridpedagogy.org/do-you-trust-your-students/; Jesse Stommel, Technologies of Meta-learning, Trust, and Power: Interview with Jesse Stommel," by HASTAC team, *HASTAC* (blog), October 16, 2014, https://www.hastac.org/blogs/superadmin/2014/10/16/technologies-meta-learning-trust-and-power-interview-jesse-stommel.
10. Catherine Denial, "A Pedagogy of Kindness," *Hybrid Pedagogy*, August 15, 2019, https://hybridpedagogy.org/pedagogy-of-kindness/.
11. Jesse Stommel, Chris Friend, and Sean Michael Morris, "Introduction: The Urgency of Critical Digital Pedagogy" in *Critical Digital Pedagogy: A Collection*, ed. Jesse Stommel, Chris Friend, and Sean Michael Morris (Washington, DC: Hybrid Pedagogy, 2020), https://cdpcollection.pressbooks.com/front-matter/introduction/.
12. hooks, *Teaching to Transgress*.
13. Sean Michael Morris and Jesse Stommel, "A Guide for Resisting Edtech: The Case against Turnitin," *Hybrid Pedagogy*, June 15, 2017, https://hybridpedagogy.org/resisting-edtech/.
14. Kit Heintzman and Molly de Blanc, "Thinking with Consent in the Digital Classroom," *Hybrid Pedagogy*, March 25, 2021, https://hybridpedagogy.org/thinking-with-consent-in-the-digital-classroom/; Shea Swauger, "Our Bodies Encoded: Algorithmic Test Proctoring in Higher Education," *Hybrid Pedagogy*, April 2, 2020, https://hybridpedagogy.org/our-bodies-encoded-algorithmic-test-proctoring-in-higher-education/; Chris Gilliard, "Pedagogy and the Logic of Platforms," *EDUCAUSE Review* 52, no. 4 (August 2017): 64.

15.   Audrey Watters, "School Work and Surveillance," Hack Education, April 30, 2020, http://hackeducation.com/2020/04/30/surveillance.

Bibliography

Beatty, Joshua F. "Zotero: A Tool for Constructionist Learning in Critical Information Literacy." In *Critical Library Pedagogy Handbook*, vol. 2, edited by Nicole Pagowsky and Kelly McElroy, 215–21. Chicago: Association of College and Research Libraries, 2016.

Benjamin, Ruha. "A Foreword to Critical Digital Pedagogy." In *Critical Digital Pedagogy: A Collection*, edited by Jesse Stommel, Chris Friend, and Sean Michael Morris. Washington, DC: Hybrid Pedagogy, 2020. https://cdpcollection.pressbooks.com/front-matter/foreword/.

Denial, Catherine. "A Pedagogy of Kindness." *Hybrid Pedagogy*, August 15, 2019. https://hybridpedagogy.org/pedagogy-of-kindness/.

Freire, Paulo. *Pedagogy of the Oppressed*, 30th anniversary ed. Translated by Myra Bergman Ramos. New York: Continuum, 2000.

Gilliard, Chris. "Pedagogy and the Logic of Platforms." *EDUCAUSE Review* 52, no. 4 (August 2017): 64–65.

Hasinoff, Amy. "Do You Trust Your Students?" *Hybrid Pedagogy*, August 22, 2018. https://hybridpedagogy.org/do-you-trust-your-students/.

Heintzman, Kit, and Molly de Blanc. "Thinking with Consent in the Digital Classroom." *Hybrid Pedagogy*, March 25, 2021. https://hybridpedagogy.org/thinking-with-consent-in-the-digital-classroom/.

hooks, bell. *Teaching to Transgress: Education as the Practice of Freedom*. New York: Routledge, 1994.

Jacobs, Heidi LM. "Falling Out of Praxis: Reflection on a Pedagogical Habit of Mind." In *Critical Library Pedagogy Handbook*, vol. 1, edited by Nicole Pagowsky and Kelly McElroy, 1–7. Chicago: Association of College and Research Libraries, 2016.

Morris, Sean Michael, and Jesse Stommel. "A Guide for Resisting Edtech: The Case against Turnitin." *Hybrid Pedagogy*, June 15, 2017. https://hybridpedagogy.org/resisting-edtech/.

Pagowsky, Nicole, and Kelly McElroy. "Introduction." In *Critical Library Pedagogy Handbook*, vol. 1, edited by Nicole Pagowsky and Kelly McElroy, xvii–xxi. Chicago: Association of College and Research Libraries, 2016.

Stommel, Jesse. "Critical Digital Pedagogy: A Definition." *Hybrid Pedagogy*, November 17, 2014. https://hybridpedagogy.org/critical-digital-pedagogy-definition/.

———. "Technologies of Meta-learning, Trust, and Power: Interview with Jesse Stommel," by HASTAC team. *HASTAC* (blog), October 16, 2014. https://www.hastac.org/blogs/superadmin/2014/10/16/technologies-meta-learning-trust-and-power-interview-jesse-stommel.

Stommel, Jesse, Chris Friend, and Sean Michael Morris. "Introduction: The Urgency of Critical Digital Pedagogy." In *Critical Digital Pedagogy: A Collection*, edited by Jesse Stommel, Chris Friend, and Sean Michael Morris. Washington, DC: Hybrid Pedagogy, 2020. https://cdpcollection.pressbooks.com/front-matter/introduction/.

Swauger, Shea. "Our Bodies Encoded: Algorithmic Test Proctoring in Higher Education." *Hybrid Pedagogy*, April 2, 2020. https://hybridpedagogy.org/our-bodies-encoded-algorithmic-test-proctoring-in-higher-education/.

Watters, Audrey. "School Work and Surveillance." Hack Education, April 30, 2020. http://hackeducation.com/2020/04/30/surveillance.

CHAPTER 13

Theories of Motivation as Inclusive Pedagogy
Strategies for Engaging and Equitable Instruction

Francesca Marineo Munk

Introduction

As an inherently interdisciplinary field, librarianship is full of inspiring ideas from across academia. The study of motivation within educational psychology, for instance, offers new grounding for librarians to deepen their understanding of equitable and inclusive theories and practices. Motivational theories explore what moves people into action and what sustains them in that action.[1] Through an educational lens, these theories shed light on how and why people learn, what maintains or impedes their engagement in the learning process, and how we as educators can support students through motivationally supportive instruction.[2] At the same time, inclusive teaching can be defined as

> the ways in which pedagogy, curriculum and assessment are designed and delivered to engage students in learning that is meaningful, relevant and accessible to all. It embraces a view that diversity stems from individual differences that can enrich the lives and learning of others.[3]

Through these definitions, we can see how both motivationally supportive and inclusive teaching share similar goals. Thus, while motivation is not explicitly an inclusive pedagogy, it offers a unique framework for educators to consider how they can create a positive, engaging, and equitable learning environment for all learners.

In this chapter, I share an overview of two motivational theories, self-determination theory (SDT) and expectancy-value theory (EVT), how these theories complement inclusive and equitable pedagogies, and how librarians can move toward praxis by adopting motivational, inclusive practices into their instruction. Specifically, I share strategies for how librarians can support student autonomy and value through engaging and equitable learning experiences that facilitate choice, practice transparency, foster relevance, and decenter the classroom. In addition, I look critically at these approaches through a social justice lens to ensure that they support all students and do not put the burden disproportionately on students from marginalized communities. Ultimately, I hope that after reading this chapter, librarians will feel inspired to explore motivational theory and implement aspects of motivation in inclusive ways throughout their own teaching.

Theories of Motivation

The study of motivation focuses on how different internal and external factors interact to produce or diminish motivation. Internal factors can include goals, emotions, and dispositions, while external factors include task or assignment design and social factors such as reinforcement and culture.[4] Motivation theories therefore provide ways of understanding how these factors interact to support positive engagement. Motivation has been researched in a wide range of contexts with an unsurprising abundance of literature coming from the field of education.[5] Motivation research is also growing within librarianship, especially library instruction research, as is evident from the recent addition of a "coming soon" category for Information Literacy on the Center for Self-Determination Theory's research page.[6] Research around motivation and information literacy has thus far focused on areas such as information-seeking behavior, information literacy self-efficacy, critical thinking, and online learning.[7] One area of research in which there is room for growth is motivationally inspired inclusive teaching.

Many parallels exist between theories of motivation and strategies for inclusive teaching. For instance, concepts such as agency, value, and relevance are important both for motivating students and for helping them feel included in and connected to their learning.[8] Because of this, recent research has begun to explore how we can facilitate inclusion and equity by employing motivational theory.[9] Research should continue to examine these commonalities and how motivational and inclusive pedagogies can work together, especially for information literacy instruction. This chapter is one step in that direction.

Self-Determination Theory (SDT)

Self-determination theory is a principal psychological theory on motivation that "examines how biological, social, and cultural conditions either enhance or undermine the inherent human capacities for psychological growth, engagement, and wellness."[10] One of the main assumptions of SDT is that humans are inherently intrinsically motivated, or motivated by internal factors such as their goals, curiosities, and emotions.[11] While these inherent capacities may exist, external factors, such as social relationships and cultural expectations, often affect the extent to which one grows, engages, and experiences wellness.[12] Within education, SDT research is particularly interested in how contextual factors, which we as instructors contribute to through how we design and facilitate instruction, enhance or undermine student capacities for learning.[13]

Another assumption of SDT is that all humans have three universal psychological needs—the need for autonomy (feeling self-governed), competence (feeling capable), and relatedness (feeling connected)—that must be met for optimal functioning (i.e., motivation).[14] According to Deci and Ryan, the founders of SDT, the most important distinction within self-determination theory is whether or not one's motivation is perceived as autonomous or controlled.[15] Motivation is perceived as autonomous when it is intrinsic, or the source of an action comes from within an individual. An example might be when someone wants to watch a YouTube video to learn a new skill that will make them better at their job for no other benefit than learning the new skill. Alternatively, motivation is controlled when it is extrinsic or viewed as external from oneself, such as when someone watches a YouTube video for a $5 gift card even though it is of no inherent interest to them. While both intrinsic and extrinsic motivation can lead to engagement, when it is perceived as autonomous or intrinsic, people are more interested, excited, and confident in their ability to succeed, and in turn, they are more likely to exhibit enhanced performance, persistence, and creativity.[16]

It is especially important for librarians to cultivate intrinsic motivation in students during the traditional one-shot model of instruction. As noted by Barefoot, "since information literacy instruction often takes place in brief formats but is a necessary skill throughout the curriculum, it is essential that students be intrinsically motivated to continue their research efforts after the individual assignment has ended."[17] In her study, Barefoot offered two back-to-back, fifty-minute information literacy sessions with an in-class activity and individual written assessment from the librarian. Formative assessment is important to intrinsic motivation as it goes beyond a grade (an external factor) to provide students with personalized feedback that supports their autonomy, competence, and relatedness needs. Splitting the traditional one-shot into two sessions allowed librarians the time to provide meaningful feedback and to connect with their students. Barefoot found that students in this study had higher levels of interest/enjoyment, perceived competence, and a decrease in pressure/tension, all of which are indicators of higher levels of intrinsic motivation.[18]

Expectancy-Value Theory (EVT) of Achievement Motivation

Expectancy-value theory from the field of achievement motivation offers another lens for inspiring motivational, inclusive pedagogy. Within EVT, motivation is directly related to how an individual expects to perform on an activity and how much they value that activity. In practice this means that students who not only find an activity attractive and valuable but also believe that their success related to the activity is attainable will be more motivated to engage in the activity.[19] The constructs and applications of expectancy and value have evolved over time with the Eccles et al. expectancy-value model emerging as a leading modern model within the developmental and educational psychology fields.[20] This model "proposes that these constructs are the most immediate or direct predictors of achievement performance and choice, and are themselves influenced by a variety of psychological, social, and cultural influences."[21] The Eccles et al. model explores four components of value, or subjective task value: attainment value or importance; intrinsic value; utility value or usefulness; and cost.[22]

The cost component of value is particularly important when working with diverse populations to ensure no student or group of students ends up unintentionally having a negative or harmful learning experience. For instance, Poort, Jansen, and Hofman used EVT to explore the costs and benefits of intercultural group work (IGW). An IGW is a collaborative learning method in which students from different cultural or national backgrounds work together. The authors provide insights on some of the possible negative effects that marginalized students may experience. They explored three previously identified costs of EVT—time, effort, and negative psychological states—and identified a new cost—compromising at the expense of personal values or standards. In their focus groups, students discussed how not only did it take more time and effort to communicate and make sense of the variety of perspectives and languages in the group, but they also experienced stereotyping and loss of personal identity by other group members. This led to a lack of motivation and increased feelings of fear and stress. When there were conflicts within the group, they were often attributed to the diversity of the group members. Things that helped alleviate these costs were the duration of the collaboration (i.e., dedicating multiple class sessions to the group dynamics) and developing intercultural communication skills ahead of the assignment itself. This allowed students to enter into the IGW better equipped to interact with one another.[23]

It is important that librarians take similar steps in evaluating the costs associated with our teaching to ensure that students do not experience loss of their identities, stereotypes, or other harmful experiences in their learning. Combining EVT with inclusive teaching principles, we can alleviate costs and increase benefits, thus contributing to increased value around a task and, ultimately, increasing engagement, perseverance, and performance. In the next section, I offer practical strategies for implementing motivation theory as an inclusive pedagogy focusing on supporting student autonomy (SDT) and value (EVT).

Motivation as Inclusive Pedagogy

As noted earlier, motivation theory is not in itself an inclusive or equitable pedagogy. Yet there are several parallels, such as the importance of agency and value, between motivationally supportive and inclusive teaching practices. The opportunity to use these theories and practices in harmony inspired this chapter and is an area for future research, especially within librarianship, where we often pull from a variety of disciplines in our inherently interdisciplinary field. When considered along with other inclusive teaching and learning frameworks, such as universal design for learning (UDL), open pedagogy, and culturally relevant pedagogy, librarians can weave motivational theory into their practice to create more equitable instruction for all learners. The next sections explore some of these concepts and how we can incorporate them into our teaching to achieve praxis. I focus on two aspects of motivation that are critical to inclusive teaching: autonomy and value. While these two concepts are central to SDT and EVT respectively, you will also see how they intertwine with each other as well as with various theories of inclusive teaching.

Autonomy

One of the three universal psychological needs of self-determination theory, autonomy is essential for an inclusive learning experience. When an action or task is perceived as autonomous, students are empowered in their own learning. Autonomy-supportive teaching provides students with a choice in not only what and how they learn but also how they demonstrate their learning. For those who have used universal design for learning, this may sound familiar. In fact, autonomy is central to the recruiting interest checkpoint 7.1 in UDL: "optimize individual choice and autonomy."[24] Two autonomy-supportive teaching strategies that librarians can use to create inclusive learning experiences are facilitating choice and practicing transparency.

FACILITATING CHOICE

Offering students choice in their learning is a powerful way to support autonomy and provide more equitable learning. As librarians, we can support student choice in many ways, especially as choice lends itself well to many modes of instruction from digital learning objects and tutorials to in-person classes and workshops. One way of facilitating choice is by providing multiple means of engagement (a central principle of UDL). For example, in the first-year English composition course at my previous institution, I provided students with the option of a printed, paper keyword development handout or a digital version in Google Docs. For both the physical and digital handouts, I also provide the activity in a linear, text-based format and a more visual, free-form format. This gave students the opportunity to choose not only the handout medium but also the flow that works best for them. For online sections of the course, students had a choice between attending a synchronous online group information literacy session with a librarian or completing an individual, self-paced, and asynchronous online tutorial. Both options met the same learning outcomes that were set for the course. Having a choice for how they could learn these outcomes supported their autonomy by giving them agency as the primary deciders of their own learning.

In addition to being autonomy supportive, having multiple means of engagement provides students flexibility in their learning, which is also essential to creating an inclusive learning experience. Griful-Freixeneta and colleagues highlight this in their study of perceived barriers and opportunities of UDL for students with disabilities. They note that meeting the needs of some students may create barriers for others, even when the intention is to be inclusive. To ensure a supportive learning environment for all students, they argue for not only flexible but also responsive teaching that goes beyond setting and curricular changes to directly addressing student needs.[25] This may be challenging for librarians who do not get to spend significant time with students due to the traditional one-shot or general nature of our instruction sessions and materials. Fortunately, there are additional ways to support choice through our work.

For instance, librarians can support student choice through multiple means of expression (also a key principle of UDL).[26] Many librarians collaborate with instructors on assignment design or teach credit-bearing courses themselves.[27] In these collaborations, we can support student autonomy by offering multiple types of assignments for students to express what they've learned. While the learning outcomes themselves do not change, students can choose how they demonstrate that they have met them. This allows students to choose the assignment type with which they feel the most comfortable and confident. While one student may prefer to write a traditional research paper, another may prefer to do an oral presentation, another a video, and yet another a podcast. Having a choice in their assignments is also inclusive in that it allows students to draw on their unique skills and interests to demonstrate their learning in a way that is meaningful and relevant to them.[28]

PRACTICING TRANSPARENCY

An important consideration of facilitating choice is that it is not the same thing as having a lack of structure. Structure may sound counterproductive to autonomy, but in practice, structure supports those who need it, while not hurting those who don't.[29] In addition, according to SDT, providing structure enhances students' competence, which leads to increased engagement and motivation to learn.[30] Librarians can provide structure by engaging in transparent teaching practices. Transparent teaching utilizes "a combination of teaching practices that are explicit in the articulation of instructor expectations for student learning and classroom success, that rely upon unambiguous language and techniques to develop and enhance analytical and critical thinking skills and deepen student learning."[31] As librarians, we can be transparent in our teaching by ensuring that we do not use jargon, and when we do (like when I would tell students to search Quick Search, my previous institution's Primo user interface), being explicit in defining confusing and new terms (i.e., this is the Libraries' "Google"; you might hear it called Quick Search or Library Search or the catalogue).

Another transparent teaching practice is to clearly articulate the *why* behind a particular task. For example, I have used a version of the information spectrum activity to facilitate discussions around information creation and privilege.[32] I let students know that this activity is important because it demonstrates the different contexts within which information exists. It helps show students the benefits and costs of different types of information and how they can be used in conversation with each other in their research. I love how this activity complicates the narrative around what types of information are valuable and why. When students understand the purpose of why they are being asked to do something, and they can see why it is important to their own lives, they are more likely to engage and benefit from the task.[33] When the library is often seen as a field trip or mandatory presentation, being transparent can help students from all backgrounds understand how the library fits into their information needs and that we are a relevant and helpful resource throughout their academic and research journey. This is also a great time to acknowledge historical and current barriers to information and research within academia and work towards breaking these barriers down by inviting student experiences into the curriculum.

Value

From an inclusive teaching perspective, specifically culturally responsive pedagogy, instructors should "seek an understanding of students' lived cultural experiences to get an idea of who they are and use this knowledge to provide engaging and relevant curriculum."[34] This is because, by doing so, instructors are adding value to students' learning experiences. In particular, aligning curriculum to students' lived cultural experiences supports students' attainment value and intrinsic value, two of the four components of value from the Eccles et al. expectancy-value model.[35] Attainment value is the importance "individuals attach to doing well on a task or how well the given task fits with the individuals' identity" and intrinsic value "is the interest and enjoyment individuals gain from engaging in a specific task."[36] Two ways that librarians can increase student attainment and intrinsic value are fostering relevance and decentralizing the classroom.

FOSTERING RELEVANCE

As educators, one way that we can help establish value for students is by ensuring that the learning activities we design are relevant to them, their communities, and their broader interests. Priniski, Hecht, and Harackiewicz note an important distinction between the standard dictionary definition of relevancy and that within motivation research: while the dictionary definition "emphasizes *objective* levels of pertinence, relevance as a motivation construct is an individual's *subjective* perception of the degree to which a stimulus (an object, an activity, a topic) is connected (i.e., has some relation) to the individual personally [emphasis added]."[37] With individual importance in mind, librarians can foster relevance by connecting specific learning outcomes or activities to a student's broader academic journey or across the curriculum (i.e., how a lower-division paper could evolve into an undergraduate thesis or how the skills learned in introductory composition courses will be essential for many of their other courses). Depending on time, capacity, and context, some strategies for fostering relevance across the curriculum include embedding in the course learning management system;[38] engaging in a flipped classroom model or workshop-intensive model instead of the traditional one-shot session;[39] and using curriculum mapping to ensure cohesive and scaffolded information literacy instruction.[40]

Another way to foster relevance is to connect learning to experiences from students' daily lives outside of academia. This could be as simple as asking students about the last time they needed information and how they found it. Often, I hear answers like they had a question about their car and watched a YouTube video or they were trying to prove their friend wrong about what year a song came out. These low-stakes conversations of information-seeking behavior can then be used to show students that they are already expert researchers and connect search strategy from everyday googling to finding academic sources. Morrison explores what this could look like on a larger scale within an information literacy classroom. Using a student asset-based approach, she demonstrates how to "develop culturally relevant (decolonized with critical race theory) and sustaining and revitalizing (cultural wealth) classrooms."[41] In her approach, Morrison had students, who were all people of color and first-generation students, voice their own assets, which became counterstories to the traditional colonized stories we often hear in academia, stories that center whiteness as a primary asset and everything, or anyone, that deviates is perceived as a deficit.

Using these counterstories, she developed a culturally relevant curriculum in which "students were able to engage with topics concerning their communities, both current and historical."[42] As a result, students noted that their classroom became a relevant and safe space to think critically and engage with their peers. It also sparked a desire for lifelong learning and a way of engaging that students hoped would happen in other classes as well.[43] I often hear librarians say, "If nothing else, I hope students come away from my sessions feeling comfortable enough to reach out to me later." For librarians, even if students don't remember specific Boolean operators or how to limit articles by year, we hope that they feel safe and inspired to continue their research beyond our classroom and come to us when they need help. Considering these ultimate goals, Morrison's research provides significant insight into the importance of fostering relevance in our teaching.

DECENTERING THE CLASSROOM

Closely related to fostering relevance and supporting student autonomy, decentering the classroom is a significant way to bring value to student learning. Like Morrison's research, wherein the students' own lived experiences and cultural assets guided the curriculum, a decentered classroom involved a student-centered curriculum that challenges the traditional hierarchy of instructor and student by "dissemination of authority to parties besides the instructor."[44] One way that librarians can support this dissemination of authority and center students in their own learning is through open pedagogy. As an inclusive practice, open pedagogy benefits students by giving them the freedom to design their own learning paths and empowering them as cocreators of knowledge.[45] Reframing these benefits from a motivational lens, we see that students have autonomy and agency in what they learn and how they learn it. Depending on time, context, and opportunities to collaborate with disciplinary instructors, there are several ways librarians can decenter the classroom through motivational and open pedagogy.

What a better way to decenter the classroom and the traditional instructor-student dynamic than by using Wikipedia, which helps "create a world in which *everyone can freely share in the sum of all knowledge* [emphasis added]."[46] From experience, one of the first things students learn about Wikipedia in their academic careers is that anyone can edit it, and, perhaps more importantly, that it should therefore not be trusted!

Thankfully, many librarians are challenging this narrative by engaging students in Wikipedia assignments and realizing the potential of this free online encyclopedia as a beneficial and meaningful experiential learning tool. One of the benefits of Wikipedia assignments is that they can be done in one-shot instruction sessions, across multiple courses as an interdisciplinary collaboration, or as an extra-curricular event with potential curricular tie-ins.[47] When students edit Wikipedia, they enter a community of content creators and engage with information in new and meaningful ways. Their motivation also improves by seeing the real-world impact and value that they themselves are creating within this community.[48] Value also increases when students are contributing information about relevant and important topics. For example, the University of Nevada, Las Vegas University Libraries have hosted Wikipedia edit-a-thons focused on increasing the content and representation of historically underrepresented groups. These have included women, nonbinary and LGBTQ+ folks, Latinx folks, and Indigenous People.[49] By focusing on topics that are not as well represented in Wikipedia, yet reflect the diversity of our student communities, we can help to democratize knowledge by amplifying the voices of marginalized groups without disproportionately putting the burden on them to do so themselves.

For librarians teaching semester-long courses or who otherwise work closely with disciplinary instructors, creating, building, and adapting open educational resources (OERs), such as open textbooks, can be profoundly transformative.[50] OER creation motivates students by incorporating and honoring the knowledge and experiences they bring from their daily lives into academic spaces. Another open pedagogical approach that connects learning with student values beyond the classroom is community-engaged research, in which nonhierarchical relationships between students and their local communities provide long-term, meaningful relationships helping both the students learn and the community meet their research needs. Community-engaged learning is also a way to promote social justice through open pedagogy. As Nizami and Shambaugh emphasize, "openness means targeting the insularity of the academic institution vis-a-vis the communities where we find ourselves."[51] Thus, as an open pedagogy, community-engaged research "enables a more critically engaged approach to community-university partnerships, which we understand as needing to be aimed at recognizing and attending to power imbalances in these relationships."[52] All work in which we can decenter the classroom brings us closer toward this goal by adding value and meaning for all students and not just those for whom the system was created.

Conclusion

When considered alongside inclusive pedagogies, motivation theory offers a powerful and meaningful approach for librarians to engage all students. Self-determination theory and expectancy-value theory from the field of motivation particularly lend themselves to information literacy instruction and educational equity. Within these theories, concepts such as autonomy and value harmonize motivation and inclusion to support student engagement, amplify diverse voices, and center all students within their learning. Strategies such as facilitating choice and practicing transparency and fostering relevance and decentering the classroom allow librarians to move from theory to praxis and incorporate autonomy- and value-supportive instruction. The benefits of these strategies go beyond student engagement to break down harmful barriers within education by amplifying diverse voices and increasing diverse representation within the classroom, across the academy, and among our local communities.

Notes

1.   Terence R. Mitchell and Denise Daniels, "Motivation," in *Handbook of Psychology, Volume 12: Industrial and Organizational Psychology*, ed. Walter C. Borman, Daniel R. Ilgen, and Richard J. Klimoski (John Wiley & Sons, 2003), 225–54, https://psihologiapentrutoti.files.wordpress.com/2011/08/handbook-of-psychology-vol-12-industrial-and-organizational-psychology.pdf.

2.   Kathryn R. Wentzel and Allan Wigfield, *Handbook of Motivation at School*, Educational Psychology Handbook Series (New York: Routledge, 2009).

3.   Liz Thomas and Helen May, *Inclusive Learning and Teaching in Higher Education* (York, UK: Higher Education Academy, 2010), 9, https://s3.eu-west-2.amazonaws.com/assets.creode.advancehe-document-manager/documents/hea/private/inclusivelearningandteaching_finalreport_1568036778.pdf.

4.   Mitchell and Daniels, "Motivation."

5.   Rory A. Lazowski and Chris S. Hulleman, "Motivation Interventions in Education: A Meta-Analytic Review," *Review of Educational Research* 86, no. 2 (June 1, 2016): 602–40, https://doi.org/10.3102/0034654315617832; Sultan Ali R. Alkaabi, Warda Alkaabi, and Glen Vyver, "Researching Student Motivation." *Contemporary Issues in Education Research* 10, no. 3 (2017): 193–202, https://doi.org/10.19030/cier.v10i3.9985.

6.   Center for Self-Determination Theory, "Research," accessed June 11, 2021, https://selfdeterminationtheory.org/research/.

7.   Reijo Savolainen, "Expectancy-Value Beliefs and Information Needs as Motivators for Task-Based Information Seeking," *Journal of Documentation* 68, no. 4 (2012): 492–511, https://doi.org/10.1108/00220411211239075; Mitchell Ross, Helen Perkins, and Kelli Bodey, "Academic Motivation and Information Literacy Self-Efficacy: The Importance of a Simple Desire to Know," *Library and Information Science Research* 38, no. 1 (January 2016): 2–9, https://doi.org/10.1016/j.lisr.2016.01.002; David B. Miele and Allan Wigfield, "Quantitative and Qualitative Relations between Motivation and Critical-Analytic Thinking," *Educational Psychology Review* 26, no. 4 (2014): 519–41, https://doi.org/10.1007/s10648-014-9282-2; Francesca Marineo, "Motivation and Online Information Literacy Instruction: A Self-Determination Theory Approach" (master's thesis, University of Nevada, Las Vegas, 2019), UNLV Theses, Dissertations, Professional Papers, and Capstones, https://doi.org/10.34917/15778503.

8.   Monique Boekaerts, "Goal-Directed Behavior in the Classroom," in *Handbook of Motivation at School*, ed. Kathryn R. Wentzel and Allan Wigfield (New York: Routledge, 2009), 105–22; Chapel Cowden et al., "Teaching with Intent: Applying Culturally Responsive Teaching to Li-

brary Instruction," *portal: Libraries and the Academy* 21, no. 2 (April 2021): 231–51, https://doi.org/10.1353/pla.2021.0014.

9. Marisa H. Fisher et al., "Applying the Self-Determination Theory to Develop a School-to-Work Peer Mentoring Programme to Promote Social Inclusion," *Journal of Applied Research in Intellectual Disabilities* 33, no. 2 (2019): 296–309, https://doi.org/10.1111/jar.12673.

10. Richard M. Ryan and Edward L. Deci, *Self-Determination Theory* (New York: Guilford, 2017), 3, https://doi.org/10.1521/978.14625/28806.

11. Ryan and Deci, *Self-Determination Theory.*

12. Ryan and Deci, *Self-Determination Theory.*

13. Thomas K. F. Chiu, "Digital Support for Student Engagement in Blended Learning Based on Self-Determination Theory," *Computers in Human Behavior* 124 (November 2021): 106909, https://doi.org/10.1016/j.chb.2021.106909.

14. Chiu, "Digital Support."

15. Edward L. Deci and Richard M. Ryan, "Self-Determination Theory," in *Handbook of Theories of Social Psychology*, vol. 1, ed. Paul A. M. Van Lange, Arie W. Kruglanski, and E. Tory Higgins (London: SAGE, 2012), 416–37, https://doi.org/10.4135/9781446249215.

16. Richard M. Ryan and Edward L. Deci, "Self-Determination Theory and the Facilitation of Intrinsic Motivation, Social Development, and Well-Being," *American Psychologist* 55, no. 1 (January 2000): 68–78, https://doi.org/10.1037/0003-066X.55.1.68.

17. Maria R. Barefoot, "Student Research and Intrinsic Motivation: Effects of Formative Assessment and the Two-Session Model of Information Literacy Instruction," *Pennsylvania Libraries: Research and Practice* 5, no. 1 (2017): 14, https://doi.org/10.5195/palrap.2017.140.

18. Barefoot, "Student Research and Intrinsic Motivation."

19. Dale H. Schunk, "Self-Efficacy and Academic Motivation," *Educational Psychologist* 26, no. 3–4 (1991): 207–31.

20. Allan Wigfield, Stephen Tonks, and Susan L. Klauda, "Expectancy-Value Theory," in *Handbook of Motivation at School*, ed. Kathryn R. Wentzel and Allan Wigfield (New York: Routledge, 2009), 55–75.

21. Wigfield, Tonks, and Klauda, "Expectancy-Value Theory," 56.

22. Wigfield, Tonks, and Klauda, "Expectancy-Value Theory."

23. Irene Poort, Ellen Jansen, and Adriaan Hofman, "Intercultural Group Work in Higher Education: Costs and Benefits from an Expectancy-Value Theory Perspective," *International Journal of Educational Research* 93 (2019): 218–31, https://doi.org/10.1016/j.ijer.2018.11.010.

24. CAST, "Universal Design for Learning Guidelines," ver. 2.2, 2018, http://udlguidelines.cast.org.

25. Júlia Griful-Freixenet et al., "Higher Education Students with Disabilities Speaking Out: Perceived Barriers and Opportunities of the Universal Design for Learning Framework," *Disability and Society* 32, no. 10 (2017): 1627–49, https://doi.org/10.1080/09687599.2017.1365695.

26. CAST, "Universal Design for Learning Guidelines."

27. Rachel Wishkoski, Kacy Lundstrom, and Erin Davis, "Faculty Teaching and Librarian-Facilitated Assignment Design," *portal: Libraries and the Academy* 19, no. 1 (2019): 95–126, https://doi.org/10.1353/pla.2019.0006; Maggie Murphy, "On the Same Page: Collaborative Research Assignment Design with Graduate Teaching Assistants," *Reference Services Review* 47, no. 3 (2019): 343–58, https://doi.org/10.1108/RSR-04-2019-0027; Spencer Jardine, Sandra Shropshire, and Regina Koury, "Credit-Bearing Information Literacy Courses in Academic Libraries: Comparing Peers," *College and Research Libraries* 79, no. 6 (2018): 768–84, https://doi.org/10.5860/crl.79.6.768.

28. Ryan Jopp and Jay Cohen, "Choose Your Own Assessment—Assessment Choice for Students in Online Higher Education," *Teaching in Higher Education* 27, no. 6 (2022): 738–55, https://doi.org/10.1080/13562517.2020.1742680.

29. Viji Sathy and Kelly Hogan, "How to Make Your Teaching More Inclusive," *Chronicle of Higher Education*, July 22, 2019, https://www.chronicle.com/article/how-to-make-your-teaching-more-inclusive/.

30. Ineke Haakma, Marleen Janssen, and Alexander Minnaert, "A Literature Review on How Need-Supportive Behavior Influences Motivation in Students with Sensory Loss," *Teaching and Teacher Education* 57 (July 2016): 1–13, https://doi.org/10.1016/j.tate.2016.02.008.

31. Tiffiany O. Howard, Mary-Ann Winkelmes, and Marya Shegog, "Transparency Teaching in the Virtual Classroom: Assessing the Opportunities and Challenges of Integrating Transparency Teaching Methods with Online Learning," *Journal of Political Science Education* 16, no. 2 (2020): 199, https://doi.org/10.1080/15512169.2018.1550420.

32. Tessa Withorn, "The Information Spectrum," CORA: Community of Online Research Assignments, May 25, 2018, https://www.projectcora.org/assignment/information-spectrum.

33. David S. Yeager et al., "Boring but Important: A Self-Transcendent Purpose for Learning Fosters Academic Self-Regulation," *Journal of Personality and Social Psychology* 107, no. 4 (2014): 559–80, https://doi.org/10.1037/a0037637.

34. Breanna N. Harris et al., "From Panic to Pedagogy: Using Online Active Learning to Promote Inclusive Instruction in Ecology and Evolutionary Biology Courses and Beyond," *Ecology and Evolution* 10, no. 22 (November 2020): 12585, https://doi.org/10.1002/ece3.6915.

35. Wigfield, Tonks, and Klauda, "Expectancy-Value Theory."

36. Gaye D. Ceyhan and John W. Tillotson, "Early Year Undergraduate Researchers' Reflections on the Values and Perceived Costs of Their Research Experience," *International Journal of STEM Education* 7 (2020): article 54, p. 3, https://doi.org/10.1186/s40594-020-00248-x.

37. Stacy J. Priniski, Cameron A. Hecht, and Judith M. Harackiewicz, "Making Learning Personally Meaningful: A New Framework for Relevance Research," *Journal of Experimental Education* 86, no. 1 (2018): 12, https://doi.org/10.1080/00220973.2017.1380589.

38. Lesego Makhafola and Martie J. Van Deventer, "Selecting Information Products and Services to Embed in a Virtual Learning Environment to Support Engineering Undergraduates in a Blended Learning Context," *Library Management* 41, no. 6/7 (2020): 579–91, https://doi.org/10.1108/LM-04-2020-0061.

39. Gerardo Gómez-García et al., "The Contribution of the Flipped Classroom Method to the Development of Information Literacy: A Systematic Review," *Sustainability* 12, no. 18 (2020): 7273, https://doi.org/10.3390/su12187273; Susan Powell and Ningning Nicole Kong, "Beyond the One-Shot: Intensive Workshops as a Platform for Engaging the Library in Digital Humanities," *College and Undergraduate Libraries* 24, no. 2–4 (2017): 516–31, https://doi.org/10.1080/10691316.2017.1336955.

40. Ladislava Khailova, "Using Curriculum Mapping to Scaffold and Equitably Distribute Information Literacy Instruction for Graduate Professional Studies Programs," *Journal of Academic Librarianship* 47, no. 1 (January 2021): 102281, https://doi.org/10.1016/j.acalib.2020.102281.

41. Kim L. Morrison, "Informed Asset-Based Pedagogy: Coming Correct, Counter-stories from an Information Literacy Classroom," *Library Trends* 66, no. 2 (2017): 178, https://doi.org/10.1353/lib.2017.0034.

42. Morrison, "Informed, Asset-Based Pedagogy," 206.

43. Morrison, "Informed Asset-Based Pedagogy."

44. Troy M. Troftgruben, "Decentered Online Bible Instruction: How Active Learning Enhances the Study of Scripture," *Teaching Theology and Religion* 21, no. 1 (January 2018): 35, https://doi.org/10.1111/teth.12418.

45. Andreia Inamorato dos Santos, *Practical Guidelines on Open Education for Academics*, technical report, EUR 29672 EN (Luxembourg: Publications Office of the European Union, 2019), https://data.europa.eu/doi/10.2760/55923; Evrim Baran and Dana AlZoubi, "Affordances, Challeng-

es, and Impact of Open Pedagogy: Examining Students' Voices," *Distance Education* 41, no. 2 (2020): 230–44, https://doi.org/10.1080/01587919.2020.1757409.

46. Wikipedia, "Wikipedia:About," ed Jim Henderson, September 20, 2021, para. 1, https://en.wikipedia.org/w/index.php?title=Wikipedia:About&oldid=1045448340.

47. John Thomas Oliver, "One-Shot Wikipedia: An Edit-Sprint toward Information Literacy," *Reference Services Review* 43, no. 1 (2015): 81–97, https://doi.org/10.1108/RSR-10-2014-0043; Angela Pratesi, Wendy Miller, and Elizabeth Sutton, "Democratizing Knowledge: Using Wikipedia for Inclusive Teaching and Research in Four Undergraduate Classes," *Radical Teacher* 114 (2019): 22–33, https://doi.org/10.5195/rt.2019.517; Brittany Paloma Fiedler, Rosan Mitola, and James Cheng, "Responding to Hate: How National and Local Incidents Sparked Action at the UNLV University Libraries," *Reference Services Review* 48, no. 1 (2020): 63–90, https://doi.org/10.1108/RSR-09-2019-0071.

48. Oliver, "One-Shot Wikipedia."

49. Fiedler, Mitola, and Cheng, "Responding to Hate."

50. Robin DeRosa and Rajiv Jhangiani, "Open Pedagogy," in *A Guide to Making Open Textbooks with Students*, ed. Elizabeth Mays (Montreal: Rebus Community, 2017), https://press.rebus.community/makingopentextbookswithstudents/.

51. Urooj Nizami and Adam Shambaugh, "Open Pedagogy through Community-Directed, Student-Led Partnerships: Establishing CURE (Community-University Research Exchange) at Temple University Libraries," *Open Praxis* 11, no. 4 (2019): 444, https://doi.org/10.5944/openpraxis.11.4.1028.

52. Nizami and Shambaugh, "Open Pedagogy," 445.

Bibliography

Alkaabi, Sultan Ali R., Warda Alkaabi, and Glen Vyver. "Researching Student Motivation." *Contemporary Issues in Education Research* 10, no. 3 (2017): 193–202, https://doi.org/10.19030/cier.v10i3.9985

Baran, Evrim, and Dana AlZoubi. "Affordances, Challenges, and Impact of Open Pedagogy: Examining Students' Voices." *Distance Education* 41, no. 2 (2020): 230–44. https://doi.org/10.1080/01587919.2020.1757409.

Barefoot, Maria R. "Student Research and Intrinsic Motivation: Effects of Formative Assessment and the Two-Session Model of Information Literacy Instruction." *Pennsylvania Libraries: Research and Practice* 5, no. 1 (2017): 13–25. https://doi.org/10.5195/palrap.2017.140.

Boekaerts, Monique. "Goal-Directed Behavior in the Classroom." In *Handbook of Motivation at School*, edited by Kathryn R. Wentzel and Allan Wigfield, 105–22. New York: Routledge, 2009.

CAST. "Universal Design for Learning Guidelines," ver. 2.2. 2018. http://udlguidelines.cast.org.

Center for Self-Determination Theory. "Research." Accessed June 11, 2021. https://selfdeterminationtheory.org/research/.

Ceyhan, Gaye D., and John W. Tillotson. "Early Year Undergraduate Researchers' Reflections on the Values and Perceived Costs of Their Research Experience." *International Journal of STEM Education* 7 (2020), article 54. https://doi.org/10.1186/s40594-020-00248-x.

Chiu, Thomas K. F. "Digital Support for Student Engagement in Blended Learning Based on Self-Determination Theory." *Computers in Human Behavior* 124 (November 2021): 106909. https://doi.org/10.1016/j.chb.2021.106909.

Cowden, Chapel, Priscilla Seaman, Sarah Copeland, and Lu Gao. "Teaching with Intent: Applying Culturally Responsive Teaching to Library Instruction." *portal: Libraries and the Academy* 21, no. 2 (April 2021): 231–51. https://doi.org/10.1353/pla.2021.0014.

Deci, Edward L., and Richard M. Ryan. "Self-Determination Theory." In *Handbook of Theories of Social Psychology*, vol. 1, edited by Paul A. M. Van Lange, Arie W. Kruglanski, and E. Tory Higgins, 416–37. London: SAGE, 2012. https://doi.org/10.4135/9781446249215.

DeRosa, Robin, and Rajiv Jhangiani. "Open Pedagogy." In *A Guide to Making Open Textbooks with Students*, edited by Elizabeth Mays. Montreal: Rebus Community for Open Textbook Creation, 2017. https://press.rebus.community/makingopentextbookswithstudents/.

Fiedler, Brittany Paloma, Rosan Mitola, and James Cheng. "Responding to Hate: How National and Local Incidents Sparked Action at the UNLV University Libraries." *Reference Services Review* 48, no. 1 (2020): 63–90. https://doi.org/10.1108/RSR-09-2019-0071.

Fisher, Marisa H., Lindsay S. Athamanah, Connie Sung, and Cynde Katherine Josol. "Applying the Self-Determination Theory to Develop a School-to-Work Peer Mentoring Programme to Promote Social Inclusion." *Journal of Applied Research in Intellectual Disabilities* 33, no. 2 (2019): 296–309. https://doi.org/10.1111/jar.12673.

Gómez-García, Gerardo, Francisco-Javier Hinojo-Lucena, María-Pilar Cáceres-Reche, and Magdalena Ramos Navas-Parejo. "The Contribution of the Flipped Classroom Method to the Development of Information Literacy: A Systematic Review." *Sustainability* 12, no. 18 (2020): 7273. https://doi.org/10.3390/su12187273.

Griful-Freixenet, Júlia, Katrien Struyven, Meggie Verstichele, and Caroline Andries. "Higher Education Students with Disabilities Speaking Out: Perceived Barriers and Opportunities of the Universal Design for Learning Framework." *Disability and Society* 32, no. 10 (2017): 1627–49. https://doi.org/10.1080/09687599.2017.1365695.

Haakma, Ineke, Marleen Janssen, and Alexander Minnaert. "A Literature Review on How Need-Supportive Behavior Influences Motivation in Students with Sensory Loss." *Teaching and Teacher Education* 57 (July 2016): 1–13. https://doi.org/10.1016/j.tate.2016.02.008.

Harris, Breanna N., Pumtiwitt C. McCarthy, April M. Wright, Heidi Schutz, Kate S. Boersma, Stephanie L. Shepherd, Lathiena A. Manning, Jessica L. Malisch, and Roni M. Ellington. "From Panic to Pedagogy: Using Online Active Learning to Promote Inclusive Instruction in Ecology and Evolutionary Biology Courses and Beyond." *Ecology and Evolution* 10, no. 22 (November 2020): 12581–612. https://doi.org/10.1002/ece3.6915.

Howard, Tiffany O., Mary-Ann Winkelmes, and Marya Shegog. "Transparency Teaching in the Virtual Classroom: Assessing the Opportunities and Challenges of Integrating Transparency Teaching Methods with Online Learning." *Journal of Political Science Education* 16, no. 2 (2020): 198–211. https://doi.org/10.1080/15512169.2018.1550420.

Inamorato dos Santos, Andreia. *Practical Guidelines on Open Education for Academics: Modernising Higher Education via Open Educational Practices (Based on the OpenEdu Framework)*. Technical report. EUR 29672 EN. Luxembourg: Publications Office of the European Union, 2019. https://data.europa.eu/doi/10.2760/55923.

Jardine, Spencer, Sandra Shropshire, and Regina Koury. "Credit-Bearing Information Literacy Courses in Academic Libraries: Comparing Peers." *College and Research Libraries* 79, no. 6 (2018): 768–84. https://doi.org/10.5860/crl.79.6.768.

Jopp, Ryan, and Jay Cohen. "Choose Your Own Assessment—Assessment Choice for Students in Online Higher Education." *Teaching in Higher Education* 27, no. 6 (2022): 738–55. https://doi.org/10.1080/13562517.2020.1742680.

Khailova, Ladislava. "Using Curriculum Mapping to Scaffold and Equitably Distribute Information Literacy Instruction for Graduate Professional Studies Programs." *Journal of Academic Librarianship* 47, no. 1 (January 2021): 102281. https://doi.org/10.1016/j.acalib.2020.102281.

Lazowski, Rory A., and Chris S. Hulleman. "Motivation Interventions in Education: A Meta-analytic Review." *Review of Educational Research* 86, no. 2 (June 2016): 602–40. https://doi.org/10.3102/0034654315617832;

Makhafola, Lesego, and Martie J. Van Deventer. "Selecting Information Products and Services to Embed in a Virtual Learning Environment to Support Engineering Undergraduates in a Blended Learning Context." *Library Management* 41, no. 6/7 (2020): 579–91. https://doi.org/10.1108/LM-04-2020-0061.

Marineo, Francesca. "Motivation and Online Information Literacy Instruction: A Self-Determination Theory Approach." Master's thesis, University of Nevada, Las Vegas, 2019. UNLV Theses, Dissertations, Professional Papers, and Capstones. https://doi.org/10.34917/15778503.

Miele, David B., and Allan Wigfield. "Quantitative and Qualitative Relations between Motivation and Critical-Analytic Thinking." *Educational Psychology Review* 26, no. 4 (2014): 519–41. https://doi.org/10.1007/s10648-014-9282-2.

Mitchell, Terence R., and Denise Daniels. "Motivation." In *Handbook of Psychology, Volume 12: Industrial and Organizational Psychology*, edited by Walter C. Borman, Daniel R. Ilgen, and Richard J. Klimoski, 225–54. New York: John Wiley & Sons, 2003. https://psihologiapentrutoti.files.wordpress.com/2011/08/handbook-of-psychology-vol-12-industrial-and-organizational-psychology.pdf.

Morrison, Kim L. "Informed Asset-Based Pedagogy: Coming Correct, Counter-stories from an Information Literacy Classroom." *Library Trends* 66, no. 2 (2017): 176–218. https://doi.org/10.1353/lib.2017.0034.

Murphy, Maggie. "On the Same Page: Collaborative Research Assignment Design with Graduate Teaching Assistants." *Reference Services Review* 47, no. 3 (2019): 343–58. https://doi.org/10.1108/RSR-04-2019-0027.

Nizami, Urooj, and Adam Shambaugh. "Open Pedagogy through Community-Directed, Student-Led Partnerships: Establishing CURE (Community-University Research Exchange) at Temple University Libraries." *Open Praxis* 11, no. 4 (2019): 443–50. https://doi.org/10.5944/openpraxis.11.4.1028.

Oliver, John Thomas. "One-Shot Wikipedia: An Edit-Sprint toward Information Literacy." *Reference Services Review* 43, no. 1 (2015): 81–97. https://doi.org/10.1108/RSR-10-2014-0043.

Poort, Irene, Ellen Jansen, and Adriaan Hofman. "Intercultural Group Work in Higher Education: Costs and Benefits from an Expectancy-Value Theory Perspective." *International Journal of Educational Research* 93 (2019): 218–31. https://doi.org/10.1016/j.ijer.2018.11.010.

Powell, Susan, and Ningning Nicole Kong. "Beyond the One-Shot: Intensive Workshops as a Platform for Engaging the Library in Digital Humanities." *College and Undergraduate Libraries* 24, no. 2–4 (2017): 516–31. https://doi.org/10.1080/10691316.2017.1336955.

Pratesi, Angela, Wendy Miller, and Elizabeth Sutton. "Democratizing Knowledge: Using Wikipedia for Inclusive Teaching and Research in Four Undergraduate Classes." *Radical Teacher* 114 (2019): 22–33. https://doi.org/10.5195/rt.2019.517.

Priniski, Stacy J., Cameron A. Hecht, and Judith M. Harackiewicz. "Making Learning Personally Meaningful: A New Framework for Relevance Research." *Journal of Experimental Education* 86, no. 1 (2018): 11–29. https://doi.org/10.1080/00220973.2017.1380589.

Ross, Mitchell, Helen Perkins, and Kelli Bodey. "Academic Motivation and Information Literacy Self-Efficacy: The Importance of a Simple Desire to Know." *Library and Information Science Research* 38, no. 1 (January 2016): 2–9. https://doi.org/10.1016/j.lisr.2016.01.002.

Ryan, Richard M., and Edward L. Deci. "Self-Determination Theory and the Facilitation of Intrinsic Motivation, Social Development, and Well-Being." *American Psychologist* 55, no. 1 (2000): 68–78. https://doi.org/10.1037/0003-066X.55.1.68.

———. *Self-Determination Theory: Basic Psychological Needs in Motivation, Development, and Wellness*. New York: Guilford, 2017. https://doi.org/10.1521/978.14625/28806.

Sathy, Viji, and Kelly Hogan. "How to Make Your Teaching More Inclusive." *Chronicle of Higher Education*, July 22, 2019. https://www.chronicle.com/article/how-to-make-your-teaching-more-inclusive/.

Savolainen, Reijo. "Expectancy-Value Beliefs and Information Needs as Motivators for Task-Based Information Seeking." *Journal of Documentation* 68, no. 4 (2012): 492–511. https://doi.org/10.1108/00220411211239075.

Schunk, Dale H. "Self-Efficacy and Academic Motivation." *Educational Psychologist* 26, no. 3–4 (1991): 207–31.

Thomas, Liz, and Helen May. *Inclusive Learning and Teaching in Higher Education*. York, UK: Higher Education Academy, 2010. https://s3.eu-west-2.amazonaws.com/assets.creode.advancehe-document-manager/documents/hea/private/inclusivelearningandteaching_finalreport_1568036778.pdf.

Troftgruben, Troy M. "Decentered Online Bible Instruction: How Active Learning Enhances the Study of Scripture." *Teaching Theology and Religion* 21, no. 1 (January 2018): 33–46. https://doi.org/10.1111/teth.12418.

Wentzel, Kathryn R., and Allan Wigfield. *Handbook of Motivation at School*. Educational Psychology Handbook Series. New York: Routledge, 2009.

Wigfield, Allan, Stephen Tonks, and Susan L. Klauda. "Expectancy-Value Theory." In *Handbook of Motivation at School*, edited by Kathryn R. Wentzel and Allan Wigfield, 55–75. New York: Routledge, 2009.

Wikipedia. "Wikipedia:About," edited by Jim Henderson, September 20, 2021. https://en.wikipedia.org/w/index.php?title=Wikipedia:About&oldid=1045448340.

Wishkoski, Rachel, Kacy Lundstrom, and Erin Davis. "Faculty Teaching and Librarian-Facilitated Assignment Design." *portal: Libraries and the Academy* 19, no. 1 (2019): 95–126. https://doi.org/10.1353/pla.2019.0006.

Withorn, Tessa. "The Information Spectrum." CORA: Community of Online Research Assignments, May 25, 2018. https://www.projectcora.org/assignment/information-spectrum.

Yeager, David S., Marlone D. Henderson, Sidney D'Mello, David Paunesku, Gregory M. Walton, Brian J. Spitzer, and Angela Lee Duckworth. "Boring but Important: A Self-Transcendent Purpose for Learning Fosters Academic Self-Regulation." *Journal of Personality and Social Psychology* 107, no. 4 (2014): 559–80. https://doi.org/10.1037/a0037637.

CHAPTER 14

Facilitating Critical Information Literacy

Using Intergroup Dialogue to Engage with the *Framework*

*Debbie Krahmer**

Land Acknowledgement

Colgate University and the town of Hamilton, New York, are built upon the ancestral lands of the Onyota'a:ká (Oneida) of the Hodinöhsö:ni´. This land was acquired through forced cession in the "Treaty" of Fort Schuyler in 1788, under the guise of "protecting" Oneida lands from greedy land speculators.[1] The state of New York as well as the United States of America owe a debt to the Onyota'a:ká, who were critical allies in the Revolutionary War. As a settler on this land and descendant of immigrants, I cannot begin to speak about equity or inclusion without recognizing the painful history of violence, dispossession, and betrayal, as well as honoring the modern Indigenous experiences of the Oneida Indian Nation of New York.

---

* Debbie Krahmer is a white, trans, queer, disabled, US-born, mid-career librarian who has lived in mostly rural areas and worked in predominantly white institutions. D comes from a working class background and is currently in a non-tenure-track library faculty position at a University in upstate New York.

Introduction

In my thirteen years at Colgate University, a predominantly white institution, I've been involved in university-wide diversity efforts, initially stemming from my experiences as a queer, trans, and disabled librarian, but also growing to focus more heavily on race as I became more aware of my own whiteness. In the fall of 2014, over 300 students staged a one-hundred-hour sit-in at the admissions office to draw attention to the unaddressed inequities and racism at Colgate, culminating in a twenty-one-point action plan.[2] The cry of "Can you hear us now?" resonated strongly with me, as it echoed my first Intergroup Dialogue (IGD) experience.

At Colgate, I was part of the second cohort of faculty and staff to participate in a two-day IGD workshop and dialogue around controversial issues in May 2014. Prior to this experience, I had stood in solidarity with my BIPOC colleagues as they shared their experiences with racism and sexism on campus. I had heard these stories. I had expressed my sympathies. I had silently sworn to enact change on this campus so these injustices wouldn't continue (though, "somehow," they just kept happening). I worked to incorporate social justice into my librarianship and collaborated with colleagues on diversity training sessions and classes.

It wasn't until I was in a room with thirty-four other faculty and staff—people that I worked with every day, people that I admired and even loved as friends—experiencing IGD for two days straight that I actually HEARD the stories and the pain of my BIPOC colleagues. I felt it all, deep inside of my core being. I understood. That day, I swore out loud that I'd do everything possible to enact real change, and I've since dedicated myself to doing the work of dismantling racism and addressing social justice through my personal life and my library work. I hope you will find something in this chapter to inspire you in your own work toward equitable and inclusive pedagogies.

What is Intergroup Dialogue?

Intergroup Dialogue (IGD) is a democratic social justice education process that involves facilitated dialogues around controversial issues with a diverse group of people over a sustained length of time.[3] Developed at the University of Michigan,[4] IGD has been grown, tested, evaluated, and used in a variety of forums to help often opposing groups come to a mutual understanding.[5]

Ione Damasco has spoken about and written extensively on using IGD in a professional development setting.[6] In a chapter in the book *Libraries Promoting Reflective Dialogue in a Time of Political Polarization*, Damasco covered the basics of the IGD process for professional development,[7] so I will speak only briefly about its design here. At the end of this chapter, I include several resources for getting started in doing your own research around IGD (see appendix).

IGD is split into four stages:[8]

- Stage 1: group beginnings (forming and building relationships)
- Stage 2: exploring differences and commonalities of experience
- Stage 3: exploring and discussing hot topics
- Stage 4: action planning and building alliances

During a sustained dialogue, the group may move between various stages, often circling back or repeating stages. The facilitator is there to guide the participants through a structured dialogue, but they are not the teachers or the experts.[9]

It's important to emphasize that IGD is a process deliberately focused on sustained dialogues. While you can use aspects and exercises from IGD to build relationships or explore differences in a one-shot or even a reference interaction, it isn't a true IGD experience without the long-term commitment to dialogue.[10] Sarah Gilchrist speaks about using the IGD exercise Ground Rules to initially engage students with the learning environment of a semester-long information literacy course.[11] IGD exercises and dialogue can be used for one-time purposes to promote emotional and intellectual engagement, but optimally IGD should be done over several class periods or in an extended (two-to-four-hour) workshop.[12]

Background

It may seem that I'm coming at this with the passion of a convert, and perhaps I am. Coinciding with my first IGD experience and the Colgate student protest of 2014, ACRL was heading toward releasing the final version of the new *Framework for Information Literacy for Higher Education*.[13] While the reception of the emerging *Framework* was chilly at best in our local conversations, I found many parallels between the equity and inclusion library work I wanted to do, the critical-dialogic approach I was learning from IGD, and the concepts presented by the *Framework*.[14]

Starting with the fall of 2015, a two-and-a-half-hour IGD experience was incorporated into the first-year orientation program.[15] I've been a frequent facilitator, leading new students in discussions of race, gender, sexuality, and class. The students are introduced to the concepts of dialogue versus debate versus discussion, set ground rules, and work through some IGD exercises to introduce them to having critical conversations at Colgate. Additionally, one-hour conversations are held throughout the academic year where students, faculty, and staff can continue to dialogue on a variety of topics. This foundation for all Colgate students also helps me to integrate IGD into my library sessions by establishing IGD as a norm on our campus so that students are prepared for and familiar with what to expect.

Ironically, my research into how I could apply IGD to librarianship led to my becoming invested in critical theory in LIS.[16] Since the introduction of the *Framework*, I've had many discussions with my colleagues around how my instruction incorporates critical theory (including the similar-yet-somewhat-distinct avenues of critical information literacy, critical librarianship, critical and inclusive pedagogies in LIS, and even critical reference dialogue[17]). The question most often asked by my colleagues is "How do you do it?" I've found that utilizing IGD exercises and facilitation is one of the ways I am able to do this work.

Connecting IGD and Critical Information Literacy

IGD is a natural fit for critical information literacy. Kate Adler, in writing about critical reference dialogue, uses Reitz's nine elements of education to illustrate the tenets of critical pedagogy for library instruction:[18] the teacher or librarian is a guide and facilitator, creating a participatory, directed dialogue with students that focuses on social problems through asking questions and unpacking logistics. The teacher or librarian must also work to establish an active rapport with the students and facilitate group solidarity into assignments that are study or action projects. Through this work, the college or library becomes an engine for social change, building alliances locally, regionally, and nationally and shedding light on where information is coming from and how to use it critically.[19]

IGD works with a similar framework. Overall, when you make the decision to use IGD in the classroom, you are recognizing that there is a need for change and that the classroom is one place to enact that change. Facilitators are not experts, but act as guides. Stage 1, group beginnings, focuses on establishing the solidarity of the group, as well as introducing the practice of dialogue. Stage 2 takes the participants through a process of exploring differences and commonalities, and the facilitators use stages 1 and 2 to determine the direction of stage 3's dialogues on hot topics. In stage 4, alliances are formed and action plans are developed.

Incorporating IGD into the Library Classroom

Stage 1 and stage 2 are the easiest to incorporate into a limited time, such as a one-shot library session. These stages create community through engaging with one's own social identity, as well as exploring the commonalities and differences of experience between oneself and others.

In every one-shot session I teach, for example, I introduce myself as a person who prefers to be referred to by name rather than gendered pronouns. I also share that I have a visual disability and how it will affect the classroom experience. By being vulnerable and sharing my own identity as someone who is often "othered," it invites the students to be more comfortable with sharing their own vulnerabilities. During one-on-one time, I find that many students with minoritized identities will introduce themselves by name and pronouns or disclose their own disabilities as it affects their ability to use our resources. This can also be used for modeling my own difficulties with searching to draw the students into a dialogue about access or the research process. Establishing classroom ground rules, or using the already established rules of the course, much as Gilchrist does in her classes, is another way to build community.[20]

With careful consideration and in collaboration with a professor who has been using IGD throughout the semester, stage 3 can also be incorporated into a one-shot. As a facilitator, you must be careful: "Group leaders must be trained to use such exercises appropriately and effectively and must be skilled in handling the personal and intergroup issues that are likely to arise from the exercises."[21] There are low-risk and high-risk exercises for engaging in hot-button or controversial topics that you can use at your own discretion, as it is appropriate or comfortable to the situation.[22] In some instances, the entire course is a hot button, such as racism in education or queering religion. Knowing how to deal with these emotions can help to keep the class session moving forward productively, as I will demonstrate later in this chapter.

The best way that I've found of reaching stage 4 in a one-shot context is to work with the professor to have an assignment rising out of the library session (or the overall course) where the students are able to effect some change or take some action rather than simply writing a report. Producing a podcast episode, editing Wikipedia pages, or presenting their findings in a short video are all ways that student research can be used in a more public and active way. For example, an introduction to Peace and Conflict Studies course started creating podcasts from their research projects on war, genocide, and ethnic cleansing.[23] The students reported that by bringing more attention to these marginalized conflicts, they felt they were actually able to help the people they were researching in some way.[24]

How I've Incorporated IGD and Critical Information Literacy into the Library Classroom

I've been integrating IGD into my classroom explicitly since 2016. In the fall of 2016, I was asked to teach three 50-minute visual literacy sessions for three different courses by Dr. Aisha Musa. I'd worked with this professor many times in the past. When we met to talk about the needs of the assignments, each class had its own focus (Legacies of the Ancient World, Sharia Law, and Introduction to the Qur'an), but the core issue was the same—the professor wanted the students to be able to engage more deeply with visual images and media and to critically examine the stories and power structures behind them. I'd been teaching visual literacy sessions for years, as well as a similar collaboration with a faculty member on Inverting the Narrative projects,[25] but this was a good opportunity to further integrate some of what I was learning through facilitator training in IGD. I asked if I could stray from my standard visual literacy lecture that I'd done for her classes before, and she was excited by the opportunity.

I structured the class session around stage 1 and stage 2 in IGD. The professor was not actively using IGD in her own classroom at the time. At the start of the class, I introduced how I expected the students to interact by both modeling and explaining dialogue while introducing some visual literacy concepts. For Legacies of the Ancient World, made up of first- and second-year students who by that point had been the first two class years to go through the required IGD program, I also asked them to recall the first-year orientation work, which most of the students readily remembered. I used images from the professor to personalize the presentation for each course, but I also used some standard images such as emojis and memes. The majority of the class was devoted to active dialogue with the students around images, power, and meaning.

For example, I used images of Darsh Preet Singh and Veerender Jubbal, two Sikh men whose images had been edited and used in various memes as a visual stand-in for "Muslim terrorist." An image of Singh, the first NCAA Sikh basketball player to wear a turban, was used as a popular meme. "Nobody at school wants to guard Muhammad, he's too explosive," one version read.[26] Jubbal, a vocal opponent of Gamergate, had a selfie edited to include a bomb vest, Qur'an, and sex toys. His image actually appeared on the cover of a Spanish newspaper after the November 2015 attacks in France, identified as one of the men involved.[27] At the time of the class session, most of the students hadn't actually seen these images but could recall similar situations. As a group we looked up newspaper articles and social media posts and discussed issues around them, focusing on how images can be misread and even deliberately used to mislead.

Toward the end of the class, I borrowed an image exercise from my colleague Sarah Keen, former head of Special Collections and University Archives. It's an image of the Salt Rush, an old tradition from the 1880s or 90s where different class years of students would wrestle and throw salt at each other.[28] Using visual thinking strategies,[29] I asked the students to tell me what they saw in the image. Students described the scene as a riot, a protest, a fire, and even a battle, while others saw the salt as smoke or tear gas. After many minutes of dialogue, I told the students what the image was and described the Salt Rush ritual. It was a fascinating piece of college history, and they all took another minute to look at the picture with the new realization. However, I shifted from my colleague's usual usage of the image and pushed the students on the issue.

"Do you think that's true? What evidence do I have that it is what I said it is?"

This caused a panic in the class, as students were insulted that I had lied to them. Out of three sessions of eighteen students each, only one student googled "Salt Rush Colgate" unprompted to double-check what I was saying. For the other two classes, I needed to prompt the students to do a little searching so they could verify the information I was sharing. It was a difficult moment of emotion in the classroom, but also a rewarding discovery for the students as they felt the power of knowledge and research. Further, it prompted a dialogue around the nature of authority, one of the tenets of the *Framework*.

This exercise is one that could be replicated in other scenarios by using your own college's history or an image with an interesting, but not well-known, backstory. *Time*'s 100 Photographs collection is a good resource for historical and iconic images, complete with evidence and copyright information for the images.[30] If the backstory can't easily be found online, you can also bring in primary documents or other sources and invite the students to fact-check your story. If you are selecting a historical image, be prepared to handle any emotions it may bring up in the classroom, especially pictures dealing with tragic or deadly events.

Even teaching basically the same session three times in a row, it was a very rewarding session. I had multiple different conversations with the students as the views they brought in were influenced by their own experiences and assumptions. I felt that the students walked away with a better understanding of images and research than in my past visual literacy classes. The professor, at the end of the semester, was extremely pleased with the depth of the students' understanding and use of images.

Another example of a library session I completely modified using IGD facilitation was for Religions of Resistance with Dr. Paul Humphrey in the fall of 2019. The course "studies African-derived religions and practices in the Caribbean, particularly the ways in which they constitute anticolonial and decolonial perspectives and practices."[31] While the professor doesn't use IGD specifically, this course, cross-listed in Africana and Latin American Studies/LGBTQ Studies, was a good opportunity to bring in stage 3. By that semester, all students currently enrolled in undergraduate classes had been through the first-year orientation IGD experience. The students were already using a critical and queer studies perspective in the classroom, so the library session needed to reflect that. It also gave me the opportunity to bring more themes of anti-racism and social justice, as they fit the overall goals of the course.

For the seventy-five-minute class, I had more time to engage the students in discussion. In addition to my typical self-introduction, I also brought attention to the fact that I was a white person and that my experience with Caribbean religions came from both a Western-biased and Pagan-based perspective. Throughout the session, I brought attention to issues of bias, especially as they concerned the commercial databases they would be searching. As the students would be doing more historical research, we discussed the fact that much of what they would find would likely be from a white, Western, and Christian bias. The professor, a white British man, brought in information from the course so far to reinforce and further prompt areas of discussion. His openness to standing in for a "typical" religion professor was especially helpful, as we both epitomized the very colonizers the Caribbean people were resisting.

For example, one of the areas of dialogue occurred around the Library of Congress Subject Heading "Vodou."[32] The spelling of the word was one of the early ideas covered in the class, so I was able to bring in the history of the LCSH change, as well as how students would be faced with historical spellings in articles. The discussion centered around both the importance of practitioners' views in religious research and how you can't automatically judge the quality of an article based on the spelling that was used without examining all the evidence. As a group, we were able to complicate the simple axiom of "peer-reviewed = good" by evaluating articles through several different lenses.

One significant situation occurred where I feel that, if I had not been trained and experienced in IGD facilitation with students, faculty, and staff, I might have had a harder time dealing with the classroom. While the class was doing some group searching, I found a small group of students talking excitedly and gesturing wildly. I asked what they found, and it was an article that used the N-word in the title. Instead of ignoring the slur in the classroom, we explored it. The student researched the professor who had written the article, looked at his other writing, and read the article to dissect the choices he made. It was an uncomfortable situation, for sure, but the students were able to tackle it in a way that demystified many aspects of scholarly communication.

Incorporating IGD and Critical Information Literacy into the Reference Consultation

With the pandemic lockdowns of 2020, courses at Colgate went completely online for the first time in its 200-year history. Typical library sessions were replaced with recorded lectures or tutorial videos as faculty scrambled to translate their face-to-face teaching to remote on the fly. With the focus on just surviving day to day for the rest of the spring semester and preparing for an uncertain fall, I found myself experiencing more burnout than usual. The video sessions were not as satisfying, and I felt despair at having another semester of database demos and "how to access our resources from off campus" videos to look forward to. It's important work, of course, where I could incorporate small areas of criticality, but not the kind of work that energizes me like IGD and critical information literacy.

So I decided if I couldn't find a way to be critical and interactive in the class sessions I had, I could use those skills to be more critical in my reference consultations, the number of which tripled from pre-pandemic times. I deliberately used more of my IGD training in my consultations with students than I had before. Time was specifically spent getting to know the student and checking in on them mentally and emotionally before addressing any research questions. This was also crucial to combat the isolation many of us were feeling due to the quarantines and lockdowns.

It was a great opportunity to discuss with them the production of scholarly information. "Why can't I find any scholarly articles on the effect that COVID-19 had on the 2020 presidential election?" was a frequent question in November that helped us to tease out many aspects of scholarly information, especially the time involved in producing and publishing articles in peer-reviewed journals, as well as the place of investigative journalism versus sensationalized news and social media posts in doing research.

While the very short interactions—usually no longer than thirty minutes—take things even further away from the "sustained" goal of IGD, they allowed me to focus on more critical interactions with the students. Until the pandemic, virtual reference interactions, regardless of length or depth, were considered purely transactional. As they became the only option for reference support, the pandemic allowed us to reconsider this lesser form of reference as being just as valuable as face-to-face consultations.

The discussions were varied, but the interactions had more depth to them. Several of the students returned to ask questions for other classes or spoke directly to the fact they would use the information and techniques in their other research projects. I also experienced more frequent follow-ups from students letting me know how the research worked out, as well as referrals from friends.

Conclusion

IGD can give librarians experimenting with critical theory in the library classroom some techniques and ways of sustaining dialogue to help them better integrate criticality in their teaching. More than just a professional development technique, IGD training is focused on facilitating dialogue on difficult discussions, a core tenet of critical information literacy. The techniques and experiences can also help the librarian to deal with difficult situations in the classroom and to bring in more critical theory into their teaching.

Appendix

Resources for Understanding IGD

Gurin, Patricia, Biren A. Nagda, and Nicholas Sorensen. "Intergroup Dialogue: Education for a Broad Conception of Civic Engagement." *Liberal Education* 97, no. 2 (2011): 46–51.

Gurin, Patricia, Biren (Ratnesh) A. Nagda, and Ximena Zúñiga. *Dialogue across Difference: Practice, Theory, and Research on Intergroup Dialogue.* New York: Russell Sage Foundation, 2013.

Humphreys, Mayra Lopez. "Intergroup Dialogue: A Pedagogical Model for Integrating Cultural Competence within a Social Justice Framework." *International Journal of Interdisciplinary Social Sciences* 6, no. 5 (2011): 199–213.

Lopez, Gretchen E., and Ximena Zúñiga. "Intergroup Dialogue and Democratic Practice in Higher Education." *New Directions for Higher Education* 2010, no. 152 (Winter 2010): 35–42.

Zúñiga, Ximena, Biren (Ratnesh) A. Nagda, Mark Chesler, Adena Cytron-Walker. "Intergroup Dialogue in Higher Education: Meaningful Learning about Social Justice." Special issue, *ASHE Higher Education Report* 32, no. 4 (2007). https://doi.org/10.1002/aehe.3204.

Resources for Facilitating Dialogues

Brookfield, Stephen D., and Stephen Preskill. *Discussion as a Way of Teaching: Tools and Techniques for Democratic Classrooms.* San Francisco: Jossey-Bass, 2005.

Landreman, Lisa M., ed. *The Art of Effective Facilitation: Reflections from Social Justice Educators.* Sterling, VA: Stylus, 2013.

Maxwell, Kelly E., Biren (Ratnesh) A. Nagda, and Monita C Thompson, eds. *Facilitating Intergroup Dialogues: Bridging Differences, Catalyzing Change.* Sterling, VA: Stylus, 2011.

Nagda, Birenee Ratnesh A., Chan-woo Kim, and Yaffa Truelove. "Learning about Difference, Learning with Others, Learning to Transgress." *Journal of Social Issues* 60, no. 1 (2004): 195–214.

Nagda, Biren (Ratnesh) A., and Ximena Zúñiga. "Fostering Meaningful Racial Engagement through Intergroup Dialogues." *Group Processes and Intergroup Relations* 6, no. 1 (2003): 111–28.

Resources on the Effectiveness of IGD

Alimo, Craig John. "From Dialogue to Action: The Impact of Cross-race Intergroup Dialogue on the Development of White College Students as Racial Allies." *Equity and Excellence in Education* 45, no. 1 (2012): 36–59

Dessel, Adrienne B., and Nancy Rodenborg. "An Evaluation of Intergroup Dialogue Pedagogy: Addressing Segregation and Developing Cultural Competency." *Journal of Social Work Education* 53, no. 2 (2017): 222–39.

Ford, Kristie, ed. *Facilitating Change through Intergroup Dialogue: Social Justice Advocacy in Practice.* New York: Routledge, 2018.

Nagda, Biren A., Patricia Gurin, Nicholas Sorensen, and Ximena Zúñiga. "Evaluating Intergroup Dialogue: Engaging Diversity for Personal and Social Responsibility." *Diversity and Democracy* 12, no. 1 (2009): 4–6.

Notes

1. Laurence M. Hauptman, "Command Performance: Philip Schuyler and the New York State–Oneida 'Treaty' of 1795," in *The Oneida Indian Journey from New York to Wisconsin, 1784–1860*, ed. Laurence M. Hauptman and L. Gordon McLester III (Madison: University of Wisconsin Press, 1999), 42.

2. Jaleesa Jones, "Colgate University Students Ask #CanYouHearUsNow," *USA Today*, September 24, 2014, https://wayback.archive-it.org/4883/20140928042224/http://college.usatoday.com/2014/09/24/colgate-university-students-ask-canyouhearusnow/; Colgate University, "Colgate for All," last modified June 29, 2015, https://www.colgate.edu/student-life/diversity-and-inclusion/colgate-all.

3. David Schoem et al., "Intergroup Dialogue: Democracy at Work in Theory and Practice," in *Intergroup Dialogue: Deliberative Democracy in School, College, Community, and Workplace*, ed. David Schoem and Sylvia Hurtado (Ann Arbor: University of Michigan Press, 2001), 6.

4. Ximena Zúñiga, Birin (Ratnesh) A. Nagda, and Todd D. Sevig, "Intergroup Dialogues: An Educational Model for Cultivating Engagement across Differences," *Equity and Excellence in Education* 35, no. 1 (2002): 15, https://doi.org/10.1080/713845248.

5. Debbie Krahmer, "Intergroup Dialogue Guide Home," LibGuide, Colgate University Libraries, last modified May 27, 2021, https://libguides.colgate.edu/IGD.

6. Ione T. Damasco, "Inclusive Library Professional Development Using Principles of Intergroup Dialogue" (presentation, Academic Library Association of Ohio, 2018 Diversity Workshop—Actively Inclusive: Libraries Speak Up! Columbus, OH, May 10, 2018), https://ecommons.udayton.edu/roesch_fac_presentations/47; Ione T. Damasco, "Incorporating Intergroup Dialogue into the Equity, Diversity, and Inclusion Conversation," *ACRL 2019 President's Program* (blog), January 4, 2019, https://acrl.libguides.com/c.php?g=899144&p=6468942&t=32314.

7. Ione T. Damasco, "Creating Meaningful Engagement in Academic Libraries Using Principles of Intergroup Dialogue," in *Libraries Promoting Reflective Dialogue in a Time of Political Polarization*, ed. Andrea Baer, Allysa Stern Cahoy, and Robert Schroeder (Chicago: Association of College and Research Libraries, 2019), 17–20.

8. Ximena Zúñiga et al., "Intergroup Dialogue in Higher Education: Meaningful Learning about Social Justice," special issue, *ASHE Higher Education Report* 32, no. 4 (2007): 26–31, https://doi.org/10.1002/aehe.3204.

9. Zúñiga et al, "Intergroup Dialogue in Higher Education," 39.

10. David Schoem and Shari Saunders, "Adapting Intergroup Dialogue Processes for Use in a Variety of Settings," in *Intergroup Dialogue: Deliberative Democracy in School, College, Community, and Workplace*, ed. David Schoem and Sylvia Hurtado (Ann Arbor: University of Michigan Press, 2001), 328.

11. Sarah Burns Gilchrist, "It's HIP to Be Square: Instruction, High-Impact Practices, and the Framework," in *Ascending into an Open Future: The Proceedings of the ACRL 2021 Virtual Conference*, ed. Dawn M. Mueller (Chicago: Association of College and Research Libraries, 2021), 339, http://www.ala.org/acrl/sites/ala.org.acrl/files/content/conferences/confsandpreconfs/2021/HIPtobeSquare.pdf.

12. Schoem et al., "Intergroup Dialogue: Democracy at Work," 6.

13. Association of College and Research Libraries, *Framework for Information Literacy for Higher Education* (Chicago: Association of College and Research Libraries, 2016), https://www.ala.org/acrl/standards/ilframework.

14. Zúñiga, Diversity and Inclusion Research Librarian at Cornell University et al., "Intergroup Dialogue in Higher Education," 3–4.

15. "Work and Play," *Colgate Scene*, Winter 2016, https://news.colgate.edu/scene/main_feature/work-and-play-3.

16. Maria T. Accardi, Emily Drabinski, and Alana Kumbier, "Introduction," in *Critical Library Instruction: Theories and Methods*, ed. Maria T. Accardi, Emily Drabinski, and Alana Kumbier (Duluth, MN: Library Juice Press, 2010), xi–xii.

17. Annie Downey, *Critical Information Literacy* (Sacramento, CA: Library Juice Press, 2016), 41–42; Eamon C. Tewell, "The Practice and Promise of Critical Information Literacy: Academic Librarians' Involvement in Critical Library Instruction," *College and Research Libraries* 79, no. 1 (2018): 11; Karen P. Nicholson and Maura Seale, "Introduction," in *The Politics of Theory and the Practice of Critical Librarianship*, ed. Karen P. Nicholson and Maura Seal (Sacramento, CA: Library Juice Press, 2018), 1–2; Michelle Reale, "Critical Pedagogy in the Classroom: Library Instruction That Gives Voice to Students and Builds a Community of Scholars," *Journal of Library Innovation* 3, no. 2 (2012): 85; John Watts, "Inclusive Cultural and Social Pedagogy in the Library Classroom," *LOEX Quarterly* 44 (2017): article 4, p. 9; Kate Adler, "Radical Purpose: The Critical Reference Dialogue at a Progressive Urban College," *Urban Library Journal* 19, no. 1 (2013): article 9, pp. 2–3, https://academicworks.cuny.edu/ulj/vol19/iss1/9/.

18. Charles Reitz, "Elements of Education: Critical Pedagogy and the Community College," *Counterpoints* 209 (2002): 199–203, https://www.jstor.org/stable/42979497.

19. Adler, "Radical Purpose," 4–5.

20. Gilchrist, "HIP to Be Square," 339.

21. David Schoem and Shari Saunders, "Adapting Intergroup Dialogue Processes for Use in a Variety of Settings," in *Intergroup Dialogue: Deliberative Democracy in School, College, Community, and Workplace*, ed. David Schoem and Sylvia Hurtado (Ann Arbor: University of Michigan Press, 2001), 330.

22. M. Lydia Khuri, "Working with Emotion in Educational Intergroup Dialogue," *International Journal of Intercultural Relations* 28, no. 6 (2004): 602.

23. Colgate University, *Marginalized Conflicts*, podcast series, 2008, https://archive.org/details/podcast_marginalized-conflicts_406995331?tab=about.

24. Colgate University, "Marginalized Podcast Project PEAC 111," February 3, 2009, YouTube video, 4:40, https://www.youtube.com/watch?v=jWlcuicMMoQ?t=282.

25. Rachel Lima, "Brown Bag Showcases Women's Studies Students' Artwork," *Colgate Maroon-News*, November 6, 2014, https://thecolgatemaroonnews.com/5119/news/brown-bag-showcases-womens-studies-students-artwork/.

26. Ismat Sarah Mangla, "Sikh-Americans Suffer Racist Abuse after San Bernardino: 'He's Too Explosive.'" *International Business Times* (US ed.), December 14, 2015, https://www.ibtimes.com/sikh-americans-suffer-racist-abuse-after-san-bernardino-hes-too-explosive-2224897.

27. Kevin Rawlinson, "Canadian Pictured as Paris Terrorist in Suspected Gamergate Smear," *Guardian*, November 15, 2015, https://www.theguardian.com/world/2015/nov/16/canadian-pictured-as-paris-terrorist-in-suspected-gamergate-smear.

28. "Salt Rush," *The Interclass Rivalry of Colgate University*, July 2015, https://colgatetraditions.wordpress.com/salt-rush/.

29. Abigail Housen and Karin DeSantis, "Directory of Studies, 1998–2003," VTS: Visual Thinking Strategies, last modified 2021, https://vtshome.org/wp-content/uploads/2016/08/6Directory-of-Studies.pdf.

30. Ben Goldberger, Paul Moakley, and Kira Pollack. "100 Photographs: The Most Influential Images of All Time," *Time*, last modified 2018, https://time.com/tag/100-photos/.

31. Paul Humphrey, "LGBT 242 AX Religions of Resistance" (course syllabus, Colgate University, Hamilton, NY, fall 2019).

32. Kate Ramsey, "From 'Voodooism' to 'Vodou': Changing a US Library of Congress Subject Heading," *Journal of Haitian Studies* 18, no. 2 (2012): 14.

Bibliography

Accardi, Maria T., Emily Drabinski, and Alana Kumbier, eds. *Critical Library Instruction: Theories and Methods*. Duluth, MN: Library Juice Press, 2010.

Adler, Kate. "Radical Purpose: The Critical Reference Dialogue at a Progressive Urban College." *Urban Library Journal* 19, no. 1 (2013): article 9. https://academicworks.cuny.edu/ulj/vol19/iss1/9/.

Association of College and Research Libraries. *Framework for Information Literacy for Higher Education*. Chicago: Association of College and Research Libraries. https://www.ala.org/acrl/standards/ilframework.

Colgate University. "Colgate for All." Last modified June 29, 2015. https://www.colgate.edu/student-life/diversity-and-inclusion/colgate-all.

———. *Marginalized Conflicts*. Podcast series. 2008. https://archive.org/details/podcast_marginalized-conflicts_406995331?tab=about.

———. "Marginalized Podcast Project PEAC111." February 3, 2009. YouTube video, 5:03. https://www.youtube.com/watch?v=jWlcuicMMoQ?t=282.

Damasco, Ione T. "Creating Meaningful Engagement in Academic Libraries Using Principles of Intergroup Dialogue." In *Libraries Promoting Reflective Dialogue in a Time of Political Polarization*, edited by Andrea Baer, Allysa Stern Cahoy, and Robert Schroeder, 13–31. Chicago: Association of College and Research Libraries, 2019.

———. "Inclusive Library Professional Development Using Principles of Intergroup Dialogue." Presentation, Academic Library Association of Ohio, 2018 Diversity Workshop—Actively Inclusive: Libraries Speak Up! Columbus, OH, May 10, 2018. https://ecommons.udayton.edu/roesch_fac_presentations/47.

———. "Incorporating Intergroup Dialogue into the Equity, Diversity, and Inclusion Conversation." *ACRL 2019 President's Program* (blog), January 4, 2019. https://acrl.libguides.com/c.php?g=899144&p=6468942&t=32314.

Downey, Annie. *Critical Information Literacy: Foundations, Inspiration, and Ideas*. Sacramento, CA: Library Juice Press, 2016.

Gilchrist, Sarah Burns. "It's HIP to Be Square: Instruction, High-Impact Practices, and the Framework." In *Ascending into an Open Future: The Proceedings of the ACRL 2021 Virtual Conference*, edited by Dawn M. Mueller, 338–48. Chicago: Association of College and Research Libraries, 2021. http://www.ala.org/acrl/sites/ala.org.acrl/files/content/conferences/confsandpreconfs/2021/HIPtobeSquare.pdf.

Goldberger, Ben, Paul Moakley, and Kira Pollack. "100 Photographs: The Most Influential Images of All Time." *Time*. Last modified 2018.

Hauptman, Laurence M., and L. Gordon McLester III, eds. *The Oneida Indian Journey: From New York to Wisconsin, 1784–1860*. Madison: University of Wisconsin Press, 1999.

Housen, Abigail, and Karin DeSantis, "Directory of Studies, 1998–2003." VTS: Visual Thinking Strategies. Last modified 2021. https://vtshome.org/wp-content/uploads/2016/08/6Directory-of-Studies.pdf.

Humphrey, Paul. "LGBT 242 AX Religions of Resistance." Course syllabus, Colgate University, Hamilton, NY, fall 2019.

Jones, Jaleesa. "Colgate University Students Ask #CanYouHearUsNow." *USA Today*, September 24, 2014. https://wayback.archive-it.org/4883/20140928042224/http://college.usatoday.com/2014/09/24/colgate-university-students-ask-canyouhearusnow/.

Khuri, M. Lydia. "Working with Emotion in Educational Intergroup Dialogue." *International Journal of Intercultural Relations* 28, no. 6 (2004): 595–612.

Krahmer, Debbie. "Intergroup Dialogue Guide Home." LibGuide, Colgate University Libraries. Last modified May 27, 2021. https://libguides.colgate.edu/IGD.

Lima, Rachel. "Brown Bag Showcases Women's Studies Students' Artwork." *Colgate Maroon-News*, November 6, 2014. https://thecolgatemaroonnews.com/5119/news/brown-bag-showcases-womens-studies-students-artwork/.

Mangla, Ismat Sarah. "Sikh-Americans Suffer Racist Abuse after San Bernardino: 'He's Too Explosive.'" *International Business Times* (US ed.), December 14, 2015. https://www.ibtimes.com/sikh-americans-suffer-racist-abuse-after-san-bernardino-hes-too-explosive-2224897.

Nicholson, Karen P., and Maura Seale, eds. *The Politics of Theory and the Practice of Critical Librarianship.* Sacramento, CA: Library Juice Press, 2018.

Ramsey, Kate. "From 'Voodooism' to 'Vodou': Changing a US Library of Congress Subject Heading." *Journal of Haitian Studies* 18, no. 2 (2012): 14–25.

Rawlinson, Kevin. "Canadian Pictured as Paris Terrorist in Suspected Gamergate Smear." *Guardian*, November 15, 2015, https://www.theguardian.com/world/2015/nov/16/canadian-pictured-as-paris-terrorist-in-suspected-gamergate-smear.

Reale, Michelle. "Critical Pedagogy in the Classroom: Library Instruction That Gives Voice to Students and Builds a Community of Scholars." *Journal of Library Innovation* 3, no. 2 (2012): 80–88.

Reitz, Charles. "Elements of Education: Critical Pedagogy and the Community College." *Counterpoints* 209 (2002): 198–206. https://www.jstor.org/stable/42979497.

"Salt Rush." The Interclass Rivalry of Colgate University. July 2015, https://colgatetraditions.wordpress.com/salt-rush/.

Schoem, David, and Sylvia Hurtado, eds. *Intergroup Dialogue: Deliberative Democracy in School, College, Community, and Workplace.* Ann Arbor: University of Michigan Press, 2001.

Schoem, David, Sylvia Hurtado, Todd Sevig, Mark Chesler, and Stephen H. Sumida. "Intergroup Dialogue: Democracy at Work in Theory and Practice." In *Intergroup Dialogue: Deliberative Democracy in School, College, Community, and Workplace*, edited by David Schoem and Sylvia Hurtado, 1–21. Ann Arbor: University of Michigan Press, 2001.

Schoem, David, and Shari Saunders. "Adapting Intergroup Dialogue Processes for Use in a Variety of Settings." In *Intergroup Dialogue: Deliberative Democracy in School, College, Community, and Workplace*, edited by David Schoem and Sylvia Hurtado, 328–44. Ann Arbor: University of Michigan Press, 2001.

Tewell, Eamon C. "The Practice and Promise of Critical Information Literacy: Academic Librarians' Involvement in Critical Library Instruction." *College and Research Libraries* 79, no. 1 (2018): 10–34.

Watts, John. "Inclusive Cultural and Social Pedagogy in the Library Classroom," *LOEX Quarterly* 44, no. 1 (2017): article 4.

"Work and Play." *Colgate Scene*, Winter 2016. https://news.colgate.edu/scene/main_feature/work-and-play-3.

Zúñiga, Ximena, Biren (Ratnesh) A. Nagda, Mark Chesler, Adena Cytron-Walker. "Intergroup Dialogue in Higher Education: Meaningful Learning about Social Justice." Special issue, *ASHE Higher Education Report* 32, no. 4 (2007). https://doi.org/10.1002/aehe.3204.

Zúñiga, Ximena, Birin (Ratnesh) A. Nagda, and Todd D. Sevig, "Intergroup Dialogues: An Educational Model for Cultivating Engagement across Differences." *Equity and Excellence in Education* 35, no. 1 (2002): 7–17. https://doi.org/10.1080/713845248.

CHAPTER 15

Drawing to Conceptualize Research, Reduce Implicit Bias, and Establish Researcher Positionality in the Graduate Classroom

Kari D. Weaver, Frances Brady, and Alissa Droog

Within higher education, equity pedagogies are accomplished through changes to teaching—methods, programs, curricula, and accreditation—and changes to research—scope, focus, methods, and interdisciplinarity.[1] There is an increasing awareness of the need to diversify the ranks of the faculty to reflect the experiences, perceptions, and needs of the broader society, but, to accomplish this, a more diverse cohort of scholars must be trained at the graduate level.[2] The academy stands to benefit from the experiences, insights, and interests of these diverse individuals, but only if it moves to conceptualize and understand research as an act that has space to grow and change, reflecting a broader range of experiences and interests.[3] In parallel, there is also a need for those with more privilege in higher education to embrace inclusivity by confronting their own implicit biases. In the ACRL *Framework for Information Literacy for Higher Education*, the frame Authority Is Constructed and

215

Contextual stresses the need to teach researchers to "acknowledge biases that privilege some sources of authority over others, especially in terms of others' worldviews, gender, sexual orientation, and cultural orientations."[4]

The qualitative practice of positionality in research offers significant promise as a method to incorporate these diverse voices and perspectives by allowing librarians and faculty to teach new researchers to see themselves, their backgrounds, and their lived experiences as valuable and present. Positionality has long been used to help scholars understand themselves in relation to their research participants.[5] Librarians can also gain significant instructional value in considering positionality as a dialogue between the researcher and the existing body of literature and research practices in their field.

Through reflection, coupled with literature to ground our thinking, this chapter discusses the experiences of three librarians with the use of conceptual drawings about research processes as an equitable pedagogical practice. This drawing technique has pushed each of us to understand research in different ways and reflect on our own positionality as researchers and as teachers in the classroom. First, Kari D. Weaver considers how drawing research shapes an individual's understanding of themselves as a scholar. Second, Alissa Droog reflects on the use of drawing to understand how research relates to our identities. Finally, Frances Brady connects drawing to further social justice discussions in the classroom. We conclude with instructional materials for others who may wish to adopt such a practice. We also acknowledge that all three of us identify as white, cisgender female librarians in a field where that is the norm. Through the interplay between communal reflection, existing literature, and lived experience, we address how drawing and discussing conceptions of research can support the growth and diversification of the next generation of scholars.

Researcher Positionality and Subjectivity: Acknowledging Diverse Voices with Kari D. Weaver

The idea of using drawing as a method for information literacy instruction is not one I ever intended to use with students at all, let alone graduate students. Over a decade ago, I first used it with some colleagues in a faculty professional development workshop. During brainstorming, the idea of having faculty draw and share their conceptions of research as a way to activate kinesthetic learning and transition them from an expert mindset to that of a novice arose. Eager to try something new, we pushed forward incorporating a drawing activity into the workshop where we asked the faculty to "Draw what research looks like" and gave them an assortment of crayons and markers to complete the task. The activity was a success and helped faculty reconnect with the experience of not knowing what to do or exactly how to answer, and I later used it again working with undergraduate research methods courses in sociology when I moved to a new institution.

Four years ago, I transitioned from a regional campus of a large state university system in the United States to a large, research-intensive university in Canada. My new job was meant to build a teaching and learning culture within the library and on behalf of the library across campus. In this role, I was tasked with identifying partnerships across academic support units. There was particular interest in increasing services for graduate students, who were traditionally underserved by our programming, as the library had long emphasized in-person supports preferred by undergraduates and built programs reflective of the corresponding statistical data that indicated significant undergraduate use. Such an emphasis on services for in-person undergraduates was not unique at my campus and has been identified as a consistent barrier to graduate student support at other institutions.[6] This experience corresponded with my own growth and development, as I completed work on a doctorate of education degree where I was trained in qualitative research methods.

A significant portion of my qualitative research training centered on considering relationships between the researcher and participants, a defining characteristic of many qualitative methods.[7] It is intensely focused on understanding who your research participants are, understanding what the power dynamics are between you and your research participants, and developing self-reflective practices that allow for critical reflection on your role, place, and experiences as a researcher.[8] These practices, which in the field are called positionality and subjectivity, helped me grapple with my own feelings of uncertainty and inadequacy as a researcher. It also drove me to begin confronting my own implicit biases as an integrated component of both teaching and research. In turn, this changed how I discussed research with graduate students, allowing me to acknowledge where my expertise lies while also understanding that I would naturally lack lived experiences that could illuminate, invigorate, and advance research.[9] Drawing to unearth the affective side of research allowed me to seamlessly integrate these ideas into my teaching. Adopting this pedagogy allowed me to honor individual lived experiences and discuss them as valid and crucial elements that support and enhance research.

The opportunity emerged to build a copresented workshop in collaboration with our campus Writing and Communication Centre on literature reviews for graduate students that would address a combination of research, writing tasks, and conventions for those in attendance. They would be at different points in their research, from just beginning to conceptualize questions to polishing writing style and citations, but given both the STEM focus of my present institution and the continuing emphasis in many fields on training students in quantitative research methods, I knew most in attendance would never have considered their own backgrounds, experiences, and relationships as influencing their research itself. Furthermore, I needed a way to explicitly address the affective components of research and expose this institutional bias in a way that supported students, including students of color, in a thoughtful and sensitive manner as affect can be both positive and negative.[10] Without these conversations, I have found students often become trapped in their own subjectivity. Thus, students often procrastinate due to a sense of inadequacy, feeling that they are the wrong person to engage in the intended research, or concerns that their own experiences are negatively biasing how they frame questions, analyze data, and engage with human subjects. For students to engage in meaningful research, I needed an approach that "maintains that the development of students' capacity to pose thoughtful questions (as opposed to clear answers) is as important as their ability to locate, access, organize, evaluate, and apply information in the research process."[11] In this need, I turned back to the drawing activity I had used so successfully with both faculty and undergraduates as a way to enter these conversations and incorporated both the drawing activity and discussions about how our own experiences, biases, and identities can influence the work we do as researchers. I coupled this with techniques for navigating these issues, including journaling or analytic memos, peer conversations, concept mapping, and note-taking practices.[12] Through the use of this activity, I often hear from students that no one has ever taken the time to speak about how emotional and personal research is, and that gives voice to the affective dimension of research, which, in turn, helps them to persevere.

Personally, using drawing as a way to engage with students continues to expose my own assumptions as a teacher and scholar and pushes me to consider how my identity and privilege interact across areas of my life and work. As an educator, this activity has encouraged me to take more creative risks in the classroom, ranging from dramatic skits to having students write works likely to be challenged or banned. As a scholar, the use of this drawing activity continues to expose how my identity and experiences shape my research agenda and practice.

Identities in Research: Deconstructing the Academy with Alissa Droog

I first encountered the "draw what research is" activity while observing Dr. Kari D. Weaver teach in a first-year experience classroom. I was a bit surprised to be drawing with first-year students in a postsecondary classroom, but quickly realized the value of the activity when students were prompted to discuss the emotions associated with their drawing. Not only did it build rapport, but also students came together to acknowledge the challenges of research as a group. I was already aware that drawing helps to surface affective and unconscious thoughts,[13] and so I began to incorporate the activity into my undergraduate and graduate classrooms to help tease out the affective component of research. I met Frances Brady after presenting this activity at the Consortium of Academic and Research Libraries in Illinois (CARLI) Instruction Showcase.[14] After discussions with Frances, I have started to dig deeper into the drawing activity, asking not just what emotions are associated with the drawings, but how our drawings of research are impacted by our various identities.

When I use this activity in the classroom, I always draw with my students. When it comes time to ask about how our drawings are impacted by our identities, I share whatever drawing I did during the activity. My drawing often shows a process of research and I share how it reflects Western conceptions of knowledge as linear and categorical, even though I know that research does not look like this. Then I turn it to the students. I state explicitly that these are vulnerable topics and that I do not expect anyone to share. I am always surprised by the overwhelming response from students who want to share and by the raw emotion and deep responses to this question.

Acknowledging emotions and identities in research often leads to conversations about how research is personal. In my experience, students often have a perception that research must be somewhat impersonal. As our experiences and identities in life impact the topics we are interested in,[15] acknowledging why we are interested in a topic can help to home in on the research question. By having conversations that acknowledge the personal dimension of research, we give permission to graduate students to connect their research interests to their identities.

Some students respond to the question about their drawing of research and identities by reflecting on how they have never considered how their identities impact research and how important it is to acknowledge this. These responses are very important for developing graduate students in education to consider, especially as they plan to go out and do their own educational research.[16] Although the activity alone is not sufficient to help students think through a framework for cultural and racial consciousness in their own research, this activity can be a starting point for some.

Students of different minority groups have responded to the question about their drawing and identities by discussing how they see their research as correcting past inequalities in their discipline. When this happens, the drawing activity allows for a critical discussion of what research is and of the academy itself. When students share what research is to them, we all encounter perceptions of research that may be different from our own. These conversations ask us to consider what research is and to see it as something that is growing and never neutral. As students share their perceptions of research and challenge existing norms in the academy, the academy itself benefits from acknowledging and grappling with past inequalities that many new, diverse graduate students are keen to solve with their own research.

Drawing research has become my favorite technique to employ in the graduate classroom. It asks difficult questions, draws on our past experiences, and challenges us to reflect on our personal connections to research. Not only have students responded very positively to the activity, but my own understanding of how my positionality relates to research continues to grow through drawing.

Researchers as Social Justice Advocates: Confronting Implicit Biases with Frances Brady

Initially, I incorporated drawing in my lesson plans to enhance student retention of concepts, given the connection of drawing to memory.[17] In 2020, I drew the concept of research during Alissa Droog's presentation of her activity regarding affect during the CARLI Instruction Showcase.[18] A few weeks later, George Floyd was murdered by Derek Chauvin, and protests erupted in response. As I engaged with anti-racism literature, I reflected on how my whiteness shapes my identity in ways often invisible to me. In reviewing my sketch of research within this light, I was disappointed by the biases implicit within it. I had depicted research as linear and individualistic. While individualism is not inherently a negative value, the unquestioned hegemony of White values (including individualism) allows those with more privilege to view their success as solely based on merit, denying how much support they received from others and ignoring how issues of systemic injustice personally benefit them. Additionally, I teach that research is iterative and collaborative, so my drawing demonstrated an internal dissonance.

Given how profoundly this dichotomy between my internalized and professed beliefs struck me, I included the activity in a workshop I facilitate for graduate-level peer teachers on teaching information literacy skills to first-year graduate students.[19] To decrease their anxiety, I exposed my vulnerability by sharing how I drew research and what I learned from it. Peer teachers reviewed their drawings and considered how their positionality impacted their conception of research. The discussion was lively and rich as they articulated their surprise at how their drawings revealed their implicit biases about what research is and who researchers are. As they are passionate about social justice and engage in anti-racism work personally and professionally, they cognitively disagreed with what their drawings depicted. This discord between implicit biases and acknowledged beliefs created an opening for learning to ensue.[20]

Bolstered by the successful discussion in the workshop, the peer teachers and I added the activity at the beginning of the lesson plan for all first-year graduate students. Although we expected these conversations to be uncomfortable, we hoped the drawing would help reveal some of students' implicit biases about research to themselves. We were pleasantly surprised to find the honesty we brought to the sessions of our own perceptions of research modeled a small shift in the distribution of power in the classroom, as it moved away from us presenting *at* students and toward a model of equity between instructor and student.

Thus, this activity centers social justice through both the content and the process itself of the discussions. Social justice must inherently involve action, not simply theory, as it refers to the equitable distribution of resources. New graduate students often conceptualize research as separate from praxis. Since many Adler students are more interested in becoming practitioners than academics, they view research as irrelevant to their future work as clinicians. I teach students that what research is done, about whom, and by whom impacts what resources are provided to which communities; how mental health experts treat their clients; which treatments doctors select for their patients; and so on. Since Adler students are interested in how their intersecting identities shape their work as clinicians, the drawing activity pushes students to consider how their positionality may impact their choice of topic, population to study, and how they evaluate authority of authors and resources, which in turn will also impact the communities they serve. For example, research in both the medical and mental health fields has traditionally been done by White people and has focused on White populations, even when making claims regarding BIPOC people.[21] Through visualizing research and the ensuing discussion, BIPOC students and faculty expressed surprise that this activity and discussion positioned them to see that they could shape not only what topics are researched, but also even impact the values that drive research.

Through scaffolded sessions I teach later in students' programs, I reiterate the connection of research to social justice, so I do not suggest that I fully address this in a short activity. However, students' visualization of their relationship to research primes them for later sessions, powerfully shaping how students conceptualize their dissertations and how they will later apply social justice as professionals.

Conclusion and Recommendations

Librarians who wish to try a version of this method with graduate students or with any other students should consider starting small by adding a drawing activity to an existing lesson or in a research consultation appointment until managing the discussions around student affect and research biases becomes more comfortable. Different challenges may arise, depending on the student population. At Adler University, the greatest difficulty was ending the exciting conversations to move to other components, so we established clear limits on how long the discussion could continue. However, if students are reticent to share with the full class, placing them in pairs might elicit more conversation. If the method is used within a one-shot rather than within a librarian-taught credit course, we recommend allowing students to simply share at their comfort level, even if this means that many students might simply listen rather than expressing themselves. Individuals wishing to build drawing techniques into their instruction in a more substantial manner may consult the brief lesson plan in the appendix.

As indicated by our collective reflections, drawing activities hold significant promise as a pedagogical method to build equity and inclusivity into conversations around graduate student research. While we reflect on our use of the technique in graduate classrooms, Kari and Alissa have used it with other learner populations too. Additionally, such activities can be readily adapted to address different needs in varied contexts, ranging from positionality and subjectivity to bias and concerns of social justice. Librarians working with graduate students have the valuable opportunity to engage by helping burgeoning scholars conceptualize what research is and take ownership of their power as new voices in academia. Using drawing to help with these processes can more readily engender conversation that exposes those biases, systemic barriers, and lived experiences that hold the potential to remake what and how research is conducted.

Appendix: Drawing Research Activity

7–25-minute session either in a classroom or synchronously online

Activity Goals

- Librarians will be able to
  - assess students' prior experiences with and affect toward research
  - create a participatory classroom culture through active learning

- Students will be able to
  - acknowledge the affective component of research
  - reflect on the ways their various identities shape their perceptions of research

Materials Needed

- In person: paper and writing utensils (instructor can have students use their own, or bring paper and colored pencils/crayons/etc.)
- Online: can be done via Zoom or other technology where students draw on their own

Directions

1. Draw the concept of research (1–2 minutes).
   a. Assure students that this is not a test of artistic skills and that it will not be collected.
   b. Provide the amount of time they will have.
   c. Draw your concept of research along with students.
2. Discuss affect (1–2 minutes).
   a. Ask students to look at their drawings and consider what emotions are there.
   b. Mode
      i. In person: this can be done in pairs.
      ii. Online: this can be entered into the chat or through Padlet, etc.
3. Discuss positionality (5–20 minutes).

    a. Share your drawing and explain how it represents your vision of research from the perspective of your own positionality.

    b. Guiding questions can include

        i. How does your drawing connect to one or more of your identities?

        ii. Did you include yourself in your drawing?

        iii. Did you draw a researcher? If so, what does that person look like? If not, why not?

    c. Depending on time, students can discuss in small groups or as a full class either in person or online.

Assessment

- Assessment *for* learning: Librarians learn students' past experiences of and current feelings toward research.
- Assessment *of* learning: Gauge student understanding of the affective component of research and the impact of positionality on research through the class discussion.

Notes

1. Cherry A. McGee Banks and James A. Banks, "Equity Pedagogy: An Essential Component of Multicultural Education," *Theory into Practice* 34, no. 3 (1995): 152, https://doi.org/10.1080/00405849509543674.
2. Crystal J. Collins and William Allan Kritsonis, "National Viewpoint: The Importance of Hiring a Diverse Faculty," *Doctoral Forum—National Journal for Publishing and Mentoring Doctoral Student Research* 3, no. 1 (2006): 2–3, 5–6.
3. Melissa Jacquart et al., "Diversity Is Not Enough: The Importance of Inclusive Pedagogy," *Teaching Philosophy* 42, no. 2 (June 2019): 107–39, https://doi.org/10.5840/teachphil2019417102.
4. Association of College and Research Libraries, *Framework for Information Literacy for Higher Education* (Chicago: Association of College and Research Libraries, 2016), https://www.ala.org/acrl/standards/ilframework.
5. Joseph A. Maxwell, *Qualitative Research Design*, 3rd ed. (Thousand Oaks, CA: Sage, 2013), 92–93.
6. Sharon Ince, "Trends in Academic Libraries Graduate Student Services: A Case Study," *Journal of Academic Librarianship* 44, no. 3 (May 2018): 426–27, https://doi.org/10.1016/j.acalib.2018.02.012.
7. Corrine Glense, *Becoming Qualitative Researchers*, 5th ed. (New York: Pearson, 2016), 29–63; Maxwell, *Qualitative Research Design*, 23–38.
8. Michael Crotty, *The Foundations of Social Research* (London: Sage, 1998), 2–9; John W. Creswell and Charyl N. Poth, *Qualitative Inquiry and Research Design*, 4th ed. (Los Angeles, Sage, 2018), 5–7; Sharon M. Ravitch and Nicole M. Carl, *Qualitative Research*, 2nd ed. (Thousand Oaks, CA: Sage, 2021), 105–8.
9. Maxwell, *Qualitative Research Design*, 39–72; Ravitch and Carl, *Qualitative Research*, 105–23.
10. Amy Catalano, "Patterns of Graduate Students' Information Seeking Behavior: A Meta-syn-

thesis of the Literature," *Journal of Documentation* 69, no. 2 (2013): 253–67, https://doi.org/10.1108/00220411311300066; Chris Linder et al., "Building Inclusive Pedagogy: Recommendations from a National Study of Students of Color in Higher Education and Student Affairs Graduate Programs," *Equity and Excellence in Education* 48, no. 2 (2015): 178–94, https://doi.org/10.1080/10665684.2014.959270.

11. Jonathan Cope, "Information Literacy and Social Power," in *Critical Library Instruction: Theories and Methods*, ed. Maria T. Accardi, Emily Drabinski, and Alana Kimbier (Duluth, MN: Library Juice Press, 2010), 13.

12. Catherine Marshall and Gretchen B. Rossman, *Designing Qualitative Research*, 4th ed. (Thousand Oaks, CA: Sage, 2006), 172–74; Maxwell, *Qualitative Research Design*, 62–63; Johnny Saldaña, *The Coding Manual for Qualitative Researchers*, 3rd ed. (London: Sage, 2016), 44–65; Jonathan A. Smith, Paul Flowers, and Michal Larkin, *Interpretative Phenomenological Analysis* (Los Angeles: Sage, 2009), 79–107.

13. Patricia Bryans and Sharon Mavin, "Visual Images: A Technique to Surface Conceptions of Research and Researchers," *Qualitative Research in Organizations and Management* 1, no. 2 (2006): 113; Lise Doucette and Kristin Hoffmann, "Conceptions of Research among Academic Librarians and Archivists," *Canadian Journal of Academic Librarianship* 5 (2019): 6, https://doi.org/10.33137/cjal-rcbu.v5.30417.

14. Alissa Droog, "What Is Research? Drawing Icebreaker" (lightning talk, 8th Annual CARLI Online Instruction Showcase, May 29, 2020), https://www.carli.illinois.edu/8th-annual-carli-instruction-showcase.

15. John W. Creswell, *Research Design*, 2nd ed. (Thousand Oaks, CA: Sage, 2003), 184–85; Kim James and Susan Vinnicombe, "Acknowledging the Individual in the Researcher," in *Essential Skills for Management Research*, ed. David Partington (London: Sage, 2002), 85–86.

16. Richard H. Milner IV, "Race, Culture, and Researcher Positionality: Working through Dangers Seen, Unseen, and Unforeseen," *Educational Researcher* 36, no. 7 (2007): 394–397, https://doi.org/10.3102/0013189X07309471.

17. Myra A. Fernandes, Jeffrey D. Wammes, and Melissa E. Meade, "The Surprisingly Powerful Influence of Drawing on Memory," *Current Directions in Psychological Science* 27, no. 5 (2018): 303, https://doi.org/10.1177/0963721418755385.

18. Droog, "What Is Research?"

19. Frances Brady, "Training Peer Teachers to Teach First Year Graduate Level Information Literacy Sessions," *Journal of Academic Librarianship* 47, no. 2 (March 2021): 102308, pp. 2–6, https://doi.org/10.1016/j.acalib.2020.102308.

20. Paulo Freire, *Pedagogy of the Oppressed*, 30th anniversary ed., trans. Myra Bergman Ramos (New York; Bloomsbury, 2014), 79.

21. Sam S. Oh, et al., "Diversity in Clinical and Biomedical Research: A Promise Yet to Be Fulfilled," *PLoS Medicine* 12, no. 12 (2015): e1001918, p. 3, https://doi.org/10.1371/journal.pmed.1001918; Steven O. Roberts et al., "Racial Inequality in Psychological Research: Trends of the Past and Recommendations for the Future," *Perspectives on Psychological Science* 15, no. 6 (2020): 1301, https://doi.org/10.1177/1745691620927709.

Bibliography

Association of College and Research Libraries. *Framework for Information Literacy for Higher Education*. Chicago: Association of College and Research Libraries, 2016. https://www.ala.org/acrl/standards/ilframework.

Brady, Frances. "Training Peer Teachers to Teach First Year Graduate Level Information Literacy Sessions." *Journal of Academic Librarianship* 47, no. 2 (March 2021): 102308. https://doi.org/10.1016/j.acalib.2020.102308.

Bryans, Patricia, and Sharon Mavin. "Visual Images: A Technique to Surface Conceptions of Research and Researchers." *Qualitative Research in Organizations and Management* 1, no. 2 (2006): 113–28. https://doi.org/10.1108/17465640610686370.

Catalano, Amy. "Patterns of Graduate Students' Information Seeking Behavior: A Meta-synthesis of the Literature." *Journal of Documentation* 69, no. 2 (2013): 243–74. https://doi.org/10.1108/00220411311300066.

Collins, Crystal J., and William Allan Kritsonis. "National Viewpoint: The Importance of Hiring a Diverse Faculty." *Doctoral Forum—National Journal for Publishing and Mentoring Doctoral Student Research* 3, no. 1 (2006): 1–7.

Cope, Jonathan. "Information Literacy and Social Power." In *Critical Library Instruction: Theories and Methods*, edited by Maria T. Accardi, Emily Drabinski, and Alana Kumbier, 13–28. Duluth, MN: Library Juice Press, 2010.

Creswell, John W. *Research Design: Qualitative, Quantitative, and Mixed Methods Approaches*, 2nd ed. Thousand Oaks, CA: Sage, 2003.

Creswell, John W., and Charyl N. Poth. *Qualitative Inquiry and Research Design: Choosing among Five Approaches*, 4th ed. Los Angeles: Sage, 2018.

Crotty, Michael. *The Foundations of Social Research: Meaning and Perspective in the Research Process*. London: Sage, 1998.

Doucette, Lise, and Kristin Hoffmann. "Conceptions of Research among Academic Librarians and Archivists." *Canadian Journal of Academic Librarianship* 5 (2019): 1–25. https://doi.org/10.33137/cjal-rcbu.v5.30417.

Droog, Alissa. "What Is Research? Drawing Icebreaker." Lightning talk, 8th Annual CARLI Online Instruction Showcase, May 29, 2020. https://www.carli.illinois.edu/8th-annual-carli-instruction-showcase.

Fernandes, Myra A., Jeffrey D. Wammes, and Melissa E. Meade. "The Surprisingly Powerful Influence of Drawing on Memory." *Current Directions in Psychological Science* 27, no. 5 (2018): 302–8. https://doi.org/10.1177/0963721418755385.

Freire, Paulo. *Pedagogy of the Oppressed*, 30th anniversary ed. Translated by Myra Bergman Ramos. New York: Bloomsbury, 2014.

Glesne, Corrine. *Becoming Qualitative Researchers: An Introduction*, 5th ed. New York: Pearson, 2016.

Ince, Sharon. "Trends in Academic Libraries Graduate Student Services: A Case Study." *Journal of Academic Librarianship* 44, no. 3 (May 2018): 426–29. https://doi.org/10.1016/j.acalib.2018.02.012.

Jacquart, Melissa, Rebecca Scott, Kevin Hermberg, and Stephen Bloch-Schulman. "Diversity Is Not Enough: The Importance of Inclusive Pedagogy." *Teaching Philosophy* 42, no. 2 (June 2019): 107–39. https://doi.org/10.5840/teachphil2019417102.

James, Kim, and Susan Vinnicombe. "Acknowledging the Individual in the Researcher." In *Essential Skills for Management Research*, edited by David Partington, 84–98. London: Sage, 2002.

Linder, Chris, Jessica C. Harris, Evette L. Allen, and Bryan Hubain. "Building Inclusive Pedagogy: Recommendations from a National Study of Students of Color in Higher Education and Student Affairs Graduate Programs." *Equity and Excellence in Education* 48, no. 2 (2015): 178–94. https://doi.org/10.1080/10665684.2014.959270.

Marshall, Catherine, and Gretchen B. Rossman. *Designing Qualitative Research*, 4th ed. Thousand Oaks, CA: Sage, 2006.

Maxwell, Joseph A. *Qualitative Research Design: An Interactive Approach*, 3rd ed. Thousand Oaks, CA: Sage, 2013.

McGee Banks, Cherry A., and James A. Banks. "Equity Pedagogy: An Essential Component of Multicultural Education." *Theory into Practice* 34, no. 3 (1995): 152–58. https://doi.
org/10.1080/00405849509543674.

Milner, H. Richard, IV. "Race, Culture, and Researcher Positionality: Working through Dangers
Seen, Unseen, and Unforeseen." *Educational Researcher* 36, no. 7 (2007): 388–400. https://doi.
org/10.3102/0013189X07309471.

Oh, Sam S., Joshua Galanter, Neeta Thakur, Maria Pino-Yanes, Nicolas E. Barcelo, Marquitta J.
White, Danielle M. de Bruin, et al. "Diversity in Clinical and Biomedical Research: A Promise
Yet to Be Fulfilled." *PLoS Medicine* 12, no. 12 (2015): e1001918. https://doi.org/10.1371/journal.
pmed.1001918.

Ravitch, Sharon M., and Nicole M. Carl. *Qualitative Research: Bridging the Conceptual, Theoretical,
and Methodological*, 2nd ed. Thousand Oaks, CA: Sage, 2021.

Roberts, Steven O., Carmelle Bareket-Shavit, Forrest A. Dollins, Peter D. Goldie, and Elizabeth
Mortenson. "Racial Inequality in Psychological Research: Trends of the Past and Recommendations for the Future." *Perspectives on Psychological Science* 15, no. 6 (2020): 1295–309. https://doi.
org/10.1177/1745691620927709.

Saldaña, Johnny. *The Coding Manual for Qualitative Researchers*, 3rd ed. London: Sage, 2016.

Smith, Jonathan A., Paul Flowers, and Michal Larkin. *Interpretative Phenomenological Analysis:
Theory, Method, and Research*. Los Angeles: Sage, 2009.

CHAPTER 16

Examining the Information Literacy Dreamfield

Applying a Sentipensante Pedagogy to Library Research Consultations

*Sheila García Mazari** and Samantha Minnis†*

---

* Growing up in a conservative Midwest city as the daughter of first-generation Mexican immigrants, Sheila found herself often struggling to reconcile her lived experiences with the narratives that have been centered in academic research. As a result, Sheila is continually learning to lean into her privileges while questioning traditional methods of ascribing value to information and information creation. Engaging in a Sentipensante approach is one of several ways that Sheila has engaged with information literacy through an inclusive pedagogical lens. However, as a tenure-track faculty member, Sheila knows that she speaks from a position of privilege and that engaging in approaches that challenge the status quo continues to be difficult for many of her peers in academic libraries. Sheila hopes to continue to examine the intersection of critical pedagogy and information dissemination within first-generation and Latinx communities, seeking to hone an increasingly equitable and inclusive librarianship practice.

† Because her mother is a university professor, Samantha has always been comfortable with how to navigate higher education and how to ask for and receive assistance. Her education and experience working with students have led her to understand the privilege of that inside view, which, combined with her whiteness, allowed her to be in higher education with confidence that she belonged. When she works with students, she brings an awareness of her privilege and works to demystify scholarly research. Before collaborating with Sheila, Samantha had not heard of Sentipensante pedagogy, but as Sheila and she worked together and talked about their approaches to their work, they noticed overlaps and connections between Sheila's grounding in Sentipensante pedagogy and Samantha's grounding in feminist theories. Samantha plans to continue to develop her approach and contribute to creating a more inclusive, anti-racist, and anti-oppressive space for students.

Introduction

As librarians, we guide students in learning about information literacy as a framework, allowing individual choices and evaluation to guide how they interpret sources and, by extension, the world around them. While information literacy instruction focuses on critically examining the context of a source, it does not focus on examining the context of the learning environment itself—an educational context that values Western notions of learning, where the student seeks one correct answer as a passive participant. Within this context, students do not have the choice in source selection that we believe they do; they search for sources that are deemed legitimate through a dominant white male narrative of knowledge production.[1] This in turn can lead to a learning process that disempowers the learner, particularly for our Black, Indigenous, and students of color, who are not equitably represented in the research landscape. In an attempt to intervene in this learning environment, the authors identified a pedagogical approach that showcased the value of both intellectualism and intuitive knowledge in Laura Rendón's model of Sentipensante (Sensing/Thinking) pedagogy. In this chapter, the authors combine the Sentipensante approach with other theories and models used in librarianship that center intuitive knowledge to survey the information literacy instructional landscape. Through a focus on the one-on-one research consultation, the authors share their personal experiences to highlight areas of opportunity toward actively practicing an inclusive Sentipensante approach.

Contextualizing Sentipensante Pedagogy

In her book *Sentipensante (Sensing/Thinking) Pedagogy: Educating for Wholeness, Social Justice, and Liberation*, Rendón applies Don Miguel Ruiz's concept of a societal Dreamfield to educational pedagogy. Don Miguel Ruiz contends that humans spend their entire lives dreaming. When our minds are physically awake, our thoughts and actions are shaped by a societal Dreamfield. The Dreamfield consists of shared societal agreements, ideas, and beliefs, many of which we do not choose but that we inherently agree to in order to be accepted as members of our societies.[2] If we attempt to resist these agreements, we are punished; therefore, we remain in a dreamlike state, as we subconsciously follow the agreements to survive in the societal Dreamfield.[3] During the times in which our minds are physically asleep, however, our dreams are not beholden to the beliefs created in the societal Dreamfield, allowing our dreams to change freely and challenge the status quo.[4] Rendón notes that the Western educational Dreamfield values intellectualism and reasoning over intuition or emotions, positing them as two separate forms of knowledge creation and ascribing value to an intellectualism/thinking approach rather than an intuitive/feeling approach.[5] Rendón makes the call to move toward a practice that values both the feeling and the thinking aspects within education; a pedagogy steeped in the difrasismo, or third space, that comes from valuing both aspects as two equal parts of a greater whole[6]—an approach that she names a Sentipensante pedagogy.

Drawn from the term used by Colombian fisherman to refer to "language that speaks truth,"[7] Sentipensante pedagogy focuses on educating for Wholeness, social justice, and the cultivation of wisdom by validating the lived experiences of students as sources of knowledge.[8] Rendón draws on Toltec wisdom and Aztec culture in her construction of the model of Sentipensante (Sensing/Thinking) pedagogy as shown in figure 16.1. The model is comprehensive, providing a total of six dialectical spaces that are constructed from the difrasismo of "sensing and thinking processes and the balance between inner and outer knowing."[9] For example, the model illustrates how Sentipensante pedagogy can be applied to research, by integrating Object and Subject toward a practice of Participatory Epistemology. Similarly, a Sentipensante assessment approach should integrate Academic Learning Outcomes and Personal Development Outcomes. For the purposes of this chapter, the authors will focus on one aspect of Sentipensante pedagogy, that which explores the difrasismo found when valuing both Intellectualism and Intuition toward a practice of educating for Wholeness.[10]

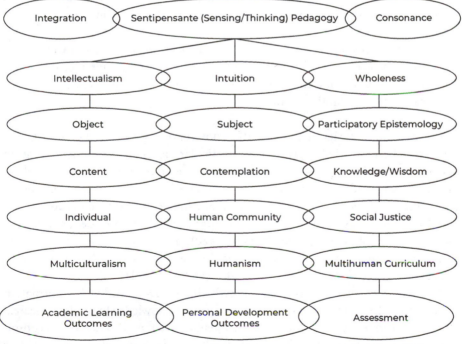

© 2014 by Stylus Publishing, LLC

Figure 16.1
Model of Sentipensante (sensing/thinking) pedagogy

Examining the Information Literacy Dreamfield

Within librarianship, the Association of College and Research Libraries' (ACRL) *Framework for Information Literacy for Higher Education* is the basis of our profession's pedagogical Dreamfield. Information literacy instruction, as defined by the authors of this article, includes, but is not limited to classroom visits, learning objects, and one-on-one research consultations. The *Framework* focuses on the ways librarians can contextualize the creation and application of information in instruction, providing six overarching frames.[11] However, within both the knowledge practices and the dispositions listed for each frame, the main focus is on the extrinsic effect of a student's choices. Students are asked to think about their audience and their responsibility to present a holistic understanding of a topic through the use of outer knowledge[12]—which includes varied and at times conflicting sources—in order to present an informed and therefore "objective" stance. This focus aligns with the "intellectualism/thinking" approach that Rendón identifies as being valued over intuitive/feeling knowledge within the educational Dreamfield.

An example of this can be found, within the frame Authority Is Constructed and Contextual. Among the knowledge practices presented is the ability to

> Acknowledge they [students] are developing their own authoritative voices in a particular area and recognize the responsibilities this entails, including seeking accuracy and reliability, respecting intellectual property, and participating in communities of practice.[13]

The *Framework* posits students as either novices or experts when engaging with the frame. This knowledge practice, in particular, notes that it is incumbent on students to seek differing viewpoints that are considered accurate and reliable, which naturally leads students to question prior knowledge. This is further reinforced through the disposition "Develop and maintain an open mind when encountering varied and sometimes conflicting perspectives."[14] While the frame does list within its dispositions that students should "Question traditional notions of granting authority and recognize the value of diverse ideas and worldviews," it does not provide language that notes how intuitive knowledge can be valuable.[15]

As the *Framework* does not speak directly to intuitive knowledge, information literacy instructors often focus more on seeking outer knowledge to validate research. When information literacy instruction is happening in a one-on-one research consultation, a teaching environment that is particularly vulnerable for the student, this focus on intellectualism can lead to harm.[16] By not acknowledging the inner knowledge that students bring with them when they engage with research, instructors may inadvertently lead them toward sources that conflict with their intuitive knowledge in a manner that disempowers them. In sum, acknowledging lived experiences as an authority requires an intentional equity lens to the frame that is currently missing.

A review of the six frames shows that the Scholarship as Conversation frame is the only instance in which there is acknowledgement of intuitive knowledge within both its knowledge practices and dispositions:

> Recognize that a given scholarly work may not represent the only or even the majority perspective on the issue; See themselves as contributors to scholarship rather than only consumers of it.[17]

These examples showcase how the *Framework* is written primarily in line with a Western pedagogical approach. Because outer knowledge is likely to have undergone a peer-review process or be built on preexisting knowledge, the education Dreamfield, and likewise, the information literacy Dreamfield views these sources as objective. As a result, the *Framework* primarily values an intellectualism or "thinking" approach to evaluating, consuming, and creating information. Through the lens of Sentipensante pedagogy and educating for Wholeness, the *Framework* lacks explicit language that speaks to the value of the intuitive aspects of knowledge creation. This omission conflicts with efforts to build and empower intuitive knowledge within the information literacy Dreamfield, which can be particularly harmful when this knowledge originates from the beliefs and values of traditionally marginalized communities.

Research as Violence

The absence of valuing intuitive knowledge in research is highlighted in Jessie Loyer's work "Indigenous Information Literacy: nêhiyaw Kinship Enabling Self-Care in Research." Loyer dedicates a section to detailing how research can be violent, explaining that Indigenous peoples are seen as "Othered objects of research and rarely as researchers…."[18] As a result, Loyer notes that information literacy instruction must include awareness of a student's physical, emotional, and spiritual health, particularly when research itself is traumatic.[19] The violence that research can inflict can be further magnified when paired with the phenomenon of stereotype threat.

Claude M. Steele, author of the book *Whistling Vivaldi: How Stereotypes Affect Us and What We Can Do,* explores stereotype threat in depth as one of several identity contingencies, which are defined as "the things you have to deal with in a situation because you have a given social identity."[20] Stereotype threat specifically stems from a desire to not confirm stereotypes about our social identities, whether they are related to gender, race, or social status, among others.[21] Steele further explains that "places like classrooms, university campuses, standardized-testing rooms, or competitive-running tracks, though seemingly the same for everybody, are, in fact, different places for different people."[22] In the information literacy teaching environment, stereotype threat can deeply affect students who did not receive the same opportunities to engage in research as their peers. The actual act of research and, further, finding research that may negate personal experiences, can compound this stereotype threat. And as Loyer has noted, when a student's prior knowledge is not represented in the academic information landscape, this can at times be a source of disempowerment rather than validation.[23]

Steele's research further shows that this violence is not limited to emotional and spiritual well-being, as short instances of stereotype threat "are enough to raise your blood pressure, dramatically increase ruminative thinking, interfere with working memory, and deteriorate performance on challenging tasks."[24] Long-term effects may lead to chronic health problems including hypertension and higher levels of visceral fat, which raises the risk of diabetes and cardiovascular disease.[25] In this way, the stereotype threat students may face from conducting research and finding sources that contradict their lived experiences can lead to physical violence.

Redefining the Dreamfield

Calls to improve upon or redefine the information literacy Dreamfield are not new. Librarians such as Laura Sanders have previously called for the addition of an Information Social Justice frame to the ACRL *Framework* that would expand on limitations of the current *Framework*; however, her draft knowledge practices and dispositions continue the focus on the extrinsic impact of research.[26] Although the dispositions in this proposed frame encourage the interrogation of outer knowledge, this interrogation also occurs primarily through an intellectualism/thinking approach.[27] While the information literacy Dreamfield at its core values an intellectualism/thinking framework to analyzing and synthesizing information, librarians have been incorporating pedagogical tools and theories from adjacent disciplines to build an increasingly holistic practice. In the following section, the authors present a general overview of two examples of practices that can shift the Dreamfield toward educating for Wholeness.

Ethics of Care

In her chapter "Feminist Reference Services: Transforming Relationships through an Ethic of Care," Sharon Ladenson names the key tenets of ethics of care as "developing and nurturing caring relations, valuing concrete experiences, and healing and transforming society as well as personal relationships."[28] Incorporating an ethics of care approach in a research consultation creates an opportunity to tend not only to students' intellectual needs, but also to the emotional and affective components of research as well. Sara Howard points out the "emphasis on listening and shared conversation" in the reference interaction in her work "Purposeful and Productive Care: The Feminist Ethic of Care and the Reference Desk."[29] Listening to students and valuing their concrete experience begins to break down the hierarchical structure that exists between librarian and student toward a collaborator model. Because ethics of care is also concerned with healing and transforming society, Ladenson discusses using a feminist approach to engage students in a critically reflective practice around their topic.[30] This helps the student reconsider their topic not only from an information-seeking perspective, but also in a way that can potentially produce social change. While both Ladenson and Howard discuss scenarios at a reference desk, these scenarios apply to the types of questions and interactions that can also happen in a research consultation.

Trauma-Informed Pedagogy

In an ACRL blog post, Karina Hagelin describes trauma-informed approaches for libraries, stating that it is impossible to tell if someone is a trauma survivor just by looking at them.[31] Because of the many circumstances that can lead to trauma, library workers can assume that we are helping traumatized people in our libraries. This is especially true in light of the current global pandemic, a collective trauma that, for some, is compounding several preexisting traumas as well. Hagelin asserts that trauma-informed approaches are important not only because of past trauma library users might have experienced, but also because we want to avoid re-traumatizing the people we are working with. This can be especially relevant to consultations where students do not see their intuitive knowledge reflected in published literature. Hagelin lists six key principles of a trauma-informed framework, any of which could be explored in the context of a research consultation. One example is "Empowerment, Voice and Choice." In a research consultation, this could look like offering a student a few different options for how to get started with searching, empowering a student by validating the work they've already done, or taking time and care with questions and listening to be sure their needs are understood.

Engaging in a Sentipensante Approach

While librarians continue to grapple with shifting practices, an area of teaching that provides great opportunity for growth is the research consultation. Symphony

Bruce speaks to this opportunity in her article "Teaching with Care: A Relational Approach to Individual Research Consultations" by explaining that these spaces require a level of vulnerability that librarians can use to "provide care or perpetuate the practices that lead to the disconnection a student may experience."[32] In the following section, the authors present our experiences engaging with Sentipensante pedagogy in one-on-one research consultations, noting areas of growth toward an increasingly intentional practice.

Sheila García Mazari: Educating for Wholeness

Prior to my current role as a liaison librarian, I was a Teaching and Learning Resident Librarian. As part of a shared curriculum, I would use an Evaluating Sources lesson plan that engaged with the Authority Is Constructed and Contextual frame for first-year students. In this activity, students were tasked with examining several information sources related to the Flint water crisis. The resulting discussion led students to understand that all the sources—from a tweet to a journal article—could be valid sources of information as they provided diverse perspectives and served to minimize bias. I encouraged students to examine their own biases as well and how these may influence how they engage with information. In response, a student asked me, "I lived in Flint when all of this started. That would make me biased, right? So I shouldn't write a paper on this topic." I backtracked immediately, noting that personal experiences were valuable, particularly for such a politically and racially charged topic.

When I started my position as a liaison librarian, the lesson learned from this interaction was instrumental in supporting students through a global pandemic. While my research consultations shifted online, I found that this allowed me to apply a Sentipensante lens in an intentional manner, building stronger relationships with students and ensuring that I could lend to their success as whole people. One common belief I encountered was that of students viewing their experiences during a global pandemic as a detriment rather than a source of knowledge. Students would share with me the competing priorities they balanced, including how the loss of peer support and structure in the asynchronous environment impacted their ability to complete assignments. Within my role as a liaison, I found an opportunity to guide students to the understanding that they knew how they learned best, and we worked together to ensure they had the tools they needed to succeed. For some students, I was an accountability partner, periodically checking progress on a research assignment. For other students, I provided structure through a set time every week during which we could co-work virtually and I would be available to answer questions. While these changes may seem small, I found students appreciated my approach to looking beyond the assignment (Intellectualism) as a marker of their success to also include the learning space they needed (Intuition) to support their individual development (Wholeness). While my university is gearing up for a return to campus in person, a subset of students will remain in an online or hybrid environment. I hope to continue to build on this approach so that I can be a source not only of knowledge, but of support as well.

Samantha Minnis: Empowering Students to Participate

There are two reference consultations that I have had multiple times throughout my time in libraries that have become almost archetypes to me. The first I think of as "the silver bullet source." The first time it happened, a student came to the reference desk looking for a source for an assignment. It eventually became clear that he was looking for one source to connect his ideas that he could lean on to prove his thesis, the one source that will bring an assignment together. As I demonstrated the databases to help him look for a source, I explained to him that there might not be one perfect article to connect his ideas and that, in fact, this was where he and his ideas came into the research process. Another type of recurring consultation I've experienced is "weird ideas," where students tell me they have an idea but they're not sure if it's right. It seems a little out there because they are not seeing it reflected in the literature and they don't know if they should pursue it. While very different from the silver bullet sources, there are similar underlying reasons for this request and similar interventions I use as a librarian when they occur in a research consultation.

In both cases, the students are experiencing elements of frustration, self-doubt, and fear. These reflect Kuhlthau's findings in her Information Search Process model, which describes the confusion and uncertainty students experience as their research becomes more complex.[33] These emotions can be compounded if a student doesn't see identities like their own reflected in the research process. Students who express doubt about their "weird" ideas or who are looking for a source to reflect their ideas back to them are doing so because it disrupts the Dreamfield they have of themselves as passive participants in knowledge collection rather than active knowledge creators, which causes discomfort.

In these reference consultations, I attempt to intervene in a way that will attend to the whole student by addressing their intellectualism and their intuition in a way that aligns with Sentipensante pedagogy, founded in ethics of care and a trauma-informed approach. I express enthusiasm for students' "weird" ideas and encourage them to pursue them. I validate their intuition by elevating their narratives in an ethics of care approach, asking questions about how they got to their ideas or, in the case of silver bullet sources, ask them questions about their topic, what got them interested in it in the first place, and what they have learned so far. I give them choices about what research steps they might want to try, whether we should try looking in some new places for more sources, or whether they're ready to move on with the sources they currently have, empowering them in their process and choices. I frequently check in with students to ask how they are feeling as well as to check that we've accomplished the goals they had for our session. I model and name frustrating moments in the research process and assure students that being frustrated or fearful are normal reactions to doing something new, as is being excited and curious about what they're discovering.

Moving Forward

In this chapter, the authors have examined the information literacy Dreamfield through the lens of Sentipensante pedagogy and, specifically, the difrasismo of educating for Wholeness. The authors offer this pedagogical tool to reframe how librarians contextualize intellectualism/thinking (outer) and intuitive/feeling (inner) sources of knowledge in one-on-one research consultations. More specifically, this chapter serves as a starting point toward intentional integration of inclusive pedagogies that can disrupt the current information literacy Dreamfield. By focusing on an intellectualism/thinking approach to research, while also elevating the intuitive/feeling knowledge that students bring to the scholarly conversation, we can begin to shape a Dreamfield that encompasses and empowers an array of voices and, by extension, redefines how we ascribe value to sources of information.

However, the authors also recognize that the information literacy Dreamfield operates within the larger context of the educational Dreamfield. This creates barriers that may seem insurmountable for the solitary instructor, and Rendón speaks to this by listing common methods that instructors have employed to engage in pedagogical dissent.[34] These include operating under the radar screen, building a scholarly reputation to legitimize their approach, adopting an ethic of working harder than others, finding supportive colleagues, assuming powerful roles on campus, and having a strong mentor.[35] Such approaches are also common within librarianship and can compound unequal labor expectations, as well as potentially lead to vocational awe.[36] To truly move forward as a profession, the value of intellectualism/thinking and intuitive/feeling knowledge must be equitably and intentionally integrated into professional expectations and practices toward a new pedagogical Dreamfield.

Notes

1.   Rebecca A. Reid and Todd A. Curry, "The White Male Template and Academic Bias," Inside Higher Ed, April 12, 2019, https://www.insidehighered.com/advice/2019/04/12/

how-white-male-template-produces-barriers-minority-scholars-throughout-their.

2. Laura I. Rendón, *Sentipensante (Sensing/Thinking) Pedagogy* (Sterling, VA: Stylus, 2008), 24, ProQuest Ebook Central.
3. Rendón, *Sentipensante*, 24.
4. Rendón, *Sentipensante*, 23.
5. Rendón, *Sentipensante*, 27.
6. Rendón, *Sentipensante*, 67–68. Difrasismo is a literary device used within Aztec ritual speech. This refers to exploring the adjacent space that two concepts or terms create when juxtaposed with one another. Laura Rendón provides the example of flowers and song being used to indicate artistic pursuits that capture beauty, such as poetry. This allows for the exploration of two seemingly contrasting terms or concepts toward a third space, where the two concepts bring to light new understandings that are not restricted to the duality through which we often understand our society.
7. Rendón, *Sentipensante*, 131.
8. Rendón, *Sentipensante*, 135–36.
9. Rendón, *Sentipensante*, 142.
10. The authors note that there is value in taking a comprehensive approach to applying a Sentipensante pedagogical lens not only to teaching information literacy, but also to library assessment practices, research, and curriculum development, among others. As novices to Sentipensante pedagogy, we have not had the opportunity to intentionally engage with the model beyond the information literacy instructional Dreamfield. There is ample opportunity to continue to explore the application of this model toward a comprehensive approach in the library profession.
11. Association of College and Research Libraries, *Framework for Information Literacy for Higher Education* (Chicago: Association of College and Research Libraries, 2016), https://www.ala.org/acrl/standards/ilframework. The six frames in the Framework for Information Literacy for Higher Education are as follows: Authority Is Constructed and Contextual; Information Creation as a Process; Information Has Value; Research as Inquiry; Scholarship as Conversation; and Searching as Strategic Exploration. There is value in a close examination of all frames individually and as a whole through the Sentipensante lens. However, such an analysis is beyond the scope of this chapter.
12. Rendón, *Sentipensante*, 27. Outer knowledge, or "outer knowing" as used by Laura I. Rendón, refers to knowledge that adheres to our societal Dreamfield and with which we interact through "intellectual reasoning, rationality, and objectivity." Inner knowledge is based on meditation and reflection and is characterized as "wisdom, wonder, sense of the sacred, intuition, and emotions."
13. Association of College and Research Libraries, *Framework*.
14. Association of College and Research Libraries, *Framework*.
15. Association of College and Research Libraries, *Framework*.
16. Symphony Bruce, "Teaching with Care: A Relational Approach to Individual Research Consultations," *In the Library with the Lead Pipe*, February 5, 2020, https://www.inthelibrarywiththeleadpipe.org/2020/teaching-with-care/.
17. Association of College and Research Libraries, *Framework*.
18. Jessie Loyer, "Indigenous Information Literacy: nêhiyaw Kinship Enabling Self-Care in Research," in *The Politics of Theory and the Practice of Critical Librarianship*, ed. Karen P. Nicholson and Maura Seale (Sacramento, CA: Library Juice Press, 2018), 147.
19. Loyer, "Indigenous Information Literacy," 149–53.
20. Claude M. Steele, *Whistling Vivaldi* (New York: W. W. Norton & Company, 2010), 3.
21. Steele, *Whistling Vivaldi*, 5.
22. Steele, *Whistling Vivaldi*, 60.
23. Loyer, "Indigenous Information Literacy": nêhiyaw Kinship Enabling Self-Care in Research,"

146.
24. Steele, *Whistling Vivaldi,* 132.
25. Steele, *Whistling Vivaldi,* 132; Isabel Wilkerson, Caste (New York: Random House, 2020), 307.
26. Laura Saunders, "Connecting Information Literacy and Social Justice: Why and How," *Information Literacy* 11, no. 1 (2017): 67–68, https://doi.org/10.15760/comminfolit.2017.11.1.47.
27. Saunders, "Connecting Information Literacy."
28. Sharon Ladenson, "Feminist Reference Services: Transforming Relationships through an Ethic of Care," in *The Feminist Reference Desk: Concepts, Critiques, and Conversations,* ed. Maria T. Accardi (Sacramento, CA: Library Juice Press, 2017), 76.
29. Sara Howard, "Purposeful and Productive Care: The Feminist Ethic of Care and the Reference Desk," in *The Feminist Reference Desk: Concepts, Critiques, and Conversations,* ed. Maria T. Accardi (Sacramento, CA: Library Juice Press, 2017), 67.
30. Ladenson, "Feminist Reference Services."
31. Karina Hagelin, "Moving towards Healing: A Trauma-Informed Librarianship Primer," *ACRLog* (blog), June 23, 2020, https://acrlog.org/2020/06/23/moving-towards-healing-a-trauma-informed-librarianship-primer/.
32. Bruce, "Teaching with Care."
33. Carol C. Kuhlthau, Jannica Heinström, and Ross J. Todd, "The 'Information Search Process' Revisited: Is the Model Still Useful?" *Information Research* 13, no. 4 (December 2008), http://informationr.net/ir/13-4/paper355.html.
34. Rendón, *Sentipensante,* 114.
35. Rendón, *Sentipensante,* 114–17.
36. Fobazi Ettarh, "Vocational Awe and Librarianship: The Lies We Tell Ourselves," *In the Library with the Lead Pipe,* January 10, 2018, https://www.inthelibrarywiththeleadpipe.org/2018/vocational-awe/.

Bibliography

Association of College and Research Libraries. *Framework for Information Literacy for Higher Education.* Chicago: Association of College and Research Libraries, 2016. https://www.ala.org/acrl/standards/ilframework.
Bruce, Symphony. "Teaching with Care: A Relational Approach to Individual Research Consultations." *In the Library with the Lead Pipe,* February 5, 2020. https://www.inthelibrarywiththeleadpipe.org/2020/teaching-with-care/.
Ettarh, Fobazi. "Vocational Awe and Librarianship: The Lies We Tell Ourselves." *In the Library with the Lead Pipe,* January 10, 2018. https://www.inthelibrarywiththeleadpipe.org/2018/vocational-awe/.
Hagelin, Karina. "Moving towards Healing: A Trauma-Informed Librarianship Primer." *ACRLog* (blog), June 23, 2020. https://acrlog.org/2020/06/23/moving-towards-healing-a-trauma-informed-librarianship-primer/.
Howard, Sara. "Purposeful and Productive Care: The Feminist Ethic of Care and the Reference Desk." In *The Feminist Reference Desk: Concepts, Critiques, and Conversations,* edited by Maria T. Accardi, 61–71. Sacramento, CA: Library Juice Press, 2017.
Kuhlthau, Carol C., Jannica Heinström, and Ross J. Todd. "The 'Information Search Process' Revisited: Is the Model Still Useful?" *Information Research* 13, no. 4 (December 2008). http://informationr.net/ir/13-4/paper355.html.

Ladenson, Sharon. "Feminist Reference Services: Transforming Relationships through an Ethic of Care." In *The Feminist Reference Desk: Concepts, Critiques, and Conversations*, edited by Maria T. Accardi, 73–81. Sacramento, CA: Library Juice Press, 2017.

Loyer, Jessie. "Indigenous Information Literacy: nêhiyaw Kinship Enabling Self-Care in Research." In *The Politics of Theory and the Practice of Critical Librarianship*, edited by Karen P. Nicholson and Maura Seale, 145–56. Sacramento, CA: Library Juice Press, 2018.

Reid, Rebecca A., and Todd A. Curry. "The White Male Template and Academic Bias." Inside Higher Ed, April 12, 2019. https://www.insidehighered.com/advice/2019/04/12/how-white-male-template-produces-barriers-minority-scholars-throughout-their.

Rendón, Laura I. *Sentipensante (Sensing/Thinking) Pedagogy: Educating for Wholeness, Social Justice and Liberation*. Sterling, VA: Stylus, 2008. ProQuest Ebook Central.

Saunders, Laura. "Connecting Information Literacy and Social Justice: Why and How." *Communications in Information Literacy* 11, no. 1 (2017): 55–75. https://doi.org/10.15760/comminfolit.2017.11.1.47.

Steele, Claude M. *Whistling Vivaldi: How Stereotypes Affect Us and What We Can Do*. New York: W. W. Norton & Company, 2010.

Wilkerson, Isabel. *Caste: The Origins of Our Discontents*. New York: Random House, 2020.

SECTION 3
Engendering Care and Empathy

Introduction

Melissa N. Mallon

As the late bell hooks reminded educators, "as a classroom community, our capacity to generate excitement is deeply affected by our interest in one another, in hearing one another's voices, in recognizing one another's presence[, and] any radical pedagogy must insist that everyone's presence is acknowledged."[1] Given our roles as educators and contributors to a service profession, generating compassion and excitement about research may seem second nature to academic librarians. However, it takes intentionality and purpose to create an environment in which students feel seen and heard. Likewise, creating a classroom culture where care is reciprocal takes effort, but it is necessary for encouraging students to build empathy for the voices and stories that are different from their own and that may be hidden from the traditional narrative.

The chapters in this section share the common thread of empathy and care. Care for students, yes, but also care for those who may share different privileges or experiences. From encouraging students to uncover hidden narratives in primary source instruction to cultivating care and connection in the classroom, these chapters encourage librarian educators to reflect and plan to intentionally create a culture of empathy and care in their classrooms.

Creating this culture is often easier when grounded in theory, which both helps librarians plan their lessons and class activities and provides students with a basis for understanding the struggles and lived experiences of their fellow humans, particularly when engaging with materials that give voice to these humans. In Chapter 17, "Empowering Students by Using Primary Sources to Research Queer and Feminist Histories," Kate Drabinski, Jo Gadsby, and Lindsey Loeper use feminist and queer theories to engage students in primary source research. In the chapter, which is cowritten by a member of the Gender, Women's, and Sexuality Studies teaching faculty, a reference and instruction archivist, and a reference and instruction librarian, the authors use zines, oral histories, and photographs in order to "help students understand that one of the fundamental ways a group of people is oppressed is by taking away their sense of history and knowledge of their roots." By focusing on primary sources, the authors have found that students think more deeply about secondary research and are able to see themselves not just as researchers but as creators of new knowledge.

Sharon Ladenson also uses a feminist lens for primary source instruction in Chapter 18, "Teaching and Learning through a Feminist Framework: Intersectionality and Primary Source Literacy." In this chapter, Ladenson shares how the Association for College and Research Libraries Rare Books and Manuscripts Section and the Society of American Archivists (ACRL RBMS-SAA) Joint Task Force's *Guidelines for Primary Source Literacy* aligns with feminist pedagogy, encouraging students to approach research critically and "challenge assumptions in order to engage in the process of creating knowledge." Ladenson provides a solid theoretical foundation and details a pedagogical strategy of using zines to teach about intersectionality in a variety of disciplines, including history, rhetoric, and gender studies.

In Chapter 19, "Black Student Union Protests and a Cemetery: Creating Space for All Learners in the Archives," Randi Beem discusses critical librarianship and the principles taught in the Librarians Active Learning Institute as pedagogical foundations to incorporate active learning when using primary sources. Beem encourages students to critically examine hidden narratives in special collections and archives, posing the questions "Why is the information that is found in a prominent library database important versus the oral traditions of marginalized communities? Why are there 'silences' of different communities within the archives? [and] Why are libraries sometimes considered neutral institutions when there are defined hierarchical systems in place with the resources we as librarians and archivists collect?" Beem's detailed lesson plan on using university archives encourages students to look for hidden biases using the Black Student Union protests at UNC and the Pinewood and Elmwood Cemetery in Charlotte, North Carolina, as case studies.

Allison McFadden-Keesling, in Chapter 20, "Human Library: Inclusion and Understanding through Dialogue," also discusses a project to engender empathy through stories, but this time through actual verbal human narratives. McFadden-Keesling describes the Human Library project, an international initiative that "fosters open and safe conversations, thereby breaking barriers that are the cornerstones of prejudice" by facilitating dialogue with human "books"—volunteers from a variety of backgrounds, including marginalized groups and those who have been stereotyped or discriminated against. McFadden-Keesling shares the history of the project and strategies for implementation in libraries, discussing safety and ethical considerations and the benefits to participants.

Switching gears from primary sources and archives as a means of building empathy, we move toward fostering a culture of care with students in our classrooms. In Chapter 21, "Flexible Pedagogies for Inclusive Learning: Balancing Pliancy and Structure and Cultivating Cultures of Care," Andrea Baer asks readers to "consider students' varying needs, interests, and passions, as well as the differing ways that they learn individually and collectively." This consideration lends itself to the adoption of flexible pedagogies that allow students agency and choice in their learning experience. Baer notes that by embracing flexibility, librarians can create more inclusive classroom experiences, which facilitates knowledge transfer and student research confidence. In addition to discussing the merits of flexible pedagogies, Baer also provides concrete examples of what this looks like in library classrooms, including one-shot sessions and online instruction.

Liz Chenevey also promotes empathy and care through Chapter 22, "Cultivating Connection: Attending to Student Affect through a Pedagogy of Care." In this essay, Chenevey reflects addressing the affective and emotional aspects of learning as grounded in a feminist ethic of care and an affective learning framework. Chenevey investigates these foundational frameworks in relation to mental health, discussing the intersection of mental well-being and information literacy instruction by weaving together personal narrative and pedagogical techniques to employ in the classroom.

Each chapter in this section approaches care and empathy in the classroom just a bit differently. For some of the authors, it's using library resources to encourage students to consider voices and stories different from their own. For others, it's considering how we, as instructors, can approach fostering a culture of care in our teaching. (This conversation is furthered in the section Instructor Identity and Positionality, coming up later in the book.) Regardless of their approach, each author brings intentionality and compassion to their writing.

Note

1.   bell hooks, *Teaching to Transgress* (New York: Routledge, 1994), 8.

Bibliography

hooks, bell. *Teaching to Transgress: Education as the Practice of Freedom*. New York: Routledge, 1994.

CHAPTER 17

Empowering Students by Using Primary Sources to Research Queer and Feminist Histories

Kate Drabinski, Jo Gadsby, and Lindsey Loeper[*]

Introduction

Teaching students how to find and work with primary sources is essential for training them as researchers, no matter the field. Working with primary sources is also about sparking and feeding the curiosity of students. We all know that rush we get when we encounter a primary text that speaks directly to us, that makes us want to know more, that gets us excited to follow the breadcrumbs in the database or archive and make new knowledge. We share these skills in classes at all levels.

We teach at the University of Maryland, Baltimore County (UMBC), a midsize regional public liberal arts institution outside of Baltimore, Maryland. Our students come largely from Maryland and the surrounding states. The student body is

---

* Kate Drabinski is a white, cis, able-bodied lesbian woman. She is a contract teaching faculty member. Jo Gadsby is a white, able-bodied, cisgender woman working as a reference and instruction librarian. Lindsey Loeper is a white, able-bodied cisgender woman. She is an archivist working in a university special collections department. Jo and Lindsey are both permanent employees with faculty status.

majority-minority, with 52 percent identifying as students of color. Of the student body, 75 percent are commuters, many working full- or part-time. The school is best known for its STEM programs and boasts the highest number of African American students continuing on to do graduate work in those fields. Bucking national trends, the school's enrollment is nearly 60 percent men. By contrast, Gender, Women's, and Sexuality Studies (GWST) courses are interdisciplinary humanities and social science courses. We serve majors and minors, but because these courses also meet general education requirements, we cannot count on the same level of interest and engagement from all students. That said, most students choose our courses precisely because they are one of the few classroom spaces where the experiences and knowledges of sexual and gender minority students are centered. Helping students understand that these are also research courses, and that our interdisciplinary research is every bit as important as what looks more traditionally like research to them, is central to the work we do.

In our projects together in GWST, we know that this work is important not just for practical research skills or for feeding curiosity, but also for political reasons, especially in an institutional context that prioritizes STEM fields. We teach these research skills to help students understand that one of the fundamental ways a group of people is oppressed is by taking away their sense of history and knowledge of their roots. This untethering from the past destroys people's ability to see themselves in the present and to imagine themselves in the future. The research process teaches students that doing historical research is itself a form of activism and self-actualization. Researching their own pasts can also induce trauma as they bump up against silences, stereotypes, and stories of violence and oppression. Part of our work is to help student researchers navigate this challenging terrain without giving up on the real potentials of finding—and making—themselves in the archive. Their research potentially builds community beyond their own classroom as they find their roots and contribute new knowledge about their own pasts and ancestries.

We started collaborating several years ago when Kate, teaching faculty from the GWST department, requested library instruction for the Feminist Activism course in order for her students to engage in archival research on social movements in Baltimore. Jo, the reference and instruction librarian, engaged in collaborative instruction with Lindsey, the reference and instruction archivist, to teach students about using primary sources, particularly those in the library's special collections. The librarian and archivist co-taught this session for a few semesters and now often teach individual sessions for courses in this department, focusing on using primary sources for assignments in Introduction to Transgender Studies, Introduction to Critical Sexuality Studies, and Queer Theory. In what follows, we will look specifically at how we work together to plan, design, and assess research-based projects in lower division undergraduate courses.

Lesson Plan and Design

Our collaborative teaching is guided by feminist pedagogy, and this shows up as we create participatory spaces for students and encourage active engagement. Our methods are also rooted in relational practice, which values mutuality, empathy, and intentional openness to change,[1] and engaged pedagogy, which focuses on the well-being of one another and values student expressions.[2] In addition, a relational approach to teaching is one that facilitates student learning through a willingness to take risks and increased receptivity to feedback from others.[3] During our classroom sessions, we want students to use the primary sources as a means to contribute to the discussion as empowered agents, and not passive receptacles of knowledge. Through this practice, we share in the growth of our students as educators, and their growth is linked with our own, both intellectual and personal.[4]

Like all good teaching, our lesson planning starts at the end. We ask ourselves, What do we want students to be able to do at the end of this assignment? What do we want them to know? And, vitally, how do we want them to *feel*? This learning outcome gets at the special nature of our courses. We want students to feel that excitement of exploring an unexpected source, of having the space to pursue genuine curiosity that we know is piqued especially when we look at primary sources. We also want our students to feel excited about making new knowledge about themselves and those who came before them. Students are actively engaged in the learning process, highlighting the feminist pedagogical approach we use in the course. As we help these students construct their own meaning from these learning experiences, they actively make connections between what they find in these sources and their own life experiences.[5]

We approach these instruction sessions as opportunities for the students to analyze artifacts of their shared histories. As instructors, we collaborate in ways that model open and equitable practices, expressing care and enthusiasm for the work and for one another, which are qualities of connected, relational teaching.[6] We share authority with our students and work on multiple levels to advance justice through primary research for our queer and transgender students as well as our larger communities. We teach the students how to think about using oral histories, photographs, zines, and other primary source collections as sources of alternative histories. As part of the review of the collection materials, the instructor discusses gaps in the archival record; this is especially relevant with historical collections created by transgender and queer communities.

Active Learning in the Classroom

During the initial session with the Feminist Activism course, Jo and Lindsey work together to provide an overview of related collections and model processes of document analysis. The students collaborate to review single items and, through discussion, unpack the process of analysis while sharing findings with their class-mates. For Introduction to Critical Sexuality Studies, Jo discusses examples of primary sources that could serve as starting points for supplementary secondary research, focusing on how these sources inform us about moments and perspectives throughout time that might otherwise be lost with more traditional academic sources. As demonstrated below, through these encounters with students, we hope to help them see themselves in history and research and empower them as creators and producers of knowledge.

As originally structured, the in-class document analysis exercise provides the students an opportunity to work directly with the selected historical documents, in this case publication issues from UMBC's Alternative Press Center collection. Founded in 1969, the Alternative Press Center is dedicated to providing access to nonmainstream serial publications; titles selected for the class include *The Ladder*, *The Advocate*, and a pamphlet for "Parents of Gays." The students examine one publication issue using a provided worksheet. The structure of the exercise is based on the "Interpret, Analyze, Evaluate" section of the RBMS-SAA *Guidelines for Primary Source Literacy*, specifically the goal to "critically evaluate the perspective of the creator(s) of a primary source, including tone, subjectivity, and biases, and consider how these relate to the original purpose(s) and audience(s) of the source."[7] This guided document analysis focuses on the factual content of the item—the who, what, where, and when of publication—but also asks the students to think about the item as an historical primary source. With that goal in mind, the students are asked to consider these two questions:

- Who was the creator, and what was their relationship to the movement or events being described?
- Who was the original intended audience of the item?

Working in small groups, the students spend fifteen to twenty minutes looking through the provided item. The guided analysis worksheet starts with several basic publication questions—date published, title, creator(s)—before moving on to the deeper analysis. The design elements, the tone of the content, word choice and terminology, and sections or layout of the content can all be helpful features for this analysis. We are looking beyond the factual content in order to interpret a sense of the mission or purpose intended by the creator for their audience.

One aspect of this analysis that is particularly relevant for this class is the membership of the creator and audience in the particular groups being documented. How events, movements, and people are described, and using what terms, can change depending on the intended audience. Is the creator seeking to educate a general audience, or are they speaking to a peer within their own community? Tracing the evolution of language within political and social justice groups is one of the strengths of the Alternative Press Center collection, and examining the words selected based on the intended audience can provide additional insight into the motivation of the creator.

Following the small-group activity, the students come back together as a group and share their items and observations with the rest of the class. This provides an opportunity for the students to learn about the primary sources available to them for their research, but also to talk through their interpretation of the creators and original intended audience. The student-led discussion, with minimal moderation and questions from the instructors, often leads to a more thorough analysis than what they have included on the worksheets. They can draw comparisons between the items and share their analysis in their own words.

In subsequent classes, we have asked the students to work with different collections, such as the Digital Transgender Archive, and several web-based oral history collections. When the students use these interviews as well as other ephemeral items in their research, we ask them to consider the perspectives represented in these materials. Is there something about these sources that makes them more accurate or representative of a moment in time? How do we determine the value of the information that these sources offer, and how is that different from complementary secondary sources? When the students present what they have learned to the class, we are all enriched by their recounting of this experience. The voices of the instructors are no longer the sole account of what happens in the classroom.[8]

Assessment

The most immediate outcome of this type of assignment is that the students know that the historical collections available in their university's special collections department are open and available to them for their own research. The document analysis exercise guides them through the initial research process of thinking about the item beyond the factual content contained—what can they learn about these movements and groups from the publications and resources that they created, distributed, and learned from at the time? We model the research process by analyzing the documents together and then discuss the experience, learning from each other and placing value on the students' original interpretations. This learning outcome is particularly powerful for students who, because of their sexual and gender identities, might not have imagined they could ever find themselves in an archive.

For example, one of the sources many students work with is the LGBT Oral Histories of Central Iowa collection. Many of our students come from rural parts of the state of Maryland, and their understanding of trans and queer life is that it is something lived only in urban areas. That might even be why they've chosen to come to college near Baltimore and Washington, DC. They discover in these oral histories, though, that rural trans lives are not only lived, but they can be lived well. Although they are bombarded by regular reports of suicide and murder in their communities, these oral histories remind them that there is more to being trans than what is in the crime blotter. They get to learn from elders, but the collection also includes oral histories of their generational peers, a reminder that their own experiences can be research as well. Students learn to critically engage oral histories as primary sources as new researchers while also feeling themselves into a place where they understand that their own stories matter, just like these ones do. Our shared library instruction sessions and research projects exemplify inclusive instruction as itself an invitation—to learning, to belonging, and to being the center of the story.

In the classroom, this assignment is one small part of the overall work for the course. The initial instruction with Jo and Lindsey shapes the rest of the conversation in the class. Particularly in sexuality and transgender studies classes, we use the source analysis questions to think about everything we read. Does it matter if the creator/researcher is transgender themselves? What difference does it make when a text is written for a general audience, an academic audience, or a specific audience of LGBTQ+ people? How do our own experiences and subjectivities shape how we read any text? Learning to make knowledge from primary sources helps students evaluate any kind of source. This has led to deeper and more critical readings throughout the class and better learning for both the instructor and the students. Student presentations of their research help the entire class understand themselves as a research team, making new knowledge together. As gender and sexual identity categories continue to change quickly, these projects are particularly useful for helping the instructor learn from students via their interpretations of primary source materials.

Conclusion

Inclusive library instruction demands that we think critically about who our students are, what support they need in order to develop a personal connection to original research, and what we need to do, as collaborative instructors, to ensure that they have the opportunity to explore and build the research skills necessary for their education.

There are several practical strategies that we use when working toward these goals. In our pedagogical approach, we pay attention to what students teach us and what they tell us they want to learn. We make sure to model our own collaboration for students to demonstrate what it looks like to work as a research team—which is precisely what their classrooms and peers are for each other. Engaged pedagogy and relational teaching ask that we share in both the empowerment and the vulnerability that enables risk taking in teaching and learning,[9] and in doing so, we can all find both joy and security in the work. Finally, essential to this practice is giving students ample time to explore and share based on their own interests. This allows students to learn from each other as we also learn from them.

Beyond these practical skills is the larger goal of teaching students to understand that they have a place in history. Historical research and analysis, as modeled in the gender studies classroom, can be a form of activism and self-actualization, a tool that can empower their present and future lives. Research like this is often emotional as students experience excitement at their discoveries, anger that it took so long to find them, and sadness as they confront trauma and violence on their research paths. In our relational approach to teaching, we encourage our students to share those feelings and dig into the affective dimensions of social science and humanities research. Inclusive teaching and learning can empower all of us to place ourselves at the center of history, even if we are gender or sexual minorities. Finding your story and your community's legacy in the collections of an archive can be very meaningful when you have not seen this representation in your life experiences.

Notes

1. Judith V. Jordan, "Empathy, Mutuality, and Therapeutic Change: Clinical Implications of a Relational Model," in *Women's Growth in Connection: Writings from the Stone Center,* ed. Judith V. Jordan, Alexandra G. Kaplan, Jean Baker Miller, Irene P. Stiver, and Janet L. Surrey (New York: Guilford Press, 1991), 283–89.
2. bell hooks, *Teaching to Transgress* (New York: Routledge, 1994), 15–22.
3. Harriet L Schwartz, *Connected Teaching* (Sterling, VA: Stylus, 2019), 23.
4. hooks, *Teaching to Transgress,* 15–22.
5. hooks, *Teaching to Transgress,* 19.
6. Schwartz, *Connected Teaching,* 32–33.
7. ACRL RBMS-SSA Joint Task Force on the Development of Guidelines for Primary Source Literacy, *Guidelines for Primary Source Literacy* (Chicago: Society of American Archivists and Association of College and Research Libraries, 2018), 4–6.
8. hooks, *Teaching to Transgress,* 21.
9. hooks, *Teaching to Transgress,* 21.

Bibliography

ACRL RBMS-SAA Joint Task Force on the Development of Guidelines for Primary Source Literacy. *Guidelines for Primary Source Literacy.* Chicago: Society of American Archivists and Association of College and Research Libraries, 2018.

hooks, bell. *Teaching to Transgress: Education as the Practice of Freedom.* New York: Routledge, 1994.

Jordan, Judith V., Alexandra G. Kaplan, Jean Baker Miller, Irene P. Stiver, and Janet L. Surrey, eds. *Women's Growth in Connection: Writings from the Stone Center.* New York: Guilford, 1991.

Schwartz, Harriet L. *Connected Teaching: Relationship, Power, and Mattering in Higher Education.* Sterling, VA: Stylus, 2019.

CHAPTER 18

Teaching and Learning through a Feminist Framework

Intersectionality and Primary Source Literacy

Sharon Ladenson

Introduction

Practitioners of feminist pedagogy can bolster their tool kit of strategies for cultivating an inclusive classroom environment by integrating primary source literacy and intersectionality into their teaching. Intersectionality strengthens feminist pedagogy by focusing on women's experiences holistically, including raising awareness about how multiple social variables (such as race, class, and gender) shape structural inequality. By interacting critically with primary sources through an intersectional lens, students have the opportunity to explore and raise questions about the lived experiences of contemporary or historical figures who have faced overlapping forms of discrimination and oppression, including racism and sexism. This chapter examines the complementary frameworks of primary source literacy, feminist pedagogy, and intersectionality. Feminist approaches for five one-shot information literacy sessions are discussed, including specific activities designed for exploring the concept of intersectionality through critically engaging with primary sources.

Primary Source Literacy, Feminist Pedagogy, and Intersectionality: Theoretical Foundations

The *Guidelines for Primary Source Literacy* provide a solid example of a framework shaped by inclusive and critical perspectives. The *Guidelines* define primary source literacy as "the combination of knowledge, skills, and abilities necessary to effectively find, interpret, evaluate, and ethically use primary sources within specific disciplinary contexts, in order to create new knowledge or to revise existing understandings."[1] Primary source literacy involves not only acquiring skills in identifying and locating archival materials, but also interacting critically with historical information sources. Through an emphasis on creating new knowledge, the definition of primary source literacy conveys a shifting emphasis on the role of students not only as reflective information consumers, but also as active producers of information. The focus on students as information producers is further underscored through the emphasis on the importance of engaging with primary sources critically and analytically. The "Core Ideas" that frame the *Guidelines* highlight the importance of critical inquiry, noting that users who engage with primary sources do so through "interpretation, critical thinking, and evaluation; they use sources to develop both questions and arguments."[2] The learning objectives outlined in the *Guidelines* also emphasize critical inquiry, most notably in the section focusing on interpreting, analyzing, and evaluating primary sources, which calls for students to "identify, interrogate, and consider the reasons for silences, gaps, contradictions, or evidence of power relationships in the documentary record and how they impact the research process."[3]

The emphasis on critical inquiry in the *Guidelines* closely aligns with feminist approaches to teaching and learning. One of the key elements of feminist pedagogy involves cultivating a learner-centered classroom environment that facilitates active engagement and critical thinking.[4] This also involves encouraging students to raise critical questions and challenge assumptions in order to engage in the process of creating knowledge. As Parry notes, a feminist approach "encourages classroom interactions that emphasize students' ability to question and explore issues deeply, and nurtures the development of motivation and skills that allow students to investigate ideas and evidence and arrive at meaning."[5] Light, Nicholas, and Bondy further underscore this point, noting that within a feminist classroom, students "challenge traditional assumptions, ask critical questions about the world around them, and make connections between and among their learning experiences, often with a view to generate social change."[6]

Emerging from the second-wave women's movement, feminist pedagogy facilitates consciousness-raising about gender discrimination and oppression.[7] The process of consciousness-raising about oppression and discrimination also facilitates critical inquiry about issues that extend far beyond the classroom and university context and, consequently, also promotes lifelong learning. Through consciousness-raising, practitioners of feminist pedagogy bring the voices of women from the margins to the center and recognize that women's experiences are shaped not only by gender, but also other factors, such as race, ethnicity, and class.[8] Intersectionality strengthens feminist pedagogy by exploring women's lived experiences holistically, underscoring that in addition to gender, other critical social variables, including race, frame challenges of systemic oppression that women face. As a theoretical framework, intersectionality illustrates how the overlap of multiple areas of identity shape individual experiences and reflect broader structural inequalities.[9] Romero notes that intersectionality conveys how systems of domination and oppression shift, causing some areas of identity to be more prominent than others in relations between individuals and groups.[10] Serving as an analytical tool, intersectionality also provides a holistic, multidimensional approach to recognizing, reflecting upon, and raising awareness about inequality. Collins and Blige assert that social inequality is not shaped exclusively by one variable (such as race or gender), but rather by many variables that work together and influence each other. As a result, intersectionality is also an important mechanism for understanding "the complexity in the world, in people, and in human experiences."[11]

Key elements of intersectionality are illustrated in social activism and theoretical writings of Black women in the late twentieth century. One notable example is the Combahee River Collective, a Black lesbian feminist organization active in Boston during the 1970s. Demita Frazier, Beverly Smith, and Barbara Smith developed the "Combahee River Collective Statement," which underscores how overlapping areas of identity, including race, gender, class, and sexuality, are subject to interlocking oppressions: "We are actively committed to struggling against racial, sexual, heterosexual, and class oppression and see as our particular task the development of integrated analysis and practice based upon the fact that the major systems of oppression are interlocking."[12] The late 1980s and1990s yielded another significant period for raising awareness about intersectionality, when Crenshaw articulated a theoretical framework for the concept. Within the context of discrimination cases, Crenshaw illustrates how focusing exclusively on either race or gender erases the experiences of Black women who encounter multiple forms of systemic inequality.[13] Furthermore, in her 1991 essay "Mapping the Margins: Intersectionality, Identity Politics, and Violence against Women of Color," Crenshaw asserts that the social category of "woman" is not uniform and that not all survivors of gender-based violence have access to the same resources or face the same challenges. For example, undocumented immigrant women who experience domestic violence often suffer in silence for fear that the security of their entire family will be jeopardized. Moreover, some shelters for survivors of domestic violence turn non-English-speaking women away due to a lack of multilingual personnel and resources.[14]

Integrating primary source literacy, feminist pedagogy, and intersectionality involves facilitating the process of raising critical questions about women's lived experiences holistically when engaging students in analysis of primary documents. *Which women's voices are included, and how are they represented?* Intersectionality aligns with primary source literacy and feminist pedagogy when students actively engage in the process of raising critical questions about ways in which overlapping areas of identity and multiple forms of oppression shape how information is conveyed. What are the challenges and struggles faced by an author who is subject to numerous forms of oppression? How do those struggles influence her perspective, contributions, and insights? Whose voices are marginalized or excluded from the documentary record? How are intersecting identities and multiple forms of oppression represented? Exploring intersectionality as part of the process of critically evaluating primary sources frames a feminist pedagogical approach of consciousness-raising about issues that shape the lives of students well beyond the classroom. Raising and exploring critical questions about multiple forms of oppression and the absence of voices and experiences of underrepresented communities also underscores key learning objectives of the *Guidelines for Primary Source Literacy*, particularly those which emphasize the analysis of power relationships and gaps and silences in the historical record.

Primary Source Literacy, Feminist Pedagogy, and Intersectionality: Women's History

Collaborating with department faculty and library colleagues to explore intersectionality within information literacy sessions has been highly engaging and rewarding. In preparation for a one-shot, eighty-minute session for an undergraduate course focused on the history of second-wave feminism, I collaborated with a history librarian to develop a twenty-minute discussion exercise designed to engage students with primary sources from the 1960s and 1970s. We selected examples of primary source documents highlighting challenges that women of color faced within dominant grassroots organizations and social movements. One of the documents selected for students to review was written by Sylvia Witts Vitale, cofounder and first Vice-Chair of the National Black Feminist Organization. Vitale's statement provides a powerful call to arms for Black women to mobilize:

Black women are finding that it is time to go one step further. We have found the Black movement and the Women's Movement to be inadequate in the area of black womanhood. In the Black movement we find men and women working …on tilted scales (with men typically in leadership positions, and women in secondary positions)…. In the Women's Movement, we find that racism has not purged itself. Some white women have no idea that by saying things like "We need more Black women in the Women's Movement," and "You are so articulate" is very oppressive to us. Those reasons coupled with your own personal experiences indicate that the time is right for a Black Feminist Movement.[15]

Working in pairs, students reviewed the documents during the session and reflected on the concerns expressed in each document, how (according to the author) the concerns could be addressed, and what questions students had about issues discussed by the author. After students completed their work in pairs, the faculty member and I co-conducted a large-group discussion in class. During the discussion, in addition to analyzing historical perspectives, some women opened up and shared information about racial discrimination they had experienced in their own lives. This exercise, rooted in feminist pedagogy, not only underscored evidence of systemic inequality and power relations in the historical record, but also provided an inclusive opportunity for the class to engage in collective learning through open conversation.

Intersectionality is a critical tool for raising awareness in the classroom about whose voices are privileged and whose are marginalized or excluded from historical documentation and analysis. Working with a different undergraduate class assigned to research and write biographical sketches of grassroots woman suffrage activists, I began this eighty-minute, one-shot instruction session with a five-minute discussion exercise by sharing pictures of Frances Ellen Watkins Harper, Susan B. Anthony, and Elizabeth Cady Stanton and subsequently asking students to identify each woman. The purpose of this exercise was to engage the students in critical conversation about how the experiences and voices of white women (including Stanton and Anthony) have been privileged and dominant in the documented history of women's suffrage, while those of Black, Indigenous, and people of color (including Harper) have been marginalized or excluded. While Harper was a prolific writer and notable activist, none of her writings or speeches on suffrage and women's rights were included in Stanton and Anthony's multivolume collection, *History of Woman Suffrage*. During the instruction session, I also asked students to engage in a twenty-minute discussion exercise of reading a biographical sketch of Frances Ellen Watkins Harper and reflecting on how she resisted racial and gender oppression. Working in pairs, students reflected and raised their own questions about Harper and shared their own search strategies for finding information about suffrage activists. Following their work in pairs, students also shared their reflections and search strategies during a large class discussion. Using an inclusive feminist approach of eliciting analyses and search strategies facilitated the process of building on the knowledge and experiences that students brought to the classroom.

Employing an inclusive, feminist approach of building on ideas and contributions of students has shaped conversations about intersectionality during my information literacy sessions for other undergraduate classes as well. For several years, I have worked with a class focused on the history of women in the United States from colonization through the end of the Civil War. One of the research assignments for the class involved reading the *Declaration of Sentiments*, a foundational document developed by nineteenth-century feminist activists. Modeled after the Declaration of Independence, the document lists grievances demonstrating the need for a women's rights movement. Students selected a specific grievance listed in the document and subsequently researched and analyzed the historical impact of the issue on women. During the one-shot, eighty-minute instruction session, students did a twenty-minute exercise that involved reading and reflecting on the *Declaration of Sentiments*. In class, I asked students to discuss in pairs what the document communicates about women's status historically, what questions they have about the grievances, and what strategies they would use for investigating the questions. During our subsequent large class discussions, students have raised key questions about *which* women's voices were authentically represented in the *Declaration of Sentiments* and, conversely, which women's voices were marginalized or excluded from feminist activism during the nineteenth century. For example, which women had the opportunity to attend the Seneca Falls Convention (where the *Declaration of Sentiments* was presented)? As voting rights for women were fundamental to the *Declaration of Sentiments*, how did racism ultimately plague the work of white women's suffrage activists who objected to the passage of the Fifteenth Amendment, which aimed to enfranchise Black men? Using a feminist pedagogical approach to elicit critical questions in the classroom has provided opportunities for raising awareness about more holistic and nuanced perspectives of the history of women's rights movements in the United States.

Primary Source Literacy, Feminist Pedagogy, and Intersectionality: Rhetorical Analysis

Raising critical questions about primary sources is key for students of not only history, but also other disciplines. Working with classes in writing and rhetoric, I have developed a variety of exercises to engage students with primary sources. One example involved working with a three-hour graduate course on queer rhetorics that required reviewing and critically analyzing texts from diverse genres (including zines) representing voices of lesbian, gay, bisexual, transgender, and queer communities. For the one-shot instruction session, I developed a thirty-minute discussion exercise that involved reviewing two zines: *Timtum* (whose author is transgender and Jewish) and *It's Complicated: Musings on Race, Ethnicity, and Identity* (written by Rachel Casiano *Hernández*, who is lesbian and Latina). I asked students to work in pairs to identify and discuss how Rachel Casiano *Hernández* conveys concerns about choosing between ethnic identity and sexuality and how the author of *Timtum* communicates concerns about "passing" as gentile and cisgender. During the subsequent large class discussion, students also talked about how the queer zine genre facilitates bringing the authentic voices of the authors from the margins to the center. Reviewing these zines provided an opportunity for students to examine the intersections of various forms of discrimination, including racism, homophobia, and anti-Semitism. Students also shared their own strategies for finding zines, which provided an inclusive opportunity for building on their background knowledge and research experiences during the information literacy session.

Zines are engaging for students at a variety of levels. I also used Rachel Casiano *Hernández*'s zine when working with an undergraduate first-year writing class. Students in the class were required to do research on the personal meaning of homeland. For this one-shot, two-hour instruction session, I developed a twenty-minute pair-share and large-group discussion exercise. The activity was designed not only to identify and discuss how Rachel Casiano *Hernández* communicates concerns about choosing between ethnic identity and sexuality earlier in life, but also what "homeland" means personally (i.e., embracing diverse areas of identity and coming out as both lesbian and Latina). In addition to illustrating the empowering experience of embracing multiple areas of identity, this exercise also provided an opportunity to raise and reinforce awareness among first-year students about intersecting forms of oppression. During the discussion activity, students also had the opportunity to share their own ideas about why Rachel Casiano *Hernández*'s zine was a primary source.

Through interacting critically with zines, students at both the graduate and undergraduate levels had opportunities to explore not only issues of structural inequality, but also how zine creators have exercised influence as agents of change. Incorporating intersectionality into information literacy instruction has been instrumental not only for raising awareness about interlocking areas of oppression, but also for sharing questions and facilitating conversation about the work necessary to yield lasting change. Through utilizing an inclusive, feminist approach, students had opportunities to learn from one another, sharing their analyses of primary source texts, their search strategies for the research process, and their lived experiences with discrimination and work to foster social change.

Conclusion

Incorporating the concept of intersectionality into information literacy instruction involves facilitating critical conversations about multiple areas of identity and oppression. Liaison librarians can facilitate these conversations by developing activities that elicit meaningful questions about ways in which overlapping areas of identity and multiple forms of oppression shape how information is conveyed. When students interact with primary sources, this provides a powerful opportunity to learn about the lived experiences of contemporary or historical subjects who have faced multiple forms of oppression. The process of engaging with primary sources is valuable for students of not only history, but also other disciplines, including writing, rhetoric, and gender studies. Practitioners of feminist pedagogy who incorporate intersectionality into their teaching embrace women's experiences more holistically, including raising and reinforcing awareness about multifaceted systemic inequality. Integrating intersectionality and primary source literacy into information literacy instruction facilitates an inclusive approach to teaching that extends the learning process far beyond the classroom and the university.

Notes

1. ACRL RBMS-SAA Joint Task Force on the Development of Guidelines for Primary Source Literacy, *Guidelines for Primary Source Literacy* (Chicago: Society of American Archivists and Association of College and Research Libraries, 2018), 1–2, https://www2.archivists.org/sites/all/files/GuidelinesForPrimarySourceLiteracy-June2018.pdf.
2. ACRL RBMS-SAA Joint Task Force on the Development of Guidelines for Primary Source Literacy, *Guidelines*, 3.
3. ACRL RBMS-SAA Joint Task Force on the Development of Guidelines for Primary Source Literacy, *Guidelines*, 5–6.
4. Sharon Ladenson, "Paradigm Shift: Utilizing Critical Feminist Pedagogy in Library Instruction," in *Critical Library Instruction: Theories and Methods,* ed. Maria T. Accardi, Emily Drabinski, and Alana Kumbier (Duluth, MN: Library Juice Press, 2010), 105–6.
5. Shirley C. Parry, "Feminist Pedagogy and Techniques for the Changing Classroom," *Women's Studies Quarterly* 24, no. 3/4 (1996): 45, https://www.jstor.org/stable/40004358.
6. Tracy Penny Light, Jane Nicholas, and Renée Bondy, "Introduction: Feminist Pedagogy in Higher Education," in *Feminist Pedagogy in Higher Education: Critical Theory and Practice,* ed. Tracy Penny Light, Jane Nicholas, and Renée Bondy (Waterloo, ON: Wilfrid Laurier University Press, 2015), 4.
7. Maria T. Accardi, "Feminist Pedagogy," in *Feminist Pedagogy for Library Instruction* (Sacramento, CA: Library Juice Press, 2013), 29–30.
8. Parry, "Feminist Pedagogy," 46.
9. Christie Launius and Holly Hassell, "Intersectionality," in *Threshold Concepts in Women's and Gender Studies: Ways of Seeing, Thinking, and Knowing* (New York: Routledge, 2015), 114–15.
10. Mary Romero, "Identifying Intersectionality," in *Introducing Intersectionality* (Malden, MA: Polity Press, 2018), 8–37.

11. Patricia Hill Collins and Sirma Blige, "What Is Intersectionality?" in *Intersectionality* (Malden, MA: Polity Press, 2016), 11.
12. Demita Frazier, Beverly Smith, and Barbara Smith, "Combahee River Collective Statement," in *Combahee River Collective Statement: Black Feminist Organizing in the Seventies and Eighties* (New York: Women of Color Press, 1986).
13. Kimberlé Crenshaw, "Demarginalizing the Intersection of Race and Sex: A Black Feminist Critique of Antidiscrimination Doctrine, Feminist Theory, and Antiracist Politics," *University of Chicago Legal Forum*, 139 (1989): 140, HeinOnline.
14. Kimberlé Crenshaw, "Mapping the Margins: Intersectionality, Identity Politics, and Violence against Women of Color," *Stanford Law Review* 43, no. 6 (July 1991): 1245–49, https://www.jstor.org/stable/1229039.
15. Sylvia Witts Vitale, "Black Sisterhood," *National Black Feminist Organization Newsletter* 1, no. 3 (September 1975).

Bibliography

Accardi, Maria T. "Feminist Pedagogy." In *Feminist Pedagogy for Library Instruction*, 23–54. Sacramento, CA: Library Juice Press, 2013.
ACRL RBMS-SAA Joint Task Force on the Development of Guidelines for Primary Source Literacy. *Guidelines for Primary Source Literacy*. Chicago: Society of American Archivists and Association of College and Research Libraries, 2018. https://www2.archivists.org/sites/all/files/GuidelinesForPrimarySourceLiteracy-June2018.pdf.
Collins, Patricia Hill, and Sirma Blige. "What Is Intersectionality?" In *Intersectionality*, 11–31. Malden, MA: Polity Press, 2016.
Crenshaw, Kimberlé. "Demarginalizing the Intersection of Race and Sex: A Black Feminist Critique of Antidiscrimination Doctrine, Feminist Theory, and Antiracist Politics." *University of Chicago Legal Forum* 139 (1989): 139–67. HeinOnline.
———. "Mapping the Margins: Intersectionality, Identity Politics, and Violence against Women of Color." *Stanford Law Review* 43, no. 6 (July 1991): 1241–99. https://www.jstor.org/stable/1229039.
Frazier, Demita, Beverly Smith, and Barbara Smith. "Combahee River Collective Statement." In *Combahee River Collective Statement: Black Feminist Organizing in the Seventies and Eighties*. New York: Women of Color Press, 1986.
Ladenson, Sharon. "Paradigm Shift: Utilizing Critical Feminist Pedagogy in Library Instruction." In *Critical Library Instruction: Theories and Methods*, edited by Maria T. Accardi, Emily Drabinski, and Alana Kumbier, 105–12. Duluth, MN: Library Juice Press, 2010.
Launius, Christie, and Holly Hassell. "Intersectionality." In *Threshold Concepts in Women's and Gender Studies: Ways of Seeing, Thinking, and Knowing*, 112–52. New York: Routledge, 2015.
Light, Tracy Penny, Jane Nicholas, and Bondy, Renée Bondy. "Introduction: Feminist Pedagogy in Higher Education," In *Feminist Pedagogy in Higher Education: Critical Theory and Practice*, edited by Tracy Penny Light, Jane Nicholas, and Renée Bondy, 1–10. Waterloo, ON: Wilfrid Laurier University Press, 2015.
Parry, Shirley C. "Feminist Pedagogy and Techniques for the Changing Classroom." *Women's Studies Quarterly* 24, no. 3/4 (1996): 45–54. https://www.jstor.org/stable/40004358.
Romero, Mary. "Identifying Intersectionality." In *Introducing Intersectionality*, 8–37. Malden, MA: Polity Press, 2018.
Vitale, Sylvia Witts. "Black Sisterhood." *National Black Feminist Organization Newsletter* 1, no. 3 (September 1975).

CHAPTER 19

Black Student Union Protests and a Cemetery

Creating Space for All Learners in the Archives

Randi Beem*

Introduction

As archivists, we know the stories our collections tell as well as the shortcomings that might exist, including archival silences, the unintentional or purposeful absence of documentation and enduring prejudices resulting in gaps and inabilities to represent the past accurately.[1] However, one constant struggle any good archivist or special collections librarian has is getting students interested in the documents that exist within their collections and selecting documents that reflect your students and the community their university or college serves.

As a white archivist who serves an increasingly diverse student population, I knew that my approach to active learning and the collections I incorporated into my teaching would have to change to give students the rush of finding a story in an archive that related to them. Through this quest, I began employing an inclusive critical librarianship pedagogy and an innovative active learning strategy from the

---

* Randi Beem is a white, Midwest U.S.-born, straight, cis, able-bodied woman. At the time of writing, she is a mid-career archivist employed in a faculty position at University of North Carolina Charlotte.

267

Librarians Active Learning Institute to create dynamic lessons that allow students to see people like themselves in the material and engage with stories that challenge accepted power dynamics of the world. I have included these lesson plans in the appendix at the end of this chapter so that you have a reference for the flow and types of materials utilized. In this chapter, I highlight two unique one-shot instruction sessions I built featuring collections in my archives and based on inclusive pedagogical principles that any special collections librarian, archivist, or librarian can adopt to engage their students with primary sources.

Critical Librarianship

The beginning principle that I employed to connect students to documents that reflect them was critical librarianship. Critical librarianship can serve as a cornerstone for creating inclusive spaces and pedagogies to engage a variety of students, including BIPOC, those identifying as queer, and those seeking to implement change on their campus and in the local community.

While I will be discussing critical librarianship in the realm of teaching, it is important to note that its principles can be used in every aspect of our tasks: from changing the neoliberal label of *customer* when we mean *patron* to developing our collection development policy to reflect the users of our spaces.[2] As James Elmborg stated in his 2006 article, "Critical Information Literacy: Implications for Instructional Practice," "Critical literacy provides a way for libraries to change this trajectory and more honestly align themselves with the democratic values they often invoke."[3]

Engaging critical literacy principles requires librarians to think outside themselves and the typical ways they present information to their students. Critical librarianship acts as a gateway framework for inclusive pedagogies since it is a building block for other pedagogies. Through undertaking this pedagogy, librarians and archivists can build lessons that engage students with uncomfortable topics while allowing them to gather thoughtful practice with library resources.

As Michelle Caswell states in her essay "Envisioning a Critical Archival Pedagogy" from *The Politics of Theory and the Practice of Critical Librarianship,* within archives, critical librarianship intersects with archival work through utilizing three key components of our work: critique, act, and imagine.[4] The portion of the outline that I utilize in my instruction falls under that of the act of being an archivist. Through instruction, I am also teaching the students the concept of critique by discussing the provenance, who created a collection, versus whose story is told within the pages of that collection. To ensure students recognize the concept of critique, I ask, "Which collection do you think these papers come from?" which gives them a touchstone of who is controlling the narrative through a collection. This intersection of critical librarianship and archives is the heart of my pedagogy and allows me to build lessons around primary sources that give the students a mirror of the past but a path forward to accurately depict history.

This pedagogy works within the context of understanding how to get students to ask the "why" of these databases, collections, and resources. The cornerstone of this pedagogy is to focus on process over product. Students are asked to question how political and social norms influence the information they have access to, such as library databases and archival collections.[5] To spur their thinking, students consider these questions: Why is the information that is found in a prominent library database important versus the oral traditions of marginalized communities? Why are there "silences" of different communities within the archives? Why are libraries sometimes considered neutral institutions when there are defined hierarchical systems in place with the resources we as librarians and archivists collect? Opening up a classroom to ask students "why?" allows them to teach us, the keepers of knowledge, something about their experience outside of the walls of our classroom.

Active Learning Academy

To make the concept of critical thinking and critical librarianship work within the archival classroom, it is important to have a specific active learning activity that serves as a foundation for the hands-on teaching that archivists want students to engage in. With archival instruction, a prominent goal is for students to become comfortable with handling archival materials and understanding how these materials work to tell a story. Routinely, archivists use active learning to teach primary source literacy skills, including recognizing, interpreting, and analyzing primary sources.[6]

An example that has become integral in my classroom is that of the Librarians Active Learning Institute (LALI). LALI, held at Dartmouth College, focuses on engaging librarians in three foundational thoughts: "meet students where they are," "engage students actively in the process of teaching and learning," and "encourage students to reflect upon and to articulate their learning process."[7]

I was introduced to this framework as part of a workshop for the Teaching Undergraduates with Archives Symposium held at the University of Michigan. The workshop was facilitated by Peter Carini, college archivist at Dartmouth, and Morgan Swan, special collections librarian for teaching and scholarly engagement. At the beginning of the workshop, we were split up into groups and given different sets of various primary documents. The documents were presented to us without explanation, but we were told that they all focused around one controversial event that occurred at Dartmouth. We first went through the folder of digitized copies as a group. We had to identify what kind of documents we had and what they were about in the first ten minutes of the workshop.

After the first ten minutes, we were told to move around the room to other groups to find out what documents they had. Our group held student records regarding a student who had been expelled from Dartmouth College in the 1920s due to selling alcohol during Prohibition. Groups around the room included the following documents: student records about the only murder on campus, documents about a student hosting parties at an off-campus house in the 1920s, and the responses of the president and board of trustees to all of the above events.

When we were done discussing as a larger class, Peter and Morgan brought us together to discuss the following questions:

- What kind of documents did you have?
- What year were your documents from?
- What were your documents discussing?
- What do you think is the overarching story of all of these documents?

All of the documents discussed the most scandalous scenarios in Dartmouth's history and the administration's feelings about and responses to them.

Peter and Morgan told us that using documents from Dartmouth College's archives increases engagement with students coming into the archives for the first time, since students always seem to be interested in stories from the college's past. The activity also allows for primary source basics to be covered when you ask students what kind of documents they have and what year they are from. Students learn about the types of documents available to research and their historical context through the activity's questions. The storytelling aspect of these documents allows students to feel comfortable engaging with each other in the larger group.

After doing this activity myself, I knew this would be a great way to engage students with historical documents while engaging them in the basics of primary source analysis. LALI's approach of using a set of "official" documents from a source of power—a university's administration or government documents—and pairing them with documents that tell the story of "others,"—such as students, student groups, or citizens—provided me with a solid pedagogy to engage students.

Atkins Library Special Collections and University Archives: Collection Development Background

Before discussing the inclusive practices that I use in the classroom, it is important to describe the collections that are at my disposal. At Atkins Library Special

Collections and University Archives, our mission and goal are to preserve the history of Charlotte, North Carolina, and the history of the University of North Carolina at Charlotte. A few examples of materials we collect include the papers of every mayor from the year 1924 on, members of the Charlotte City Council, local activists, and everyday citizens.

Charlotte's history influences our collection and by extension the type of items we can use in the classroom. Charlotte has a unique history among Southern towns, from its different economic standards due to not having large plantations but still maintaining a large population of enslaved people, to its rise as a mill town in the 1900s, to its cornerstone status today as a hot spot for the financial world. As with many cities in the South, Charlotte has had its own growing pains with the issues that many Americans are discussing today, including urban renewal and desegregation. Our collections are rich when it comes to telling the history of not just a city, but also the folx who have lived here.

The University of North Carolina at Charlotte also has a distinct and unlikely history. The university was founded by a woman, Bonnie Cone, who ran the first iteration of the school, a junior college night school that began in 1946 as a response to the needs of GIs returning from World War II. When the school moved to its current location, the university saw it as a chance to expand. The beginning class consisted of fewer than one hundred students, and today the enrollment is over 30,000 students. In many ways, the university has been overwhelmingly responsive to the times and contains a microcosm of many of the events that occurred on campuses before, during, and after the Southeast Asia War—historical events that students can relate to and that encourage them to question social norms.

The following portions of this chapter will focus on two examples that incorporate the ideals around critical librarianship and critical literacy and the LALI methods that I use in the classroom: the Black Student Union protests at the University of North Carolina at Charlotte, and the case of the Pinewood and Elmwood Cemetery in Charlotte.

The Black Student Union Protests

The Black Student Union protests are the perfect incident in UNC Charlotte history to get students comfortable with primary documents and begin to build the landscape of our "why" questions for them. These protests began in 1968 and are an example of the student activism that was a large part of campus culture across the country during the Southeast Asia War.

The University Archives hold various documents surrounding these events. I use the following documents to tell the Black Student Union's side of the story: the Black Student Caucus request for a black flag to be flown in recognition of the Orangeburg (South Carolina) massacre; the Ten Demands of the Black Student Union; a statement to the press from the Black Student Union; and *The Utter Truth*, a newsletter created by the Black Student Union after the administration invited them to a meeting to halt the protests. For the administration's side of the protest, I include Chancellor Dean Colvard's response to the Ten Demands, a memo from Academic Affairs Vice President William McEniry, and another memo from McEniry regarding *The Utter Truth*. These materials come from Student Affairs Vice Chancellor (Bonnie Cone) papers, 1965–1975, and Chancellor (Dean W. Colvard) records, 1964–1979.

When I use this experience in a classroom outside of the library, I employ digitized printed copies of the materials. One-half of the class receives the Black Student Union story, and the other half receives the administration documents. Each individual student receives one pack of the documents depicting one side of the story: either the story from the viewpoint of the Black Student Union, or the "official" story from the viewpoint of the administration. If I conduct this in the Reading Room, I take the folders that hold these materials out of the boxes of the collections that they come from and place them around one of the tables in the Reading Room. I then lead the whole class to the table, where they split up into pairs to look through the documents. Whether we are working online or in person, the documents are presented without context to support the lesson plan's objectives, which include students identifying types of primary sources, utilizing context clues, and using collective analysis to build the story together as a class.

During the session, students have ten minutes to either read the packets or look through the folders that contain the materials. I then ask the students these questions:

- What kind of documents did you see? (letters, memorandums, newsletters)
- What year are your documents from?
- Do you recognize any names from your documents?
- What are your documents discussing?

From these questions, students piece together the events of the Black Student Union protests.

Those questions cover the basics of the LALI and get students feeling comfortable with a discussion. However, to incorporate the idea of critical thinking and the principles of critical librarianship, I use more pointed questions:

- Why do you think these students were protesting?
- What are some demands of the Black Student Union? (The demands range from a fair minimum wage to the creation of a Black Studies program and the hiring of Black faculty, among other requests.)
- What does the administration's reaction to the Ten Demands tell you about its feelings toward this protest?

- Why is this event important to campus history?

These questions expand on how students think about questioning authority. The administration's reaction to the Ten Demands held a tone of "we are trying" rather than listening to the requests from the students.

The story of the Black Student Union is one that works very well with many different classes. The Black Student Union is still active on campus, so students have a knowledge of the organization. Present-day students enjoy this activity since it gives them an idea of how former students have spoken to power and an opportunity to understand how changes can occur on campus. Students also get interested in archival terms, such as *onionskin* (which some of the documents are printed on), so this activity leaves a lasting impression on them beyond just the subject matter.

Prior to the protests and demonstrations that occurred during the summer of 2020, students enjoyed learning about this interesting aspect of campus history because it felt like a connection to a well-known club on campus and allowed them to learn about the history of administrators whose names appear on many buildings on campus. During the fall and spring semester of 2021, many students have reflected on protests they may have been involved in and discussed how the administration was strongly lacking in its response to the students. This activity engages students in understanding how to speak truth to power and is a direct example of how institutional hierarchy doesn't necessarily look out for the interests of those it is meant to serve.

Pinewood and Elmwood Cemetery

The second scenario I use for classes is one rooted in local city government and can be used to illustrate the power local officials have to enact change. This activity focuses on the story behind the Pinewood and Elmwood Cemetery, which is in the center of Charlotte. This cemetery is the second oldest in the city and has an interesting history to match.

For this activity, I utilize the following collections: our Special Collections map collection, the Frederick D. Alexander papers, and Charlotte (N.C.) City Records. When conducting this activity virtually, I use two copies of early Charlotte, North Carolina, maps, some pages from the graveyard index from the early 1900s that come from the Charlotte (N.C.) City Records, and constituent letters from the records of Charlotte's first Black city councilman post-Reconstruction, Frederick D. Alexander. When I can hold class in the Reading Room, I take all of these materials and place them around a table where the class works in pairs to look at the materials and discover their context.

Again, students have ten minutes to either read the digital copies or look through the folders that contain these materials and discuss the same questions:

- What kind of documents did you see? (letters, memorandums, newsletters)
- What year are your documents from?
- Do you recognize any names from your documents?
- What are your documents discussing?

This variety of materials allows students to get acquainted with the story and to experience that it takes many archival materials to build an accurate retelling of historical events representing multiple viewpoints.

Pinewood and Elmwood Cemetery was segregated until the 1960s. I use the maps to showcase how Charlotte has grown over the years and expose students to maps as primary documents. The Pinewood and Elmwood Cemetery Indexes from the early 1900s are labeled "White" and "Colored" on the inside cover. The constituent letters showcase the anger many residents felt toward City Councilman Fred Alexander because he was leading the charge to take down the fence at the cemetery that was the dividing line between the deceased white citizens and the deceased Black citizens.

These documents allow students to see a local landmark that has a connection to a larger historical theme of segregation. After we cover the basics of identifying the documents, I then ask the critical thinking questions:

- Is any of this surprising to you?
- Why do you think the cemetery was segregated?
- Why do you think the constituents from the Fred Alexander papers are angry? Looking at the maps and where the cemetery is in the city, do you think these concerns are valid?
- What does this tell you about a society that separates people even after death?

Many students are surprised that people were segregated even in a cemetery, and the case works well to increase awareness of prejudices. It also has been helpful to use this example during an election year since it reminds students that they are citizens and that local elections have an impact, even when the impact feels small or elusive.

Conclusion

If you want to attempt this type of instruction for yourself, the best way to do this is to find within your archives or special collections an event that employs two different viewpoints that you know will engage students. It could be a protest on your campus or a time when a local official sought to change one small thing about your community to help foster a sense of equality and justice. When you find a case like this, there are almost always two sides to each story, so be sure to find at least two different collections to choose from for these types of activities. Since one lesson objective with this active learning activity is to have students be able to identify types of documents, gathering a variety is key.

Another point of this activity is that while I do supply a range of questions, I also allow the students to lead the discussion. As a result, I have had students dive deeper into the mechanics of power structures or ask for more information about the documents, such as what a constituent letter is and what the further involvement was of different players in the stories. Being able to come up with a variety of questions that encourage students to dig deeper into existing issues while demonstrating documents exemplifying those issues is integral to creating a lesson plan like this.

When incorporating the pedagogy of critical thinking and critical librarianship with the principles from the LALI, the opportunity to engage students with stories of marginalized communities questioning common social structures can be achieved. Creating a space of inclusivity can be accomplished by choosing primary source documents from collections of past students and diverse perspectives and using a class structure that allows students to understand that the classroom is a place to challenge norms. By drawing on the past, students can understand and recognize present and past events that may require them to think critically about how the official story that is being told reinforces an oppressive power dynamic.

Appendix

Lesson Objectives

Students will be able to explain what primary documents are and how they can contribute to research.

Students will investigate subjects across various materials and formats using primary documents.

Students will engage in object-based learning activities to connect the context of the documents to the time period they are studying.

Lesson Plan

Special Collections and University Archives overview (10 minutes)

Looking at different ways of understanding primary documents (split this up into three activities to cover all of it):

- Pinewood Cemetery Documents: Fred Alexander Papers, City of Charlotte Records, and Charlotte-Mecklenburg Historic Landmarks Commission records

Primary documents that focus on one event over time (use the Black Student Union of UNC Charlotte protest; 20 minutes)

- Exposure of North Carolina–specific materials, including mayoral papers, textile mill papers, Julius Chambers papers, LGBTQ community, and family papers

FIRST ACTIVITY: PINEWOOD/ELMWOOD CEMETERY: WHAT ARE PRIMARY SOURCES AND HOW DO WE USED THEM? (20 MINUTES)

What are primary documents? How can you use them to understand the history behind one city? Students will have ten minutes to look at constitution letters from the Fred D. Alexander Papers and the financial ledger for the Pinewood and Elmwood cemeteries from the City of Charlotte, N.C. Records. Students will be presented these materials with the idea that these items are connected and the students need to discover what is the connection. They will have ten minutes to discover the connection and we will discuss using the questions below.

1. What kind of documents did your folder have?
2. Are you surprised by what kind of documents you saw?
3. What names do you recognize from your documents?
4. What kind of situation do you think your documents are covering?

5. What does even being segregated in death tell you about Charlotte's perceptions about race?

SECOND ACTIVITY: STUDENT PROTESTS AT THE UNIVERSITY OF NORTH CAROLINA AT CHARLOTTE (20 MINUTES)

How do we find bias in primary documents? This activity will engage students with various materials around one event so we have an idea of what may be going on from just a few documents. Students will spend 10 minutes looking at their documents and then we will discuss what one event these materials relate to.

Collections

- Student Organizations, Black Student Union
- Black Studies Program, 1969–1974
- Loose papers
- Stokley Carmichael's speech
- Chancellor subject files—Black Student Union

We will answer the following questions:

1. What set of documents did you all have?
2. What year are your documents from?
3. What do your documents discuss?
4. What do you think all these documents have to do with each other?
5. What further questions do you have after reading your documents?

THIRD ACTIVITY: GETTING CREATIVE WITH PRIMARY SOURCES (25 MINUTES)

Students will spend some time looking at the different North Carolina–based collections we have. These collections will be placed in the pairs listed below to focus on different themes.

Collections

- Harvey Gantt Mayoral Papers and Sue Myrick Mayoral Papers
- Reginald A. Hawkins and Kelly Alexander, Sr. NAACP
- Donaldson Wells King and Sue Henry papers
- Caldwell and Davidson Family Papers and Jetton Family Papers
- Julius S. Chambers Papers and North Carolina School Desegregation Collection

Discussion Questions

1. What collections did you have?
2. What kind of materials did you find?
3. What time period are your items from?
4. Why do you think these two boxes are together?

Notes

1. Society of American Archivists, Dictionary of Archives Terminology, 2005, https://dictionary. archivists.org/index.html.
2. Sam Popowich, "'Ruthless Criticism of All That Exists': Marxism, Technology, and Library Work," in *The Politics of Theory and the Practice of Critical Librarianship*, ed. Karen P. Nicholson and Maura Seale (Sacramento, CA: Library Juice Press, 2018), 39–62.
3. James Elmborg, "Critical Information Literacy: Implications for Instructional Practice," *Journal of Academic Librarianship* 32, no. 2 (March 2006): 192-198, https://doi.org/10.1016/j.acal-ib.2005.12.004.
4. Michelle Caswell, "Envisioning a Critical Archival Pedagogy," in *The Politics of Theory and the Practice of Critical Librarianship*, ed. Karen P. Nicholson and Maura Seale (Sacramento, CA: Library Juice Press, 2018), 159–65.
5. Maria T. Accardi, Emily Drabinski, and Alana Kumbier, "Introduction," in *Critical Library Instruction: Theories and Methods*, ed. Maria T. Accardi, Emily Drabinski and Alana Kumbier (Duluth, MN: Library Juice Press, 2009), ix–xiii.
6. Anne Bahde, Heather Smedberg, and Mattie Taormina, "Introduction," in *Using Primary Sources: Hands-On Instruction Exercises*, ed. Anne Bahde, Heather Smedberg and Mattie Taormina (Santa Barbara, CA: Libraries Unlimited, 2014), xiii–xx.
7. Dartmouth Library, "About: Librarians Active Learning Institute," 2020, https://www.library. dartmouth.edu/lali/about.

Bibliography

Accardi, Maria T., Emily Drabinski, and Alana Kumbier. "Introduction." In *Critical Library Instruction: Theories and Methods*, edited by Maria T. Accardi, Emily Drabinski and Alana Kumbier, ix–xiii. Duluth, MN: Library Juice Press, 2009.

Bahde, Anne, Heather Smedberg, and Mattie Taormina. "Introduction." In *Using Primary Sources: Hands-On Instruction Exercises*, edited by Anne Bahde, Heather Smedberg and Mattie Taormina, xiii–xx. Santa Barbara, CA: Libraries Unlimited, 2014.

Caswell, Michelle. "Envisioning a Critical Archival Pedagogy." In *The Politics of Theory and the Practice of Critical Librarianship*, edited by Karen P. Nicholson and Maura Seale, 159–65. Sacramento, CA: Library Juice Press, 2018.

Dartmouth Library. "About: Librarians Active Learning Institute." 2020. https://www.library.dart-mouth.edu/lali/about.

Elmborg, James. "Critical Information Literacy: Implications for Instructional Practice." *Journal of Academic Librarianship* 32, no. 2 (March 2006): 192–99. https://doi.org/10.1016/j. acalib.2005.12.004.

Popowich, Sam. "'Ruthless Criticism of All That Exists': Marxism, Technology, and Library Work." In *The Politics of Theory and the Practice of Critical Librarianship*, edited by Karen P. Nicholson and Maura Seale, 39–62. Sacramento, CA: Library Juice Press, 2018.

Society of American Archivists. Dictionary of Archives Terminology. 2005. https://dictionary.archi-vists.org/index.html.

CHAPTER 20

Human Library
Inclusion and Understanding through Dialogue

*Allison McFadden-Keesling**

What Is a Human Library?

The Human Library is an international movement to promote diversity and inclusion initiatives by people having one conversation at a time. The concept is simple. Instead of physical paperback and hardcover books, a human library is a collection of people who serve as human books. These human books are volunteers who have been marginalized by society and generously share their stories with "readers." Through these intimate conversations, both the reader and the human book gain a better understanding of another individual. These encounters help humanize the stereotype they represent and give a voice to the marginalized. It is harder to discriminate against a group of people when you have met, and chatted with, someone from that group as they are no longer faceless.[1]

The Human Library fosters open and safe conversations, thereby breaking barriers that are the cornerstones of prejudice. As these conversations unfold, readers are encouraged to ask difficult questions they would not typically feel comfortable asking in any other social setting. These conversations "lead to greater acceptance, tolerance and social cohesion in the community."[2] These open and sincere conversations held in a safe and encouraging environment give a voice to those who have been stigmatized and marginalized so readers can grow in their understanding of diversity and inclusion.[3]

279

History

In 1993, in response to violent unrest in Copenhagen, Denmark, a group called Stop the Violence was formed. The group encouraged peaceful solutions to conflict.[4] By 2000, they had grown to 30,000 members. Ronni Abergel (a cofounder of the group) asked, "Why are people willing to commit acts of violence against people they don't know? One of the reasons is that they don't have a previous relationship with that person. This is when we came up with the concept of The Human Library. If you could build relationships between groups in the community that think they don't like each other, that think they don't have anything in common, then we might be able to change that attitude."[5]

Concerned about potential unrest at their four-day annual music festival, the Roskilde Music Festival organizers contacted Stop the Violence. Ronni Abergel, Dany Abergel, Asma Mouna, and Christoffer Erichsen developed the project, and in 2000 the first Human Library was held at the music festival.[6] Fifty human books were checked out by over 1,000 readers during that four-day event.[7] Ronni Abergel subsequently established and continues to run the nonprofit *HumanLibrary.org. The Australian government funded the National Living Library Strategy: Living Libraries Australia, a three-year national project (2007–2010) to promote tolerance and inclusion.[8] These Living Libraries were "a way of interrupting a politics of fear and division that was prevalent in Australia in the early and mid 2000s by bringing people together."[9]

Human Libraries continue to address social issues of fear and division within a community by facilitating events focused on that community's specific needs. The Human Library is trademarked, and therefore those interested in facilitating an event must register at https://humanlibrary.org. Human Library events are always free. Organizers and participants are volunteers, and there is no charge to attend the event. Today, there are Human Libraries in over eighty countries around the world.[10]

Why Should You Have a Human Library in a College Setting?

Human Libraries promote experiential learning. Instead of simply studying about people from various cultures or lifestyles from a textbook, the student experiences hands-on learning by meeting and having personal conversations with individuals

---

* I am a white, middle class, U.S. born, grey haired, able-bodied, cisgender straight woman. I've been happily married for 35 years and have three grown children I'm proud to know and love.

from other walks of life they may not otherwise have met. The human books do not give a speech but instead have a conversation with the reader and encourage any and all questions. These events allow the reader/student "to focus and reflect on their own prejudices and stereotypes, and to establish a peaceful, positive and fun meeting with one's own worst prejudice."[11] The Human Library brings those prejudices into the light and asks individuals to bravely look at their personal prejudices and learn more about another human being. "It's easy to have prejudices about another group of people from a distance, but far more difficult to maintain the stereotypes in direct personal contact with someone. We often heard things like 'I hate immigrants, but Mohammad from my school is okay because I know him.'"[12] The Human Library forges real connections.

Students today are often so connected to their social media that they lack the social skills to have an intimate conversation. The Human Library promotes the development of those conversational social skills, which are essential in the workplace. Students learn to listen to the human book, make eye contact, and ask questions. Initially students may feel uncomfortable, but with a little encouragement, they thrive and gain confidence in their ability to communicate with someone who is different.

Critical thinking and reflection are important aspects of the Human Library experience. Many instructors incorporate it in their assignments to strengthen the student learning experience. The week before an event, we meet with the classes that plan to attend and share more information about the event. We share the history and purpose of the event as well as the specific human book titles (and their book descriptions) that will be available at the upcoming event. Some students are hesitant at first, so we work to assuage any fears or concerns they may have as well as encouraging them to think about what topics they may want to learn more about and what questions they may want to ask. "The Human Library® is a place where difficult questions are expected, appreciated and answered."[13] After the event, the students frequently are required to write reflective papers on their experiences.

It is difficult to feel connected and empathize with people we don't know or understand but easy to make snap judgments about people that we feel are different. Those judgments "rob people of their dignity. It makes our recognition of our equal humanity difficult. It emphasizes how we are different rather than how we are similar."[14] The Human Library lets you meet and learn about people who are different from you, which helps you feel connected to people from other cultures. It provides individuals the opportunity to check out their prejudice and unjudge someone.

Community colleges universally struggle to create opportunities for students to bond with their school and each other outside the classroom. The conversations and connections made at the Human Library help foster a sense of community and belonging. That sense of community enhances students' education by broadening their perspective. That connection and camaraderie continue long after a Human

Library event has ended. Students greet each other in the halls with a warmth seldom seen on campus before the event. I've run into former students years later and they enthusiastically share that they remember me because of the wonderful experience they had at one of our Human Libraries. The sense of community these events help create for all involved, especially the human books and the readers, is meaningful, powerful, and long-lasting.

The Human Library books form a connection all their own; they become like a family, and every Human Library event feels like a family reunion! The human books excitedly look forward to seeing one another, so we schedule to meet an hour before each event to allow human books the opportunity to catch up with old friends and meet new ones. We've scheduled several online Human Book Socials so human books can meet virtually and share their stories with one another. They have such interesting stories to share, and this is an opportunity for just human books to meet and "read" one another. The Human Library forges multilayered connections.

How the Human Library Works

Like any endeavor, Human Library events grow and improve through practice and trial and error. Reading and watching videos about how others facilitate Human Libraries has proved helpful. Attending virtual or in-person events and talking directly with facilitators was even better. And finally, reading articles and watching videos featuring Ronnie Abergel as well as e-mailing and talking with him directly has shaped the direction of our Human Library events.

We have facilitated two types of Human Libraries: Traditional and Reading Hall Style. Both allow readers and books to have honest conversations in a safe, nonjudgmental environment. A Traditional Human Library allows readers and books to have intimate one-on-one conversations. As in a real library, readers select human book titles of interest from a catalog of titles and book blurbs. Readers are also given a library card from Humanlibrary.org, which includes expectations of the event, encourages questions, and stipulates the rules. "The 'Rules for readers' is simple, respect the book, be curious, bring the book back on time and in the same condition in which given to you. Both parties have the right to end the loan at any time."[15] A Reading Hall Human Library is similar to a Traditional event except instead of an individual reader checking out a human book, small groups of four to seven readers check out a human book. These small groups talk with three different human books throughout the event.

Each human book writes their title and book jacket summary of what they intend to share as a teaser to spark the interest of potential readers.[16] Some titles and summaries are straightforward, for example:

- Addicts: They die—Why not me?

o "Darkness couches at the door. Its urge is toward you yet you can be its master." Everyone can change—but first, we must uncover the strength to step from darkness toward brightness.
o Chapter 1: Early Years—The Happy, "Normal" Suburban Life
o Chapter 2: Age 18—Overdose No. 1
o Chapter 3: Age 20 and the First Night
o Chapter 4: From Casual Use to Full Blown Addiction
o Chapter 5: Withdrawal: Pain, Misery, and Suffering
o Chapter 6: Second and Last Overdose
o Chapter 7: …the monk and meditation…
o Chapter 8: The Anomaly, Survivor's Guilt, and the Good Samaritan Law

- Being Black and Deaf

o How I survived through the struggling years growing up.

Some titles are less direct and include creative wordplay, for example:
- Do Ask, Do Tell: non-secret lives of a married Lesbian couple

o Chapter 1: Growing up Lesbian in the 60s (before "Ellen"): The Era before Role Models
o Chapter 2: Jesse has two mommies
o Chapter 3: Three Weddings and Two Funerals: Partners without benefits; Discrimination in everyday life
o Chapter 4: Married life without the Rights of Marriage in Michigan

Each title and summary reflect the personality of the human book and give the reader the opportunity to select their readings accordingly. Students/readers check out a human book through a circulation system created by the librarian.[17] Librarians share the catalog of human book titles and summaries with readers, explain the rules and expectations of the event, and encourage individuals to step outside their comfort zone and check out their prejudice. Both types of events can be in person or online.

Collection Development

Every Human Library features different topics based on the needs of its community, and the human books reflect these individual community needs. Organizers actively observe their community to address what diversity is lacking, misunderstood, and even feared. A good library has a carefully developed and well-balanced collection. The Human Library should include a variety of topics from which readers can choose. The "Pillars of Prejudice" (see figure 20.1), which include Religion, Ideology, Ethnicity, Health, Addiction, Victim, Social Status, Disabilities, Gender/Sexuality,

Occupation, Lifestyle, and Family Relations serve as a guide.[18] Human Libraries should strive to have a balanced collection that includes six or seven Pillars of Prejudice when possible.

Figure 20.1
"Human Library, Unjudge someone, Pillars of Prejudice." Southern Connecticut State University, Buley Library's Research Guide Human Library: Themes and Topics, accessed August 22, 2021 https://libguides.southernct.edu/c.php?g=960661&p=6936953.

After deciding which prejudices to address, it's time to recruit human book volunteers. Some students, staff, and faculty volunteer to be human books, and many volunteers come from the community at large. Local organizations (Alzheimer's Association, affirmations, Holocaust museum, police, mosque, etc.) are good places to recruit human book volunteers because they reflect your community, but the best way to find volunteers is through word of mouth. Our community college campus Diversity, Equity, Inclusion, and Justice Committee members often know people who would be a good human book. Additionally, after each Human Library event, several readers are so impressed by their experience that they volunteer to participate to share their stories in future events as a human book.

Recruiting and vetting human books is the most time-consuming and challenging part of the process but also a lot of fun. It's the opportunity to meet new people and hear their stories. We send potential human books an e-mail of introduction including an application.[19] After receiving their application, we chat with them two or three times to go over expectations in more detail and allow them time to practice telling their story and answer questions by simulating a real Human Library event.

Because these individuals are asked to share personal, often difficult, stories with strangers to help break down social barriers, it's important to make sure they are prepared and feel confident in their role as a human book. Human books must be open, comfortable in their own skin, and willing to share their personal stories without having an agenda or wanting to proselytize; promoting a specific philosophy or group is not allowed. To achieve this goal, each human book must be carefully vetted. After this process, they may decide to not participate, or the facilitator may decide they are not a good fit. Being a human book isn't for everyone.

It's important to constantly build, grow, and improve your human book collection. The needs of the community served will change over time, and the collection of titles should change accordingly. As a human book collection is comprised of volunteers, the collection will decrease for a multitude of reasons, so it's best to have a surplus of human books in your collection.

After every Human Library event, the readers and the human books complete separate evaluation forms. We make improvements based on those evaluation forms. The reader evaluation form also encourages those interested in being a human book to complete an application form.

Encouraging Participation

We strive to have the right balance of human books and readers so no human book is left on the shelf waiting for a reader. We work with classroom faculty to encourage interest. When classroom faculty recognize the power and impact of the event and see how it supports their course content, they often bring their entire class during their class time or offer extra credit. Communication, English, ethics, psychology, and speech faculty often bring their class (or offer extra credit) as they recognize the connection between their course curriculum and the event focus. Nursing, dental hygiene, and early childhood development faculty teach empathy and work with diverse populations, so they too offer extra credit or bring their class to these events. We schedule event dates and times accordingly.

As a small thank-you gift for their time and generosity in sharing their personal stories, we purchase and give each human book a Human Library T-shirt. The T-shirts attracted the attention of the readers, who wanted to buy them, so instead we allowed students the opportunity to earn a T-shirt by checking out four human books at a Human Library. This proved hugely successful! Students would enthusiastically check out four human books, then proudly wear their Human Library T-shirts following the event. The T-shirts served to encourage potentially hesitant readers to check out multiple human books as well as advertising for future Human Library events.

Events have grown in popularity and size because these inclusive events are an exciting and creative way to encourage honest dialogue. Some of our events attracted over 200 readers, which caused long lines and wait times to check out a human book. To mitigate the long wait time and to facilitate a more relaxing and intimate atmosphere, we select a Traditional or Reading Hall Style event according to the number of readers expected at a given event. This is the rare opportunity for readers to ask any questions about which they are curious and is a safe space to learn more about another person and about themselves. Human books are not experts on their topic but are experts on their personal stories, which they generously and bravely share. This honest dialogue allows the reader and human book to get to know one another and break down barriers, which will help end prejudice. The idea is to learn about one another and ask questions to gain a better understanding of the human book. Students are encouraged to attend and to bring their family, friends, and neighbors, which promotes diversity among the readers who check them out.

Safety and Planning

We recognized that the Human Library events have the potential to be perceived as controversial, and therefore we make every effort to secure the safety of our human books and readers. We actively work to make sure the events are safe whether in person or virtual.

At in-person Human Libraries, we make sure we can physically see all the human books during the entire event for their safety and to make sure they get a drink, a break, or to answer a question if necessary. Each human book sits at a table a few feet from one another, adding to the sense of community as well as safety.

At virtual Human Libraries, we use the Reading Hall Style event, during which readers are divided into small groups (four to seven readers per group). These online events were refined during the restrictions of the current COVID-19 pandemic. Each breakout room includes a human book, a moderator, and a small group of readers. The moderator serves as a layer of security at these online events as they may redirect or even remove patrons or chat if needed.

It takes time to organize the Human Library but very little money. A successful Human Library will necessitate buy-in from college administration, faculty, staff, and students. Planning should start four to six months before the first event. It's time-consuming but fun to organize! Future events will take less time to prepare.

Conclusion

There is a real need for connection and inclusion today. The Human Library recognizes that need and that we all have biases, both conscious and unconscious. Readers have the opportunity to grow and "unjudge" individuals they may not agree with or someone they may even fear in a safe, nonthreatening, nonpolitical environment with no agendas. Both parties, human books and readers, learn they have more in common than they may have otherwise realized. Our experience matched Ronni Abergel's belief that Human Library events "make space at the table for everyone"[20] and promote genuine dialogue between people who may not otherwise meet. Individuals who have been discriminated against or stereotyped share their truth as a human book, which enables readers the opportunity to confront their personal biases and prejudices in a safe space where they learn about another human being and themselves. We found that "Open and honest conversations …lead to greater acceptance, tolerance and social cohesion in the community. Real people in real conversations within a framework setup to help facilitate and accommodate the process."[21]

The Human Library is an amazing experience to facilitate or attend. Most everyone involved, as a reader, human book, or facilitator, gains a better understanding of another individual and themselves. That understanding leads to a more inclusive outlook and ultimately a more inclusive society. I've observed readers attend, confront their personal prejudice, and leave changed for the better. I personally learn and grow with each Human Library I facilitate, as I'm confronted by prejudices I didn't even know I had. I know I'm a better person for my involvement with the Human Library and believe you will be too.

Notes

1.   Human Library home page, accessed May 1, 2021, https://humanlibrary.org.

2.   Human Library, "Organizers," accessed August 15, 2021, https://humanlibrary.org/human-library-organizers/.

3.   Human Library, "Organizers."

4.   Ronni Abergel et al., *Don't Judge a Book by its Cover!* (Budapest, Hungary: Council of Europe, Directorate of Youth and Sport, 2005), 13, https://amics.eu/allin/wp-content/uploads/2018/07/Living-Library-book.pdf.

5.   Ronni Abergel, quoted in Robert Bright. "Why I Formed a Library Where Humans Replaced Books," HuffPost, last updated October 3, 2017, https://www.huffingtonpost.co.uk/entry/why-i-formed-a-library-where-humans-replaced-books_uk_5935500be4b02478cb9d19c4.

6.   Human Library, "The Early Years," accessed August 11, 2021, https://humanlibrary.org/about/the-early-years/.

7.   Human Library, "Early Years."

8.   Gregory John Watson, "'You Shouldn't Have to Suffer for Being Who You Are': An Examination of the Human Library Strategy for Challenging Prejudice and Increasing Respect for Difference" (PhD diss., Curtin University, 2015), 48, https://espace.curtin.edu.au/bitstream/handle/20.500.11937/1344/234254_Watson%202015.pdf?sequence=2.

9.   Rob Garbutt, "The Living Library: Some Theoretical Approaches to a Strategy for Activating Human Rights and Peace," in *Activating Human Rights and Peace: Universal Responsibility Conference 2008 Conference Proceedings*, ed. Rob Garbutt (Lismore NSW Australia: Southern Cross University Centre for Peace and Social Justice, 2008), 274, https://researchportal.scu.edu.au/discovery/delivery/61SCU_INST:ResearchRepository/1267029310002368?l#1367452730002368.

10.   Human Library, "About the Human Library," accessed July 23, 2021, https://humanlibrary.org/about/.

11.   Abergel et al., *Don't Judge a Book*, 15.

12.   Abergel et al., *Don't Judge a Book*, 15.

13.   Human Library home page.

14.   Chimamanda Ngozi Adichie, "The Danger of a Single Story," recorded July 2009 at TEDGlobal 2009, TED video, 18:22, https://www.ted.com/talks/chimamanda_ngozi_adichie_the_danger_of_a_single_story?language=en.

15.   Human Library, "The Human Library Book FAQ," accessed August 22, 2021, https://humanlibrary.org/meet-our-human-books/the-human-library-book-faq/.

16.   Abergel et al., *Don't Judge a Book*, 31.

17.   Abergel et al., *Don't Judge a Book,* 32.

18.   Southern Connecticut State University, Buley Library, "Human Library," research guide accessed August 22, 2021, https://libguides.southernct.edu/c.php?g=960661&p=6936953.

19.   Human Library, "Get Published," accessed August 22, 2021, https://humanlibrary.org/meet-our-human-books/get-published/.

20.   Bright. "Why I Formed a Library."

21.   Human Library home page.

Bibliography

Abergel, Ronni, Antje Rothemund, Gavan Titley, and Peter Wootsch. *Don't Judge a Book by Its Cover! The Living Library Organiser's Guide.* Budapest, Hungary: Council of Europe, Directorate of Youth and Sport, 2005. https://amics.eu/allin/wp-content/uploads/2018/07/Living-Library-book.pdf.

Adichie, Chimamanda Ngozi. "The Danger of a Single Story." Recorded July 2009 at TEDGlobal 2009. TED video, 18:22. https://www.ted.com/talks/chimamanda_ngozi_adichie_the_danger_of_a_single_story?language=en.

Bright, Robert. "Why I Formed a Library Where Humans Replaced Books." Huff-
Post, last updated October 3, 2017. https://www.huffingtonpost.co.uk/entry/
why-i-formed-a-library-where-humans-replaced-books_uk_5935500be4b02478cb9d19c4.

Garbutt, Rob. "The Living Library: Some Theoretical Approaches to a Strategy for Activating Human
Rights and Peace." In *Activating Human Rights and Peace: Universal Responsibility Conference 2008
Conference Proceedings*, edited by Rob Garbutt, 270–78. Lismore NSW Australia: Southern Cross
University Centre for Peace and Social Justice, 2008. CiteSeerX.

Human Library. "About the Human Library." Accessed July 23, 2021. https://humanlibrary.org/about/.

———. "The Early Years." Accessed August 11, 2021. https://humanlibrary.org/about/
the-early-years/.

———. "Get Published." Accessed August 22, 2021. https://humanlibrary.org/
meet-our-human-books/get-published/.

———. "The Human Library Book FAQ." Accessed Aug, 22, 2021. https://humanlibrary.org/
meet-our-human-books/the-human-library-book-faq/.

———. "Organizers." Accessed August 15, 2021. https://humanlibrary.org/human-library-organizers/.

Human Library home page. Accessed May 1, 2021. https://humanlibrary.org.

Southern Connecticut State University, Buley Library. "Human Library." Research guide. Accessed
August 22, 2021. https://libguides.southernct.edu/c.php?g=960661&p=6936953

Watson, Gregory John, "'You Shouldn't Have to Suffer for Being Who You Are': An Examination of the Human Library Strategy for Challenging Prejudice and Increasing Respect for
Difference." PhD diss., Curtin University, 2015. https://espace.curtin.edu.au/bitstream/
handle/20.500.11937/1344/234254_Watson%202015.pdf?sequence=2.

CHAPTER 21

Flexible Pedagogies for Inclusive Learning

Balancing Pliancy and Structure and Cultivating Cultures of Care

*Andrea Baer**

When we think about or enact equitable and inclusive pedagogies, we are in many ways engaging in a practice of flexibility. We consider students' varying needs, interests, and passions, as well as the differing ways that they learn individually and collectively. This can then inform how we design and facilitate learning experiences, as we structure learning experiences that provide a helpful degree of focus and guidance and that at the same time are flexible enough to allow room for student choice and agency.

This is essentially what *flexible pedagogies* are: "giv[ing] students choices about when, where, and how they learn" in order to foster student agency and engaged learning.[1] Research on self-regulated learning and intrinsic motivation suggests that being able to exercise such choice fosters a sense of agency and purpose.[2] In this essay, I reflect on flexibility as a concept and as a practice that has informed my teaching, in particular since adapting to online library instruction in March 2020 due to the COVID-19 pandemic, and how flexible pedagogy principles and

---

* Andrea Baer is a white, US-born, cis, able-bodied woman. At the time of this writing, she is a mid-career academic librarian in a tenure-track position. Her career has focused primarily on teaching and learning in higher education.

practices can be catalysts for reflective and inclusive teaching and a culture of care in all teaching contexts.

Flexible pedagogy, like the very concept of flexibility, is not rigidly defined. As David Harris points out, the term *flexible learning* (closely tied to *flexible pedagogy*) has been "itself used pretty flexibly." It "does not seem to refer precisely to any particular kind of educational system but acquires its meaning only from its location in particular discourses" that often describe existing educational systems as lacking flexibility.[3] While Harris understandably expresses skepticism about much of the discourse surrounding *flexible learning* (which at times seems more oriented to business models of education that prioritize discrete workplace skills over the broader skills of critical thinking), the basic principle of flexibility in teaching and learning remains powerful. In this essay, I focus less on the wide-ranging uses of the term *flexible learning* and instead concentrate on how the concept of flexibility can enrich teaching and learning, when used with the goal of fostering inclusive learning environments in which students exercise choice and grow a deeper sense of agency in their learning process.

My discussion of flexible pedagogies (and relatedly flexible learning) in this essay might also be considered flexible. I use the term *flexible pedagogy* not to describe a fixed set of teaching practices, but rather to consider more broadly ways that we might design learning experiences and cultivate learning environments with the intention for all students to experience greater choice and agency in their learning process. Flexible teaching and learning can be processes through which both educators and students gently bend and stretch beyond familiar habits that often unnecessarily limit student choice and agency. This process can cultivate holistic learning, a recognition of students' full lives and communities, and a culture of care.

The flexibility that I describe is not about librarians and educators breaking ourselves or giving up all agency in teaching. To the contrary, it is about cultivating connective and inclusive learning environments and experiences that are vital to both agentic learning *and* agentic teaching, as we balance the degrees of structure and choice that are part of those environments and experiences.

Flexible Pedagogies as Inclusive Practices

Often we apply principles of flexible pedagogy and flexible learning intuitively. This happens any time we present students with choices about how they will learn or how they will engage in a task or project. But intentional reflection on how we integrate opportunities for student choice, and how we design learning experiences and environments accordingly, can help us further expand how we encourage agency and motivation among students who have a wide variety of interests, backgrounds, experiences, personalities, preferences, and passions. Creating room for student choice affirms a valuing of difference in people's learning processes and experiences and may help students grow a sense of agency and purpose. Flexible pedagogy can be enacted in a number of ways, including through pacing and timing, instructional content, instructional approach or design, and delivery methods or spaces.[4]

In considering flexible learning in connection to inclusive pedagogies, I find Ryan and Tilbury's discussion of flexible pedagogies to be particularly useful.[5] In their report on flexible pedagogies for the Higher Education Academy (HEA) in the UK, Ryan and Tilbury describe flexible pedagogies in relation to "new pedagogical ideas" that help both learners and educators strengthen their capacity "to develop flexibility as an attribute or capacity" as they "think, act, live and work differently in complex, uncertain and changeable scenarios."[6] Ryan and Tilbury present these concepts as a response to questions about higher education at a time of rapid and increasing technological change, globalization, and changing employer expectations.[7]

Recognizing that efforts to grow the flexibility of higher education can have both beneficial and deleterious effects, Ryan and Tilbury challenge an uncritical celebration or acceptance of technology and of "work-readiness" training that often overlooks social inequities and systems of power and privilege and instead are interested in the potential through flexible pedagogies for "democratic and emancipatory approaches to teaching and learning."[8]

Though Ryan and Tilbury do not foreground the phrase "inclusive pedagogy" in this report (they do refer twice to "inclusive learning"), their discussion relates directly to inclusive pedagogies. This is evident in the following pedagogical ideas that they outline:

- learner empowerment: "actively involving students in learning development and processes of 'co-creation' that challenge learning relationships and the power frames that underpin them"
- future-facing education: "refocusing learning towards engagement and change processes that help people to consider prospects and hopes for the future across the globe"
- decolonising education: "deconstructing dominant pedagogical frames that promote only Western worldviews"
- transformative capabilities: "creating an educational focus beyond an emphasis solely on knowledge and understanding, towards agency and competence"
- crossing boundaries: "taking an integrative and systemic approach to pedagogy in HE"

- social learning: "developing cultures and environments for learning that harness the emancipatory power of spaces and interactions outside the formal curriculum"[9]

These principles reflect a flexibility in thinking that involves looking both inward and outward—considering individual experiences, relational and collective experiences, and systems and structures. This flexibility occurs largely through continually examining experiences and situations from different angles (e.g., challenging traditional power relations and Western-centric pedagogies, valuing not only knowledge but also agency) and through enabling a range of individual and relational experiences (e.g., co-creation, social learning and engagement beyond formal curricula). Similar language might be used to describe equitable and inclusive pedagogies, even though Ryan and Tilbury don't explicitly refer to inclusive pedagogies.

Considerations for Putting Flexible Pedagogies into Action

These ideals of flexible pedagogies may sound lofty to some readers, particularly as librarians look at the realities and confines of our everyday work (e.g., the prevalence of one-shot sessions that are usually structured around completing an assignment that a librarian did not design, the difficulty of building a rapport with students within the confines of a stand-alone workshop). At the same time that the limitations of our day-to-day teaching contexts are real, the creative approaches that librarians repeatedly bring to their work within and beyond classroom settings demonstrate the potential power of intentional flexibility as a pedagogical practice.

Because of the many shapes and forms that flexible learning can take, it can be hard to know where to start in integrating it more intentionally into one's teaching.[10] I think it's helpful to remember that there are multitudes of ways to encourage student choice and that each approach will depend on one's teaching context at a particular moment in time. For those interested in expanding their engagement with flexible pedagogy principles, Per Bernard Bergamin and colleagues recommend beginning by asking several key questions: In what ways are students engaged as active and constructive learners who exercise some control over their learning? and How are learning materials designed to respond to learners' varying needs?[11] I would add to these questions a consideration of how activities can be constructed as welcoming invitations for participation and as expressions of valuing students' unique and varying perspectives and contributions.

While flexible pedagogies may at first glance seem too involved for short periods of instruction like library one-shot sessions, often a small tweak to a class session or an activity can open considerably more room for student choice and agency. For example, in a one-shot instruction session, perhaps students have the choice to work individually or in small groups when looking for relevant sources. Or students might be given the option either to explore a topic of their own choosing or to select from one or two sample topics. During an in-class discussion, students might have the option to reflect and express their individual and collective ideas in various ways (for example, through individual reflective writing, creating a visual, contributing to a collaborative Google Doc, or speaking in small groups or in the larger class). In a hands-on research workshop, students could choose to focus on different aspects or stages of the research process depending on their particular process and needs. (Practices like these align with Ryan and Tilbury's emphasis on flexible pedagogy principles like co-creation and the valuing of all participants' voices and contributions.) Credit courses open a still wider range of possibilities for flexible pedagogies, including choosing among assignment options that target the same learning outcomes or having the option to engage in additional learning activities through which students can engage more deeply with a course-related issue or project or an assignment.

Of course, too much choice or flexibility can also be overwhelming and can contribute to an experience of cognitive overload, in which a person is presented with more information than they can process in a given moment. According to John Sweller's theory of cognitive load theory, individuals can process only a certain amount of information in a given moment, and instructional design can be used to make cognitive load more manageable.[12] Experiences of cognitive overload tend to feel paralyzing, rather than being empowering and motivating. Cognitive load differs among individuals. Relatedly, some learners may prefer a higher degree of structure, which limits the number of choices they need to consider, while others benefit from more flexibility. For example, when students are asked to reflect or to articulate their thoughts, some students may immediately have much to say without being given any specific prompt, while others might be unsure how to respond without being given any more specific prompts or examples.

As this suggests, flexible pedagogy involves balancing pliancy and structure: just as things that are too rigid are likely to break, those that are too bendable may not be able to hold a form. In a class with too many rules, people may feel boxed into formulas that lack meaning or purpose. On the other hand, in a classroom that has no structure, people are likely to feel adrift, and a classroom in which the teacher bends so much that they strain their bodies ultimately becomes counterproductive. Flexible pedagogies can present a healthy and bendable amount of structure—for example, giving students the option to respond to specific questions about the issue at hand or to generate and answer their own questions.

Bringing Flexible Pedagogy Principles to Online Teaching during the Pandemic

I am writing this essay in spring 2021, after a little over a year of social distancing, remote work, and a good amount of isolation due to the COVID-19 pandemic. Flexible thinking and flexible structure have been key to the synchronous online class sessions and workshops that I've facilitated during this time, probably more so than when I taught almost exclusively in person. I've been pleasantly surprised that the move to online teaching has helped me create more opportunities for all students to engage in idea sharing and conversation than had previously been the case in my in-person classes.

Reflecting on my recent experiences with online library instruction and my intention to cultivate flexible and inclusive learning environments, I see Ryan and Tilbury's description of flexible pedagogy principles mirrored back in several ways in terms of both content and approach. Though I focus in this essay primarily on pedagogical approach (and less on learning content), it's worth noting that flexible pedagogy principles are relevant to both. In terms of content, the many social, cultural, structural, and ethical dimensions of information literacy are certainly relevant to Ryan and Tilbury's description of a "future-facing education," through which people "consider prospects and hopes for the future across the globe and …anticipate, rethink and work towards alternative and preferred future scenarios."[13] Issues and skills about which I and other librarians teach—evaluating online information, valuing and acknowledging different types of expertise and knowledge, algorithmic bias, digital privacy and digital wellness—have real and everyday significance to students and to societies more broadly. Engaging with such issues is about more than merely acquiring new knowledge; it also points to, in Ryan and Tilbury's words, "transformative capabilities" that involve students' expanding their experiences of agency and competence.[14] The pandemic has drawn this into sharp relief, as trustworthy information sources and supportive online communities and platforms have had real impacts on virtually all aspects of human and global health and well-being.

Whether diving into the complexities of online information environments and systems or focusing on the practicalities of a source-based research project, I have found with a shift to online instruction that flexible pedagogy principles can be integrated into my teaching about almost any learning content. Like many fellow librarians and educators, I have done this partly through collaborative digital tools, which can encourage a more inclusive and participatory learning environment that involves co-creation and social learning, as well as time for individual and shared reflection.

One practice that I've adopted that has been particularly valuable for cultivating more flexible and inclusive learning environments has been the use of collaborative writing tools like Google Docs, Padlet, and Google Jamboard. Since the move many of us made to online instruction in spring 2020, many readers have likely become familiar with incorporating these tools into their teaching. Collaborative writing tools are an example of how simple teaching practices can help to open up choices and avenues for class engagement, participation, and even community building.

Here is what that has often looked like for me in practice. The majority of online library classes and workshops that I've taught over this past year have been synchronous meetings that primarily involve an online meeting platform like Zoom and use of a collaborative Google Doc. I give all attendees Google Doc editing privileges and retain a master template to which only I have access so that I can easily recover portions of the original document if needed (for example, on the rare occasion that someone inadvertently removes content from the collaborative document). Students and workshop participants frequently comment that they enjoy the engagement and interaction that the Google Doc enables and find it highly effective.

The Google Doc includes essential information, links to multimedia like short videos, and collaborative activities and discussion prompts. It also includes "grounding principles" that describe how we will strive to engage with one another, with an appreciation of what we each bring to the class and with an appreciation of difference. Presenting these grounding principles at the start of a class conveys the collaborative and communal spirit of the session and encourages a sense of community and mutual support in which individuals value what both they and others bring to the learning process. In a credit course in which there is more time, I would take the time for the class to build on and revise these guidelines in order to feel more ownership of them.

As we move through the class session, important concepts and information about which I speak are represented in the text and resources included in the Google Doc. The document also includes links to multimedia content like videos. Such content is accompanied by collaborative activities and discussions. For example, in a workshop on algorithmic bias, I begin with a quick poll within the Google Doc on the degree to which Google is neutral (with 1 being completely unneutral and 5 being completely neutral), followed by the open-ended prompt "After rating Google's neutrality in the online poll, please share the reasoning behind your ranking of Google's neutrality." We take a few minutes for everyone to add thoughts to the Google Doc so that each person has time to reflect while also seeing what others are saying. Sometimes people respond to one another's thoughts within the Google Doc (for example, using "+1" to indicate agreement or referencing and making a connection to someone else's idea). This provides another means for engagement. It may be particularly appreciated by students who are otherwise reluctant to share their thoughts aloud and by those who benefit from more reflection time before articulating their ideas. In short, there is more time and space for everyone to contribute to the conversation and for everyone to see, reflect, and perhaps build on what others are saying.

When the writing has slowed down or the allotted time has passed, I invite participants to speak about things that they have shared or noticed in the Google Doc. Sometimes this generates richer conversation; at other times the group may be fairly quiet. In either case, I skim the document for points that may be worth further emphasizing or expanding on. I use a similar approach when introducing new content like a short video: before showing the video, I often present questions to consider about the video content, usually including at least one very open-ended question that invites students to share any thoughts, questions, or impressions related to the video that aren't explicitly addressed in the other question prompts. Participants can then respond to those questions while and after watching the video. This again creates an opportunity for reflection and sharing, as well as an opening for further discussion. Such questions provide a flexible structure that leaves room for choice (e.g., answering those questions that interest them most, having the opportunity to see what others have written, introducing new ideas or questions that aren't already represented in the question prompts).

The interactive components of the document also present opportunities during and after the session for formative assessment (through which the teacher/facilitator checks student understandings and can revise their pedagogical approach in order to respond to participants' interests and needs). During the session, I can immediately see evidence of many participants' thinking and areas of interest; after the session, I can return to the document to analyze and to reflect more deeply on participants' thoughts and processes. An additional benefit of this approach is that the resources and ideas shared during the session continue to be available to the class after the class. The Google Doc serves as a record for both participants and teachers; it offers a way to continue engaging with learning content at a later time.

The affordances of online learning that are reflected in this approach, of course, don't erase the fact that many inequities persist (e.g., the availability and speed of internet connections, the digital devices and physical spaces through which students obtain online access, the time and resources available to students to engage in learning on- and offline). Online learning no doubt can exacerbate educational inequities, as the pandemic has brought into sharp relief. But many aspects of online learning can also work to foster a more inclusive and flexible learning environment in which students have meaningful choices about ways to engage and participate. Collaborative digital writing tools like Google Docs, Padlet, and Jamboard are just a few examples of technologies that help to flexibly structure learning environments and experiences that foster inclusion and social learning, alongside student choice and agency.

When these technologies are available to all students, they may help to increase inclusion in the physical classroom as well. When I return to the physical classroom in the coming months, I will continue to offer students a wider range of choices and possibilities for both individual and collaborative work. In both in-person workshops and one-shot sessions, I'll continue to use collaborative tools like Google Docs as a means for students to reflect on and share about their process. Similar to my approach in online sessions, I'll create time and space in which we can view what others have shared and speak aloud or in large and small groups about our observations and experiences and how they relate to those of others. While presenting different participant options, I'll also remain cognizant that using too many tools or having too many choices can be distracting or overwhelming. With this in mind, I'll aim to choose tools based on goals, intentions, and an appreciation of where I am asking students to focus their attention.

In short, as I integrate in-person and digital means of communication and interaction, I will continue to learn and to practice ways to balance structure and flexibility. For me this largely involves providing a helpful degree of guidance alongside manageable and meaningful options for individual and collective student expression and engagement, as well as an appreciation of the ways that students contribute to and shape both their own learning and the class's collective process.

A Final Reflection

The importance of balancing structure and flexibility in both teaching and in everyday life has become especially apparent to me in this past year. A healthy amount of flexible structure has helped me to get up in the morning and often to regain some sense of purpose on days when I felt that I and many others around me were losing that.

Amid so much loss across the globe and in our everyday lives, it can feel trivial to write practical teaching recommendations. At the same time, I find hope in the thought that sometimes even one small action or interaction has positive ripple effects, even if those ripples aren't immediately visible or felt. Those ripples can come from fostering more inclusive learning environments, which are often also more flexible environments: in them we interact with and respond to others in the moment, hopefully seeing, hearing, and appreciating one another as human beings with unique experiences, thoughts, and voices, and at the same time with a shared humanity.

Notes

1.   Ryerson Mental Health and Wellbeing Committee, "Flexible Learning Resource," Ryerson University, accessed May 21, 2021, 2, https://www.ryerson.ca/content/dam/learning-teaching/teaching-resources/teach-a-course/flexible-learning.pdf.

2. Richard M. Ryan and Edward L. Deci, "Self-Determination Theory and the Facilitation of Intrinsic Motivation, Social Development, and Well-Being," *American Psychologist* 55, no. 1 (2000): 68–78, https://doi.org/10.1037/0003-066X.55.1.68; Jack Martin, "Self-Regulated Learning, Social Cognitive Theory, and Agency," *Educational Psychologist* 39, no. 2 (2004): 135–45, https://doi.org/10.1207/s15326985ep3902_4.
3. David Harris, "The Paradoxes of Flexible Learning," in *Flexible Pedagogy, Flexible Practice: Notes from the Trenches of Distance Education*, ed. Elizabeth Burge, Chère Campbell Gibson, and Terry Gibson, Issues in Distance Education Series (Edmonton, AB: Athabasca University Press, 2012), 275.
4. Stuart R. Palmer, "The Lived Experience of Flexible Education: Theory, Policy and Practice," *Journal of University Teaching and Learning Practice* 8, no. 3 (2011): article 2, https://doi.org/10.53761/1.8.3.2.
5. Alex Ryan and Daniella Tilbury, *Flexible Pedagogies* (York, UK: Higher Education Academy, November 2013), https://www.heacademy.ac.uk/sites/default/files/resources/npi_report.pdf.
6. Ryan and Tilbury, *Flexible Pedagogies*, 4.
7. Ryan and Tilbury, *Flexible Pedagogies*, 4.
8. Ryan and Tilbury, *Flexible Pedagogies*, 4.
9. Ryan and Tilbury, *Flexible Pedagogies*, 5.
10. Andrea Baer, "Gently Stretching to Reach All Students: Inclusive Learning through Scaffolding and Flexible Pedagogy," *College and Research Library News* 82, no. 4 (April 2021), https://crln.acrl.org/index.php/crlnews/article/view/24890/32733.
11. Per Bernard Bergamin et al., "The Relationship between Flexible and Self-Regulated Learning in Open and Distance Universities," *International Review of Research in Open and Distributed Learning* 13, no. 2 (2012): 101–23, https://doi.org/10.19173/irrodl.v13i2.1124.
12. John Sweller, "Cognitive Load during Problem Solving: Effects on Learning," *Cognitive Science* 12, no. 2 (1988): 257–85.
13. Ryan and Tilbury, *Flexible Pedagogies*, 5.
14. Ryan and Tilbury, *Flexible Pedagogies*, 5.

Bibliography

Baer, Andrea. "Gently Stretching to Reach All Students: Inclusive Learning through Scaffolding and Flexible Pedagogy." *College and Research Library News* 82, no. 4 (April 2021). https://crln.acrl.org/index.php/crlnews/article/view/24890/32733.

Bergamin, Per Bernard, Simone Ziska, Egon Werlen, and Eva Siegenthaler. "The Relationship between Flexible and Self-Regulated Learning in Open and Distance Universities." *International Review of Research in Open and Distributed Learning* 13, no. 2 (2012): 101–23. https://doi.org/10.19173/irrodl.v13i2.1124.

Harris, David. "The Paradoxes of Flexible Learning." In *Flexible Pedagogy, Flexible Practice: Notes from the Trenches of Distance Education*, edited by Elizabeth Burge, Chère Campbell Gibson, and Terry Gibson, 275–84. Issues in Distance Education. Edmonton, AB: Athabasca University Press, 2012.

Martin, Jack. "Self-Regulated Learning, Social Cognitive Theory, and Agency." *Educational Psychologist* 39, no. 2 (2004): 135–45. https://doi.org/10.1207/s15326985ep3902_4.

Palmer, Stuart R. "The Lived Experience of Flexible Education: Theory, Policy and Practice." *Journal of University Teaching and Learning Practice* 8, no. 3 (2011): article 2. https://doi.org/10.53761/1.8.3.2.

Ryan, Alex, and Daniella Tilbury. *Flexible Pedagogies: New Pedagogical Ideas*. York, UK: Higher Education Academy, November 2013. https://www.heacademy.ac.uk/sites/default/files/resources/npi_report.pdf.

Ryan, Richard M., and Edward L. Deci. "Self-Determination Theory and the Facilitation of Intrinsic Motivation, Social Development, and Well-Being." *American Psychologist* 55, no. 1 (2000): 68–78. https://doi.org/10.1037/0003-066X.55.1.68.

Ryerson Mental Health and Wellbeing Committee. "Flexible Learning Resource." Ryerson University. Accessed May 21, 2020. https://www.ryerson.ca/content/dam/learning-teaching/teaching-resources/teach-a-course/flexible-learning.pdf.

Sweller, John. "Cognitive Load during Problem Solving: Effects on Learning." *Cognitive Science* 12, no. 2 (1988): 257–85.

CHAPTER 22

Cultivating Connection

Attending to Student Affect through a Pedagogy of Care[*]

Liz Chenevey

"How do you feel when asked to do research?"

The question sat at the top of the screen displayed to the computer lab classroom. This was the first time I was attempting to have this discussion with students to talk about emotions, research, and support.

The students, faces mostly hidden behind large monitors, were anonymous to me. Their responses, also anonymous, started to populate the page so everyone could see, and I began to read them aloud. *Stressed. Overwhelmed. Ugh.* Most of the responses were ones I had seen before and were expected. But one came through that caught my off guard: *like killing myself.*

My breath caught and I stumbled over my words for a moment. These students were strangers to me, and I a stranger to them. It was just me and them, as their professor had introduced me and then left the class in my hands, as we had always done in sessions prior.

I finally found a simple response. "I'm hoping this is an exaggerated statement, but if not, I want to encourage whoever feels this way to please see the Counseling Center for support." And we moved on, talking about how research is stressful and difficult and highlighting strategies, tools, and services to help. But I was shaken and in my post-class reflection commented on not feeling prepared for this kind of response and needing to have a better method for addressing this should it come up again.

---

[*] Content warning: suicidal language.

I continue to ask this question, or a variation of it, in most of my instruction sessions in an effort to talk about the affective side of research and have not yet had another response as concerning as that one. But it was a wake-up call to me that if I was going to attempt to attend to the affective needs of students I do not know, that my pedagogy needed to adapt.

Campus Mental Health: An Introduction

The increase in mental health concerns among college students has been well documented.[1] According to the 2018 Healthy Minds Study, about one-third of students struggle with issues of anxiety, depression, self-harm, and other mental health conditions.[2] Students seeking help on campus almost doubled over a ten-year period,[3] which has burdened understaffed and underresourced counseling centers.[4] To compensate for this increase in need, some have begun to advocate for faculty and staff training in mental health literacy and how to support students and connect them with mental health support services.

A 2021 Boston University report found that a majority of faculty have observed the increasing needs of their students and want more training and development in how to assist them; about 60 percent feel training should be mandatory upon hire.[5] However, this perspective is controversial, as many faculty and staff also struggle with their own mental health, which is exacerbated by precarity, family responsibilities, and even supporting their students' wellness.[6] When Inside Higher Ed published an article on this report, the critical response on academic Twitter was swift. The common thread of critique among those who replied or retweeted was for institutions to hire more mental health professionals and to stop asking faculty to continually do more.[7]

As someone who has struggled with my own mental health, I completely empathize with these critics. We are too often asked to do more, give more, care more, without any forms of tangible returns. Further, issues of mental health are not trivial. They require paid and trained professionals who understand the intricacies of harm mitigation strategies to ensure that students—as well as faculty and staff—are receiving the best support possible to keep them safe and well. But I was struck by a quote from the report's lead author Sara Ketchen Lipson:

> There's a lot of really low-hanging fruit that we can be thinking about in terms of how we can be flexible with students, how we can convey to them that we want them to succeed, and bring in this empathy and humanity to our instruction. It's not written into the job description, but it really is fundamental to teaching young people.[8]

Having an understanding of the mental health concerns facing our students is imperative to providing inclusive and equitable instruction. Mental health is an intersectional issue that connects to race, gender, and class. There is a higher prevalence of mental health problems in women, students who experience discrimination, and students of lower socioeconomic status.[9] Students of color are less likely to be diagnosed with mental health problems and seek help, despite experiencing similar rates of mental health concerns as white students.[10] This means we have students in our classrooms who are struggling, who may not be able to name *why* they are struggling, and who are not receiving support.

We know that students' academic performance is likely to be impacted by mental health concerns and that academics can in turn impact students' mental health.[11] If we have potentially large numbers of students not seeking help, we won't receive accommodations requests for those students to ensure our classrooms are equitable. Therefore, our teaching practices may at best be not effective and at worst be actively harmful to some students. But there are pedagogical changes we can make as a part of a critical and reflective practice that can care for not only students who are struggling, but also all students.

Connecting Mental Health to the Information Literacy Classroom: A Process of Care

As a feminist instructor who prioritizes a reflective and care-based approach to my teaching, I have been long interested in how to build meaningful relationships and attend to students' emotional needs in the classroom in an effort to transform the learning environment. With the rising concerns around mental health on campus, this interest has become more acute.

In my exploration of the intersections of mental health and teaching and learning practices, much of what I have found is geared toward more traditional teaching faculty. Suggestions of syllabus statements, flexible assignments and deadlines, and incorporating mindfulness practice throughout the semester abound. But because I am a librarian who teaches largely one-shot sessions, many of these practices are not available to me. I have started to adapt some of these suggestions and look to the fields of librarianship, critical pedagogies, and affective science to find my own path forward in recognizing students' mental health in my classroom.

The majority of these practices are rooted in questions of connection. How do students connect with the learning environment, with me, with each other, with themselves? How does this connection influence students' learning, particularly in the affective domain, which is notoriously harder to measure?

What I aim to do with this piece is to connect with you, the reader, in reflecting on these practices I have been cultivating over the last few years and how I hope to carry them forward in a process of continual adaptation. They may not work in every situation or for every librarian, but I hope they can serve as a starting point for others who are interested in the emotional needs of our students to find ways to bring this care into their classrooms.

Connect with Services

An incredibly simple change to my instruction following the previous story is including referral information to various services on campus, including mental health support. White and LaBelle cite the *referral source* as one of four communicative roles faculty can play in supporting student mental health.[12] These referral sources can demonstrate care for their students by broaching the topic of mental health, while still maintaining personal and professional boundaries. As a librarian, I am already often acting as a point of connection for students, and even faculty, who aren't sure what office or department will best help them with their need. This is a natural point of engagement for me, as someone with institutional knowledge, to briefly share an array of support services both in and out of the library. It is an accessible, easily incorporated extra minute or two of my lesson that can set a supportive tone and reinforce other support messages they may see in their syllabus or other campus messaging.

Connect with Librarian

In my first year as a liaison librarian, I was teaching a session with a very enthusiastic professor. We had discussed goals in advance, and I had planned a lesson to tie in with a semester-long literature review assignment. As I began the session, the professor kept interrupting me, asking questions about myself, my background, and my interests. As a new librarian whose academic background is not in the discipline with which I liaise, I felt nervous and anxious, like an imposter. I quickly shared a bit about me, rushing past this while also trying to retain my authority.

As I continue to grow as an instructor, however, I have realized that this kind of honest and somewhat vulnerable introduction is an important part of connecting with the students. Cavanagh highlights the importance of first impressions on creating lasting impressions in the classroom.[13] Because the majority of my instruction is in one-shot format, I often have only one chance to make a connection with these students, so cultivating an authentic first impression is important. The main goal of these sessions for many professors—and really, I have come to realize for myself—is that students know me, remember me, and feel comfortable with me to reduce barriers to help-seeking. I also now use this opportunity to talk about expertise and how it can fluctuate based on scenario; for example, in a reference consultation, the student is the expert in their discipline while I am the expert in search strategies. This is a way for me to share power in the space, model vulnerability, and allow the students to see me as a whole person to whom they can reach out.

Connect with Process

A main benefit I have found in being a librarian who largely teaches one-shots is that I do little to no grading. Not only is this helpful to my own stress levels and mental health, but it allows me to create a space for students where they can try and fail, and reflect on that process, with low stakes. Because academics can have an effect on students' mental health, creating learning environments in which they can learn how to fail and come back from that can have a beneficial impact.[14] I often find myself reminding students, in both instruction and reference consultations, that I have no control over their grade. This is a space where they can ask "dumb questions," learn from their mistakes, and not feel that those "failures" will be held against them in the form of a grade.

Typically, I have students explore databases without demonstrating first. I want them to see what they know on their own, share what they did, and reflect on the search process in an effort to encourage longer term recall. Trying something and "failing" elicits an emotional response, just as trying and succeeding does. Cavanagh writes, "One of the best predictors of whether an event or information will be remembered is how emotional it is."[15] If we can cultivate a space for students to experience various emotions in the classroom, again, where there is little to no perceived risk, students may retain this information for longer, which is what we want.

Moving forward, I want to encourage students to determine learning goals for themselves so that they feel empowered to take control over their own learning and can set the boundaries within which they take these risks.

Connect with Peers

Finding ways for students to connect with one another can also have an encouraging effect on their affect. In the previous story in which I asked students how research makes them feel, I used a Padlet site so that students can anonymously, but synchronously, share their responses. I started using this format instead of print pre-assessments or even think-pair-share activities because I wanted students to connect across the whole class and normalize whatever they are feeling.[16]

Thanks to Kuhlthau, we know that the process of seeking information elicits an affective response,[17] but our students may feel like they are the only ones who feel overwhelmed, frustrated, or anxious. Normalizing and affirming academic challenges and feelings about research—or even the library in general—is an effective way to attend to students' affective needs in the classroom.[18] This connection and normalization process also grabs their attention and can make the content feel more self-relevant, which is a key component to paying attention and learning.[19]

The use of peer-to-peer confirmation has proven effective with "positive relational and emotional outcomes for students."[20] As I continue to evolve these practices, I plan to expand on the affirming of experiences to encourage students to work in small groups or dyads to discuss strategies and reflect on one another's processes together.

Connecting It All Together

Intentionally caring for my students and incorporating that care into how I approach my pedagogy has become a form of self-care that has reinvigorated me as an instructor and an individual. I have been able to transform my teaching and assessment practice into something that reflects my values and acknowledges everyone in the classroom as whole people, with our own values, concerns, and needs. I feel more confident in adapting my practices to set boundaries, be flexible, adapt in the moment, and build authentic connections. I am embracing and attempting to practice what Veronica Arellano Douglas calls "assessment as care," in which students, relationships, intention, and ourselves are valued and a part of the practice.[21]

I have attempted to weave care through my whole process. When I plan lessons, I write outcomes that address not only cognition and behaviors, but emotions as well. While teaching, I rely on formative, observational, and reflective assessment practices to notice and acknowledge what students are feeling, thinking, and taking with them. I continuously reflect on my own presence in the classroom and how I am demonstrating care for them and myself, before, during, and after a session.

In her ACRL 2021 panel presentation, Allison Jennings-Roche summed up my thoughts eerily well:

> Do they [students] feel good, do they feel supported? Do they feel listened to cause then they'll come back, right? And if they don't, then they won't, it doesn't matter how good my information was if I wasn't able to really provide that space socially and emotionally for students.[22]

If a student is struggling with their mental health, they are unlikely to care much about what database is going to be best for their needs. Of course, I want my students to learn something about the information landscape, but ultimately, I want them to feel valued, supported, and empowered to ask for help when they need it.

Notes

1.   Sarah Ketchen Lipson, Emily G. Lattie, and Daniel Eisenberg, "Increased Rates of Mental Health Service Utilization by U.S. College Students: 10-Year Population-Level Trends (2007–2017)," *Psychiatric Services* 70, no. 1 (January 2019): 60–63, https://doi.org/10.1176/appi.ps.201800332; Gary H. Bischof, Alexander J. Hamilton, and Adrian J. Hernandez, "Mental Health Matters: College Student Mental Health in the Twenty-First Century," *Honors in Practice* 16 (January 2020): 228–30; Karishma Collette, Sara Armstrong, and Christine Simonian Bean, *Supporting Students Facing Mental Health Challenges*, CRLT Occasional Paper No. 38 (Ann Arbor: Center for Research on Learning and Teaching, University of Michigan, 2018), https://eric.ed.gov/?id=ED592877.

2.   Daniel Eisenberg et al., "College Student Mental Health: The National Landscape," in *Promoting Behavioral Health and Reducing Risk among College Students: A Comprehensive Approach*, ed. M. Dolores Cimini and Estela M. Rivero (New York: Routledge, 2018), https://doi.org/10.4324/9781315175799.

3.   Lipson, Lattie, and Eisenberg, "Increased Rates."

4.   Peter LeViness et al., *The Association for University and College Counseling Center Directors Annual Survey: 2019* (Indianapolis, IN: Association for University and College Counseling Center Directors, 2019), 56.

5.   Boston University School of Public Health, Mary Christie Foundation, and Healthy Minds Network, *The Role of Faculty in Student Mental Health* (Boston: Boston University, 2021), https://marychristieinstitute.org/wp-content/uploads/2021/04/The-Role-of-Faculty-in-Student-Mental-Health.pdf.

6.   Boston University School of Public Health, Mary Christie Foundation, and Healthy Minds Network, *Role of Faculty*.

7.   Inside Higher Ed (@insidehighered), "'Given the importance of faculty and the frequency of faculty-student interactions, Cawley said, mental health literacy training, or gatekeeper training, should…'" Twitter, April 11, 2021, 11:02 p.m., https://twitter.com/insidehighered/status/1380355286788141062.

8.   Inside Higher Ed (@insidehighered), "Given the importance."

9.   Sarah Ketchen Lipson et al., "Mental Health Disparities among College Students of Color," *Journal of Adolescent Health* 63, no. 3 (September 2018): 348–56, https://doi.org/10.1016/j.jadohealth.2018.04.014.

10. Lipson et al., "Mental Health Disparities."

11. Sara LaBelle, "Addressing Student Precarities in Higher Education: Our Responsibility as Teachers and Scholars," *Communication Education* 69, no. 2 (2020): 267–76, https://doi.org/10.1080/03634523.2020.1724311.

12. Allie White and Sara LaBelle, "A Qualitative Investigation of Instructors' Perceived Communicative Roles in Students' Mental Health Management," *Communication Education* 68, no. 2 (2019): 133–55, https://doi.org/10.1080/03634523.2019.1571620.

13. Sarah Rose Cavanagh, *The Spark of Learning*, Teaching and Learning in Higher Education 1 (Morgantown: West Virginia University Press, 2016), 40.

14. Collette, Armstrong, and Bean, *Supporting Students*.

15. Cavanagh, *Spark of Learning*, 40.

16. Liz Chenevey, "An Emergent Pedagogy of Presence and Care: Addressing Affect in Information Literacy Instruction" (presentation, ACRL 2021 virtual conference, April 13–16, 2021).
17. Carol C. Kuhlthau, "Inside the Search Process: Information Seeking from the User's Perspective," *Journal of the American Society for Information Science* 42, no. 5 (1991): 361–71, https://doi.org/10.1002/(SICI)1097-4571(199106)42:5<361::AID-ASI6>3.0.CO;2-%23.
18. Collette, Armstrong, and Bean, *Supporting Students*; Sara LaBelle and Zac D. Johnson, "The Relationship of Student-to-Student Confirmation in the Classroom to College Students' Mental Health and Well-Being," *Communication Quarterly* 69, no. 2 (2021): 133–51, https://doi.org/10.1080/01463373.2021.1887310; Constance A. Mellon, "Library Anxiety: A Grounded Theory and Its Development," *College and Research Libraries* 47, no. 2 (1986): 160–65, https://doi.org/10.5860/crl_47_02_160; Erin McAfee, "Shame: The Emotional Basis of Library Anxiety," *College and Research Libraries* 79, no. 2 (March 2018): 237–56, https://doi.org/10.5860/crl.79.2.237.
19. Cavanagh, *Spark of Learning*.
20. LaBelle and Johnson, "Relationship of Student-to-Student Confirmation," 144.
21. Veronica Arellano Douglas, "Moving from Critical Assessment to Assessment as Care," *Communications in Information Literacy* 14, no. 1 (2020), https://doi.org/10.15760/comminfolit.2020.14.1.4.
22. Bria Sinnot, Allison Jennings-Roche, and Elisabeth White, "Radically Reimagined: Open-Hearted Instruction Strategies for the Library Classroom" (presentation, ACRL 2021 virtual conference, April 13–16, 2021).

Bibliography

Arellano Douglas, Veronica. "Moving from Critical Assessment to Assessment as Care." *Communications in Information Literacy* 14, no. 1 (2020): 46–65. https://doi.org/10.15760/comminfolit.2020.14.1.4.

Bischof, Gary H., Alexander J. Hamilton, and Adrian J. Hernandez. "Mental Health Matters: College Student Mental Health in the Twenty-First Century." *Honors in Practice* 16 (January 2020): 228–30.

Boston University School of Public Health, Mary Christie Foundation, and Healthy Minds Network. *The Role of Faculty in Student Mental Health.* Boston: Boston University, 2021. https://marychristieinstitute.org/wp-content/uploads/2021/04/The-Role-of-Faculty-in-Student-Mental-Health.pdf.

Cavanagh, Sarah Rose. *The Spark of Learning: Energizing the College Classroom with the Science of Emotion.* Teaching and Learning in Higher Education 1. Morgantown: West Virginia University Press, 2016.

Chenevey, Liz. "An Emergent Pedagogy of Presence and Care: Addressing Affect in Information Literacy Instruction." Presentation, ACRL 2021 virtual conference, April 13–16, 2021.

Collette, Karishma, Sara Armstrong, and Christine Simonian Bean. *Supporting Students Facing Mental Health Challenges.* CRLT Occasional Paper No. 38. Ann Arbor: Center for Research on Learning and Teaching (CRLT), University of Michigan, 2018. https://eric.ed.gov/?id=ED592877.

Eisenberg, Daniel, Sarah Ketchen Lipson, Peter Ceglarek, Adam Kern, and Megan Vivian Phillips. "College Student Mental Health: The National Landscape." In *Promoting Behavioral Health and Reducing Risk among College Students: A Comprehensive Approach*, edited by M. Dolores Cimini and Estela M. Rivero, 75-86. New York: Routledge, 2018. https://doi.org/10.4324/9781315175799.

Inside Higher Ed (@insidehighered). "'Given the importance of faculty and the frequency of faculty-student interactions, Cawley said, mental health literacy training, or gatekeeper training, should…" Twitter, April 11, 2021, 11:02 p.m. https://twitter.com/insidehighered/status/1380355286788141062.

Kuhlthau, Carol C. "Inside the Search Process: Information Seeking from the User's Perspective." *Journal of the American Society for Information Science* 42, no. 5 (1991): 361–71. https://doi.org/10.1002/(SICI)1097-4571(199106)42:5<361::AID-ASI6>3.0.CO;2-%23.

LaBelle, Sara. "Addressing Student Precarities in Higher Education: Our Responsibility as Teachers and Scholars." *Communication Education* 69, no. 2 (2020): 267–76. https://doi.org/10.1080/03634523.2020.1724311.

LaBelle, Sara, and Zac D. Johnson. "The Relationship of Student-to-Student Confirmation in the Classroom to College Students' Mental Health and Well-Being." *Communication Quarterly* 69, no. 2 (2021): 133–51. https://doi.org/10.1080/01463373.2021.1887310.

LeViness, Peter, Kim Gorman, Lynn Braun, Linda Koenig, and Carolyn Bershad. *The Association for University and College Counseling Center Directors Annual Survey: 2019.* Indianapolis, IN: Association for University and College Counseling Center Directors, 2019.

Lipson, Sarah Ketchen, Adam Kern, Daniel Eisenberg, and Alfiee M. Breland-Noble. "Mental Health Disparities among College Students of Color." *Journal of Adolescent Health* 63, no. 3 (September 2018): 348–56. https://doi.org/10.1016/j.jadohealth.2018.04.014.

Lipson, Sarah Ketchen, Emily G. Lattie, and Daniel Eisenberg. "Increased Rates of Mental Health Service Utilization by U.S. College Students: 10-Year Population-Level Trends (2007–2017)." *Psychiatric Services* 70, no. 1 (January 2019): 60–63. https://doi.org/10.1176/appi.ps.201800332.

McAfee, Erin. "Shame: The Emotional Basis of Library Anxiety." *College and Research Libraries* 79, no. 2 (March 2018): 237–56. https://doi.org/10.5860/crl.79.2.237.

Mellon, Constance A. "Library Anxiety: A Grounded Theory and Its Development." *College and Research Libraries* 47, no. 2 (1986): 160–65. https://doi.org/10.5860/crl_47_02_160.

Sinnot, Bria, Allison Jennings-Roche, and Elisabeth White. "Radically Reimagined: Open-Hearted Instruction Strategies for the Library Classroom." Presentation, ACRL 2021 virtual conference, April 13–16, 2021.

White, Allie, and Sara LaBelle. "A Qualitative Investigation of Instructors' Perceived Communicative Roles in Students' Mental Health Management." *Communication Education* 68, no. 2 (2019): 133–55. https://doi.org/10.1080/03634523.2019.1571620.

A Call to Action

This book started with a call to action by Nicole A. Cooke and Miriam E. Sweeney:

> "We challenge you to be the instructors our students need."[1]

The editors would like to issue a similar call to action to readers of these volumes. We encourage you to consider how you might apply some of the pedagogical strategies, such as reflecting on methods of fostering an anti-racist classroom, using primary source materials to engender empathy for different voices, and/or considering potential partners on your campus to increase the accessibility of your instructional materials. We posit several questions for contemplation and action:

- How does your own positionality affect the way you approach equitable and inclusive pedagogies?
- How have the theories and practices related to equitable and inclusive pedagogies inspired your teaching in the past, and might continue to inspire it in the future?
- How can you thoughtfully articulate your teaching practices to promote an inclusive and equitable classroom for all learners?
- How can we, as academic librarians, lift up and amplify the voices of our students, our colleagues, and learners all over the world?

We hope the chapters in this manuscript have inspired you as much as they have inspired the editors. No matter what has resonated, we encourage you to make positive changes, to include a philosophy of inclusive and equitable teaching and learning in your praxis, and, above all, to center the learner.

Notes

1. Nicole A. Cooke and Miriam E. Sweeney, *Teaching for Justice: Implementing Social Justice in the LIS Classroom*, Library Juice Press 2017. p. 288.

Bibliography

Cooke, Nicole A., and Miriam E. Sweeney. *Teaching for Justice: Implementing Social Justice in the LIS Classroom*. Library Juice Press, 2017.

About the Editors

Robin Brown, BSFS, MLS, MA is professor and head of public services for the library at Borough of Manhattan Community College (CUNY). She identifies as a person with disabilities and has published significant work on universal design for learning and disabilities studies. She identifies as a white, cis gender person and acknowledges that she has benefited from privileges on many different levels.

- Brown, R. and S. Sheidlower. *Seeking to Understand: A Journey into Disabilities Studies and Libraries.* Sacramento: Library Juice Press, 2021.
- Brown, R, Z. Welhouse, and A. Wolfe. "Keeping up with Universal Design for Learning." ACRL, 2020. http://www.ala.org/acrl/publications/keeping_up_with/udl
- Brown, R. "Wheelchair Warrior: Gangs, Disability, and Basketball." In *Disability Experiences: Memoirs, Autobiographies, and Other Personal Narratives*, edited by G. Thomas Couser and Susannah B. Mintz, 825-828. Vol. 2. Farmington Hills, MI: Macmillan Reference USA, 2019.
- Brown, R. and S. Sheidlower. "Claiming our Space: A quantitative and qualitative picture of disabled librarians." *Library Trends* (67:3, Winter 2019).

Elizabeth Foster, MSLS, is the social sciences data librarian at the University of Chicago. She serves as the subject expert for sociology and provides research and instructional support for data-driven research. Her research interests include anti-racist pedagogy, reflective practice, and data privacy.

Melissa N. Mallon (she/her), MLIS, is associate university librarian for teaching & learning at Vanderbilt University. She has published, presented, and taught professional development courses in the areas of online learning, instructional design, and the impact of information and digital literacies on student learning. Her previous books include *Partners in Teaching & Learning: Coordinating a Successful Academic Library Instruction Program* (2020); *The Pivotal Role of Academic Librarians in Digital Learning* (2018); and the co-edited volume, *The Grounded Instruction Librarian: Participating in the Scholarship of Teaching & Learning* (2019). Positionality Statement: I identify as a white, cis-gendered woman, which affords me an acknowledged place of privilege. Through my teaching and research, I strive to use this privilege to give voice to those that may be underrepresented or unheard in both libraries and higher education. I strive to lead with empathy and humility, and endeavor to not stop listening and learning.

Jane Nichols provides research and instructional support as a humanities librarian and a liaison to the Undergrad Research & Writing Center at Oregon State University. Reflecting the variety of roles she has taken over her career, she has published and presented on myriad topics aimed at improving library services and spaces for all. Her scholarship extends to editing "The Americas" volume of *Women's Lives around the World: A Global Encyclopedia*. A white, cis-gendered queer lesbian, she lives and works in the traditional homelands of the Marys River or Ampinefu Band of Kalapuya.

Ariana Santiago (she/her) is the head of open education services at the University of Houston Libraries. She has published, presented, and contributed professional service in the areas of open educational resources, information literacy, and library outreach. Ariana earned an M.A. in applied learning and instruction from the University of Central Florida and an M.A. in library and information science from the University of South Florida.

Maura Seale is the history librarian at the University of Michigan, providing research and instructional support for students and faculty in the history department. Maura holds an M.S.I. from the University of Michigan School of Information, an M.A. in American studies from the University of Minnesota, and a graduate certificate in digital public humanities from George Mason University. Her research focuses on critical librarianship, library pedagogy, political economy and labor in libraries, and race and gender in libraries. She is the co-editor, with Karen P. Nicholson, of *The Politics of Theory in the Practice of Critical Librarianship* (2018). Her work can be found at www.mauraseale.org and she welcomes comments via @mauraseale.

About the Authors

Andrea Baer is a public services librarian at Rowan University in the Campbell Library and has been an academic instruction librarian for over ten years. She has worked at both teaching-centered and research-intensive universities. Andrea holds a master's in information sciences from the University of Tennessee and a PhD in comparative literature from the University of Washington. Prior to entering librarianship, she taught and studied comparative literature and writing, which has informed her approach to information literacy education. Her research interests include the intersections between information literacy and writing studies, digital literacies, affect and learning, critical reflective practice, and librarians' development as teachers. For more about her research please see https://orcid.org/0000-0002-6361-948X.

Kelsa Bartley is the education and outreach librarian in the Learning, Research and Clinical Information Services Department at the Louis Calder Memorial Library, University of Miami Miller School of Medicine. Her role includes providing library education and research services, in addition to outreach and promotion of library services and resources. Her research interests include diversity, equity and inclusion in libraries, library marketing, outreach and social media, library instruction and instructional design and also wellness and wellbeing in libraries.

Randi Beem is the instruction archivist at University of North Carolina at Charlotte, where she uses primary document instruction in her Reading Room classroom across various subjects from the African American experience post-1865 to feminist resistance theory in cartography. A born and bred Hoosier, Randi attended Saint Mary's College, Notre Dame, Indiana, receiving a bachelor's in history, and Indiana University Bloomington, receiving a master's in library science with a specialization in archives and records management.

Selinda Adelle Berg is currently the university librarian at the University of Windsor, Canada. She holds a PhD in library and information studies from Western University, a master's in library and information studies from the University of Alberta, and a bachelor of science in nutrition from the University of Saskatchewan. Selinda maintains an active research program that intersects with her professional interests, including research culture in academic libraries, information inequities for 2SLGBTQ+ communities, and tacit knowledge in the health and information professions.

Ashley Blinstrub (she/her) is the student success and inclusion librarian at George Mason University Libraries. She has a master of science in information from University of Michigan. Her research interests include accessibility of information, inclusive teaching practices, and assessment of student learning.

Katie Blocksidge is the library director at The Ohio State University at Newark and Central Ohio Technical College. As part of this role, she works with colleagues and faculty to integrate information literacy into the student learning experience. Katie has an MLIS from Kent State University and an MA in learning technologies from The Ohio State University.

Faith Bradham is a community college librarian in California. Originally a Texan, she obtained her MLS from Indiana University Bloomington before moving to the West Coast. As a community college librarian, she has a role that extends into reference, instruction, liaisonship, and outreach. Her research interests focus on critical librarianship and inclusive teaching practices. When she's not in the library, Faith can be found on one of California's many beautiful hiking trails.

Frances Brady, MS, is the reference and instruction librarian at Adler University, where she coordinates, teaches, and assesses scaffolded information literacy sessions for graduate students and mentors student workers as peer teachers. Her research interests include information literacy instruction, social justice, and mentoring student workers as co-teachers.

Ava Brillat is the program lead for information literacy and instructional design. She also serves as a liaison librarian to the departments of English, English composition, theatre arts, and classics. Ava Brillat received her MLIS from the University of South Florida in 2010 and her MA in liberal studies from the University of Miami in 2019. Prior to coming to the University of Miami, she worked as an instructional design librarian. Born and raised overseas in Saudi Arabia, she enjoys the cross-cultural experiences Miami has to offer. Her personal research is focused on mentoring, collaboration, and diversity in librarianship.

Angie Brunk is an experienced public services librarian who also holds a MAS in human factors. Her primary research interest is accessible and inclusive design in libraries.

Sam Buechler, MLIS (they/them), is the student success faculty resident librarian at Washington State University, Vancouver. Prior to their current position, Sam worked in circulation and access services departments at a variety of four-year and community college libraries. Sam is also a member of the Library Freedom Project. These experiences provide the foundation for their research interests, which center privacy and surveillance on college campuses, outreach services, and critical information literacy.

Heather Campbell is a mother, teacher, librarian, and educational developer. She is an uninvited settler on lands connected with the London Township and Sombra Treaties of 1796 and Dish with One Spoon Covenant Wampum, the traditional lands of Anishinaabek, Haudenosaunee, Lūnapéewak and Chonnonton peoples. Now Curriculum Librarian at Western University, Heather worked as a library assistant, librarian, and educational developer at Brescia University College from 2006 to 2020. Heather's work in supporting the creation of Brescia's first-year seminar, along with her leadership in Brescia's articulation of values-based degree outcomes, helped solidify her teaching identity as a feminist pedagogue. Heather spends her professional time navigating academia's third-space, with the hopes of contributing to the decolonization and Indigenization of the academy. She is happiest, though, when playing LEGO with her five-year old son.

Allison Carr serves as the Academic Transitions Librarian at California State University, San Marcos. Her current area of research is centered around the sense of belonging of transfer students and creating a robust Common Read program. She has a Master of Library and Information Science from San Jose State University.

Liz Chenevey is a health and behavioral studies librarian at James Madison University in Virginia. She is interested in affective learning, ethics of care, zines, and critical pedagogies. Outside of the library, she enjoys gardening, quilting, and making up silly songs for her daughter.

Melissa Chomintra is an assistant professor in the Purdue Libraries and School of Information Studies. She received an MA in criminal justice from the University of Nevada, Las Vegas, and her MLIS from Kent State University.

Maggie Clarke is the reference services coordinator, an instruction librarian, and liaison to the humanities at CSU Dominguez Hills. She has worked in both academic and public libraries since 2016 and is currently pursuing research focused on the politics of student workers in academic libraries.

Scott R. Cowan is an information services librarian at the University of Windsor, Canada. His research has centred around teaching and learning within a library context; information and access needs of the LGBTQ2S+ community; and social justice issues within the classroom. In his previous career, Scott taught middle school and high school instrumental and vocal music in Saskatchewan. He received his master of library and information science (MLIS) from Western University and his bachelor of music education and bachelor of education from the University of Saskatchewan. Currently, Scott is also working on a PhD in educational studies.

Breanne Crumpton is the Information Literacy Librarian for the Humanities and Assistant Professor at Appalachian State University. She is a cis, settler, able-bodied, white, middle class, heterosexual female. Her research interests include DEIA work in libraries, social and racial justice to overcome systemic barriers, inclusive pedagogy practices and critical information literacy.

Kyle Denlinger is the digital pedagogy and open education librarian at Wake Forest University's Z. Smith Reynolds Library, where he collaborates with faculty and students to develop scholarly digital projects, advocates for and supports open educational practices, and contributes to the library's information literacy efforts through teaching and student support.

Emily Drabinski is interim chief librarian at the Graduate Center, City University of New York.

Kate Drabinski is principal lecturer in Gender, Women's, and Sexuality Studies at UMBC, where she also directs the Women Involved In Learning and Leadership (WILL+) program. She teaches courses in sexuality studies, queer theory, transgender studies, and activism. She is coeditor with Nicole King and Joshua Davis of *Baltimore Revisited: Stories of Inequality and Resistance in a U.S. City.*

Alissa Droog, MLIS, MA, BEd, BA, is an assistant professor and the education and social sciences librarian at Northern Illinois University, where she works primarily with faculty and graduate students in the College of Education. Alissa's research interests include information literacy, library assessment practices, LGBTQ+ children's literature, biblical reception history, and children's Bible stories.

Sara Durazo-DeMoss is the director of mentoring and academic advising at California State University, San Bernardino. Her work focuses on student mentoring and college transition, experiential learning and career readiness, and academic advising for undergraduate students. Her research interests include representations of higher education in popular culture, leadership identity development of college women, critical mentoring, and the dualism of mentoring as both an oppressive and liberating practice.

Erin Durham is a reference and instruction librarian at the University of Maryland, Baltimore County (UMBC), and provides research instruction and support to the history, english, music, theatre, dance, and language, literacy, and culture departments. She received an MLIS and MA in History from the University of Maryland, College Park. Her research interests include critical pedagogy, open educational resources, the intersection of libraries and writing centers, and she seeks to engage in conversations about information privilege and inequities. In addition to her library pursuits, Erin is a violin performer and teacher and an enthusiast for the outdoors.

Christine R. Elliott is a reference and instruction librarian at UMass Boston. Christine's interests include universal accessibility, library marketing, innovative technologies, information literacy instruction, and open educational resources. She loves cross-stitching, and her favorite flavor of toaster pastry is blueberry.

Rachel Fager is Head of Resources Management at Saint Joseph's University. She first became interested in accessibility while working with students at a community college ten years ago and has continued to seek opportunities to learn and to support students. She has co-presented accessibility webinars for national and regional organizations..

Carol Fisher, MLIS (she/her), is a collections and technical services librarian at Washington State University, Vancouver. She holds an MLIS from University of Washington and a BS in psychology from Penn State University. Prior to working in academic libraries, Carol served on active duty in the United States Navy, where she worked in tropical cyclone forecasting. Her research interests currently involve veteran identity and the intersection with academic libraries, focusing on outreach and programming.

Rebecca Fitzsimmons is special collections librarian and liaison to the Women's, Gender, and Sexuality Studies program at Illinois State University. She is the curator of the Children's and Historical Textbooks Collection and works extensively with the Rare Books and Manuscripts Collection. She provides instruction, reference, and collection development services and engages in a variety of digital projects and initiatives in the library.

Amanda L. Folk is an assistant professor and head of teaching and learning at The Ohio State University Libraries. Amanda works with her teaching and learning colleagues to develop a vision and strategy for developing students' information literacy through instructor development, reference interactions, cocurricular programming, credit-bearing courses, and learning objects. Amanda has both an MLIS and a PhD from the University of Pittsburgh.

Shanti Freundlich is an assistant professor and the assistant director for online learning and assessment at MCPHS University in Boston, Massachusetts.

Joanna Gadsby works as the instruction coordinator/reference and instruction librarian at University of Maryland, Baltimore County. Her research interests include relational practice, critical and constructivist pedagogies, and gendered labor in librarianship. She is coeditor, along with Veronica Arellano Douglas, of the recently published volume *Deconstructing Service in Libraries: Intersections of Identities and Expectations.*

Rachel W. Gammons is head of teaching and learning services at the University of Maryland (UMD) Libraries, an affiliate faculty member in the UMD College of Information Studies (iSchool), and a PhD candidate in higher education, student affairs, and international education in the UMD College of Education.

Sheila García Mazari, is the online learning librarian at the University of California, Santa Cruz. Formerly, she was a professional programs liaison librarian at Grand Valley State University. Sheila has an MLIS from Wayne State University and is a 2016 American Library Association Spectrum Scholar as well as a 2019 Emerging Leader. She is an active member of the Asian Pacific American Librarians Association (APALA) and the Michigan Academic Library Association (MiALA) and has served as the 2020–2021 Residency Interest Group convener of the Association of College and Research Libraries (ACRL).

Jane Hammons is an assistant professor in the University Libraries at The Ohio State University. As the teaching and learning engagement librarian, she focuses on supporting the integration of information literacy into the curriculum through instructor development. Jane has an MSLIS from the University of Illinois Urbana-Champaign and an MS in instructional design from Western Kentucky University.

Beth Heldebrandt has been the public relations director at Booth Library since 2012. She is the sole person responsible for the library's PR, publicity, and communications, with her work including social media, photography, graphic design, media relations, grant writing, and internal communications. Prior to working at Booth Library, Beth was a newspaper editor for more than twenty-two years. She also works as a media research specialist for Ad Fontes Media, home of the Media Bias Chart, and is an adjunct instructor of journalism at Eastern Illinois University.

Barbara Herrera is the coordinator of the Student Mentoring Program at California State University, San Bernardino. Her work focuses on the hiring, training, and supporting professional development of student mentors. She has partnered with the library to co-facilitate the Library Ambassador Initiative.

April Ibarra Siqueiros is the User Experience Librarian at CSU San Marcos and was formerly in reference and instruction. She has a Master of Library and Information Science with a User Experience concentration from Pratt Institute. Her research interests range from zines to critical user experience design in libraries.

Darren Ilett is a Teaching and Outreach Librarian and Assistant Professor at the University of Northern Colorado. He serves as a liaison for two TRIO programs supporting first-generation students (Student Support Services and McNair Scholars Program), the DREAMer Engagement Program (supporting DACAmented and undocumented students), and Go On and Learn (supporting students with intellectual and developmental disabilities), as well as the College of Education and Behavioral Sciences. Darren teaches information literacy credit courses and one-shot instruction sessions. His research centers on how librarians can work with students typically underserved and underrepresented in higher education, particularly first-generation students.

Allison Jennings-Roche is the library instruction coordinator for Towson University and a PhD student in information studies at the University of Maryland. Her research interests include information policy, advocacy, and human rights, critical information literacy, and inclusive leadership. She has an MLIS with a focus on diversity and inclusion from the University of Maryland, as well as an MA in legal and ethical studies and a graduate certificate in organizational leadership from the University of Baltimore. Allison has professional experience in higher education, libraries, and undergraduate teaching, and has previously worked at UMBC and the University of Baltimore.

David Kelly, Jr. is the writing services coordinator at the University of Baltimore. He received his MS in negotiations and conflict management from the University of Baltimore. Focusing on writing as a conflict in institutions of higher education, David works to transform students' relationships with writing through advocating writer autonomy; collaboration; and development of rhetorical awareness, genre expectation, and audience identification; through demystifying the curriculum of higher education. Some of his interests include rock climbing, hiking, daydreaming, and finding meaningful ways to interrogate and disrupt the everyday practice of racism and white supremacy in higher education spaces. I do what I do for my people. You know who you are!

Amanda Kalish has a BA in History and a Master's of Library and Information Science from UCLA. She has worked in both public and academic libraries and is currently an Instruction & Reference Librarian at California State University, San Marcos. Her research interest revolves around figuring out the best methods of effectively teaching information literacy that can cut through the deliberate disinformation spread through social media, foreign influences, and other bad actors.

Sara C. Kern is the student success and outreach librarian at Juniata College in Huntingdon, Pennsylvania. She earned her MA in history from the Pennsylvania State University and her MSLIS from Syracuse University. She loves library instruction and hiking, and her favorite flavor of toaster pastry is cinnamon.

Maria Kingsbury, PhD, works at Southwest Minnesota State University in Marshall, Minnesota, where she serves as the director of the Center for Online Teaching and Learning in the McFarland Library.

Stacey Knight-Davis is the head of circulation services at Booth Library, Eastern Illinois University. She also serves as the systems librarian and as the librarian for nursing and public health. She earned an MS in library and information science from the University of Illinois at Urbana-Champaign and an MS in technology from Eastern Illinois University. Stacey joined the EIU library faculty in 2002 as a reference librarian.

Glenn Koelling is an instruction librarian and English department liaison at the University of New Mexico in Albuquerque. Her research focuses on information literacy and instruction.

Debbie Krahmer is the diversity and inclusion research librarian at Cornell University in New York State. As a white, queer, fat, trans, and disabled librarian, D has been incorporating social justice into D's librarianship for many years and using IGD actively since 2016. Debbie has presented on accessibility, instructional technology, queer and trans issues, and assessment at library and higher education conferences for many years.

Pamela Nett Kruger is the institutional repository librarian at California State University, Chico, Meriam Library. She has an MA in anthropology from California State University, Northridge, and an MLIS from San José State University. Her research interests include communities of practice, tech equity, and inclusive and constructivist pedagogies.

Sharon Ladenson is gender and communication studies librarian and coordinator of diversity, equity, and inclusion education at the Michigan State University Libraries. Her commitment to equity, diversity, and inclusion and anti-racist practices informs her work, particularly in the areas of teaching and learning. She has presented independently on intersectionality and critical information literacy at the California Conference on Library Instruction and collaboratively at the European Conference on Information Literacy and at the Charleston Conference. Her writing on feminist pedagogy and information literacy is included in works such as *Critical Library Instruction: Theories and Methods* (from Library Juice Press) and the *Critical Library Pedagogy Handbook* (from the Association of College and Research Libraries).

Tricia Lantzy is the Health Sciences & Human Services Librarian at California State University San Marcos. She has a MS in Information Studies from the University of Texas at Austin and a BA in Anthropology from the University of California, San Diego. Her current research focuses on investigating how students learn and experience their education in a variety of different learning environments.

David X. Lemmons (he/they) is the instruction coordinator for George Mason University Libraries. They have a master of science in library science from the University of North Carolina at Chapel Hill and a master of arts in political science from Appalachian State University. Their research interests include student-centered pedagogy and critical information literacy.

Lindsey Loeper has served as the reference and instruction archivist at the University of Maryland, Baltimore County (UMBC), since 2019, following her role as the special collections archivist since 2007. In this position she coordinates the Special Collections reading room, reference and researcher services, and instruction and archival literacy and serves as the primary student supervisor. She has previously written and presented on EAD-XML finding aids, participatory learning in archival literacy instruction, and team-based instruction portfolios.

Christopher Lowder (he/him) is the online learning specialist at George Mason University. He has a master of library and information science with a specialization in diversity and inclusion from the University of Maryland. His research interests include information accessibility, online learning, and inclusive teaching in library instruction.

Elaine MacDougall is a lecturer in the English department and director of the Writing Center at the University of Maryland, Baltimore County (UMBC). She is currently a doctoral student in the Language, Literacy, and Culture program at UMBC with research interests in mindfulness and writing studies, embodiment pedagogy, tutor and student self-efficacy and advocacy, and anti-racist pedagogy in the writing center and writing classroom using frameworks from critical race theory and feminist theory, especially Black feminism. Additionally, her background as a yoga instructor influences her practices in the writing classroom and made her more aware of the importance of being present with and listening to her students. Elaine is excited to continue growing from and learning about positionality in her roles as a writing center director, instructor, colleague, and student.

Kelleen Maluski is a student success and engagement librarian at University of New Mexico Health Sciences Library.

Francesca Marineo Munk is the education liaison and humanities and social sciences librarian / coordinator of library student research assistants at the University of California, Los Angeles. She wrote this chapter while in her previous position of teaching and learning librarian for online education at the University of Nevada, Las Vegas, one of the nation's most diverse universities for undergraduates. In addition to her MLIS, she holds an MS in educational psychology, which is where she was first introduced to motivation theory. She is a first-generation college student and an emerging mid-career librarian. Her current research focuses on fostering a culture of educational equity through communities of practice and designing inclusive learning experiences especially within an online environment. Francesca is a white, Canadian-born dual citizen of the United States and Canada. She is a queer, cis, and able-bodied woman, and her pronouns are she, her, hers.

Talitha R. Matlin is the STEM Librarian at CSU San Marcos. She has a Master's of Learning, Design, and Technology from San Diego State University and a Master's of Library and Information Science from San Jose State University. Her research interests focus on applying instructional design methodologies to nontraditional instructional settings.

Allison McFadden-Keesling received her BA from Albion College (1982) and MLIS from the University of Michigan (1984) and has been a reference librarian for thirty-eight years at academic and public libraries. An active member of Diversity, Equity, Inclusion and Justice initiatives, she was honored and humbled to receive the Oakland Community College (OCC) Diversity Champion award in 2017 for her work on the Human Library. She read about the Human Library in an article in a London paper in 2008. Impressed and intrigued by the concept, she researched and contacted the Humanlibrary.org and facilitated her first Human Library in 2009 at OCC in Michigan. She has facilitated over thirty Human Library events over the last thirteen years. Recognizing the immediate and positive effects for all involved, she continues to be passionate about meeting and vetting potential human books and facilitating human libraries. These events foster empathy and understanding in both the reader and the human book.

Samantha Minnis is the information literacy and outreach librarian at Grand Rapids Community College. After working in a variety of areas of librarianship in both public and academic libraries, she earned her MLIS from Kent State University in 2016. Samantha is an active member of Michigan Academic Library Association (MiALA). Her research interests include critical librarianship and critical pedagogy.

Michelle K. Mitchell is the Reference and Instruction Librarian at Syracuse University. She holds a MSLIS from Simmons College and a BA in English from Le Moyne College. She is a cis, settler, able-bodied, white, middle-class female. Michelle is passionate about critical librarianship, inclusive instruction techniques and practices, assessment strategies, and technological literacy.

Madeline Mundt is head of the Research Commons at the University of Washington Libraries, where she is responsible for planning, managing, and coordinating services for student researchers in this interdisciplinary physical and virtual space. She is also particularly interested in bringing graduate student researchers into public and open scholarship. She is a cis white woman who has been working in libraries for fifteen years.

Megan Mulder is the Special Collections Librarian at Z. Smith Reynolds Library, Wake Forest University. She teaches classes on the history of material texts and provides instruction for undergraduate and graduate students, and she collaborates with teaching faculty to embed primary source materials from Special Collections and Archives into the classroom and the curriculum. She holds an MA in English literature from the University of Virginia and an MLIS from the University of North Carolina at Chapel Hill.

Yvonne Nalani Meulemans has been the Head of Teaching and Learning at the University Library at California State University at San Marcos since 2010. Her research interests include the use of threshold concept framework to support students' transformational learning and reflective practice in library leadership and management.

Lalitha Nataraj is the Social Sciences Librarian at California State University, San Marcos. She holds an MLIS from UCLA and a BA in English and Women's Studies from UC Berkeley. Her research interests include relational-cultural theory, critical information literacy, and South Asian Americans in librarianship.

Clanitra Stewart Nejdl is head of professional development and research services librarian at the Alyne Queener Massey Law Library at Vanderbilt University, as well as a lecturer in law at Vanderbilt Law School. She teaches both first-year and advanced legal research classes. Clanitra presents and publishes on topics related to academic law libraries and legal research instruction, including cultural competence and DEIA awareness for law students, legal information preservation, and professional development for law librarians. Clanitra is the 2021 recipient of both the American Association of Law Libraries (AALL) Emerging Leader Award and the AALL Spectrum Article of the Year Award. She is also the 2017 recipient of the AALL Minority Leadership Development Award. Clanitra is an active member of the American Association of Law Libraries, the Southeastern Chapter of the American Association of Law Libraries, the Mid-America Association of Law Libraries, and the Chicago Association of Law Libraries. She is a licensed attorney in Georgia and in South Carolina.

Zach Newell served as dean of library services at Eastern Illinois University from 2018 to 2022 and is currently dean of libraries and learning at the University of Southern Maine. Zach earned a BA in philosophy from Susquehanna University, Selinsgrove, Pennsylvania; an MA in history of art from University of Massachusetts Amherst; and an MS in library science from Clarion University, Clarion, Pennsylvania. He is a PhD candidate in library and information science at Simmons University, Boston, Massachusetts.

Judy Opdahl is the Business and Economics Librarian for the College of Business and Department of Economics Department at California State University San Marcos. Her research interests include practices of embedded librarianship and how the academic library can support ADHD and other neurodiverse students.

Nicole Pagowsky is an associate librarian at the University of Arizona Libraries and adjunct faculty with the University of Arizona School of Information.

Roxane Pickens is the community engagement librarian and head of External Engagement at New York University Libraries, having formerly served as the director of the Learning Commons at University of Miami Libraries. She received her MA and PhD in American studies at the College of William and Mary, and her scholarly work explores identity and festivity in Harlem Renaissance/Jazz Age literature and expressive culture. Her current research and teaching interests include library outreach and engagement, interdisciplinarity and cultural literacies in library settings, teaching with primary resources, diversity/equity/inclusion in academic spaces, American studies, African American literature/culture, US identity construction, and the rhetorical dimensions of ethnic festive/expressive culture.

Hanna Primeau is the instructional designer at The Ohio State University Libraries. In this role, she is involved in a range of projects from redesigning for-credit online courses to consultations with fellow librarians on how to best use teaching technology in their sessions or how to transition from in-person to virtual instruction. Hanna has an MSI from the School of Information at the University of Michigan.

Torie Quiñonez is the Arts and Humanities Librarian at CSU San Marcos. Her research interests include exploring the role validation plays in the intellectual development of learners of all kinds.

Madeline Ruggiero is a collection development librarian at Queensborough Community College in Queens, New York. In addition to an MLS from Pratt Institute she also has a masters degree in Art History from SUNY Stony Brook. Her research and publications focus on ways to support community college students academically and holistically.. In addition to an MLS from Pratt Institute She also has a masters degree in Art History from SUNY Stony Brook. Her research and publications focus on ways to support community college students academically and holistically.

Zohra Saulat is a graduate of the School of Information Sciences at the University of Illinois, Urbana-Champaign. She is the student success librarian at Lake Forest College. Her passions include student success, the first-year experience, and critical library pedagogy.

Laura Saunders is a Professor at Simmons University School of Library and Information Science, where she teaches and conducts research in the areas of reference, instruction, information literacy, and intellectual freedom. She has a strong interest in the connections between information literacy and social justice issues, as well as in the impact of mis- and disinformation.

Her most recent books include *Reference and Information Services: An Introduction*, 6th edition, co-edited with Melissa Wong, and the open access textbook *Instruction in Libraries and Information Settings: An Introduction*, co-authored with Melissa Wong. Her articles have appeared in a variety of journals, including *College & and Research Libraries*, The *Journal of Academic Librarianship*, and *Communications in Information Literacy*. Laura has a PhD and a Master of Library and Information Science, both from Simmons College, and a Bachelor of Arts in English Literature from Boston University. She has served a Trustee for the Somerville Public Library in Somerville, Massachusetts. She is the 2019 recipient of Simmons University's Provost Award for Excellence in Graduate Teaching.

Gina Schlesselman-Tarango is a librarian at Des Moines University and was previously the coordinator of library instruction at California State University, San Bernardino. In addition to co-facilitating the Library Ambassador Initiative in partnership with the Student Mentoring Program, she facilitated library instruction and led professional development for faculty on topics related to critical information literacy. Her research interests include gender and race in librarianship, critical library pedagogy, and information labor as it relates to reproductive failure.

Melanie Sellar is head of instruction and assessment at University Library, Santa Clara University. In this role she develops, enhances, and implements the Library's instruction and assessment programs and priorities. She has twelve years of accrued experience specializing in the public services of academic libraries, with scholarships interests spanning inclusive and critical pedagogy, algorithmic literacy, and instructional design.

Anne Shelley is scholarly communication librarian and music librarian at Illinois State University, where she manages the institutional repository ISU ReD, gives workshops, and provides instruction, reference, and collection development services. She has written or cowritten book chapters published by ALA Editions, ACRL Publications, IGI Global, Neal-Schuman, and A-R Editions.

Kathy Shields is the Research and Instruction Librarian for History and Social Science and Research Services Lead at Wake Forest University's Z. Smith Reynolds Library. In those roles, she provides research and instruction support to students and faculty, primarily in the areas of History and Psychology, teaches credit-bearing information literacy courses on primary sources and social science research, and coordinates the library's liaison program. Her scholarship has primarily focused on the value of collaboration between librarians and disciplinary faculty. She holds an MLIS from the University of North Carolina at Greensboro.

Tierney Steelberg is a Digital Liberal Arts Specialist at Grinnell College's Digital Liberal Arts Collaborative. Prior to joining Grinnell, she was the Digital Pedagogy & Scholarship Technologist at Guilford College's Hege Library. She is passionate about supporting the critical and thoughtful implementation of technology in teaching and learning, as well as empowering students to create digital projects across disciplines and modalities. She earned her MSI from the University of Michigan in 2016.

Elliott Stevens is the English studies and research commons librarian at the University of Washington, Seattle. With Madeline Mundt, he has done research and written about the value of undergraduate student library workers doing written reflections while on the job. He is also interested in the digital humanities and digital scholarship and to what degree they are accessible. He is a forty-year-old, white, cis, able-bodied man who is six years into full-time library work.

Alicia G. Vaandering is an assistant professor and the student success librarian for the University Libraries at the University of Rhode Island. In her role, she supports the learning and research of students, with an emphasis on undergraduate first-year, international, first-generation, and transfer students. She received a bachelor of arts in history from Willamette University and master of library and information studies and master of arts in history at the University of Rhode Island. Her research interests include the history of public libraries, the representation of the LGBTQIA+ community in children's picture books, library collaborations with academic services, and the use of dialogic pedagogy in information literacy instruction.

Kari D. Weaver, MLIS, EdD, is the learning, teaching, and instructional design librarian at the University of Waterloo, where she oversees the development of online instruction, advances teaching culture, and explores strategic partnerships related to teaching and learning. Her research interests include accessibility, censorship, co-teaching, information literacy, and academic integrity, particularly in the STEM disciplines.

Megan Wilson is an assistant professor and research and instruction librarian at Murray State University. She serves as the library liaison for the Jones College of Science and the Hutson School of Agriculture as well as serving as an instructor for courses about information literacy and intellectual property. Her research interests include virtual reference, inclusive teaching and learning, library outreach, and online learning.

Lauren Wittek is a librarian and instructor at Central Washington University's James E. Brooks Library. She earned her MLIS from the University of Washington in 2018 and has worked in higher education for over 15 years. Her research interests include addressing accessibility and privacy issues in the library.

Mir Yarfitz is an Associate Professor in the Department of History at Wake Forest University and the Director of the Jewish Studies Program. His teaching and scholarship bridge Latin American History, Gender and Sexuality Studies, and Jewish History. He incorporates library visits into undergraduate classes at all levels, collaborating with librarians to make primary source research accessible to every student. His current research explores multiple interpretations and assertions of what might fruitfully be framed as trans lives in Argentina circa 1900-1930. His monograph Impure Migration: Jews and Sex Work in Golden Age Argentina was published in 2019 by Rutgers University Press. He holds a PhD in History from UCLA.

Perry Yee is the senior online learning support manager at the University of Washington, Seattle. As part of the libraries' Instructional Design unit, he designs, develops, and delivers online learning opportunities for UW students, staff, and faculty while providing digital pedagogy and instructional technology training and support to libraries staff members. He offers his viewpoint as a mixed-race, cisgender, able-bodied man who has been working in libraries for seven years.